STAGECRAFT
FUNDAMENTALS

SECOND EDITION

STAGECRAFT
FUNDAMENTALS
A GUIDE AND REFERENCE FOR THEATRICAL PRODUCTION

RITA KOGLER CARVER

SECOND EDITION

Focal Press
Taylor & Francis Group

NEW YORK AND LONDON

First published 2013
by Focal Press
70 Blanchard Road, Suite 402, Burlington, MA 01803

Simultaneously published in the UK
by Focal Press
2 Park Square, Milton Park, Abingdon, Oxon OX14 4RN

Focal Press is an imprint of the Taylor & Francis Group, an informa business

Library of Congress Cataloging in Publication Data
Carver, Rita Kogler.
  Stagecraft fundamentals : a guide and reference for theatrical
production / Rita Kogler Carver. — 2nd ed.
    p. cm.
  Includes index.
1. Theater—Production and direction. I. Title.
  PN2053.C32 2012
  792.02—dc23
                          2012003641

ISBN: 978-0-240-82051-4 (pbk)

Typeset in ACaslonPro Regular
by TNQ Books and Journals, Chennai

CHAPTER III

CHAPTER IV

CHAPTER V

CHAPTER VI

CHAPTER XV

PART SIX: STAGE MANAGEMENT AND CAREERS   409

CHAPTER XVI

CHAPTER XVII

As always during acknowledgments, there are so many people to thank. And, like any good award acceptance speech, there are going to be people I forget to thank. So, first and foremost, I thank all of the people I am about to forget. I couldn't have done it without them, even though I can't remember their names at the moment. I'm sure their contributions helped me in more ways than I can remember.

I would like to thank Wonder Woman© DC Comics. That's right, Wonder Woman. I grew up knowing that she was the one female superhero who didn't need a guy to swoop in and rescue her. She wasn't afraid to achieve her goals, to enlist help as needed, or to try new and different things no matter what public opinion said or thought. She is my hero!

Since this is a textbook, let me start by thanking my high school art teacher, Fred Beaver. This insightful instructor told me that I didn't have a creative bone in my body, then he sent me to the office to drop his class. Way to go! On a much more serious note, I was privileged to study with an amazing man by the name of John Gleason while I was getting my MFA. John taught me that using your eyes is the best kind of research available, that you must learn to pick your fights, and that magenta doesn't actually occur anywhere in nature.

Many designers and friends who happen to be designers gave so generously of their time to share with me their insights. This truly has been a collaboration. They are Campbell Baird, Fernando Bermudez, Michael Clark, Pat Collins, Geoff Dunbar, M. L. Geiger, Tim Mazur, John McKernon, Linda Mensching, Curt Ostermann, Michael Rizzo, Mimi Jordan Sherin, Sal Tagliarino, Andy Warfel, and D. M. Wood. Michael Fink has been amazing with his talent for imagery. He graciously designed all of the chapter opening images. Beth Bergman openly searched her archives for opera images from the Metropolitan Opera amongst others.

The same has been true of so many of the manufacturers in the industry. I interviewed, asked for favors, pleaded for documentation. I would like to thank Randy Altman, Altman Rentals; David Barbour, *Lighting and Sound America*; Grace Brandt; Charlie Davidson, Arri; Celia Donnoli, Arri; Gary Fails, City Theatrical; Anne

Hunter, Rosco; Anne Johnston, PRG; Jenny Knott, Rosco; Robert Kulesh, Matthews; Neil Mazzella, Hudson Scenic; Andrew Nikel, City Theatrical, Patricia Saite-Lewe, Ben Nye; Carrie Silverstein, Hudson Scenic; Ame Strong, Rosco; Tom Sullivan, Hudson Scenic; Joe Tawil, GAM Products; and Jackie Tien, *Lighting and Sound America*.

■ Albert H. Kogler, Jr., my dad, doing what he loved—sitting on a boat, fishing.

■ John C. Carver, my husband, enjoying the gorgeous scenery in Nova Scotia.

■ John Gleason, my mentor, posing for a GAM Products color advertisement in 1992.

My sister-in-law, Wendy Herron, created most of the illustrations for this book. She is an awesome artist, and a wonderful friend. My research assistant, William Domack, stayed with me through all the craziness that ensued during the writing and the rewrites. He kept me caffeinated with chai, relatively focused, and always seemed able to find the files I had inadvertently deleted from the server—oops!

Please indulge me while I thank my family. My entire family has supported me throughout the whole process of getting this book published. They have been nothing short of amazing, even rallying in the final week before my deadline. My mother and sister Angela baked and cooked to keep us energized. Niece Katie and nephew Zack happily descended to complete many of "techno geek" duties. Duke (Australian shepherd), Milo (PBGV), and Polly (bassett hound) have finally figured out when *not* to disturb me. My dad, who is still with me every day in spirit, believed that his daughters should know how to use tools as well as his sons—and gave me my first 10-inch Crescent© wrench when I started in the theatre.

Cara Anderson, my first editor, believed in this book—and in me—from the first moment I spoke with her about my ideas for *Stagecraft Fundamentals*. She has been at my side leading, guiding, and supporting for several years. Her instincts for my process are superb, and with my sense of humor, that really says something. I could not have done this without her. Stacey Walker, my new editor, has been as supportive and wonderful as any editor could be.

Last, and most important, there is my wonderful husband, John. It is simply this: Without him there is nothing.

Why do we need yet another book on technical theatre? What a good question!

I have always been fascinated by the combination of history and the newest trends. For example, I love fountain pens *and* computers! I believe we must know what has come before, who first did something, and how they did it. In essence, we must know where we come from and honor that history. Otherwise, we spend a great deal of time reinventing, well, the wheel—literally. At the same time, we must continue to push, pull, and stretch ourselves as both designers and technicians, using the newest materials and technology currently available. This new technology allows us to do things that were previously unavailable to us. It also can make our lives easier on some of the more routine tasks. Technology is only as good as the use you have for it. It can be your best friend or your worst enemy, depending on how you choose to use it.

Theatre is a relatively small business. I have been fortunate to interview a great many working designers and technicians. I have quoted them throughout the book. I have also researched a great many of the superstitions or traditions we have all come to know in theatre, trying to find their origins. I also include this information, a little in each chapter, as a part of the industry's overall history. We always hear people saying "break a leg" or "the Scottish play." Now, we try to find out, as best we can, where these sayings started.

Useless Factoid: Opening Night and Paying Customers

There is a superstition in theatre about the opening-night customers. As we all know, some tickets are given away through various connections with the production. These are called comps, or complementary tickets. Supposedly, the first customer to be admitted into the auditorium must be a paying customer. This is said to ensure the financial success of the production. House managers have been known to refuse admittance to someone with a comp ticket prior to seating a paying customer.

Stagecraft Fundamentals uses examples of past and current design ideas to make interesting comparisons. Not to say that one is right and the other is wrong—anything but that! What is truly wonderful is that we who work in the theatre are constantly reinventing it. We do this not only through our concepts and ideas, but also through our implementation. Think of the classic musicals from the 1950s and 1960s like *Hello Dolly*, *My Fair Lady*, or *Camelot*. Then, think more recently to the musicals like *Spring Awakening*, *Wicked*, and *Young Frankenstein*. What are the differences from a design point of view?

Don't immediately jump to the conclusion that the newer shows couldn't have been done 50 years ago. They absolutely could have, but they would have been different. We look at the differences that may have been incorporated in the design and implementation process. This will clearly show how scripts have been able to expand their scope, at least in part, to the expanded possibilities in design and implementation now available. The bigger we can dream, the more we can accomplish!

My goal in writing this book is to bring the newest ideas and technologies available in professional theatre to the attention of anyone with an interest in backstage theatre. Each chapter goes into enough historical detail to give you a background and a perspective. Visual examples as well as explanations of current techniques bring you not only into the present but also into the future.

Wow—sure does sound like an awful lot of information for one book! Well, it is. But I organized it in such a way that ideally it will make sense. We start slow, and with each new chapter, we build a little more on what has come before. Always keep in mind that this is a "fundamentals" book. There is more in-depth information to follow. My goal is to get you excited about the theatre! Here is how we'll do it.

We start by honoring the history I talked about earlier. It all started with the Greeks, right? Our overall organization in the theatre as well as some of the basic conventions we still use all have their roots in Greece. If you've ever been backstage in a theatre, it may seem like the technicians are speaking an entirely different language. Well, in some ways they are. In Chapter 1, we discuss many of the terms that form the foundation we build on in later chapters, as we continue to expand our new theatre vocabulary.

You want to be a technician, or you are at least interested in the topic, and you wonder why you should also be learning about design. The best way to be a good technician is to understand the designer's process. And, the best way to be a designer is to understand what the technicians go through to realize your design. Then, as questions arise or perhaps problems needing creative solutions, you can be a part of the final answer. Chapter 2 discusses the design process. And, yes, it is a process. Designers don't sit down and just draw pretty pictures. They read scripts, do research, go to production meetings, and so forth.

The next logical step in the conversation is to discuss composition and color theory. Any visual artist needs to understand composition. Chapter 3 and Chapter 4 explore the basics of these topics. All the images that an audience sees and perceives are directly relayed to them through composition and color. Composition is the basis for all things visual. At its most basic, we can discuss whether a line is straight or curved. Does it have pattern or rhythm? This begins our discussion of composition. Color adds to the conversation about composition. It adds another element or layer. *Color* is usually defined and thought of in terms of primary and secondary colors. We discuss this and so much more. How we perceive the world around us is directly related to how we see color.

Chapter 5 begins the implementation phase of the book. So, you have all these great ideas. How do you get these wonderful ideas out of your head and into the theatre? We jump right into our discussion of drafting, drawing, and rendering. This is the first tangible step for any designer. You have to get the ideas out of your head and onto paper. That is the only way others can see *visually* what you've been describing *verbally*. The "old way" to do this is with a pencil and a piece of paper. And many designers still work this way. The "new way," with technology, adds the use of computer drafting software and photo manipulation software as well as other programs written specifically for the theatre. The goal of creating drawings and drafting is still very simple. Get the ideas out of your head so they can be realized.

My students all know one of my favorite sayings: "*I've never had to call 911 for a student, and you're not going to break my record.*" Chapter 6 talks about safety, both backstage in the theatre and in the various shops related to implementation of the designs. There are standards for safety, and they are practiced for a reason. The theatre can be a dangerous place. We are always trying to accomplish things that aren't supposed to be done inside a building, never mind in the dark! If you follow some basic safety rules, you will have a much better chance at staying safe. And, let's face it, most of us got into theatre because it looked like fun. Let's keep it that way.

Scenic tools and materials are discussed in detail in Chapter 7. You might need to do so many different projects, and I give you the basic information you need to walk into a scene shop and get the job done. This chapter has tons of information about the nuts and bolts—literally—of theatre. I also talk about how to choose the right tool or material for the job at hand.

Chapter 8 is all about scenery. Yes, we finally will get to talk about scenery. Did you think that scenery was going to be Chapter 1? As we get into the "down and dirty" of implementing scenic ideas, you'll see how the first seven chapters have given you a background you didn't think you'd need but is now coming in very handy! This chapter gives you a background in the traditional scenic elements: flats, platforms, stairs, doors, and the like. As always, we honor the past before moving into the future. And, keep in mind that, when the budget is tight, you need this "historic" information to come up with a well-rounded solution to whatever problems might arise. Once we get the basics under hand, we discuss some of the new technologies available today. These include advancing in the capabilities of decks as well as other technologies that can help your vision come alive.

The next logical topic is a discussion on paint. Chapter 9 addresses a range of painting tools and techniques. You might wonder how painting has changed or what new technologies there are. It's just a paintbrush and some paint right? Wrong! There are many new developments in this area. Some changes are small, some are large, but all are important. There has been a resurgence of painted faux finishes both in the theatre and in homes. These techniques help to complete our picture of what is possible from a scenic point of view, and they might even help you make your living room look better!

Chapter 10 follows with a discussion on rigging. Now that the scenery is built, how do you get it into place? How do you get it into its storage position? Does it fly in and out, does it track on and off, or does it just sit there? Once you know the answers to these questions, the solution lies with the rigging department. Rigging at its most basic is all about knots. Where do these knots come from? Again, we look at the history of knots, which all come from sailors! Once we learn about the knots that make theatre rigging safe and easy, we move on to more complicated rigging, where new technology has really made a huge impact. Fifty years ago, if you wanted a platform to move across the stage, somebody had to push it. It sure is different today with the advent of hoist, motors, winches—and computers to control them.

From all things scenic to all things lighting, Chapter 11 discusses lighting. With the same concept as other chapters, we discuss the history of lighting through a variety of developments straight through to today's fixtures. Automation is the biggest overall change. Conventional lighting (meaning nonmoving lights) and intelligent lighting (meaning the fixture automatically moves in some way) are both viable options in today's theatres. In some ways, this is one department where both old and new coexist on the stage seamlessly.

Chapter 12 is all about costumes. Now, you may be thinking, "How can costumes use new technology?" Well, of course, we look at history a bit, as many of those same techniques are still in use today! Many of the newer technologies that costume designers and shops use are not obvious in the actual costumes but in how they get built. Sewing machines have come a long way since the old treadle machines. Patterning software has had huge developments that may change the way a costume shop functions.

From costumes, the next logical step is makeup. In Chapter 13, we explore the basics of makeup starting with evaluating the face. Makeup can show the era of the play, the age of the character, and so much more. We discuss street, or everyday, makeup, as well as aging and some special effects. Street makeup is what works to enhance the features of a face. Aging takes it to the next level by not just enhancing but changing features. Aging makeup can give you insight into how you will look in 10, 20, 30, or more years. Additional effects makeup can include everything from a broken nose, to scarring, to injuries, to all sorts of fantasy characters.

Chapter 14 explores sound. There are many aspects to what sound can do for a theatrical production. At the very least, sound can reinforce the spoken word. Sound can also create everything from a source of the individual sound to wild effects. With the advent of digital technology, the impact sound can have has drastically improved. Sound can now follow a performer around the stage, or around the entire theatre. Digital delays can ensure that audiences of 50 to 50,000 all hear the same thing at the same time.

Special effects will be the focus of Chapter 15. We explore all varieties of effects. Effects can fall into any of the departments we already discussed, or the production may add a special effects department if there is a need for many effects. A prop may need to explode into flames, rain or snow might be needed for a certain scene, one character might be portrayed as having some awful scar, and another character might need to fly through the air. All these effects can be handled in a variety of ways depending on the theatre space and the budget. Bringing in an expert in special effects is sometimes the only way to safely do these effects. Other times, if the effects are done simply enough, someone already on the production team can supervise it.

Now that we've done all the technical stuff, what next? The culmination of working in the theatre is always the actual performance. I don't think we'd ever get much of an audience if all we did was put the set and lighting on stage. Audiences have come to expect actors! Chapter 16 talks about stage management. The stage manager is responsible for organizing the initial rehearsals. The true test of a stage manager comes into play during the technical rehearsals and performances. Without the stage manager, we would never get as far as *house to half*. The stage management team, and yes it is a team, is responsible for everything that happens during the actual performances. Stage managers have to be organized, they have to love paperwork, and they need to work well with a variety of people.

OK, great, you learned all this stuff. What is next? Chapter 17 discusses all the places you might find employment. There are many job opportunities out there, some of which are directly related to the theatre. Many of these possibilities are in related fields, and some are in what seems at first to be totally unrelated fields. We explore all of these options to make sure your training gets put to good use in an area where you will be happy.

Now, let's talk about the web site! In addition to the printed book, there is a matching web site full of information.

Check it out at www.StagecraftFundamentals.com. There is so much information out there to reference that it could take an entire room full of bookshelves. Never mind the fact that the information is ever changing. The more information we can store digitally, the easier it is to search for the one exact thing you are looking for. The information takes all forms:

1. There are lists of schools, theatres, and associations. This combination of organizations will help you find the right place to continue to study and learn your craft. The lists then give you some of the contacts you will need to begin to make the transition from student to successful professional.

2. There are also lists of other textbooks that specialize in one specific area of theatre. They can go into much more depth than I can in this book, so keep them in mind as you continue to yearn for knowledge!

3. Manufacturers, suppliers, and other vendors have allowed me to include their catalogs in PDF form. This can be the beginning of a resource or reference library that I hope you will return to again and again. I listed these companies in a PDF file as well, with their web sites and other contact information.

4. *Lighting and Sound America* worked closely with me to allow reprints of a number of its articles. I excerpted them in the book, but you can access the complete articles on the web site. Don't miss this special chance.

Ideally I've given you enough of an idea of what fun theatre can be that you aren't running out of the classroom screaming. Theatre is fun! I wrote this book so you can learn some of the information you will need while having fun at the same time. Now let's get started!

And remember, this book is a jumping off point—don't stop here!

PART
ONE
History and Art

Where We've Been and Where We're Going

A Brief History and Introduction

We start this chapter by honoring the history I talked about in the Introduction. I'm sure you either have or will be taking a full class on theatre history, so this first chapter is meant more as a refresher. Think of it as an abridged history, as the full history of theatre takes up a whole book the same size as this one and has its own class as well.

Theatre history as we know it started with the Greeks. Our overall organization in the theatre as well as some of the basic conventions we still use have their roots in Greece. If you have ever been backstage in a theatre, it may seem like the technicians are speaking an entirely different language. Well, in some ways, they are. In this chapter, we discuss the history of many of the terms that form a foundation on which we build in later chapters, as we continue to expand our new theatre vocabulary.

Let's begin at the very beginning. I don't mean in time; I mean, what does the word *theatre* mean and where do we get it? Theatre comes from *theatrum* in Latin or *theatron* in Greek. It means a space designated for dramatic performances and spectacles. Only in more modern times have we come to use the same word for the actual buildings and performances.

GREEK THEATRE

Let's dive right into history and begin with the genre created by the Greeks. Since I said much of what we still do today is based on the Greek theatre, what does that actually mean? Well, keep in mind that what we actually know of the Greek theatre we gather from ruins of architecture as well as from artwork. With that said, most of today's scholars agree that the Greek theatre evolved from religious performances; in fact, most of theatre around the world did. The church has always contained an amount of pageantry that is easily transformed in our thoughts to theatrical performances. In fact, many major religious festivals encouraged theatrical performances and often prizes were awarded.

Very few texts from Ancient Greece survive today. But we do know that Thespis, Aeschylus, Aristophanes, Sophocles, and Euripides were the important playwrights. All these playwrights wrote with similar conventions and themes. The plays were written in what we would consider today to be four acts. The first three acts were concerned with everyday issues. The fourth act was often based more on mythology and usually had a lighter subject matter than the first three.

These plays rarely had more than a few actors (all men, by the way), who played all the roles, using masks to change characters as needed. Have you heard of a Greek chorus? Or, have you possibly seen the Woody Allen film *Mighty*

Aphrodite? Well, the chorus was a group of people, sometimes as many as 50, onstage, who sang or chanted in unison to give the audience additional information that was usually moral in tone. Musicians often accompanied the chorus.

The Greek amphitheatre was a huge cavernous space. It was simple in its design, which is actually based on a circle. That circle often had a diameter of close to 80 feet. That is at least two times the size of most theatres we use today! The amphitheatre was most often built into the slope of a hill, which allowed for seating a large number of people, often up to many thousands. Figure 1.1 shows all of these features.

Once the Greeks decided to perform a play and built the amphitheatre, the next thing to worry about was sound. Would the audience be able to hear the actors? Remember all that math in high school you never thought you'd use again? Well, the Greeks used it and used it well. Mathematics played a huge role in the construction of these theatres and in the acoustics. In an audience that seats up to 15,000 people, how could anyone possibly hear the actors' voices? Many people today believe the Greeks were very advanced on the subject of acoustics, maybe even having a better understanding of it than we do today. However, how the Greeks were able to use acoustics is still not completely understood. Lost in the sands of time, so to speak. They needed to understand it. They couldn't turn to microphones and speakers for help.

So, here is what they did. By building the theatre into the side of a hill, they used the natural acoustic properties of the hill to bounce sound up toward the audience (Fig. 1.2). Also, the acting stage was angled higher as it went away from the audience. This created a bowllike effect where the sound could bounce around to all areas of the audience.

■ **Fig. 1.1** The Epidaurus theatre during 4th century BCE.

■ **Fig. 1.2** Greek theatre, showing playing area, seating, and surrounding hillside.

This type of angled stage is called a **rake**. The rake also serves as our basis for modern stage directions.

The further away from the audience, the further "up" in the air the actor was physically. This is why we call the area of the stage furthest from the audience **upstage** (Fig. 1.3). Obviously, that means that the area closest to the audience is considered **downstage**. The other terms we use all the time are **stage left** and **stage right**. These two terms are based on the actors' point of view. What does that mean? Well, picture an actor standing on the stage facing the audience. To the actor's left is stage left, and to the actor's right is stage right.

Let's discuss the physical theatre for a second. The first seats built for the audience were temporary wooden benches. Fairly quickly, these were changed to inlaid stone, which created permanent seating. Once the audience seating was set in stone, so to speak, the rest of the theatre areas

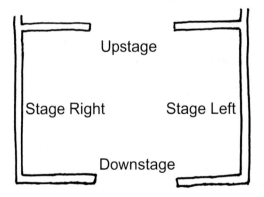

■ **Fig. 1.3** Key areas of today's stage as defined by the Greek's angled stage.

could be figured out. The next development came when the back wall was painted to help create the environment for the play. This **backdrop** served two purposes: It helped the audience better understand where the play was taking place, and it provided a space for the actors to change their costumes and masks out of the sight of the audience. This eventually developed into walls with doors and windows, eventually becoming the type of sets we use today. Another addition was to add columns on either side of the stage. This slowly transformed into what we call our proscenium arch.

The proscenium arch is what formally separates the audience from the acting area. It creates a frame around the stage just like a picture frame for a painting, and some are as ornate. It lets viewers know where to look, and more important, where not to look. The proscenium is one of the most popular theatre types today, and we discuss it more fully later in this chapter.

Theatre is all about the focus. The next logical step was to try to vary the audience's focus for effect. This meant the development of more complex scenery. Sets started to be two stories high. This gave many more possibilities for the actors in terms of entrances and exits. It also helped in the development of the new career path of set designing.

ROMAN THEATRE

Let's march onward to the Romans. They built the next viable genre of theatre. Roman theatre came directly on the heels of the Greeks and continued to build on the traditions already established. The initial plays were produced using Greek scripts and Greek staging. Two of the major playwrights from Rome were Seneca and Plautus. Although they primarily were doing translations, they were still very important to this era of theatre.

There are a few basic differences between Greek and Roman theatre. The Greeks, as we discussed, dealt with earthly and mystical topics within the same performance. The Romans lived much more in the here and now. They didn't just talk about war in a play, they acted it out. This is definitely a reflection of the times. The audience in Rome started to participate more, cheering, booing, and applauding, as they deemed necessary. The audience was so loud at times that the plays would become more of a pantomime—actions without words.

The main Roman performance spaces were still circular, similar to the Greeks. But, whereas the Greeks built their theatres into a natural amphitheatre, the Romans tended to construct artificial walls to create their theatres. The colosseum (Figs. 1.4 and 1.5), as the Romans called it, was still circular in shape. The audience seating was raised, as if it had been built into the side of a hill. The playing area was flat and at the lowest part of the colosseum. At one end of the colosseum was the stage with a scenic wall behind it.

> He means "well" is useless unless he does well.
>
> —Plautus

Another major addition to the architecture of the Roman theatre was the vomitorium. Most likely this is not what you are thinking! The vomitorium was, and still is, a hallway where the actors could enter unseen from the middle of the audience. This area usually led directly underneath the audience risers. The Roman theatre had at least two vomitoriums, one on each side. Not only did actors use these for entrances and exits, but also the audience was often ushered in and out of the theatre using them.

Once the Greek plays had been seen repeatedly, original Roman scripts started to emerge. One big change at this time was in the structure of the Roman plays. They started to develop standard characters who would become very popular during Commedia del'Arte. More on that later though—back to Rome. The actors used various costume pieces to let the audience know with just a glance which "character" they were playing. For example,

- Young men wore black wigs and purple robes.
- Old men wore gray wigs and white robes.
- Slaves wore red wigs.
- Women wore yellow robes (keep in mind that men played the women).

Now this is really important: An actor playing a god wore a yellow tassel. I'm not sure why a tassel meant a god, but hey, it's one of those fun facts of theatre history.

THE MIDDLE AGES

The Middle Ages were an interesting time, to say the least. There was much upheaval of the political, economic, and religious life of the time. So, basically everything was changing. What survived in the theatre was the base that had been established through the Greek and Roman genres. What emerged as new forms were the mimes, minstrels, and jugglers, who traveled from town to town to make

■ **Fig. 1.4** Roman colosseum, as it exists today.

■ **Fig. 1.5** The Roman Odeum in Pompeii, Italy.

their living. This makes perfect sense if you think about it. During any kind of upheaval, planning something to stay in one place can be problematic. Small shows that could easily move around would much better suit the situation of the time.

The next style of theatre was the liturgical drama. Based solely on religious stories from the Bible, this filled a need within the community. Quickly thereafter, the liturgical drama expanded to include dramas based on historical events and mysteries. These plays, taught through moral lessons, often used allegorical characters representing virtues and faults.

Useless Factoid: The Green Room

The green room in a theatre is known for being the one room where you can just go and hang out. You can meet with people and talk before or after a performance. Actors sometimes even meet their fans in the green room. But it is very rare that I've ever seen a green room that is actually green! So how did it get its name?

One story says that the Gaelic word *grian* means sunlit, which is where we get the word *greenhouse*. Since the green room is often one of the few rooms in the theatre with windows, it was labeled the *green room*.

As this was the era of mobile theatre, the sets were often set up on wagon stages with wheels so that they could be moved more easily from one town to another. England was the only country to continue the use of exclusive male casting. Other countries were now integrating casts with both men and women—finally.

Other styles of plays that developed during this time are the passion plays and cycle plays. The passion plays were often performed once a year during specific times of the religious calendar. A passion play is still performed in Oberammergau, Bavaria, during the Lenten season, but now it is every 10 years instead of every year. The cycle plays were massive extravaganzas that often involved hundreds of actors and multiple wagons in a processional. Keep in mind that both were religious in nature, as the church had money to sponsor these events.

Sponsorship became a major part of this period. Much of the control for theatre began to shift during this time from the church to political control. Kings and queens were often the patrons of the arts, commissioning plays to be written for special events and festivals. Not only was patronage in the form of sponsorship to come to the forefront at this time but so was licensing and censorship!

COMMEDIA DEL'ARTE

Commedia is a very interesting part of theatre history (Fig. 1.6). Many of today's theatre characters are still based on the development during this era. Commedia was largely improvised around a base story with an established cast of characters. This gave the actors a great deal of freedom during each performance, as you can imagine. Scenery and props were minimal, although masks were still used to change actors from one character to another. Based on this outline, it was easy for the players to make a performance timely and pertinent to the goings on about the village or town. A Commedia troupe often consisted of 12–15 actors, most of whom were (still) men. A major change is that the actors were paid by receiving a share in the profits from each performance. Commedia is the forerunner of today's improvisation.

There were four topics or basic stories: adultery, jealousy, old age, and love. Sometimes topics were combined within a story. Think about the last play or movie or TV shows

■ **Fig. 1.6** A commedia troupe coming to town on their show wagon.

Fig. 1.7 The Pierrot Commedia del'Arte character.

that you saw. Did the plot line fit into one of these topics? I bet it did. It's amazing how the themes of life haven't changed over time.

The stock characters fell into four basic categories: lovers, masters, servants, and clowns (Fig. 1.7). Again, think about recent shows you've seen. If you break down the characters you'll see categories at the base of each one. The characters were then divided into very specific types within each category. Each specific character had a certain costume and mask that easily identified him or her to the audience.

> The world is a beautiful book, but of little use to him who cannot read it.
>
> **—Carlo Goldoni**

There are many characters within each type; it is really an almost endless list. This should at least give you an idea of how Commedia was established and able to work with the various stories. Each troupe had specialties. What really

survived from this era are the characters and the plots. They are eternally current because they address the basic parts of our lives.

THE RENAISSANCE

At the beginning of the Renaissance, there were still no formal theatre buildings. Performances were mostly still outside at various celebrations. Commedia continued for a time until the masques came into being. Masques were elaborate spectacles, often performed in ballrooms. No expense was spared on these events. An entire ballroom might be transformed into heaven or some exotic location. There were often clouds on the ceiling, angels and cherubs flying about, and chariots racing into view. The story of the masque didn't matter; it was all about the spectacle! This may also sound eerily familiar in today's culture.

> We know what we are, but know not what we may be.
>
> **—William Shakespeare**

Our next step forward in time takes us to Shakespeare. Finally, something you've all heard of! You've heard of Shakespeare, right? Obviously, there other playwrights from this era, and you might even have heard of some of them: Sir Francis Bacon, Ben Johnson, Christopher Marlowe, Sir Thomas More, and John Webster. Anyway, during this time, two big developments occurred. One was to move the performances inside a building that had been specifically built for this purpose. The other change was that people actually began to make a real living doing theatre. Yay!! These two things combined to become a huge turning point for the future of the theatre.

Let's discuss the layout of this new theatre building. There was, of course, a transition phase. Initially, the performances were held within the courtyards of inns. They would lay a platform down to cover watering troughs. Spectators (or audiences) would stand or sit at the opposite end. Properly planned theatres were built fairly quickly from this point. The most famous of these were The Curtain, The Rose, and, of course, The Globe (Fig. 1.8).

The Globe is the theatre where many of Shakespeare's plays were first produced. The architecture of The Globe

■ **Fig. 1.8** Old Globe Theatre, Shakespeare's "home" theatre.

became a reference for new theatres, for years to come. The Globe was built as a hexagon that spanned 55 feet across. Now, think back to the Greeks. Their amphitheatre was 80 feet across. The Globe was a much smaller space. Also the audience area could hold only about 1500 people. How did this new space change or dictate the plays? Well, a smaller space allowed the shows to be much more intimate. We could now deal with more quiet and subtle plot lines with a show.

The Globe had a platform for the stage that was about half the size of the whole building. The stage had two levels for acting. The lower level contained a curtained area and usually two doors. The upper level had another curtained area and two windows. This is the beginning of the "inner above/inner below" idea, where good things happened on the upper level (closer to heaven) and bad things happened on the lower level (closer to hell). Can you see how the Greeks and Romans led us along the path to this type of theatre?

The audience had two basic choices for viewing the show, which affected their proximity to the stage and their ticket cost. If they wanted a less expensive ticket and were willing to stand, there was the open courtyard at the end of the stage, which was called the *pit*. The other option, if the audience wanted to sit and a pay a little more, was the galleries. In today's terms, these were basically semicircular balconies. By the way, speaking of "pits," have you ever heard of some other place near the edge of the stage being called a kind of pit? Always be thinking about today's words and where they come from. It is an interesting thing to study, but more important, it helps us figure out who we are by knowing where we come from.

It is hard to keep this all in chronological order, as so many different cultures were developing their theatre simultaneously. I want to change here from Western theatre to Eastern theatre. Let's do a brief tour of Japanese and Chinese

■ **Fig. 1.9** Noh performance.

theatre to really explore the differences between the genres of theatre and see where more of our traditions are based.

JAPANESE THEATRE

There are three main styles of Japanese theatre: Noh, Bunraku, and Kabuki. You may have images in your head of Kabuki as it is the best known, but each style has very specific characteristics and it is important to know all three.

NOH

Noh theatre is the oldest style of Japanese theatre. It evolved slowly from acrobatic techniques and became popular with both the common folk and aristocrats (Fig. 1.9). Noh uses masks (Figs. 1.10 and 1.11) and is known for its slow, graceful movements. Noh is also a chanted form of drama. Repetitive passages lacking melody are very reminiscent of a much newer form of poetry, haiku.

Noh has four basic categories or topics for the plays: gods, warriors, women, and demons. Other topics occasionally were thrown in, however, these were the main four. Isn't it interesting to see how closely some of these conventions and topics fall in with what Western theatre was doing during a similar time frame?

■ **Fig. 1.10** Noh facial mask of a woman.

Fig. 1.11 Noh facial mask of a man.

BUNRAKU

Bunraku-style theatre flourished after a period of wars that left the culture longing for some form of entertainment. The more a culture is trying to divert itself from the reality of war, the more stylized the art form chosen. This is indeed the case with bunraku. There is one known playwright, Chikamatsu Monzaemon, who wrote thousands of plays during his lifetime, most of which are still used in Japan today. Plot topics included, as usual, conflicts between social obligations and human emotions. We've seen it before, and we'll see it again: Bunraku is a highly stylized performance using puppets that are about one third to one half the size of a human. Bunraku is still one of the most elaborate and sophisticated uses for puppets in the world.

Do not seek to follow in the footsteps of the wise. Seek what they sought.

—Matsuo Basho

Most of the puppets require three performers to manipulate them. Performers can train their entire lives to become master puppeteers. Only masters can operate the head and right arm of the puppet. Lesser puppeteers control the rest of the puppets' movements. One person will speak all the dialogue, changing his or her voice as needed for the various characters. Puppeteers perform in full view of the audience. To heighten the experience for the audience, performers wear black robes and hoods. Only the master puppeteer goes without a hood as a tribute to his or her training and talent.

KABUKI

Kabuki, as I said before, may be the one form of Japanese theatre with which you are familiar (Fig. 1.12). When you hear the word *Kabuki*, what is the first thing that comes to mind? For me, it's kimonos and white face makeup. Kabuki actors were trained in many areas, including dancing, singing, pantomime, and even acrobatics. Kabuki was similar to many other styles of the time, in that men played all the roles in a given play!

This style of play has three main categories or plot topics: the historical play, the domestic play, and the dance. The sets for Kabuki plays are always similar (Fig. 1.13). A walkway or ramp that extends into the audience is used for the actors' entrances and exits. This type of staging brought the actors much closer to the audience and made a more personal and intimate approach. Over time, the sets became more complicated as innovations, like trap doors and revolving stages, were invented.

There are a few traditional characteristics of Kabuki. I already mentioned the kimonos and makeup. The white makeup is made from rice powder base and is used to exaggerate facial features to help create animal and more mystical characters. Another traditional part of Kabuki is posing (Fig. 1.14). The actors pose, creating traditional silhouettes that are easily recognizable to the audience. This helps further the different plot lines. Have you ever seen posing used in a different art form, perhaps with music?

CHINESE THEATRE

Chinese theatre has a very long history, which has been complex at times. Let me explain. The first documented Chinese theatre took place around 1500 BCE. That's

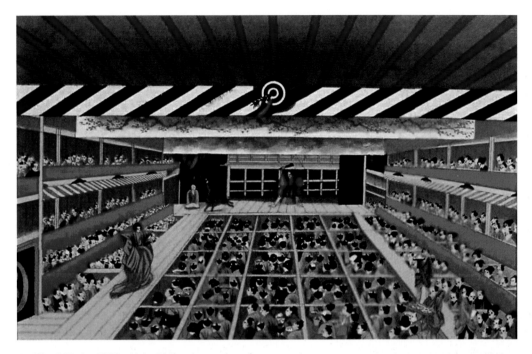

■ **Fig. 1.12** An 1860s Kabuki theatre and performance.

■ **Fig. 1.13** A modern Kabuki production showing actors and scenery.

right, BCE! These were simple performances, which often included music, clowning, and acrobatics. This led directly into shadow puppetry, with two styles of shadow puppets, Cantonese (from the south) and Pekingese (from the north).

Both genres generally performed the same style of plays. These plays were based heavily in adventure and fantasy. As opposed to other theatres we discussed, the Chinese had no interest in depicting the political struggles of the day on stage. Entertainment was a diversion from the struggles of real life.

The two genres differentiated themselves mainly in the making of the puppets. Cantonese puppets were larger and built using thick leather, which created strong shadows. Colors were used symbolically—a black face represented honesty while a red one meant bravery. Pekingese puppets were smaller and more delicate. They were built using thin leather, which was almost translucent. Paint was used in vibrant colors that cast very colorful shadows. Keep in mind that this is the first extensive use of shadows.

> You should examine yourself daily. If you find faults, you should correct them. When you find none, you should try harder.
>
> **—Xi Zhi**

One interesting story from this time is that the head of the puppet was removable. This allowed the heads to be removed when not in use, especially at night. There was a superstition at the time that, if the head was left on a puppet, the puppet might come to life. Imagine the nightmares children must have had when told of this legend. Some puppeteers went so far as to store the heads in a totally separate area from the body.

Puppet theatre was popular for many centuries. As centuries of time passed, more complex plots were developed. The plays were also transformed into a four- to five-act structure. Shadow puppetry reached the height of its popularity in the 11th century. Eventually, the government began to use the theatre for its own needs, at which point, the plots expanded to include more politically based stories.

OK, are you about ready to talk about the modern day and get to some information that may seem more familiar? Well, we've finished with our brief history lesson, but keep it in mind, as we are not leaving it behind. We are taking it with us forward in time, as it is truly the basis for everything that we do today. That is why we had to look at the history before looking at the modern stuff. OK. Ready? Let's begin—or continue.

■ **Fig. 1.14** A modern Kabuki production showing an actor in a classic kabuki pose.

THE 20TH CENTURY

Modern theatre comes in many types, and to complicate our discussion even further, it has many venues, each with its own variations. Let's start with the types, then get into the actual venues. There are basically five types of performance space: proscenium, thrust, arena, black box, and environmental. We break them down one by one. Sometimes, two styles are combined to form a hybrid. But, let us talk about the classical ideas behind these for now. Watch out for lots of new terms.

> Go on failing. Go on. Only next time, try to fail better.
>
> —Samuel Beckett

PROSCENIUM THEATRE

The proscenium theatre is possibly the most recognizable type of theatre today (Fig. 1.15). This design has been the most popular for the 18th, 19th, and 20th centuries (Fig. 1.16). *Proscenium*, as we learned earlier when discussing the Greeks, refers to an archway that separates the acting area from the audience. Usually, but not always, the proscenium arch is close to the downstage edge of the stage.

This type is called an *end stage* on occasion, which references the fact that the stage is at one end of the building and the audience is at the other. The audience directly faces the stage but does not interact with the actors. As with the Greeks, the proscenium becomes a frame through which the audience views the play. This frame is often referred to as the **fourth wall**. The actors treat the fourth wall as if it is a real wall and ignore the audience. Some plays call for the actors to look right at the audience and deliver their lines. This is called *breaking the fourth wall*.

Often a curtain is placed directly upstage of the proscenium and acts as a **house curtain** (Fig. 1.17). The house

■ **Fig. 1.16** The 1869 Bardavon Opera House side boxes.

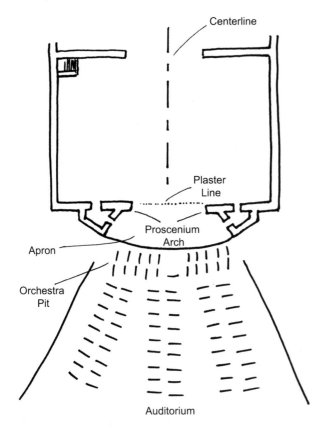

■ **Fig. 1.15** Layout of a proscenium-style theatre.

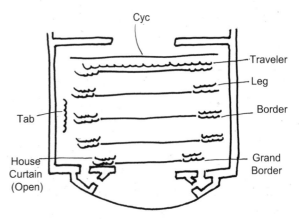

■ **Fig. 1.17** Sample borders and curtains for the theatre.

curtain is used to mask the stage from the audience's view prior to the performance. The house curtain is not always used in this manner today, as some less-traditional productions choose to expose the stage (and the scenery) rather than hide it. Downstage of the house curtain usually hangs the **grand border**. A border is a short curtain that hangs up in the air and goes all the way across the stage from left to right. It helps to mask the workings of the theatre from the audience's view. In this case, the grand border is the one closest to the audience. It is often made of fabric to match the house curtain, rather than the plainer fabric traditionally used for other borders.

Let's talk about some of the architectural details of this type and what we call them. If the stage extends downstage of the proscenium arch, that area of the stage is called the **apron**. The audience sits in seating located in the **auditorium**. This seating can be fixed or moveable. Most often the seating area in the auditorium is raked, similar to the Greek and Roman theatres. It is good not only for acoustics but for seeing the stage unobstructed.

While we're discussing seeing, let's introduce the term **sight lines**. If you draw an imaginary line between the audiences' eye and the stage, that is called a *sight line* or *line of sight*. The common practice is to draw the line from a variety of places using the most extreme angles for both the audience and the stage. The goal for scenic designers is to make sure that the important parts of the set and action fall within this line and are therefore visible to as many audience members as possible.

There is often an area between the stage and the auditorium. It is called the **orchestra pit**. This is an obvious term to explain. The orchestra occupies this space if there is an orchestra. If there is no orchestra in the show, the pit may be covered to provide extra acting area. The name *pit* comes from the fact that most often this area is lower than the auditorium floor, creating a "pit," similar to the standing room area in Shakespeare's time.

There are many more terms to learn. Since these terms apply not only to the proscenium type but to the others as well, I spread them out a bit as we go on to the next type.

THRUST STAGE

The **thrust stage** is usually considered to be a hybrid of the proscenium (Fig. 1.18). There is most often a proscenium of some kind, but it is usually much less ornate. The big difference is with the apron. We talked about how the apron is the part of the stage that extends downstage between the proscenium and the auditorium. Well, in a thrust stage, the apron becomes much larger and "thrusts" into the auditorium. Many people compare it to a tongue or a fashion

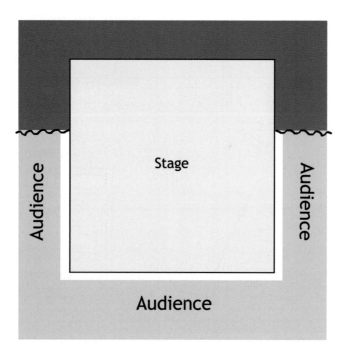

■ **Fig. 1.18** Layout of thrust-style theatre.

runway. There is no rule about its shape or size, just that it extends substantially into the audience area.

The nice effect of a thrust stage is to bring the actors much closer to the audience while still keeping some backstage space for technical support. The audience ends up being located on three sides of the stage. This is a much more intimate setup for everyone. The audience members now feel like they are participating in the play, not just watching it. Another change with the thrust setup is the addition of the vomitorium. Remember these from the Roman theatre? They also add to the intimacy of the experience. The audience can reach out and touch the actors. Not that I recommend this, but it's possible.

> Just say the lines and don't trip over the furniture.
>
> —Noel Coward

In terms of the scenic changes, both the proscenium and the thrust allow the possibility of a backdrop or **cyclorama**. A backdrop in today's theatre is a curtain placed upstage of all, or at least most of, the action. We see the actors against it, and usually, it helps to inform us of where we are: the location or setting for the play.

A cyclorama is slightly different. Traditionally, the cyclorama was a backdrop placed upstage, however, it was wide enough that the sides wrapped around and came downstage toward the audience. This was a more enveloping type of theatre. Eventually the cyclorama starting getting called the **cyc** and now *backdrop* and *cyc* are used almost interchangeably.

Other scenic issues involve the fact that the audience is seated on three sides of the stage. This means that furniture needs to be kept low for sight lines. Remember sight lines? Well, imagine a tall-backed chair placed on the edge of the stage, right in front of an audience member. He or she would see nothing but the chair. Any actual scenery needs to be kept to a minimum and placed carefully, checking sightlines.

ARENA STAGE

For the **arena stage**, think boxing ring and you've the right idea (Fig. 1.19). Arena stages are truly theatre in the round. The stage is in the center of the space and the audience is seated on all sides. There are vomitoriums in each diagonal corner, allowing the audience to be seated, as well as for the actors' entrances and exits. There are many more challenges for the actors and director on this type of stage. The actors' movements are almost always on a diagonal, allowing the

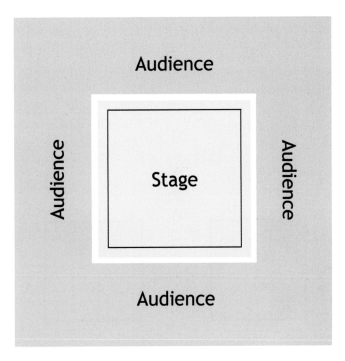

■ **Fig. 1.19** Layout of an arena-style theatre.

maximum number of audience members to see their faces. Arena is reminiscent of some ancient Greek and Roman theatres. It wasn't until the mid-20th century that the arena type became truly popular.

Think back to the discussion of the fourth wall. Arena basically has four fourth walls. Acting with four fourth walls is a very different experience for the actors as well! Scenery is a bigger challenge than in thrust, as there is no backstage area. Scenic design for an arena is about the furniture placement and the floor. Occasionally, the vomitoriums have scenery in them as well. This can ease the transition of the scenery ending and auditorium beginning.

> If I see an ending, I can work backwards.
> —Arthur Miller

BLACK BOX

The **black box** is the most flexible of all the spaces so far. Basically black box is just what it says—it's a big black room with absolutely nothing in it (Fig. 1.20). Very simple, very plain. It's a space in need of a production. The production brings in chairs and maybe risers for the audience. They also bring in a stage, raised or not. This allows for infinite possibilities within one space. It is very flexible and this can be really wonderful for some productions. It allows the production to truly make its mark on the whole experience of the performance.

The black box is very popular with colleges and other training schools, as it is easily reconfigured to the needs of the production. This allows the school to set up the room in any configuration to give the students the greatest experience with varying theatre types. Black box theatres are usually fairly small. This makes them perfect for experimental works, which may have a smaller budget and expect smaller audiences. Keep in mind that, if every production had to exist in a 1200-seat house, it would preclude some productions from ever being mounted.

> Don't live down to expectations. Go out there and do something remarkable.
> —Wendy Wasserstein

ENVIRONMENTAL THEATRE

Environmental theatre came about during the 1960s with the help of many avant-garde groups. The basic idea is to provide integration between the audience and the actors. The audience is expected to participate in the performance at some greater level than usual. Another aspect of this type is that there are multiple areas of focus in the performance simultaneously. I said that theatre is all about the focus. This is one type of theatre where the chaos created by dividing the audience's focus is the whole point of the style. The best example I can think of is a three-ring circus. There is always something to look at. You need not watch everything, nor can you. But, ultimately, you get to see the performance you choose based on what you watch.

The actual spaces for these performances range from converted garages to parks to castles to monuments. Scenery is used at a minimum, as the whole point is to go to a "realistic" setting. As the name suggests, environmental theatre brings the audience to the environment instead of creating a manufactured environment through traditional theatrical conventions.

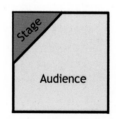
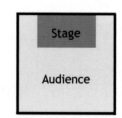
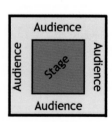

■ **Fig. 1.20** Layout of black box–style theatre.

THEATRE VENUES

Theatre venues are our next topic. This is the fun part—a list of the various places you might get to work someday. Let me preface this list by saying that the best theatre in the world is not found in a specific venue. The best theatre in the world is found in the hearts of the performers and the audience. Do not allow yourself to be swayed by what the reviewers say. If you go to a performance, no matter where it is, and you are really moved and touched by it, *it is good theatre*. Please keep in mind, as we begin to discuss venue, that the type of venue is in no way linked to the quality of the production.

Broadway (New York) and the West End (London) are considered the crème de la crème of theatre. Refer to the last paragraph for my thoughts on this. I will admit that these two venues have the biggest budgets. They are also the best known worldwide. Opera happens all around the world, from the Metropolitan Opera in New York to Covent Garden in London to the Staatsoper in Vienna. These all have huge shows having more special effects than almost anything except blockbuster films. Most of these venues have a traditional proscenium stage.

Off-Broadway in New York and the Fringe in London are the places for the smaller shows. The venues become a little less glamorous and vary from proscenium to thrust to arena. Off-Off-Broadway is known for smaller, more remote, and less traditional spaces. These spaces can include gymnasiums, church basements, and black box theatres on the 10th floor of an office building.

Next, let's talk about regional and repertory theatres. In my opinion, some of the best theatre happens here. Both venues are often not-for-profit and therefore depend on donations for their annual budget. Since they are not actually trying to make money, their goal is to create great theatre. Working for this type of venue is very freeing . The regional theatres are just what they sound like. They are located around the world in various geographic regions. The repertory theatres, by their name, are theatre companies that produce more than one show at a time and may have alternating performances within the schedule.

Summer stock and community theatres are the next group of venues. Summer stock, as its name suggests, occurs during the summer. A "season" often consists of five separate productions being produced during a 10-week season. This is a major part of the training for young performers and technicians. The experience you get in such a short time is unrivaled anywhere else in the industry. Community theatres often operate during the normal season, not the summer. It is a similar experience to summer stock although at a slower pace.

Dinner theatre is a unique experience where your ticket price covers not only the show but also your meal. The room where you sit and eat your meal is the same room where the performance happens. Some people find this a little strange, but it can be a very enjoyable experience. You stay at your table continuing to eat and enjoy the cuisine—and a show starts at the end of the room on a stage, or better yet, the actors wander through the dining room and it becomes more of an environmental theatre type.

Fringe festivals, street theatre, and improvisational theatre fall into a similar category. These are all examples of smaller, more avant-garde performances that are easily moved from one venue to another. Festivals are a great way to see a large number of performances in a short time. Street theatre is just plain fun. You simply walk down the street, and who knows what you will see or who will be performing.

The last venue I want to address is themed entertainment. This is when theatre-type shows take place inside an amusement park, casino, or something similar. This is one of the fastest-growing venues in the industry. Think of it as theatre on vacation! The shows that take place in this type of venue are often more extensively designed and created than for other venues. This venue tends to also put on the show for the long term, even permanently.

We finish our discussion by talking about the different styles of theatre. Differing styles are chosen by writers and directors based on the needs of the play and what they are trying to achieve. The following is a list of some, but certainly not all, of the styles prevalent in today's productions. This list is incomplete, as space is somewhat limited, and a complete list could become a book of its own. The glory of today's theatre is that parts of each style may be borrowed and combined to create new styles. This is an ever-changing and evolving list. I have tried to list, at the very least, the basics that we call on today.

- **Comedy:** This style is not always full of humor, but usually focuses on a problem that has a happy outcome. Lighter themes are used and often the comedy comes out of stressful situations.

- **Fantasy:** These plays are often set in another realm. The interesting thing is that the characters are still dealing with the universal themes we've been discussing throughout.

- **Farce:** Farce is a more extreme form of comedy. The plot lines in farce tend to push the limits between physical and verbal stereotypes. Often, this includes a physical layout that does not follow conventional construction.

- **Melodrama:** This is a sentimental drama similar in themes to daytime soap operas. Melodramas feature stock characters, such as the noble hero, the long-suffering heroine, and the cold-blooded villain.

- **Romantic comedy:** Romantic comedy is comedy in which the main characters are often romantically linked.

- **Theatre for social change:** Such theatre addresses social issues with the ideal of achieving societal change.

- **Tragedy:** This is a drama that deals in a serious and dignified way about sorrowful or terrible events.

So, here is the brief history and introduction. You now have a basic understanding of where we, as theatre geeks, come from. You should have enough knowledge in your head to take on the next chapter and begin moving forward to the glory we in the know, call theatre!

Apron

Arena

Auditorium

Backdrop

Black box

Cyclorama

Cyc

Downstage

Environmental

Fourth wall

Genre

Grand border

House curtain

Orchestra pit

Proscenium arch

Rake

Sight lines

Stage

Stage left

Stage right

Thrust

Upstage

Vomitorium

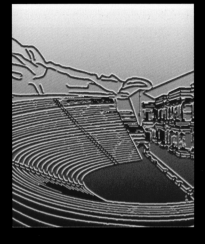

CHAPTER ONE
Study Words

BROADWAY - OFF BROADWAY - OFF-OFF BROADWAY - LORT - REGIONAL - COMMUNITY -TOURING - EDUCATIONAL INTERACTIVE COMEDY TROUPS - CORAL GROUPS CIRCUS ROCK & OPERA TRADE - MIME

THE SHOW

PRODUCER – DIRECTOR – AUTHOR – COMPOSER

COMPANY MANAGER – ACCOUNTANT – LAWYER – INVESTORS

SET DESIGNER – LIGHTING DESIGNER – FX DESIGNER – COSTUME DESIGNER

MUSICAL DIRCTOR – CHOREOGRAPHER – CASTING DIRECTOR – PUBLACIST

STAGE MANAGER – ASSISTANT STAGE MANAGER – TECH DIRECTOR – MASTER ELECTRICIAN

PRINCIPAL CAST & UNDERSTUDIES – CHOURUS – DANCERS – REHERSAL PIANIST – MUSIC ARRANGER

SCENE SHOP – ELECTRICS SHOP – AV HOUSE – MUSICIANS – LOAD IN CREW STAGE/ELECTRICS – PROP MASTER

FLYMEN – RUNNING CREW – CHANGERS – HEAD CARPENTER – BOARD OPERATOR – SOUND OPERATOR – PROJECTIONIST

ASSISTANT COMPANY MANAGER – HOUSE MANAGER – BOX OFFICE MANAGER – HOUSE STAFF – CONSESSIONS MANAGER

ASSISTANT COMPANY MANAGER – TICKET SALES PEOPLE – PHONE SALES PEOPLE – PRODUCTION ACCOUNTANT

MAINTENANCE CARPENTER – SCENIC MAITENANCE ARTIST – ON CALL FOCUS CREW – THEATER CLEANING CREW

CLEANING / LAUNDRY SERVICE – PICK UP SERVICE – PROFESSIONAL ENGINEER – BUILDING DEPARTMENT – FIRE DEPARTMENT

USHERS – USHERS – USHERS – USHERS – USHERS – USHERS – USHERS – USHERS – USHERS – USHERS – USHERS

AUDIENCE – AUDIENCE – AUDIENCE – AUDIENCE – AUDIENCE – AUDIENCE – AUDIENCE – AUDIENCE – AUDIENCE

It's All About Collaboration

Design for Theatre

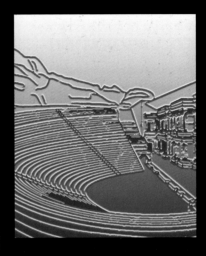

You want to be a technician (or think you might) and are wondering why you should be learning about design. The best way to be a good technician is to understand the designer's process. And the best way to be a designer is to be prepared and learn from others who have been doing it longer than you. Then, as questions arise or perhaps problems needing creative solutions, you can be part of the final solution. We reached the point where we discuss the process of design. And, yes, it is a process. Designers don't sit down and just draw pretty pictures. They read scripts, do research, go to production meetings, and so forth.

> The director calls to ask if you're interested and you read the play to decide whether to say yes or no. Liking the play is most important! If you don't care about the play there's no point to doing it; you'll never come up with good ideas. After that, you and the director start to have conversations.
>
> **—Derek McLane**

PRODUCTION TEAM COLLABORATION

We start at the beginning. There is an order to the production staff. Each position reports to another. This order is what keeps the team organized and the production moving forward to opening night. Whatever position you might be interested in having, it is very important to know how the team works. Take a look at Figure 2.1 to see how the whole production team is shown from producer all the way to the running crew. Where do you think you want to fit in?

Let's move on to our discussion of designers. There are a number of reasons for taking a job. Maybe the director is someone you have always wanted to work with or someone you have worked with many times before. Maybe the script is new, exciting, or earth-shattering or a revival of a play you always loved. Maybe the design team (the other designers) is composed of people you always wanted to work with or have worked with many times before. Maybe the director is assembling a team of people who know each other so well that the creative **collaboration** is already in place and you can communicate intuitively with each other's creative choices. Maybe the production is going to start out of town and move to Broadway. Or maybe, just maybe, the rent is due and you have no other job.

> I read a script until I understand that either I have something to contribute or I don't. If I don't, I don't take the job.
>
> **—Geoff Dunbar**

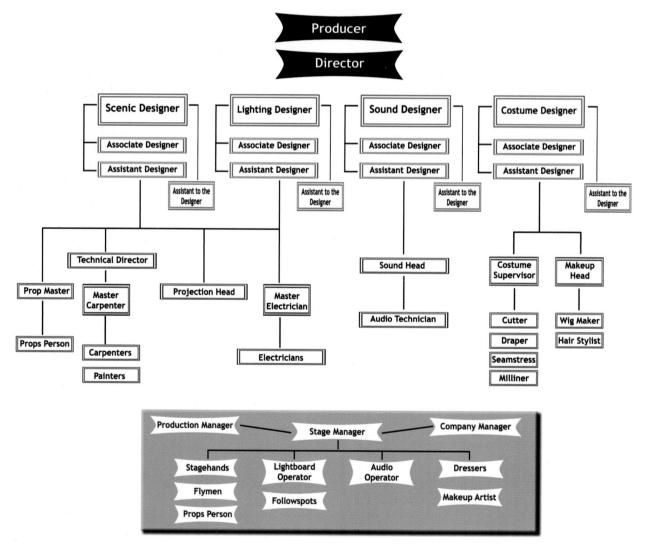

■ **Fig. 2.1** Some of the employment positions on a production and how the hierarchy is laid out.

To be perfectly honest, all these reasons can be the right reason to take a job. The hope is always that several of these will be why you take the job. If you take the job just to cover the rent, be aware that this is what you are doing. If you have grander ideas about collaborating with your "dream team" of designers, be aware of that, too. Know why you are accepting a job and how that will influence your work. What do I mean by *influence*? Well, if you take a job because of the dream team, will you expect to work harder than if you take the job to pay the rent? Your answer should be *no*.

You should be willing to work as hard as possible on every job you accept. There is no such thing as an inferior production, unless you make it one. There is also no such thing as a guaranteed career-making show. If you ask people how they got to where they are in their careers, you will hear a different story every time. This is important to know and remember, because there is not just one way to a successful career. Everyone must find his or her own path. And it always starts with the first step.

So, what does that mean to you? Well, let's look at some possibilities. You accept a job even though the production is in a church basement, in some town that isn't even on the map yet. It turns out that a friend of a friend of someone connected to the show knows a "big-time" director and the director will be attending opening night. Wouldn't you be disappointed if you had done mediocre work because you thought of the production as a throwaway? The reverse can also be true. You have what you think will be the production to take your career to the next level, then no one "important" comes to see it. Are you disappointed? Does this make your work any less good? Absolutely not.

> It's not Show Fun . . . it's Show Business.
> **—M. L. Geiger**

My goal has always been to do the best work I can, every single time. If I am happy with my work, then I can assume that someone will eventually see it and agree with me. This is how I started out my career, how I continued my career, and how my career has gotten to where it is today. Keep in mind that every production should be a learning experience as well. I do not say that because this is a textbook and you are a student. I say that because, when we stop learning, we stop growing. As artists we always want to be pushing ourselves to be better, to learn more, to strive for the next level. This is a mindset as much as anything else. If you stop striving, you stop creating.

OK, so, I got off on a tangent. Let's talk about *collaboration*. This is the single most important word to remember as a designer. Before you go off to work on your own part of the design and production, you must first begin the process of collaboration that will take you all the way through to opening night. If we as theatre artists wanted to work by ourselves, we would be studio artists doing painting or sculpture. What makes us different, and unique, is that we actually enjoy the input other designers give us. The goal is to work as a team and collectively create a production where there once was none. We continue to discuss collaboration throughout the chapter as it is at the base of every good design.

DESIGN PROCESS

Now, let's talk about the steps to design. Each design discipline has some similarities and some differences. We discuss the similarities here, then go into detail in the individual chapters about the specific process during implementation. That is where things vary a bit. So the phone rings and you are offered a design job or asked for an interview. It used to be that you had to sit at home waiting for that phone call. Today's technology means you may get a phone call at home or on your cell phone; a message on your answering machine, or a fax, email, instant message, or whatever. There are so many ways to keep in touch—maybe you'll get a text message that asks you for a meeting. All these ways are valid forms of communication, and you have to be aware that they are now a necessary part of our world.

READING THE SCRIPT

What do you do next? Well, everybody has his or her own way of working. The design process varies slightly from one project to another. There is no one formula that works for everyone. With that said, certain things do have to happen in a certain order. The first thing most designers do is get a copy of the script and meet with the director. The script is really your road map (Fig. 2.2). It should inform all your decisions and choices. The director is the driver, to continue the analogy. These are your first two points of contact with any production and possibly job.

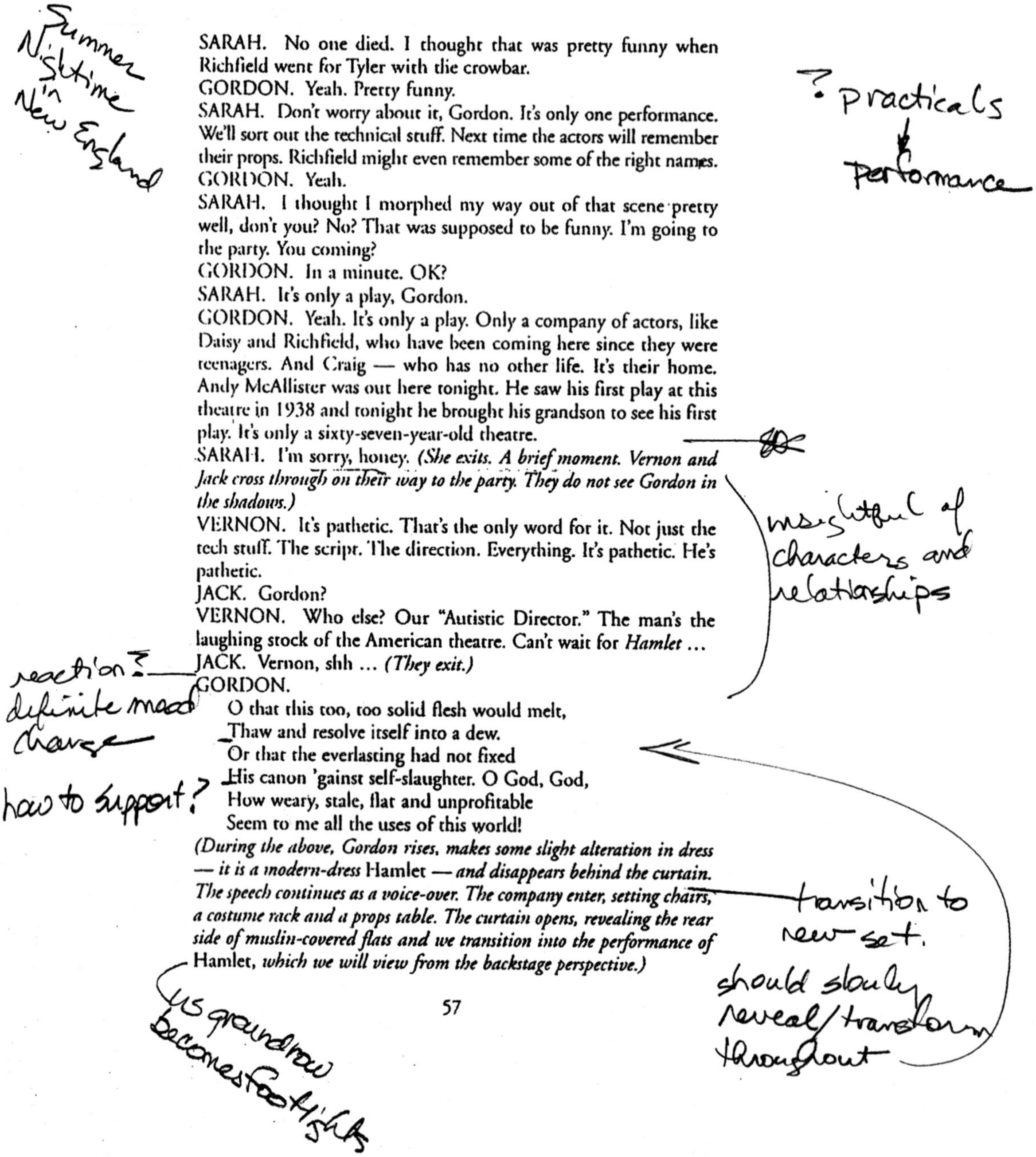

Summer
Nightime
in
New England

? Practicals
↕
Performance

SARAH. No one died. I thought that was pretty funny when Richfield went for Tyler with the crowbar.

GORDON. Yeah. Pretty funny.

SARAH. Don't worry about it, Gordon. It's only one performance. We'll sort out the technical stuff. Next time the actors will remember their props. Richfield might even remember some of the right names.

GORDON. Yeah.

SARAH. I thought I morphed my way out of that scene pretty well, don't you? No? That was supposed to be funny. I'm going to the party. You coming?

GORDON. In a minute. OK?

SARAH. It's only a play, Gordon.

GORDON. Yeah. It's only a play. Only a company of actors, like Daisy and Richfield, who have been coming here since they were teenagers. And Craig — who has no other life. It's their home. Andy McAllister was out here tonight. He saw his first play at this theatre in 1938 and tonight he brought his grandson to see his first play. It's only a sixty-seven-year-old theatre.

SARAH. I'm sorry, honey. *(She exits. A brief moment. Vernon and Jack cross through on their way to the party. They do not see Gordon in the shadows.)*

VERNON. It's pathetic. That's the only word for it. Not just the tech stuff. The script. The direction. Everything. It's pathetic. He's pathetic.

JACK. Gordon?

VERNON. Who else? Our "Autistic Director." The man's the laughing stock of the American theatre. Can't wait for *Hamlet* …

JACK. Vernon, shh … *(They exit.)*

GORDON.
    O that this too, too solid flesh would melt,
    Thaw and resolve itself into a dew.
    Or that the everlasting had not fixed
    His canon 'gainst self-slaughter. O God, God,
    How weary, stale, flat and unprofitable
    Seem to me all the uses of this world!

(During the above, Gordon rises, makes some slight alteration in dress — it is a modern-dress Hamlet *— and disappears behind the curtain. The speech continues as a voice-over. The company enter, setting chairs, a costume rack and a props table. The curtain opens, revealing the rear side of muslin-covered flats and we transition into the performance of* Hamlet, *which we will view from the backstage perspective.)*

57

msightful of characters and relationships

reaction?
definite mead
change
how to support?

transition to new set.
should slowly reveal/transform throughout

us groundrow becomes footlights

■ **Fig. 2.2** A script page with designer notes from one of the first reads.

> The only reading that counts is the first; it determines if I will take the project. The script has to say something to me, and I have to see where my visions will best represent the author's vision.
>
> **—Michael A. Fink**

Most designers admit to reading the script several times. The first time through the script is usually to read and enjoy the story, plot lines, and characters. Nothing more. If you read it through and you enjoy it, most likely you will accept the project. This first reading is like a first date. It should be a glance into the future. You will spend a good amount of time working on a play, and this is the critical moment when you have to decide whether you like the script enough to dedicate the next months or years of your life to it. Don't take this lightly.

MEETING WITH THE DIRECTOR

The next step is almost always the initial meeting. This meeting is often between you and the director. Many designers prefer that the initial meeting is with the whole team: the director, set designer, costume designer, lighting designer, sound designer, and any specialty designers who may be needed. Specialty designers can include projections, pyrotechnics, and various other special effects. It is important to have the whole team together for several reasons. In design, the most important word I can think of is *collaboration*. I know I said it before, but this is the major difference between theatre people and everyone else.

During this initial meeting it is best to discuss what the play means. Why are we doing it? One main topic of conversation is usually about the **style** of the production (Fig. 2.3). You may ask, what is style? The terms *presentational* and *representational* are the most often-used styles of production. Let me explain the difference between the two. A **presentational** style offers a performance in which everyone is fully aware that the actors are at work on a stage, speaking and acting out a script, under lights, and in costumes. There is

■ **Fig. 2.3** A sketch for Verdi's *Macbeth*, designed by Salvatore Tagliarino.

no attempt to disguise the fact that a theatrical performance is taking place to entertain the audience.

The **representational** style of production differs in that it shows naked truths about ordinary existence within specific situations. This style can be broken into two substyles: realism and naturalism. **Realism** is based in our own world, with recognizable characters having no supernatural powers. The characters do the sorts of things that ordinary people do every day. **Naturalism,** on the other hand, is much more specific. There are no stereotypes per se but specific characters in specific environments. The purpose of this very detailed world is to show how a person's character and life choices are determined in part by the environmental or social forces. Production elements are as specific to the environment as the characters' descriptions. Often "real" props, furniture, clothing, and lighting are assimilated into the production for that added feel of realism. Once a style is decided on, it becomes the reference for your next set of choices.

Once the initial meeting is over, you sit down and start to think. You take in the information about style and how the director is approaching the script. You should now begin to come up with your **concept,** which is your unique way of looking at the show. Keep in mind that the director also has a concept, and that your concept *must* work with the director's. Again, collaboration. You may find an image, photograph, or painting that strikes you as the essence of the production. You can use this concept to guide your choices of color, shape, direction, and all the other choices you need to make.

SCRIPT BREAKDOWN

OK, so the first meeting is over and you decided to stick with it and make this the best design you ever did. What is next? Go back to the script. You should now read the script again, paying more attention to detail while keeping in mind all the information that came out of that initial meeting. How does the newly chosen style help you to start visualizing the production? This reading is where you begin to break down the script.

The design process for Michael A. Fink is all about questions:

- **Who:** How many characters, in what age range or attitude? What is my vision of them from what is in the script and my own internal perceptions from life? Have

I worked with the director before and do we share a common language?

- **What:** Is there is driving theme to the script or story or concept that it embodies? What is the vision—natural, farcical, strange, normal?
- **Where:** Do the events in the script take place in an English drawing room, old fort, or bordello? What is the size of the theatre and its capabilities?
- **When:** When does the play take place: period play, time of day, season? Do we witness events as they unfold, as flashbacks, or as dreams?
- **Why:** Why are the characters driven to do what they do? Why is there an interest in presenting this story?
- **How:** How will each moment tell this story? If you can visualize your idea properly it can come from the ethereal to the material.

The script breakdown will vary depending on which design you will do. The basic idea is to identify the circumstances of the play. You need to determine whether the play takes place during the day or night. What season is it? Do the scenes take place inside or outside? Is there a specific geographic location? It doesn't matter what the style is, you have to determine these things before you can either follow them or abstract from them.

RESEARCH

The next step is to do your **research**. Now, what does that mean? You have to decide what the script requires and find out what is available to achieve that. Geoff Dunbar told me, "If a script needs a fire, I will research how fires are being done this year (in addition to already knowing how fires were done last year)."

Research also means that, if your production is set in 1818 London, you better find out what 1818 London looks, feels, and smells like. Do not guess, and certainly don't make it up. All designers should research the architecture, clothing, lighting, political events, atmosphere—everything you can think of. Your research should include shapes, lines, and colors that are appropriate. You are looking for pictures. They can be photos or drawings and paintings (Fig. 2.4).

■ **Fig. 2.4** Stained-glass art, *Long Beach*, by Isabella Rupp.

Even sculpture can be research. Any visual reference that helps inform your choices is considered research. Once you have done your research and before you start making choices, you must consider the style decided on in the first meeting.

The style, together with your research, helps you choose the right direction in which to move forward. You should be starting to form ideas now for your design. You might even be doing rough sketches.

Disregarding the audience's expectations (or failing to research what those expectations might be), is basically disregarding the audience. This is a failure of the most basic reason for presenting a work: to make some sort of connection with an audience! Of course, one can (and should) trump/trash/exceed the expectations. But if one doesn't know what the expectations are to begin with, then it's less than a gamble . . . it's just arrogance! If you're not doing it for an audience, then it's just something that you should work out on paper at home, and save everyone else the hassle . . . and money!

—Andy Warfel

At this point, let's talk for a minute about audiences. After all, the audience is who actually pays to see our work. Andy Warfel has some interesting thoughts on audiences:

Wow, I couldn't have said it better. So always, always keep the audience in mind while you research.

Part of the research process is to know about symbols. Huh? You might be thinking, Why are symbols important? Well, first, let's define what a symbol is. A **symbol** is a picture, object, or color that stands for something else (Fig. 2.5). As you start to get ideas of what you want the design to look like, you have to be aware of what things will mean when the audience sees them. Take some of the most common symbols. The eagle is used as symbol of freedom; the skull and crossbones are a sign of danger (Fig. 2.6); the lightbulb is often used as a symbol for an idea. Have you got the idea? Every image has some meaning that comes along with it like baggage (Fig. 2.7). The audience already knows these meanings, so you have to be aware of them before you use something that conjures a meaning other than what you intended.

Let's take research in a slightly different direction. There are things about the history of architecture that you have to

Fig. 2.6 The skull and crossbones are a symbol that can have many differing meanings, but they all refer to some kind of danger.

Fig. 2.7 The cross and crown are a traditional Christian symbol, appearing in many churches as well as in heraldry.

know. There are styles of architecture, periods of architecture, orders of architecture–you get the idea. You need to understand the basic ideas of each, realizing you can always reference a history when needed for more details. So, here we go!

STYLES OF ARCHITECTURE

The following examples relate to the stylistic feel of all elements for the visual part of a production. Think about art history as you read this section and start to make correlations between these periods and artistic trends. Bear with me, there are lots of new words, but they will come back again and again. Periods of architecture are usually named for the styles from which they came:

- **Classicism:** This style is based on idealistic models or established conservative standards. It embraces a high level of taste, sobriety, and proportion. Conventional formality is another way to think of classicism.

- **Romanticism:** This is an imaginative emphasizing individualism in thought and expression in direct opposition to the restrictive formality of classicism. Other traits of this period are freedom of fancy in conception and treatment, picturesque strangeness, or suggestions of drama and adventure.

- **Realism:** This is a representation of nature without idealizing (as in classicism) or inclining to the emotional or extravagant (as in romanticism). There is an interest in the accurate and graphic that may degenerate into excessive detail and preoccupation with the trivial.

- **Impressionism:** This is a type of realism and romanticism combined that seeks to allow the artist to define the personality of the subject matter. Through the use of color and light, the subject matter's personality is revealed.

- **Expressionism:** This is a style in which the artist seeks to express an emotional experience placed onto the subject matter. This style allows the artist and the art to combine and form an altered reality.

- **Postmodernism:** This style rejects the preoccupation with purity of form and technique. Mixtures of style elements from the past are applied to sparse modern forms. The observer is asked to bring his or her opinions of this combined form, as there is no real standard or unity.

ORDERS OF ARCHITECTURE

Again, keep in mind that this is key to understanding where things come from and how to use them today. Different column types fall into the five so-called classical orders, which are named *Doric, Ionic, Corinthian, Tuscan,* and *composite.* Each order is made up of the column, its base, shaft, and capital. Each has its own distinctive proportions and character (Fig. 2.8).

In Greece, the Doric was the earliest order to develop, and it was used for the Parthenon and for most temples. It has no base and was developed around the 5th century BCE. The Ionic with scroll-like capitals soon followed it. The Corinthian was rarely used until the Romans adapted it. This order includes leaves on the capitals in a more natural replica and dates from the end of the 5th century BCE. The Roman orders made greater use of ornaments than the Greek orders, and their column proportions were more slender. The Romans, in their temples and other public buildings, used all three of the Greek orders, together with two others of their own devising, the Tuscan and the Composite orders. The composite first appeared on the arch of Titus in Rome in 82 CE. Although no Tuscan columns survive, this order was thought to originate in the Etruscan times. There is obviously a lot more to the orders, but that is enough for now!

DESIGN MEETING

So, you did the research. What is next? At about this point, there is usually another design meeting. This is the time to discuss with the design team any research you might have found and explain how you might use it. A true collaboration continues during this step, as each designer brings his or her thoughts to the table. Thoughts exchanged freely at this meeting are the way to a wonderful production.

Everyone's ideas are as valid and important as everyone else's. This meeting is to exchange those ideas. Each person brings his or her own perspective on what was discussed at the first meeting. This is the best way to collaborate and eventually produce a well-designed show.

After the meeting, you may want to do some additional research, based on new thoughts and ideas that came through the discussion. The next phase is to sketch. Scenic and costume designers will begin to sketch out their rough ideas. A working ground plan should be coordinated with the lighting designer and then further developed through collaboration of ideas (Figs. 2.9 and 2.10). Did I mention collaboration again? Yes, yes, I did. It is the key. Working in a void makes for a disjointed production. Working together is definitively the way to go.

Design meetings continue to happen throughout the rehearsal process. In addition, designers often attend rehearsals. This gives them the opportunity to spend time with the director prior to the pressures of technical rehearsals. It also allows the designers to see the development of the characters and blocking. It may seem that this is unrelated to design, but it is not. It's that collaboration thing again. The better informed you are about every aspect of the production, the better you can do your individual job.

DESIGNERS DRAW, RENDER, AND DRAFT

We are now at the part of the process where designers do what we think they do: draw, render, and draft. All of this is discussed in detail in Chapter 5. But let me give you a brief look at what is in store. Drawing, rendering, and drafting are the best ways to get visual ideas across. The first thing that needs to happen is for the director to see what is in the designer's head. If the ideas stay inside your head, it does no good. You have to get the ideas out of your head so others can see them, react to them, and help you implement them.

Another aspect of being a designer is keeping a morgue. No, not for dead bodies, for images. If you want to be a designer, you should start a morgue. A morgue is an organized collection of images. There is no need to invent ideas when you have the whole world at your Internet fingertips. Different designers organize their morgues in different ways. Set designers may keep architectural research, landscaping research, furniture research, and the like. Costume designers may keep research of each period in history, organizing separately by men and women or hairstyles and

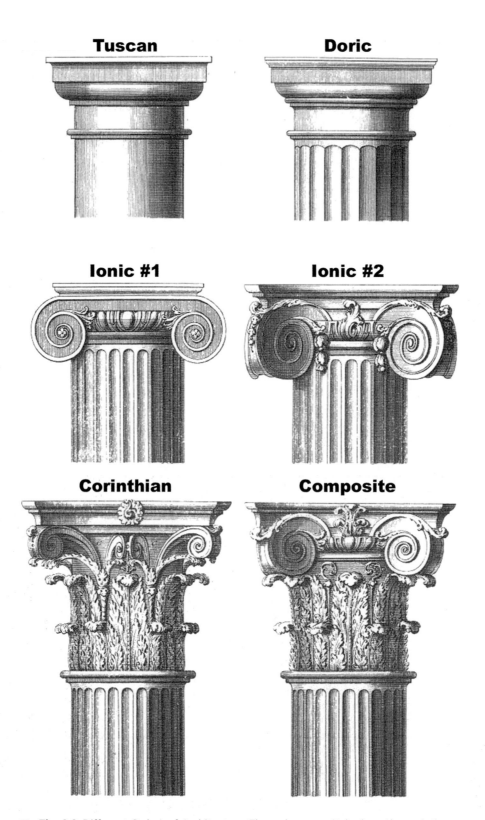

Tuscan

Doric

Ionic #1

Ionic #2

Corinthian

Composite

■ **Fig. 2.8** Different Orders of Architecture. The column capitals show the varieties possible. Also how they grew and progressed throughout time.

■ **Fig. 2.9** *Camelot Opening Scene*, watercolor rendering by Oliver Smith. © Rosaria Sinisi.

■ **Fig. 2.10** *Camelot Outside Camelot*, watercolor rendering by Oliver Smith. © Rosaria Sinisi.

■ **Fig. 2.11** *The Crucible* at the NYU Department of Graduate Acting/Department of Design for Stage and Film in April 2005. Director, Tazewell Thompson; Scenic Designer, Alexandre Corazzola; Costume Designer, Meg Zeder; and Lighting Designer, G. Benjamin Swope.

accessories (Fig. 2.11). Lighting designers may keep images that evoke different moods, different times of day, or different seasons. The goal is to have research at your disposal to help trigger ideas as you work on various productions.

We're now going to look at two plays sharing four productions from the Shakespeare Theatre Company. Look at the differences between two different productions of *Coriolanus* that took place 9 years apart (Figs. 2.12 and 2.13)

and two productions for *Othello* that took place 14 years apart (Figs. 2.14 and 2.15). Based on all our discussions in this chapter about the design process and the importance of the audience, look at the four photos and really start to "see" how the designs are different. Are the differences based on a change in the audience's expectations or changes due to the materials and techniques available, different designers, or all of these?

■ **Fig. 2.12** *Coriolanus* at the Shakespeare Theatre Company in 2000. Director, Michael Kahn.

■ **Fig. 2.13** *Coriolanus* at the Shakespeare Theatre Company in 1991. Director, William Gaskill.

■ **Fig. 2.14** *Othello* at the Shakespeare Theatre Company in 2005. Director, Michael Kahn. (Cast: Gregory Wood-dell, Avery Brooks, Colleen Delany, Patrick Page, and Lise Bruneau.)

■ **Fig. 2.15** *Othello* at the Shakespeare Theatre Company in 1997. Director, Jude Kelly. (Cast: George Causli and Lana Buss.)

Classicism
Collaboration
Composite
Concept
Corinthian
Doric
Expressionism
Impressionism
Ionic
Naturalism
Postmodernism
Presentational
Realism
Representational
Research
Romanticism
Style
Symbol
Tuscan

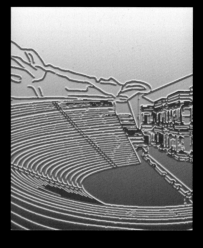

CHAPTER TWO
Study Words

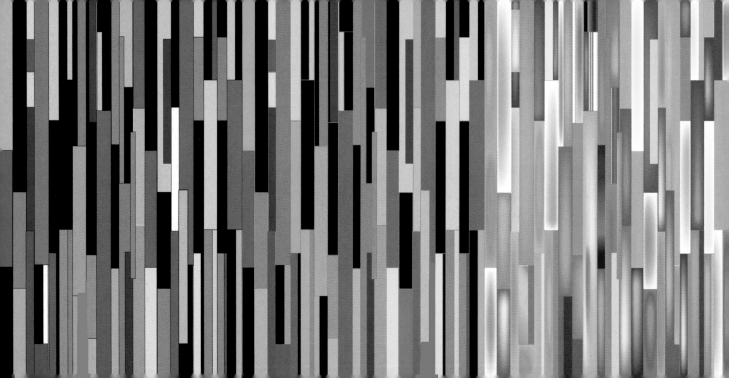

Making It Visual

Composition

The next logical step in the conversation is to discuss composition. Theatre is a visual art form. To plan any production, the producers must hire visual people. These people are called *designers*. Designers are visual artists who need to understand composition. Let's explore the basics of this topic. All that the audience sees and perceives is directly relayed to them through composition and color. Composition is the basis for all things visual. At its most basic, we can discuss whether a line is straight or curved. Does it have pattern or rhythm? This begins our discussion of composition.

> Before you compose your picture it's a good idea to ask yourself why you're doing it.
>
> **—Anonymous**

We start by defining *composition*. As simply as I can say it, composition is the placement or arrangement of objects. Objects are placed in relation to other objects to form a grouping. This grouping is called a *composition*. The goal is to inform your viewers where you would like them to look within the composition. The theatre stage is a dynamic composition. Scenery, lighting, and actors constantly move around the stage, reconfiguring the composition. In artwork, whether it be a painting on canvas or a sculpture, compositions are static. Another word for composition is *focus*.

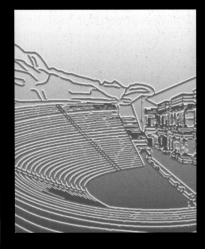

CHAPTER THREE

In this chapter

- **Rule of Thirds**
- **Putting the Composition Together**
- **Line Weight**
- **Study Words**

RSC'S NEW STAGE

Royal Shakespeare Company gets a new home, conceived expressly for the demands of classic theatre

by Sarah Rushton Reed

Excerpt 1

Like an artisan-crafted musical instrument, the newly-transformed Royal Shakespeare Theatre is crying out to be played. Full of tension, the intimate thrust stage auditorium is bursting with exciting creative possibilities, artistic vision, clever design, and invention. The new RST has been four years in the making and much longer in the planning. The transformation scheme has been client-led, using an unusually theatrical and collaborative approach. Every contractor and trade and craft person who has worked on the project has been hand-picked by the RSC and supervised by a construction management team.

Designed by the architecture firm Bennetts Associates, with auditorium, backstage planning, and technical design by theatre consultant Charcoalblue, the result is a direct response to RSC artistic director, Michael Boyd's unwavering vision for an intimate thrust stage arena in which to perform Shakespeare. Charcoalblue's managing director, Andy Hayles, says, "Our task was to transform Elisabeth Scott's 1932 cinema-style Royal Shakespeare Theatre into the definitive environment in which to perform and enjoy Shakespeare."

The previous theatre had been reworked to its limit, and was struggling to accommodate the modern day needs of a busy repertory company. The auditorium prevented all but the most distant relationship between audience and players; some of the furthest seats from the stage were 90' away.

A project of such magnitude demanded a formidable RSC team: RSC executive director Vikki Heywood, artistic director Michael Boyd, associate designer Tom Piper, chairman Sir Christopher Bland, deputy chair Lady Sainsbury of Turville CBE, and project director Peter Wilson OBE all ensured the design team created a performance environment that Shakespeare himself might recognize, which could comfortably accommodate 1,000 people around a thrust stage. Nothing was left to chance—so much so that the RSC, along with Ian Ritchie Architects and Charcoalblue, built a 1:1 prototype of the intended RST thrust stage format—the Courtyard Theatre—just up the road from the main house. It opened in 2006 and has since served a number of significant purposes. It provided a temporary home for the RSC while its flagship space was transformed. It also allowed the company to test the possibilities of a thrust stage, iron out any issues, and fine-tune the detail of the new RST auditorium. And it acclimatized the RSC audience to the new format.

"Our designs for the Courtyard really helped inform the new RST theatre design," says Charcoalblue's design director, Gavin Green. "We constantly re-examined and retested every part of the Courtyard for the new RST. The new theatre is a more personal and compact space. It has a stronger geometrical basis, which reinforces the compression and focus of the room and makes it a really rewarding place to be." The result is a highly scenic, three-dimensional and sculptural space, and Boyd is delighted: "We've been more privileged than any arts capital project in the world in that we had one year in the Courtyard to try it out before we agreed to the final designs for the RST. That's why this is a miracle of a space that combines the epic and the intimate, the hugest metaphysic, and the tiniest psychological detail in one space. Here we have all the possibilities of the heavens above the stage from which we can bring down the Forest of Arden, while all our deepest fears can rise up from the depths of hell in the basement."

Source: Originally published in *Lighting and Sound America*, February 2011.

RULE OF THIRDS

Many factors can affect a composition. Let's start with some basics. The basic rule of composition refers us directly to the **rule of thirds**. As you start to really look at images, analyze them (Figs. 3.1–3.3). Draw lines through an image both horizontally and vertically, dividing the image into thirds in both directions. Important compositional elements should be placed along these lines. People who follow this rule believe that following it creates more tension, energy, and interest than simply centering the image in the frame.

Notice how the "focus" in both photographs of rowboats is not in the center of the image. Your eye is drawn around the photo. In Figure 3.1, the row of boats creates the reference horizon line. The water in the background, as well as the tree line on the left and right, comes to an apex above and to the left of the boats. The tree on the left side angles in toward the center. This has the effect of bringing your eye back into the photo. Figure 3.2 has a much more

obvious circular composition, continually leading your eye around and around.

The goal with any good composition is to have the audience's eyes continually moving around the image. Each area within the lines should be its own smaller composition. Our instinct is to look at the center of whatever we are looking at (Fig. 3.4). Think about it for a second. When you look at a person, do you look at his or her whole body? No, you look at his or her face. And within the face, you concentrate on the eyes. The eyes are the center of the face.

By keeping the main subject of the composition outside of the center area and near the intersection of the lines, you assure the viewer will look at the whole image and not be drawn to one detail to the exclusion of all others (Fig. 3.5). If you want to simplify a composition that has only one focal point, obviously the best place to put the focal point is in the center of the image. Even with the central focus, you still need to help the composition. Blurring or darkening the background often helps to achieve this.

■ **Fig. 3.1** Photograph of rowboats lined up on the shore. Analyze the composition.

■ **Fig. 3.2** A different photograph of rowboats. On the left, white lines show the rule of thirds. On the right is the same image with white lines showing the true center as well as diagonal lines. Which do you think is more dynamic?

■ **Fig. 3.3** Photograph of a stone wall and sidewalk. Follow the lines of the composition. Where does the composition lead your eye?

■ **Fig. 3.4** Stained-glass art entitled *Sunday* by Isabella Rupp. The two circles are a focal point, and the swirling lines keep your eye moving.

Now, let's translate the idea to the theatre (Fig. 3.6). Think about a single actor on the stage, standing at the edge of the stage on the center line. This is one of the few situations when simplifying the composition to this extreme will work in the theatre.

PUTTING THE COMPOSITION TOGETHER

OK, that is the background information. Now the question is, How do we do it? Well, creating a composition is like putting a puzzle together. You have a whole bunch of pieces that all have to be put together in the right order to make it all work.

> Nothing goes by luck in composition. It allows for no tricks. The best you can write will be the best you are.
>
> —Henry David Thoreau

COPYRIGHT © BETH BERGMAN 1991

■ **Fig. 3.6** *Ghost of Versailles* at the Metropolitan Opera in 1991. Director, Colin Graham; scenic and costume designer, John Conklin; and lighting designer, Gil Wechsler.

LINE AND DIRECTION

The first element, or puzzle piece, to consider is the line (Fig. 3.7). The mathematical definition of a **line** is the shortest distance between two points. Sounds easy, right? Well, a line also has **direction**. The designer or artist often infers what that direction is, as part of the composition. Direction gives you movement. This is critical to the composition, as I said before. The use of movement in a composition helps the viewer to know where to look next.

■ **Fig. 3.7** A basic line, by Salvatore Tagliarino.

SHAPE

Next, let's talk about shape. **Shape** is the definition of any two-dimensional (2D) or three-dimensional (3D) object. Keep in mind that 3D drawing is simply an illusion. The line you draw holds the shape you see (Fig. 3.8). Shapes can have light or line to help define them. You have to use shadow to turn a 2D image into a 3D image by giving it volume. The shape of the highlight, middle tone, and shadow are what add up to create the illusion. Shapes can be geometric or organic.

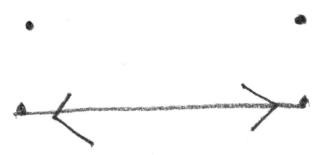

■ **Fig. 3.8** Basic shapes, by Salvatore Tagliarino.

The arrangement of how the shapes go together creates the image. The visual images we see are all made up of shapes. These shapes are 2D images described by a line or series of lines. When put together in the right way and the right **proportion**, they create a compositional image. You can distort the image by screwing up the shapes—or not. It's up to you, and this is what designers play with to create their designs.

> No matter what the illusion created, it is a flat canvas and it has to be organized into shape.
>
> —David Hockney

TEXTURE

Texture is our next puzzle piece. Texture represents a 3D detail that we observe in a 2D drawing (Fig. 3.9). It also represents the properties that differentiate objects of similar shapes from each other. Textures can be either tactile or nontactile. Think of tactile texture as the surface detail you can feel when you touch something. It can be soft or hard, fuzzy or flat, wet or dry, and so forth.

Nontactile textures can be patterns that are scaled up or down to differentiate objects when using line alone to describe the object (Fig. 3.10). Keep in mind that, in two dimensions, you can only allude to real texture.

The drawings in Figure 3.10 might be grass, brick, concrete block, and stone. The difference between the brick

■ **Fig. 3.9** Leonardo da Vinci's self-portrait. Notice the lines and how they create shapes and textures.

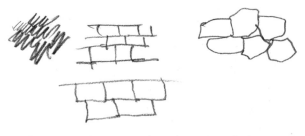

Fig. 3.10 Basic textures, by Salvatore Tagliarino.

and the block is the difference in proportion. Start keeping a mental log of everyday items and what they look like. For example, you probably have an idea in your head about the difference between traditional TV screens and how they differ from the HD sets. This is proportion, which we define in a minute. The difference between bricks versus blocks is that exact same thing. The more you keep in your mental log the easier it will be for you to draw these things.

RSC'S NEW STAGE

Royal Shakespeare Company gets a new home, conceived expressly for the demands of classic theatre

by Sarah Rushton Reed

Excerpt 2

"The most important thing to crack is the relationship with the actors and the audience," says Flip Tanner, the RSC's project coordinator. "We've changed what essentially was a cinema experience, with the audience in one room and the actors in another, to a one-room space, where the actors can't ignore the audience. When they're doing a soliloquy, stood downstage center, they have to include the audience. I saw Kenneth Branagh doing Hamlet in the old space and, because he was staring into blackness, the way that he delivered his soliloquy was internalized, in a sense. David Tennant, delivering the same speech last year in the Courtyard, had to talk to the people in the stalls, because you can't ignore the fact that there are people in the room. So the relationship between actor and performer makes it much closer to the sort of space that Shakespeare wrote for."

Enclosed in a new brick drum structure, the new auditorium sits comfortably in the void left by the demolished cinema-style auditorium, which sat between the retained Elisabeth Scott-designed Art Deco foyer at the front of the building and the proscenium arch at the back. The original rear wall of the auditorium has been left as a reminder of how far away the rear seats were from the stage, and the 1932 boards of the old stage have been reused to deck out the newly created inner foyer between the original rear wall and the curved drum wall of the new auditorium.

Inside, it's intimate and stripped-back, yet it provides a three-dimensional universe for the dramatic treatment of Shakespeare's universal themes. It also facilitates an unusually direct audience connection with Shakespeare's dramatization of the human condition and all the comedy, tragedy, and complexity that entails.

The thrust stage strides confidently into the room and, careful not to upstage it, the brick proscenium of the original stage stands behind. Wraparound seating allows for eyeball-to-eyeball contact between audience and players (as well as audience and audience). It's all about shared experience—and the success of that for Boyd clearly lies in audience involvement and reaction. Helping to recreate the natural and supernatural themes of Shakespeare's plays in an enclosed space relies on clever design, planning, and innovative utilization of entertainment technology, and Charcoalblue, along with Tanner and a technical working party of backstage staff, developed the specification for the entertainment technology that now

furnishes the new theatre. Instrumental in this working party were RSC's head of lighting Vince Herbert, head of sound Jeremy Dunn, and deputy technical manager Peter Bailey, all under the eye of head of production Geoff Locker.

Source: Originally published in *Lighting and Sound America*, February 2011.

LINE WEIGHT

Next comes **line weight**. Any pencil, depending on its size and softness, has a thickness it can create (Fig. 3.11). **Contrast** in line weight is created by your choice of pencil and the pressure you apply. This adds interest to your composition. It can also help focus the viewers' eyes. The better and more varied your line weight, the less you need other factors to define your shape. Keep in mind though, that it is just another piece to the overall puzzle. Take a look at some of the drawings by da Vinci and Raphael—look at the contrast in the line weight. It's important that they use line weight, but it's more important *how* they use it!

■ **Fig. 3.11** Basic line weights, by Salvatore Tagliarino.

BALANCE AND PROPORTION

Balance is next. OK, picture an acrobat on a tightrope. That is **balance**, right? Right. It is similar in art. You have to get the composition balanced, and this usually means the contrast between all the different characteristics we already discussed. If the composition looks awkward, that means the contrast in the line, shape, texture, or line weight is out of whack.

Proportion is the most important thing and goes hand in hand with balance. **Proportion** is a mathematical thing. It defines the relationship between two objects or two parts of the same object. You can measure proportion mechanically, and most people should. That is what a scale rule is about; that is what a tape measure is about. You might be one of those rare people who can look at something and know exactly how big it is. I can't do this, and neither can most people. So, if you can't "eyeball" the size and proportions of an object correctly, get a ruler and measure it. To relay graphical information clearly, that information, in scale or actual size, needs to be noted on the paper.

> Even in front of nature one must compose.
>
> **—Edgar Degas**

Let's talk for a minute about the best example of proportion known in the art world today. It is Leonardo da Vinci's *Vitruvian Man* (Fig. 3.12). Vitruvius was a Roman writer, architect, and engineer born during the 1st century. He studied proportion in all things, culminating in understanding the proportions of the greatest work of art: the human body. This led Vitruvius to define verbally his concept for what has come to be known as the *Vitruvian man*. Leonardo da Vinci later illustrated this concept magnificently by showing the human body inscribed within a circle and a square.

Da Vinci's drawing is good because the line weight is good, the understanding of human anatomy is incredible,

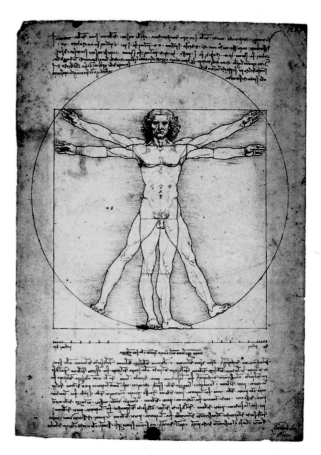

■ **Fig. 3.12** Leonardo da Vinci's *Vitruvian Man*. Balance and proportion to perfection.

Fig. 3.13 A really cool tree. How many pieces of the composition can you identify?

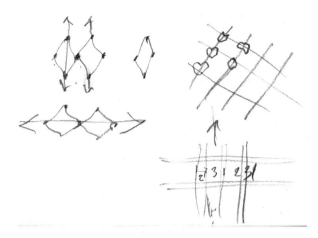

Fig. 3.14 Basic patterns, by Salvatore Tagliarino.

and the draftsmanship of the square and the circle is totally mathematical. Try to copy it! It may look simple, but trust me it's not. All the elements we've been discussing in the chapter are done to perfection in this figure. Don't be intimidated—look at the drawing. No, really look at it. Look at the line weight. See the differences in the lines that form the outside of the body versus the ones that are used for contour on the inside of the body. Look also at the lines around the body and notice how they help to set the body apart from the paper background.

OK, another way to look at proportion is to think of that gimmick when artists hold their arm out in front of themselves and look at their thumb—it is all about proportion. You can measure a tree with your thumb (Fig. 3.13). It could be five thumbs tall versus three thumbs wide. This is a different way to measure the world, similar to using a tape measure or scale rule. All of these are just different techniques or tools. Each is valid and appropriate. You just have to determine which is right for which situation.

PATTERN

Our next puzzle piece is pattern. A **pattern** is a repeated element within a composition, such as a stripe or zigzag (Fig. 3.14). Make any shape; if you repeat it, it becomes a pattern. Think about wallpaper or fabric for a second. They contain great examples of repeating patterns. Patterns can be horizontal, vertical, or diagonal. Plaids are a kind of pattern with multiple directions. Plaids are complex. They are made up of various line weights into a grid.

SCALE

Scale is the next piece to the puzzle. **Scale** is a term that relates to how big or small the object is, as well as the drawing of the object. The world we live in has a set scale. In set design, the measure of the scale is the human being. In theatre, we generally use 6' feet as the height of a "standard" person. When we are determining relationships and the surrounding proportions, the 6-foot human height divides out easily in halves: 3 feet + 3 feet. A standard chair seat height is 16–18 inches. Tabletops are generally 30 inches high. The height of doors, windows, and other architectural elements are all based on this same scale. How the human body moves and bends determines how all of these details come together. A comedian once said, "Imagine what chairs would look like if our knees bent the other way." I rest my case—it's all about the scale of the human body.

> Man is the measure of all things.
>
> —Vitruvius

It's all about the human ratio and how it translates onto the stage! Fashion designers aren't costume designers. Architects aren't set designers. Marc Chagall and David Hockney bridged the gap between the art world and the theatre world. They took visual style based on good line weight, proportion, and the like and, with help, translated the ideas into stage sets.

Now, let's put it all together: line, direction, shape, texture, line weight, balance, proportion, pattern, and scale. These are the pieces of a composition. You can put them together in an infinite variety of ways to create the compositions that are in your head. The way to put the pieces together to form a good composition is by using contrast to create an **emphasis** or focus.

Useless Factoid: Break a Leg

One possible explanation for this expression is its relation to "taking a knee," which itself has roots in chivalry. Meeting royalty, one would "take a knee"—in other words, bend down on one knee. That breaks the line of the leg, hence "break a leg," a wish that the performer will do so well that he or she will need to take bows.

Balance
Contrast
Direction
Emphasis
Line
Line weight
Pattern
Proportion
Rule of thirds
Scale
Shape
Texture

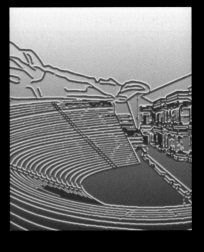

CHAPTER THREE
Study Words

Black and White Are Colors TOO!

Color Theory

A whole chapter on color! Why, you may ask—you just want to learn how to build scenery. Well, if you want to work in any of the departments in a theatre, you need to know about color. The scene shop doesn't just build the scenery and props, it also paints them. The costume shop deals with color in the fabrics, threads, and accessories. The lighting department uses gel. And don't even get me started on the makeup department, where it is all about color! We think we know all about color from the moment we open our eyes and begin to see. Yeah, you know all about color—the grass is green, the sky is blue. Big deal, right? Right.

> Mere color, unspoiled by meaning, and unallied with definite form, can speak to the soul in a thousand different ways.
>
> **—Oscar Wilde**

Color helps us perceive, distinguish, and recognize everything in the world around us. If you look at something in the distance, you may recognize it by its color long before you can actually "see" what it is. In fact, advertisers depend on this ability. Think of your favorite fast food restaurant or your favorite snack food. The logo jumps into your head, doesn't it? These are all images that are recognizable while driving on the highway at 55 mph! Now try something a little different. Imagine the world without color for a while! It's a strange concept, I know. It's hard to picture the world in black and white.

CHAPTER FOUR

In this chapter

- **Pigment and Light**
- **Tints, Shades, and Tones**
- **Interpreting Color**
- **Black and White**
- **Reference White**
- **Study Words**

Everybody loves a good sunset. Think about the most beautiful sunset you have ever seen. It can be a sunset at the beach, in the mountains, in the woods, or even a skyline of a big city (Fig. 4.1). Any sunset will do. How does it make you feel? Is it pretty, or relaxing, or peaceful? Maybe it's even romantic. Now try to analyze the sunset you are imagining. Picture all the rich and vibrant colors: the reds, oranges, and yellows. Think about how those colors contrast with whatever small amount of blue is left in the sky.

What a nice sunset Figure 4.1 shows. Is it similar to what you were picturing in your head? If it is different, the differences are most likely in the subject matter, not the color. Now let's put a twist on our image. What happens if we take away the color? Imagine if that image were in black and white. Take a look at Figure 4.2.

Pretty different image, no? Suddenly, the thoughts that come to mind are ominous, scary, and dark. What happened to pretty, relaxing, and peaceful? Those warm and fuzzy feelings disappear when the color does. This is why I say

that color helps us perceive the world. We take color for granted. We see it everywhere, and we know what an object is not just by its shape but also by its color.

And, that is only one example. Let's try it a different way. Think about the differences between an orange and a grapefruit. They can be about the same shape and have similar texture, but they are usually different sizes and different colors, right? What if you put a large orange and a small grapefruit side by side and photographed them in black and white (Fig. 4.3)?

PIGMENT AND LIGHT

Color is often organized and displayed using something called a *color wheel*. The important thing to know right away is that there are actually two color wheels. There is the color wheel most of us are familiar with, the one for paint or pigment. The other color wheel is for light. Yes, that is right—there are two color wheels. It can be confusing when you are first learning it, but stay with me and I'll explain it.

The way you are most likely accustomed to using color is based on the pigment color wheel. The first three colors to know are the **primary** colors (Fig. 4.4). Primaries are colors that cannot be created by mixing any other colors together. The primary colors in pigment are red, blue, and yellow.

> There is no blue without yellow and without orange.
>
> **—Vincent Van Gogh**

Fig. 4.1 Beautiful sunset overlooking the Hudson River.

Fig. 4.2 Sunset photo converted to black and white.

Fig. 4.3 If you eliminate the color, an orange and a grapefruit can look pretty similar. Can you tell which is which?

The next three colors to learn are the **secondary** colors (Fig. 4.5). Combining any two primary colors creates a secondary color. Secondary colors in pigment are purple, green, and orange. If you compare the two figures showing primary and secondary colors, you will see how mixing any two primary colors creates a secondary color. If you take red and blue and mix them together, you get purple. Mix blue and yellow, you get green. Mix yellow and red, you get orange. It's that easy! At least, it's that easy at first.

So, basically, you mix two colors together, and their sum total becomes a new and unique third color. You can take two secondary colors and mix them together. The result is that you have now created what is called a **tertiary** color. In this way, you can continually divide the color wheel into smaller and smaller sections. Mixing color in this way is known as **subtractive** mixing. Simply explained, subtractive color mixing means that when all three primary colors are mixed together in equal parts they "theoretically" make black. Thus, you are always mixing toward black, which equals subtractive color mixing.

OK, now that you have the basics, let us mix it up a little. The primary colors in light (instead of pigment) are red, blue, and green (Fig. 4.6). That is right, green, not yellow. Secondary colors in light are magenta, cyan, and yellow (Fig. 4.7). Of course, we need different color wheels now that we have different primary colors. Although the

■ **Fig. 4.4** Primary colors for pigment.

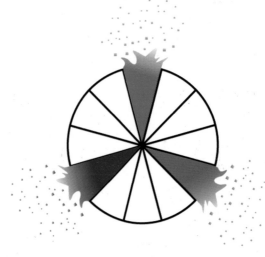

■ **Fig. 4.6** Primary colors for light.

■ **Fig. 4.5** Secondary colors for pigment.

■ **Fig. 4.7** Secondary colors for light.

primary colors of light may be different, mixing the secondary colors happens the exact same way.

Another difference between pigment and light that makes it more confusing is that color mixing in light is called **additive**, not subtractive. Additive color mixing means that, when all three primary colors of light are mixed together in equal parts, they make white light. You can also do subtractive color mixing in light. Are you ready for this one? If you put one piece of color in front of a light, it is considered additive color mixing. If you put two pieces of color in front of the same light, you've now changed into subtractive color mixing for that one light. That means you change back to the pigment color wheel and all the rules that go along with it.

Making black paint or white light by mixing all the respective color wheel's primaries is theoretical at best. Making black or white in this manner really works properly only in a laboratory with the purest version of each color. It is interesting to try it though and see the results. If you try to do this in a theatre or shop, you will most likely get a murky brown or a tinted version of white.

> I cannot pretend to feel impartial about colors. I rejoice with the brilliant ones and am genuinely sorry for the poor browns.
>
> **—Winston Churchill**

The full color wheel, meaning 12 colors, looks very similar to a rainbow. Look at Figures 4.8 and 4.9. Start at one color and work your way around to see how each color progresses from one to the next. Can you see how mixing two colors together can make the one in between? Is it starting to make sense?

Now that we have the basics of color theory, let's move on to the next step.

Complementary colors are those colors that are opposite each other on the full color wheel as shown in Figures 4.8 and 4.9. For example, in pigment, red and green are complementary. Purple and yellow are as well. Complementary colors, when paired together, make each color appear more vibrant. They achieve this vibrancy because they have no colors in common. That is why they are

■ **Fig. 4.8** Full color wheel for pigment. Notice how when the colors overlap they combine to form other colors using the subtractive method of mixing.

■ **Fig. 4.9** Full color wheel for light. Notice how when the colors overlap they combine to form other colors using the additive method of mixing.

opposite on the color wheel. Remember how they are made? Think of some typical color pairings for holidays, sports teams, or corporate logos. Often you will see complementary colors or a primary color combined with white or black. These combinations tend to "pop" and be more recognizable (Fig 4.10). That makes it more memorable, which is the kind of recognition a logo wants.

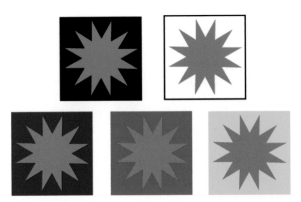

Fig. 4.10 Primary green shown in direct comparison to black, white, blue, red, and yellow. Notice the extreme contrast between the complementary colors of green and red.

> All colors are the friends of their neighbors and the lovers of their opposites.
>
> —Marc Chagall

TINTS, SHADES, AND TONES

Let's explain some more definitions for various terms used to describe color. These terms work for either pigment or light. **Hue** is another word for color. *Color* and *hue* can be used interchangeably. Say, your favorite color is green, then your favorite hue is also green. A **tint** is a hue mixed with white. We often think of these colors as pastels. When any amount of white is added, the hue is called a *tint*. The opposite of a tint is a **shade**. A shade is a hue mixed with black. Tones exist between tints and shades. A **tone** is a hue mixed with gray.

Saturation describes the amount of pure color a hue contains. **Chroma** is a word often used instead of *saturation*; they can be used interchangeably. It is a term that describes a hue in its purest form. Primary colors are very saturated; they have a high chroma level (Fig 4.11). Tints, shades, and tones are all less saturated because, by definition, they are a hue mixed with something else. Tones are the colors we see most often in everyday items such as clothing, cars, and houses. They are muted and tend to be less vibrant. The color makes less of a statement or impact. They, therefore, appeal more to our general sensibilities.

Two other color terms to be aware of are value and intensity. **Value** is the lightness or darkness of a color. **Intensity** is

Fig. 4.11 Paint samples of four different greens. From left to right: primary green, green tint, green tone, and green shade.

the brightness or dullness of a color. These two terms help describe our perception of a color. This perception dictates how we react to colors. For example, green is the color of money, the color of greed, and the color of envy. Green is also the color of grass, leaves, and much of nature. Each of these items contains different tints, tones, and shades of green, with differing values and intensities that give each item its individual characteristics.

When an entire composition is made up of tints, shades, and tones of the same hue, it is called a **monochromatic** composition. Each single color on the color wheel can have an infinite number of variations. The color violet, for example, can range from a shade of deep eggplant to a tint of light lavender. Using variations like this of a single color can create a monochromatic design.

> In a sense, light makes potential colors into actual colors.
>
> —Aristotle

Often, to create more interest, you will want to use a number of different hues, instead of just one, but still from within the same area of the color wheel. This is called an **analogous** color palette. To take your design to the next level of color contrast, and therefore add more interest, add one more step to the process. For this technique to work, design your background with analogous colors. Then pick one item in the foreground, the focal point of your image, and make it an entirely different hue. This contrast helps to focus the eye on your chosen point. See an example of this in Figure 4.12.

■ **Fig. 4.12** *The Sorcerer* by Michael A. Fink, is an example of an analogous composition with a one-color contrast.

Figure 4.12 uses a palette of almost exclusively cool colors. There is a range of blues and greens that make up almost 85 percent of the image. The central focus of the composition is all pinks and oranges. Notice how your eye keeps returning to the center. This is because it is the area of highest color contrast. The rest of the composition helps to focus your eye, as some of the lines point toward the center. Without the color contrast in the center, this would not be nearly as interesting an image. Color is really an amazing thing. It can focus your eye, and it can sway your emotions. Color, just simple color, can do all that.

INTERPRETING COLOR

Interpreting color is the next step in our discussion. We start by dividing colors into cool and warm. It sounds easy, and it is, to a point. Warm colors are reds, oranges, and yellows. Cool colors are greens, blues, and purples. Now, here is the confusing part. Within the hue of red, for example, there are cool reds and warm reds. This goes for every color! It's really all about contrast again. If you put a warm red next to a cool red you will see them both in comparison to the other (Fig. 4.13). It is an exercise for your eyes to play

■ **Fig. 4.13** Example of three different reds. The top center is primary red. The bottom left is a cool red created when primary red is mixed with a little blue. The bottom right is a warm red created when primary red is mixed with a little yellow. Can you start to see how purple and orange are made?

with. Look out at someone's front yard or into the woods behind your house. How many different greens do you see?

When working on a color composition you should think about warm and cool colors. These two ideas can help you to choose the right color for a specific part of your design. Cool and warm colors also have emotional impact. A warm color palette can often benefit from a touch of coolness to create balance. Warm colors are more dominant and tend to appear as if they are coming toward you. That also means warm colors are more challenging, more energized, more vivid. Cool colors are more recessive and tend to appear as if they are receding into the background. This also means that cool colors are more calming, more soothing. Similarly, a cool palette can be livened up by a touch of warmth. Look again at the image of *The Sorcerer* in Figure 4.12. Try to imagine it without the warm colors in the middle. Very different, right?

All of these words have emotional counterparts that go along. This is how we react to color, and more important, why we react to color. Choices you make, from what you wear to the color of your car or the color you choose to paint your room, all define who you are and how other people will react to you. Keep your eyes open for color all around you. Look at the clothing you are wearing. What color choices did you make this morning? What about your classmates or your teacher? Look at the color choices in your classroom. Why do you think the school chose those colors?

Colors can also have very specific meanings. Some meanings have a historical basis. Other meanings may be cultural and will vary from one country to another. For example, in the United States, the traditional color for a funeral is black, while in China the funeral color is white. Red can mean anger, danger, warning, or passion, depending on how it is used. Think for a second about a traditional traffic light: red means stop, yellow means caution, green means go. Where else in your life do these colors have the same meanings?

BLACK AND WHITE

Now that we're beginning to get a handle on color, let's leave it behind for a second. What? Isn't this a chapter on color? Yes, it is. To better understand color, we need to better understand black and white. Most people think black and white are not colors. Now, you know better, based on our color wheels. We know that in pigment black is the presence of all color. Even though it may seem strange, we also know that in light the presence of all color is white. We also talked about tints, shades, and tones, all of which have to do with the amount of black and white added to a color. So, let's spend a little time talking about the grayscale chart.

■ **Fig. 4.14** Grayscale chart from black to white in 10 percent increments.

Figure 4.14 is a **grayscale** chart showing stepped gradations from black to white. Moving from left to right each successive tint has 10 percent more white added to the black until we finally reach pure white. When different gray samples are organized like this, it is a called a *grayscale chart*. Often these charts are used to calibrate computer monitors, printers, and much more. A very important thing to know is where a color falls on this grayscale chart (Figs. 4.15 and 4.16). When you are combining colors to create interest, you will be far more successful if the colors are also in different areas of the grayscale chart. This is where tints, shades, and tones come into practice. From primary red to the palest pink, these colors are all based on the same hue. However, they create interest in different ways dependent on their value and intensity.

Did you think red and green would be so dark in black and white? Did you think they would be almost the same value? Did you think yellow would look almost white? These details are important to know and remember. Colors are tied not only to our designs but also to our emotions. All the qualities of a particular color—not just the actual hue but all its inherent qualities—inform how perception happens.

Perception is the key to it all. As you paint (whether it is with pigment or light), you may perceive a color as burgundy or dark red or a shade of red. Someone else may look at the same color and perceive it is a warm brown. All your intended emotions associated with using red are now thrown out the window. If you want your ideas to be clear, the implementation of your ideas must be clear as well. Your intentions need to be informed by how others may choose to perceive any individual part of your work. Simply put, know your audience. Their reaction to your choices is really what matters most.

How we perceive color is critical. Let's talk a little more about perception. **White balance** is a phrase often used when shooting video or film, but it is equally important to us in the theatre. You "teach" your camera (or in our case, our eyes) what white really looks like, then all other colors

■ **Fig. 4.15** Pigment color wheel in color and converted to gray scale.

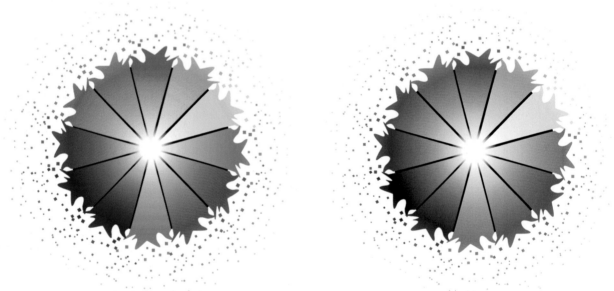

■ **Fig 4.16** Light color wheel in color and converted to gray scale.

are seen in relation, or in perspective, to this newly defined "white." If you don't teach the camera what white looks like, it will mistake a different color for white and your whole image will be altered (Fig. 4.17).

REFERENCE WHITE

There is no right or wrong, only what you intentioned. *White balance* and **reference white** are terms linked to each other as a baseline for all that we use to compare colors. Consider white balance to be the standard by which you judge all other colors. In actuality, white may not exist in your work. Then, the reference you establish can be any color that you want the audience to perceive as white. Reference to white's affect can change depending on what it is next to in a composition. Almost any color can be made to look white, simply by putting a color next to it that is more saturated.

Daylight   Warm Fluorescent   Incandescent

Fig. 4.17 The same photo, without white balancing the camera, taken under three different kinds of light. See how the entire image is changed. Which one is "right"?

> White is not a mere absence of color; it is a shining and affirmative thing, as fierce as red, as definite as black.
> —**Gilbert K. Chesterton**

In Figure 4.18, I demonstrate this concept in a series of steps to show how quickly your eye can get used to a certain color. As your eye adjusts, it tends to desaturate the color. This means it pulls the chroma out of a given color, making it appear paler to the eye. Look at the photos one at a time. Cover up all the photos, except the first, with your hand. Then, slowly move your eye from one photo to the next as you uncover them. Isn't it amazing how white, pink, and magenta can all change their appearance from being saturated to being white? I go back and do this exercise all the time, and it never fails to amaze me how much the human eye wants to adjust everything it sees back to white.

This demonstration is created in a very simple, methodical way. Let me explain how it works. You set up a mannequin at center stage with a white cloth draped around it. Then, you add a white light from either side. *White* in this instance means that there is no color in front of either light. The only color comes from the inherent qualities of the lightbulb. Now you have the basic setup.

The next step is for you to add the palest pink you can find to the light on the left side. Then, find a pink that is slightly more saturated, and put it on the light on the right side. The left side now looks white, even though you know it still has a pink color. Continue substituting more saturated pinks, alternating one side at a time, slowly progressing all the way to magenta. Look very closely to each step along the way. One color may look very pink. Then, you change the color on the opposite side, and suddenly the first color looks like white.

I have one last image for you on the topic of color. Keep in mind all that you learned in this chapter. Don't take color for granted. Remember for a second how you thought of color before reading this chapter. Now, look closely at Figure 4.19. Start immediately to analyze the color with your new knowledge and skills. What hues are used? How are they organized? What hues are next to what other hues? How does that affect your perception? What emotions do you feel as you look at it?

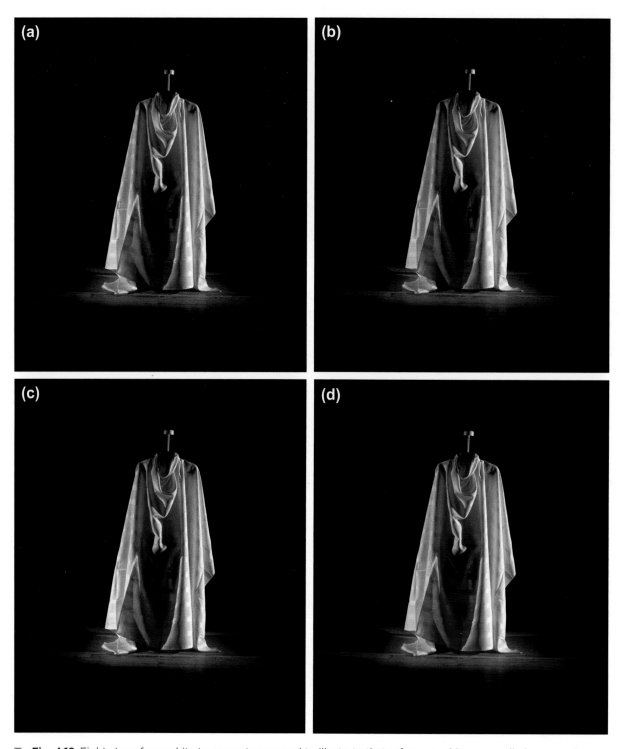

■ **Fig. 4.18** Eight steps from white to magenta are used to illustrate that reference white can really be any color you choose it to be.

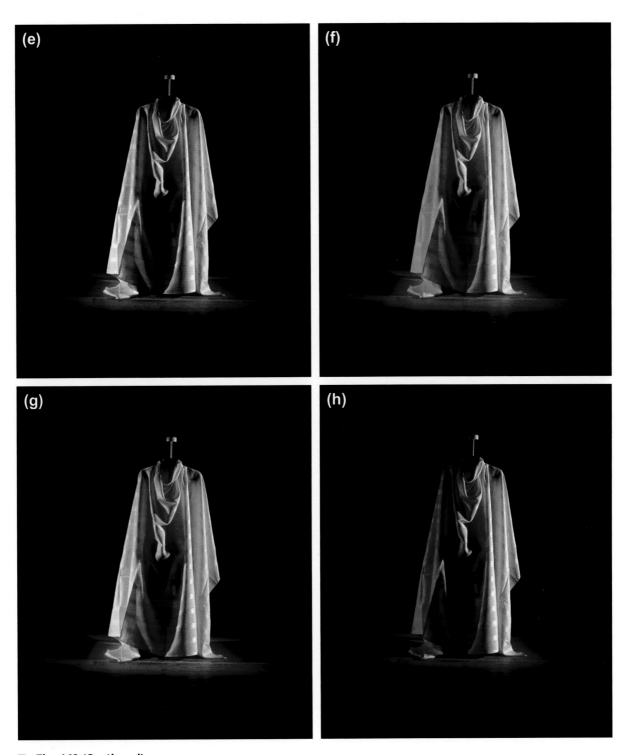

■ **Fig. 4.18 (Continued).**

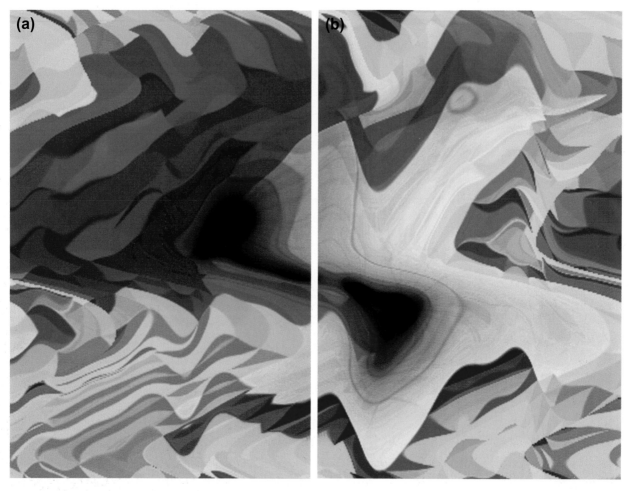

(a)

(b)

■ **Fig 4.19** *The Turtle* by Michael A. Fink, is a gorgeous explosion of color.

Useless Factoid: Green Is a Bad Color

Don't wear green onstage. Actors used to perform outdoors on the green grass, so actors wearing green weren't seen very well. Also, a green light was often used to illuminate characters, and this limelight would make anyone wearing green appear practically invisible.

Additive

Analogous

Chroma

Complementary

Grayscale

Hue

Intensity

Monochromatic

Primary

Reference white

Saturation

Secondary

Shade

Subtractive

Tertiary

Tint

Tone

Value

White balance

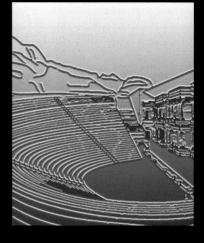

CHAPTER FOUR

Study Words

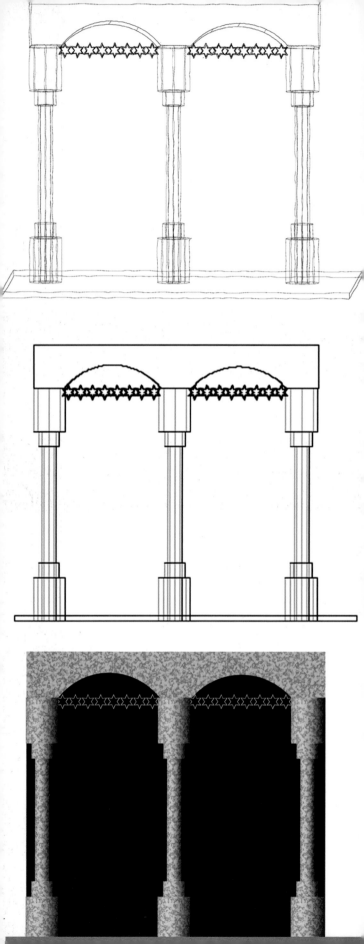

Creating the Stage Picture

Drawing, Rendering, and Drafting

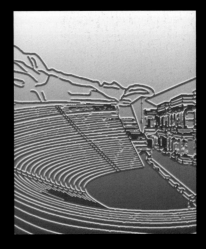

So, you have all these great ideas. How do you get these wonderful ideas out of your head and into the theatre? We jump right into our discussion of drafting, drawing, and rendering. This is the first tangible step for any designer. You have to get the ideas out of your head and onto paper or the computer screen. That is the only way others can see *visually* what you've been describing *verbally*. The traditional way to do this was with a pencil and a piece of paper. And many designers still work this way. The modern way, using technology, is to use computer-aided drawing and drafting (CAD) software, photo manipulation software, as well as other programs written specifically for the theatre. The goal of creating drawings and drafting, no matter how you do it, is still very simple. Get the ideas out of your head so they can be realized.

> When I sit alone in a theater and gaze into the dark space of its empty stage, I'm frequently seized by fear that this time I won't manage to penetrate it, and I always hope that this fear will never desert me. Without an unending search for the key to the secret of creativity, there is no creation. It's necessary always to begin again. And that is beautiful.
>
> **—Josef Svoboda**

Semantics can be a nasty word. Picture this: You and the director are having your first conversation. He or she says his or her favorite color is green. He or she wants the whole set to be green. Let us ignore his or her motivation for a second. If you are not careful, you'll walk away from this meeting thinking, OK, I can do that. Then, at the next meeting, when you show the director your sketch in glorious sage green, he or she screams in horror and says, "Not that green!" Theatre is a visual business—I said it before and I say it again. Sometimes, words just don't cut it. Remember the saying "A picture is worth a thousand words"? Well, it sure is true. Whenever possible, your ideas will come across much clearer if they are presented in a visual way. That is what this chapter is all about. So, let's get on with it.

What is the big deal about drawing? You don't like to draw? You think you are no good at it? Well, here is the scoop. Drawing is simply an extension of seeing. You can use drawing as an exercise to better look and see. The more closely you observe the world around you, the better you can relate it visually to others. Don't give up on drawing and sketching. It takes practice like everything else. But, it is some of the best training I ever received (Fig. 5.1).

WHAT ARE THE DIFFERENCES?

Drawing, drafting, and rendering—let's break them down and discuss the basic ideas of each before moving on to the technical how-to. **Drawing** is often used interchangeably with sketching. I find it interesting that the dictionary tends to define *draw* as a pulling toward yourself. The artistic definition of draw is much further down the list. Well, think

Fig. 5.1 Gustav Rehberger was my instructor at the Art Students League. He drew this sketch in two minutes, without a model.

about it for a second. Maybe we can use that part of the definition to indicate that we are pulling our ideas together and allowing them to form on the outside of our heads. Esoteric at best, but I think there is something interesting here. **Sketch** has similar combinations of definitions. It is not only defined as a rough drawing but as a brief description. Here is another one—**render**. Today, we instantly think of a computer-generated image. From the dictionary, this time I find one meaning for render is to give back. I like that—giving back. I think, in a way, that is the key to design. Last, we get to **drafting**. In racing, *draft* means to stay close behind. Well, drafting is usually done shortly after the drawing and rendering are complete.

So, now that we know how these terms are defined and why they are important to us, the next question is, How do we do them? In grammar school, you are taught how to write the alphabet and the numerals. These are the basic and most simplistic forms of communication. From those building blocks, you learn how to read and write. You still have to have some information (dog, cat, tree) to turn the information into a vocabulary. Drawing and painting are exactly the same. First of all, you need to have a graphic alphabet for it to work. The graphic alphabet is made up of all the things we discussed in Chapters 3 and 4—composition and color.

Now that you understand the graphic alphabet, you need the ideas for the information you want to write down. Drawing equals information. The better your information, the better the drawing. Masters of the art world like Raphael, da Vinci, and Michelangelo were so good at this, the information they relayed to us was sublime. Once you reach sublime, you've got *art*. This level of drawing shows information that is so well organized, the transfer of information to the audience is perfectly clear. Keep in mind that sublime is very hard to achieve, but as long as we keep striving for it, we might just make it.

> Look! Look at everything! Remember things! Make your eye your strongest instrument, because it's through looking at what you see that you're able to absorb and use it. I'm never bored at airports—I spend my time looking at people and thinking, "Now what do they do?" and "Why did they choose to wear that?" and "Who are they?"
>
> **—Jane Greenwood**

Let's talk about insight for a moment. Insight is key to designing for the theatre as well as being a technician. **Insight** is observing the world around you and forming opinions. We do it every day. Most of the time, we don't realize we are doing it. Theatre artists need to consciously observe every small detail of the world around them. We then need to take that information and form an opinion. One of the reasons Shakespeare's writing is so eternally viable is that it's poetry, good poetry. But also, and more important, he had an amazing insight into the human condition. He could observe and form opinions. Then, he translated these observations into amazing literary pieces. This is our hope. To observe, form opinions, and translate them onto the stage. Easy, right? Not exactly.

Drawing is like a puzzle, where you need all these characteristics, or pieces, to have a chance at making it good (Fig. 5.2). All of these things coming together makes a good design. The well-designed part, however, is the result. You can't start out with a good design! You have to work your way to it using all these techniques and parts of the process we discussed earlier. The visual context we grow up in (our family, neighborhood, time frame) is the one we memorize. What we call good art and bad art is a matter of taste. Most people criticize art based on the information that is either clearly conveyed or not. Does it look like a rabbit or a chair? Any artist who starts a new style is often thought to be crazy. It seems to take about 40 years for the general public to accept something new and catch up. When you have time, look up the following artists: Pollock, Rothko, Warhol, and Seurat. They all started new movements in the art world, and it took quite some time for their work to be accepted.

SAL'S TEST

Let's put all this information to work for us. Are you ready? Here is your first test, and the most enjoyable test you'll ever take. On a piece of paper, draw four things: a cube, a chair, a rabbit, and human being. Now, I have to acknowledge that the test is not my own idea. Sal Tagliarino, one of my instructors from NYU, came up with this idea. I love it so much. I use it all the time and think it is an important idea to put into this book. Now, draw your four images. When you're done, keep reading.

Useless Factoid: Umbrella Problems

For over a century, opening umbrellas on stage has been perceived as bad luck. Hugget reports that the belief actually started in 1868, when an orchestra leader named Bob Williams said good-bye to his theatre company before going away for the weekend. He opened his umbrella while standing on the stage, then walked out into a very rainy day. An hour later, he was standing on the stern of a boat, waving good-bye to a group of friends. As it sailed away from the dock, one of the engines exploded and Williams was instantly killed. The publicity seemed to

■ **Fig. 5.2** A lighting sketch for *Ancient Voice of Children*.

say that the accident and the opening of the umbrella were connected. A theatre superstition was born and lives to this day. As with many of the other superstitions, there is a "counterspell." This was especially needed with this belief, because occasionally an actor must open an umbrella as a stage direction in a play. If an actor opens the umbrella facing the ground, good luck is restored.

OK, now, look at your drawing. This test is all about a way of learning to think and create. The outcome of those two things should be a relay of information. The test is used to explain information. Remember what I said earlier: Every day you should be observing and forming opinions. The test gives you several challenges that are easily solved if you've been observing the world around you and forming opinions.

Let's take each of the drawings individually. The cube is all about mathematical information. You can't even draw a cube properly unless you've taken plane geometry and learned the rules of 3D constructs. Keep in mind that it also helps to observe the world around you, like cardboard boxes, and notice how they are made as well. A cube, by definition, is the same exact length on all sides. A cube has a ratio of 1:1:1. This is very specific. If the cube you drew has a ratio closer to 1:1:2, then it's a rectangle not a cube. Understand?

The chair is structural information. This is the kind of information that architects use the most. There are all sorts of rules that govern this. Gravity, strength, and balance come to mind. Does your chair look like it will float away? Does it look like someone could actually sit in it without it breaking? Does it look like all the feet touch the floor? Now here is the hard question? Does it look like a "specific" chair?

The rabbit is organic. Most people tend to draw a cute rabbit because they have no good reference of stock information in their head about rabbits. How many of us were lucky enough to grow up seeing rabbits every day? I bet your drawing is good if you had a pet rabbit when you were younger. The more you are around something, the more time you have to observe it and file that information away for a later time.

The artist Albrecht Durer didn't make it up. He observed a rabbit to make his drawing, shown in Figure 5.3. If you observe what exists and you like it, methodically note it down with lines in the correct proportion you observe—your drawing should be as good as the thing you're copying if you copy the right proportion. If you do not copy the right proportion, you mess up. Now compare Durer's very famous *Hare* to your little bunny rabbit. What are the differences? And don't fall into the trap of saying, "His is better than mine!" That is not the point of what we are doing. The point is not only to look but to see the differences. A major difference is most likely in the details. Durer has drawn almost every hair. He has obviously studied this hare. Look further for ways to compare your drawing to his. What about the parts of the body? For example, did you draw a short-eared bunny or a long-eared one? Look at your line weight, shape, and value. Now look at Durer's.

Now for the last drawing: the human being. We all know what they look like, right? I mean honestly, we are human beings! But, have you ever taken the time to really look at the

proportions of the human being. From a mathematical point of view it's pretty amazing. Symmetry is considered to equal beauty. You may not like an individual's specific symmetry, but we are all based on a symmetrical mold. Of course, everybody has a variation here or there, so let's take a look for a second at the ideal person. No it's not a supermodel!

PUTTING IT IN PROPORTION

Leonardo da Vinci read a paper by a Roman architect named Vitruvius. In his paper, Vitruvius described the basic proportions for the male human body and related them to mathematical calculations. For your reference, here is an excerpt from Vitruvius's paper so you can see exactly what da Vinci read:

> The navel is naturally the exact centre of the body. For if a man lies on his back with hands and feet outspread, and the centre of a circle is placed on his navel, his figure and toes will be touched by the circumference. Also a square will be found described within the figure, in the same way as a round figure is produced. For if we measure from the sole of the foot to the top of the head, and apply the measure to the outstretched hands, the breadth will be found equal to the height, just like sites which are squared by rule.
>
> —Vitruvius

Da Vinci chose to try and illustrate this theory and called it the *Vitruvian Man*. The basic information from the full text goes something like this:

- A palm is the width of four fingers.
- A foot is the width of four palms.
- A cubit (term for a measurement) is the width of six palms.
- A man's height is 4 cubits or 24 palms.
- A pace is 4 cubits.
- The length of a man's outspread arms is equal to his height.

Fig. 5.3 Albrecht Durer's 1502 *Hare*.

- The distance from the hairline to the bottom of the chin is one 10th of a man's height.

- The distance from the top of the head to the bottom of the chin is one eighth of a man's height.

- The maximum width of the shoulders is one quarter of a man's height.

- The distance from the elbow to the tip of the hand is one fifth of a man's height.

- The distance from the elbow to the armpit is one eighth of a man's height.

- The length of the hand is one 10th of a man's height.

- The distance from the bottom of the chin to the nose is one third of the length of the head.

- The distance from the hairline to the eyebrows is one third of the length of the face.

- The length of the ear is one third of the length of the face.

Yikes! I bet you didn't realize drawing had anything to do with math. Drawing does have to do with observing. Any "tool" you use to help you observe is a valid tool. Math helps. So use it. Reread that list again; take it slowly; and I bet it will all start to make sense. Go look at a photograph of yourself. Check the measurements—I bet they are pretty close. Now, here is the thing, no one is actually perfect. But, we are all based on the same mold.

The *Vitruvian Man* is the perfect blending of art and science. Mathematical precision and a keen interest in proportion is what drove da Vinci forward with this piece. This is clear observation. You need to use everything at your disposal to truly observe the world around you. Here is a fun idea: Wait until next year, then take Sal's test again. Don't wait for a teacher. Just do it. Keep the one you just finished. Put it away somewhere. Then, next year, do another test and compare them. I bet with every succeeding year your observations will be keener and more accurate. Notice I didn't say *better*. *Better* is relative.

VARIOUS SUPPLIES AND TOOLS

We start our next section by talking about what is involved in drawing, rendering, and drafting. It is important to have all the tools you need within reach so you need not hunt around for something at a critical moment of creative inspiration. This is the point where you have to start making choices. Many tools achieve similar results, but one is usually more appropriate for the job than another. If you have to go from New York City to Chicago you could fly, drive, take a train, ride your bike, or walk. All these options get you to Chicago. It depends greatly on the circumstances of your travel. Do you have to arrive by a certain time? Is your budget limited? Are you participating in a marathon fundraiser? Many things affect your choices. Got it?

Start with writing implements. You can use anything that leaves a mark. Of course, pens and pencils are much easier than grabbing a big hunk of burnt wood and trying to write with that. So, let us explore the options that are a little more realistic. I like to break them down into two categories: dry stuff and wet stuff.

DRY STUFF

Pencils

Let's start with pencils. You may be thinking, "Yeah, yeah, I know what a pencil is." I'm sure you do. But, do you know how many different kinds of pencils there are? The basic pencil that most people know has a graphite core surrounded by hexagonal-shaped wood with a pink eraser at the opposite end. If you've ever taken a standardized test in school and they required you to use a "#2 pencil," this is the kind of pencil you used. Did you ever wonder what that "2" stood for?

Pencil graphite is labeled by hardness (Fig. 5.4). The harder the lead, the lighter a mark it makes. Conversely, the softer the lead, the darker is the mark. Leads are divided into three groupings. The middle range we use mostly to write with consists of H (harder), F (fine), and HB and B (blacker). Pencils ranging from 2B to 9B are softer and are used primarily for sketching. The 2H to 9H are harder than average and used mostly for drafting. So your #2 pencil equals an HB on this scale. In order, the variety of leads available are (from hardest to softest) 9H, 8H, 7H, 6H, 5H, 4H, 3H, 2H, H, F, HB, B, 2B, 3B, 4B, 5B, 6B, 7B, 8B, 9B.

Let's dispel a quick misconception. The part of the pencil that does the writing is called the *lead*, however, it is not made of lead. Let me explain. Pencils originally had lead in them. It was sandwiched between two pieces of cedar wood. During the late 18th century, graphite became the substitute for lead. At this point, it was also discovered that, by mixing clay with the graphite, you could get different rates of hardness and softness. More clay makes the pencil harder; more graphite makes it softer.

The next kind of pencil is a mechanical pencil (Fig. 5.5). Most of you have seen this type as well. Mechanical pencils use a very thick "lead" that comes in the same hardness and softness as regular pencils. The diameter of the lead varies from 0.3 mm to 0.9 mm, and the mechanical pencil is specific to that size. There is no need to sharpen these

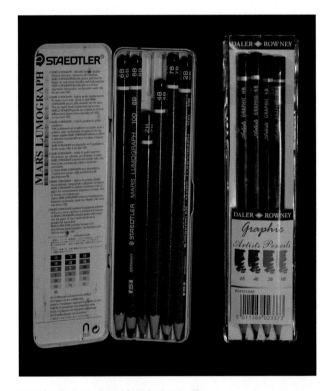

Fig. 5.4 Various drawing pencils.

leads as they are too thin. When the lead starts to get too short, you simply extend the lead, usually by pushing on the end cap of the pencil. A larger diameter lead, 2.0 mm, is used in a lead holder. This is a much thicker lead than the regular mechanical pencils and is usually used for drafting. This lead will not fit in a regular pencil sharpener. It needs what is called a lead pointer to sharpen the tip.

Charcoal is our next drawing option. Charcoal comes either compressed in pencils or blocks or uncompressed in what is usually referred to as *willow* or *vine charcoal*. Willow and vine are usually much softer (and therefore darker) than compressed pencils and blocks.

Moving into color now, we are probably all familiar with color pencils (Fig. 5.6). The biggest difference is that they come in a variety of colors instead of a variety of hardness and softness. Most colored pencils get darker simply by pressing harder. That is the only way to control the light

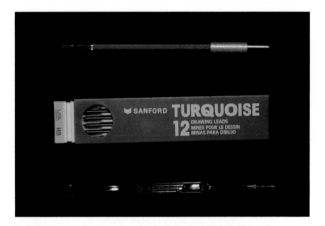

Fig. 5.5 Lead holder, leads, and mechanical pencil.

Fig. 5.6 Colored pencils.

and dark qualities. The oil color pencil is much creamier in texture than the traditional colored pencil. Pastel pencils are able to draw sharp lines while still maintaining their ability to blend easily.

The last type of pencils we discuss are watercolor pencils. These pencils are unique in that there are two very distinct ways of working with them. The first way to use them is like any other colored pencils—you draw. You can use them like this and they never change. However, if you draw and then use a brush with some water, the pencil lines turn into paint. If you are going to do this, make sure you have watercolor paper. We talk about paper choices soon.

Pastels and Crayons

Moving away from pencils, let us talk about pastels and crayons. Pastels come in two varieties, soft and hard. Pastels usually have a much more intense color than pencils (Fig. 5.7). The color is very concentrated. Soft pastels are more powdery and therefore make more of a mess. But, if you can work with the powder dust, they are a great tool. Hard pastels are, well, harder. This means less dust, less powder, and unfortunately less vibrant color. Both hard and soft pastels are often described as "chalky." Oil pastels, on the other hand, are more "waxy." They are less intense than regular pastels and also less messy.

Our last dry item is the crayon. I am talking about the "64 pack" you grew up with and much, much more. Crayons take on all different forms for the adult artist. Crayons traditionally used a binder of wax. This means they were harder to blend and the colors tended to be less intense. Newer versions of crayons have different binders. These forms include everything from products resembling hard pastels to water-soluble crayons that work similarly to the watercolor pencils. The key to remember is that there are

■ **Fig. 5.7** Pastels.

options. Try as many as you can before you decide what you like and what you don't.

WET STUFF

Pens and Markers

We start off the wet stuff category with pens. Basic writing pens include everything from ballpoints to the newer gel ink pens. Fountain and calligraphy pens are other types of pen. They have replaceable nibs. Nibs determine the thickness of the line. They also differ in terms of how they use ink. There are two ways they can get ink. First, there is the simple basic dip pen. You have to sit with a bottle of ink and continually dip the nib into the ink bottle. The other style has a refillable bladder, cartridge holder, or other replaceable ink supply. Technical pens come in a variety of sizes, similar to mechanical pencils. Each size produces a different thickness of line.

Let's talk about markers (Fig. 5.8). Markers contain a hidden reservoir of ink that is pulled into the tip. Many different styles of markers are on the market today. Many

■ **Fig. 5.8** Markers.

are known by their brand name only. Let me try and explain the different styles.

Permanent markers use ink that is waterproof. This category includes the brand name Sharpie®, among others, as well as all styles of highlighters.

Artists of all kinds use layout and brush markers to do a variety of sketching techniques. Brush markers are just what they sound like. The tip is shaped liked a paintbrush instead of like a pen. Layout markers often come with a writing tip at each end, usually in different sizes. Brand names to think of in relation to this type are Pantone® and Prismacolor®.

Paint markers are an aptly named hybrid. They are in the style of a regular marker, however, they actual dispense paint instead of ink. This can be useful for any number of reasons. A brand name to know is Pentel®.

Paint

Our next topic is paint. Let's start with watercolor. As the name suggests, in watercolor paints, the pigment is suspended in water and can therefore be thinned with water. Transparency, or at least the ability for it, is the main characteristic that sets watercolor apart from other paints. You can see the paper through the colors and layers of paint.

These paints come in both tubes and pans. Tubes of watercolor come in many quality levels. The biggest differences are the intensity of the pigment and range of colors. The paint-by-number kit you had when you were little most likely had pans of paint. Pans of paint still exist but are no longer the norm. Similar to tubes, they come in a range of qualities. Gouache is another type of watercolor paint. The difference between regular watercolor and gouache is that gouache is opaque. It is often used in conjunction with watercolor paint for the shadows and highlights.

Acrylic paint differs from watercolor in that the pigment is suspended in an acrylic polymer emulsion. It can be thinned with water, but once it is dry, it becomes water resistant. Oil paint is rarely used in theatre, as it has a very slow drying time. As I bet you can guess, oil paint gets its name because the pigment is suspended in oil. Oil paint is opaque. Oils are often applied in fairly heavy layers. This gives them a deep color saturation that is often not possible in any other medium.

FIXING THE OOPS

Now, I prefer to think of it as a design change rather than a mistake. However, there will always be the inevitable "oops." A number of different eraser styles are available from which to choose (Fig. 5.9). The type of eraser you use depends

■ **Fig. 5.9** Erasers.

entirely on what you are drawing with and how much of an "oops" you have. Let's go through each kind of eraser and look at the differences.

We start with the basics. A pink eraser is on the end of most of our pencils. The brand name for the bigger version of this is the Pink Pearl®. It has beveled ends for getting into those small details. This is a longtime favorite, as it leaves no smudges on the paper. Gum erasers are another popular type of eraser. They are made of a soft, coarse rubber and work really well if you are trying to erase a large area. They leave a residue on the paper and are not extremely precise. Another form of the gum eraser is the dry cleaning pad. This is a mesh fabric pouch that is stuffed with powdered gum erasers and sewn closed. This is a much messier process. You are meant to tap the pad on your drawing before or after you finish. It will remove smudge marks and oily deposits such as visible fingerprints.

Kneaded erasers are known for removing pencil, chalk, charcoal, and pastel. You can use them to create a highlight in a drawing or to make a change to part of the image. These erasers have wonderful powers of rejuvenation. You can pull this eraser apart slightly, fold it into itself, and it is clean. You can shape it to a point for getting into fine detail. Another benefit is that kneaded erasers leave no residue on the paper.

Vinyl is another kind of eraser. This is a great eraser for use on drafting vellum, film, and tracing paper. It rarely smudges and leaves a minimum of residue. Brand names for this style include Sanford Magic Rub® and Alvin Erase Clear®. Vinyl erasers remove pencil and some pen.

There are electric erasers that can either plug into an outlet or run on batteries. They are great for doing large amounts of erasing, particularly on drafting. Refills for this type of eraser can include white vinyl, pink styles, or special ink erasers. The ink erasers are similar to compressed sand paper. You have to be very careful when using them or you can rip a hole in your paper.

I keep mentioning residue left behind. How do you fix that, you may ask? Well, the mighty and all-powerful drafting brush is the tool of choice. It has a long handle and very soft bristles. It whisks away eraser gunk without damaging or smudging your drawing. I usually have several of these handy, mostly because my cats like to play with them.

When all else fails, there are always correction fluid and tape. They come in a variety of colors now. They are opaque and cover up just about anything. However, they do not blend into the rest of your drawing very well. So use this option only as a last resort.

PAPER

There are many different types of paper that come in a variety of sizes and shapes (Fig. 5.10). They all have very specific purposes, however. Newsprint paper is often used for quick sketches with pencil or charcoal. Newsprint is an inexpensive paper and doesn't hold up to repeated erasing or pressure with the drawing tool. Drawing paper is sturdier than newsprint and is meant for a dry medium—pencil, charcoal, pastel, and crayon. Specific drawing papers are intended for use specifically with pencil or with charcoal. The major difference is the "tooth" or texture of the paper.

Illustration board is heavier and meant for a wet medium, like pen and ink, marker, watercolor, and airbrush. Watercolor paper is just what it sounds like, paper for painting with watercolor paints. Watercolor paper is very specific and comes in a number of finishes that vary in texture. The texture changes how the paint adheres to the paper, giving very different effects.

For hand drafting, vellum is used. It is translucent, so that you can trace an object from another drawing below the vellum. Speaking of tracing, there is actual tracing paper, which is similar to the tissue paper you use when wrapping a gift. It is a more fragile paper, tearing easily and not being of archive quality. It is, however, great for quick sketches during research or meetings.

TOOLS

Let me start by talking about hand drawing and drafting and the tools you need for each. This discussion applies to all areas of technical theatre! Whether you are drawing a **ground plan**, a **light plot**, a clothing pattern, or the spread of an effect projector's lens, you need the skills we are about to discuss. Later in this chapter, we discuss computer software and hardware. Keep in mind that, if you understand the basics of hand drafting, your computer drafting will go faster and be easier to understand.

The **scale rule** is possibly the most important tool of all (Fig. 5.11a). It is the basis for our shorthand way of

Fig. 5.10 Pads of paper.

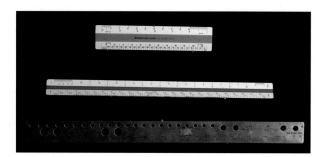

Fig. 5.11 Scale rulers.

drawing. I carry one with me at all times; you just never know. Here is how it works. If you wanted to draw the theatre in its actual size, you would need a pretty big piece of paper. And that is not practical. Scale allows you to draw things smaller, or in some cases larger, than they actually are. You have to keep the proportion right, so you choose one of several scales to have your object fit on the page. You

need a scale rule not only for creating your drawings but also for reading other people's drawings.

In the USA, we use the scales of ⅛, ½, 1, 1½, and 3 inches. There are lots of others in metric, but let's limit ourselves to these. A scale rule is normally a triangular-shaped ruler with six sides containing 11 scales. One of the six sides is a regular ruler, just like you are used to looking at. The other sides have two scales on each side. One scale reads from right to left, the other from left to right. Let's pick one scale and I'll explain how it works. Now keep in mind that there are separate scale rules for Imperial measure (used in the US) versus Metric measure (used almost everywhere else). Look at Figure 5.12 for conversions back and forther between Imperial and Metric.

Drawing in ½-inch scale means that every 12 inches in reality will equal ½ inch on the paper. It's that simple.

Conversion of US Linear Measure to Metric System	
1 inch	2.54 centimeters
1 foot	0.3048 meters
1 yard	0.9144 meters
1 mile	1.6093 kilometers
1 millimeter	0.03937 inches
1 centimeter	0.3937 inches
1 decimeter	3.937 inches
1 meter	39.37 inches
1 kilometer	0.62137 miles

■ **Fig. 5.12**

Instead of making you figure out all the math in your head, someone came up with the brilliant idea to put the different conversions on a ruler. Trust me, it saves a lot of time! It may sound really confusing, but after you make your first drawing this way, it will seem as easy as the proverbial riding of a bike.

The next thing you need is a surface on which to draw. **Drafting tables** are often used for sketching and layout as well as for drafting (Fig. 5.13). This is because you can change the angle of the tabletop to whatever is comfortable for you. Sometimes, I sit while I draw and stand while I draft. I can adjust the table height and angle to whatever is the most comfortable. You need a good drafting chair or **drafting stool**, one that goes up and down to adjust to the height of your table. It should be comfortable and support your back. You will sit in this chair for long periods of time, so make sure it's comfy. Next, you need light. Drafting table lights usually clamp onto your table. This allows you to have consistent light whenever you change the angle of your desk. A good fluorescent lamp gives you a bright, even amount of light. The other nice thing about fluorescence is that it doesn't get hot. If you are working underneath the light for hours at a time, it is good to keep cool.

Most tables come with a **parallel rule** or offer an upgrade to a drafting machine. A parallel rule is a straight edge that travels up and down your table on two cables. The cables are on either side of your table. The rule typically has a brake to hold it in place when you let go. The parallel rule allows you to draw horizontal lines that are consistently parallel to each other. A drafting machine tracks on left and right

■ **Fig. 5.13** A designer's studio with drafting table with drafting machine, chair, and lamp. You can also see storage for rolled drawings as well as in filing cabinets and drawers.

and up and down on one arm that is mounted to the table. The machine has two scale rulers, one vertical and one horizontal. The main advance in the drafting machine is that it can adjust to any angle you need. The older method you can choose, and the cheapest, is a **T square**. The T square is a tool shaped like a T (Fig. 5.14). The short part of the T leans against the side of your table. By sliding it up and down the length of your table, the long part of the T becomes an edge you can use to draw a horizontal line. It is a replacement for the parallel rule. The T square doesn't lock into place, it doesn't track easily, and it has no brake. However, it is more portable, meaning you can use it on any table you sit down at.

OK, you're doing great. You can draw a horizontal line. There all sorts of lines types that mean different things on a drawing (Fig. 5.15). Lines can show curtains, centerlines, broken lines, and the like. Each has a different look. Line

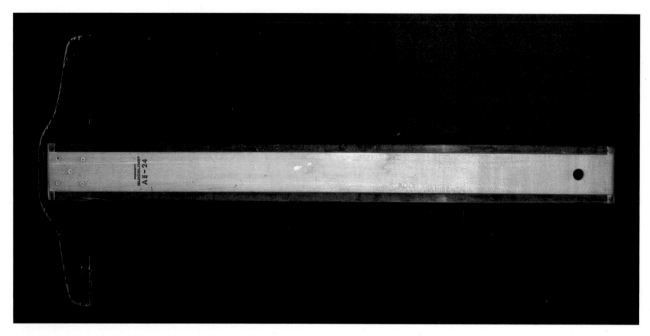

■ **Fig. 5.14** T square.

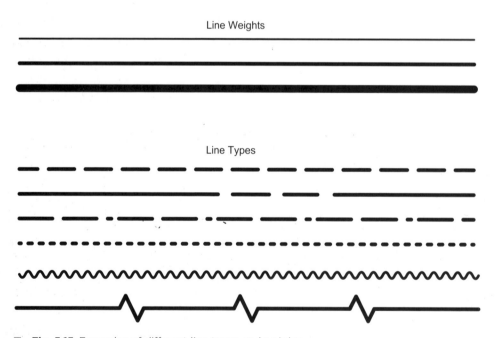

■ **Fig. 5.15** Examples of different line types and weights.

weights are also important. Heavier lines are generally more important on a drawing than lighter weight lines.

What about vertical lines? Well, there is a great way to draw vertical and angled lines. The tool you need is called a **triangle** (Fig. 5.16). There are many different styles, and you will most likely need at least two or three. There are two ways to consider which triangle to purchase. The first and most important consideration is the angle of the triangle. Triangles come in two fixed configurations: 30/60 degree and 45/90 degree. You need both of these, and using them in combination gets you many more angles. Another consideration is the adjustable triangle. These are usually able to adjust from 0 to 90 degrees. I do not recommend using an adjustable triangle exclusively. I find the best way

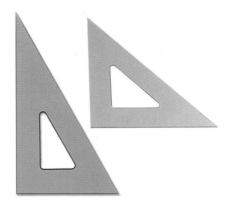

Fig. 5.16 Triangles.

Fig. 5.17 French curves.

to go is to use a combination of fixed and adjustable. The other consideration that affects all triangles is their overall size. They can come as small as 4 inches on the longest side all the way up to 18 inches. All triangles should be see-through, so that you can line up the edge of the triangle to your drawing underneath.

Now that you can draw straight lines in many directions, what happens if you need a curve? Not a problem. Let me introduce you to the **french curve** (Fig. 5.17). It is a template for drawing curves. It has curved edges and several scroll-shaped cutouts in the middle. The french curve is used by tracing one of its edges. Then, you carefully move the template to the end of the curve you just drew, and continue the curve tracing the template. You repeat this as many times as you need to create the proper curve. You can now repeat this curve, using the template again, if it appears somewhere else in your design. This is a technique that needs practice, but it can produce great effects.

There are many different templates that may come in handy (Fig. 5.18). Scenic designers can find templates with furniture in different scales. Lighting designers can find a wide variety of lighting fixture templates. Everybody can use shape templates that include circles, squares, triangles,

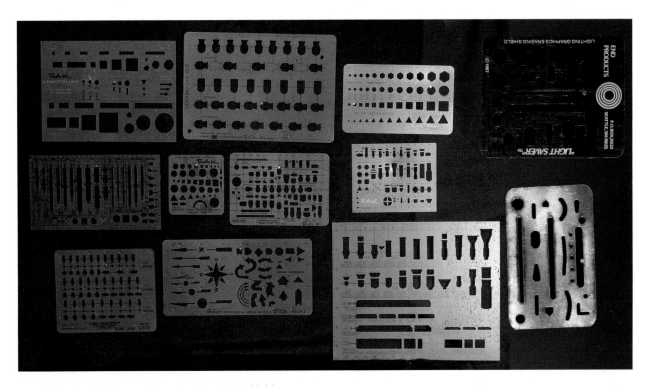

Fig. 5.18 Drafting templates and erasing shields.

Schoolhouse Printed

ABCDEFGHIJKLMNOPQRSTUVWXYZ

abcdefghijklmnopqrstuvwxzy

0123456789

Bradley Hand ITC

ABCDEFGHIJKLMNOPQRSTUVWXYZ

abcdefghijklmnopqrstuvwxzy

0123456789

Papyrus

ABCDEFGHIJKLMNOPQRSTUVWXYZ

abcdefghijklmnopqrstuvwxzy

0123456789

Tekton Pro

ABCDEFGHIJKLMNOPQRSTUVWXYZ

abcdefghijklmnopqrstuvwxzy

0123456789

■ **Fig. 5.19** Samples of various computer fonts for lettering styles. All these can be replicated with hand lettering.

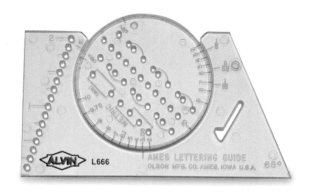

■ **Fig. 5.20** The Ames Lettering Guide is a favorite of mine, as it can be adjusted in many ways. I always keep one with me!

arrows, or just about any shape you can think of. They come in handy whether you are drawing, drafting, or just doodling.

Another type of template is the **erasing shield**. In my opinion, this is one of the coolest things ever invented. It is a small, thin piece of polished steel with different shapes cut out of it. You lay the shield over your drawing, specifically the part you want to erase. Then, while holding it in place, you erase the offending line without the possibility of your eraser touching anything else on the paper. It's like magic, only better!

Let us talk about lettering for a minute (Fig. 5.19). Sloppy lettering can make a good drawing look terrible. If you want to look professional, practice your lettering. It is the quickest, easiest way to make your presentation jump up a couple of notches. The Ames **Lettering Guide** (Fig. 5.20) is going to be your best friend. It is yet another template. The left side is at a 90-degree angle to the bottom of the template; use this for making your vertical lines. The right side is at a 60-degree angle; use it for angled letters like *v* and *w*, for example.

Now for the really cool part! The center of this template is a circle that rotates. Inside the circle are a variety of little holes. You rotate the circle until you get the little holes the right distance apart for the desired height of your letters. Put your pencil in any of the little holes, and slide the guide along your parallel rule or T square to make guidelines.

The last tool to think about is tape (Fig. 5.21). **Drafting tape** and drafting dots are made by a variety of companies. This tape looks like regular masking tape, but it is less sticky. That means you can pull it up without leaving a residue or tearing your paper. This is important, as you will sometimes need to pull up the tape, reposition your paper, and put down new tape.

Computers

Some people use computers with software—OK, most of us do. Heck, I'm sitting at a computer right now writing this book. Computers are the way of not only the future but the way of *today*! I still maintain that learning hand drafting and drawing is always helpful. The conventions for one technique are the same as another. It's really only a matter of whether you have to go to someone with a blueprint machine or a plotter. So, let us talk hardware and software.

Hardware first. The big debate I always hear is "Should I use a Windows computer or Apple computer?" Well, it's easy. It's the simplest choice of all. This is a true no brainer. The answer is—it doesn't matter. Get whichever you are more comfortable with. You will, almost always, find programs made specifically for your computer's operating system. All of the big software companies have finally

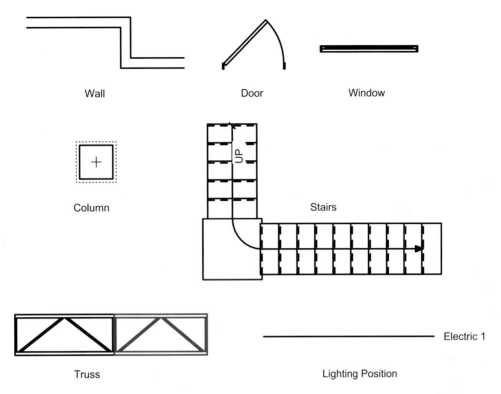

Fig. 5.21 There are conventions for drafting different parts of the scenery. See this figure for examples.

figured out that both platforms are here to stay. You'll see what I mean when we talk about software.

When you are buying a new computer, my advice is simple. Get the fastest processor with the biggest hard drive and the most RAM. Whatever you buy will be outdated within 2 years. You have a better chance of keeping your machine longer if you get the newest, best, and greatest now. The same advice goes for peripherals: digital cameras, scanners, printers, plotters— everything. We are not going to suddenly discover that we want to store everything at low resolution, right? So, use your student discount and get the best you can.

Now for the software. There are specific programs that everybody uses. Before I give you the list, I have to share something. Long before there were programs dedicated to theatre needs, we all still got the paperwork done. So keep in mind that, if you don't find exactly what you need, be creative! Find a work-around for whatever task you're trying to do. We are theatre people, we're creative, it is what we do for a living!

Let's discuss the specific software developed with our intended purposes in mind. Let me explain something first. The lighting department generates more paperwork, I think, than any other department. Various pieces of paperwork are

updated on a daily basis, sometimes even hourly during tech. So, the first thought that comes to mind is John McKernon's Lightwright®. Lightwright began life officially as ALD® (Assistant Lighting Designer) in 1982 on a TRS-80 computer! What humble beginnings, and now it is the industry standard for lighting paperwork. Lightwright is the new name for the program, and new versions come out regularly. Lightwright works on both the Mac and PC.

If you want to try one integrated software package that can generate all versions of the required lighting paperwork, try Stage Research's Light Shop®, Soft Plot®, and Soft Plot 3D®. The Soft Plot programs allow you to create and maintain all the necessary paperwork. Light Shop allows you to view the photometric data of over 1500 fixtures. Don't worry, we discuss photometrics in Chapter 10. Keep in mind that many people will use your paperwork. Everyone will need to use the software to make updates and changes.

Previsualization is a hot topic today for many designers. Often referred to as *pre-vis*, it means just what you think. It's a way to "see" what the show will look like before you get to the theatre. Everyone has very strong opinions about it. Some say it's a waste of time, while others say they wouldn't

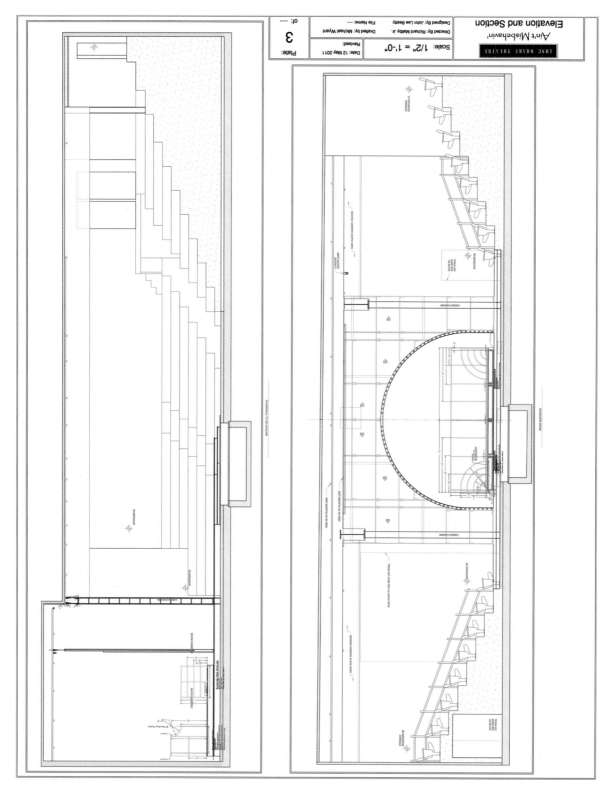

The drawing's title block reads:

LONG WHARF THEATRE

Ain't Misbehavin'

Elevation and Section

Designed By: John Lee Beatty	
Drafted by: Michael Wyant	File Name: ——
Directed By: Richard Maltby Jr.	

Scale: 1/2" = 1'-0"	
Date: 12 May 2011	
Revised:	

Plate: **3** of: ——

■ **Fig. 5.22** Computer drafted elevation and section for *Ain't Misbehavin'* at Long Wharf Theatre, designed by John Lee Beatty.

do a show without it. Pre-vis is a slow process. It is used mostly when time in the theatre will be at a minimum. Software today has gotten to a point where you can actually cue lights in the computer, then load the disk into your light board and run cues. It's not a fast or easy process though.

Lighting and scenery require drafting many plans, **sections**, and other drawings for every show. Computer-aided drafting is now the standard (Figs. 5.22 and 5.23). The granddaddy of all CAD programs is AutoCAD® by Autodesk. It is a massive, expensive program used primarily by architects. If you have access to it, try it out. Many plug-ins are now to help us in theatre work. The most popular program for this purpose, however, is Vectorworks® by Nemetschek. Vectorworks worked closely with the theatre industry to create palettes for scenic objects, trusses, and hardware. There is also a version called Spotlight® that allows for the insertion of lighting instruments. This is truly one of the rare times when a commercial software package has actually catered to a small niche industry.

Costumers, don't feel left out. A few options are available for you as well. Dress Shop® and My Pattern Designer® were developed by the same team to cater to two different markets. Patternmaker® is another option created by people with a theatre background who understand our needs.

> Clothing is architectural . . . it's construction, just different construction methods.
>
> **—William Ivey Long**

Dress Shop has two versions, Standard and Pro, and is geared toward those of us who make clothing for others. Standard includes 150 patterns with a wide assortment of mix-and-match possibilities. You can also vary how many measurements you want to take or if you want to use standard sizes. Pro expands on all the options within Standard, adding more patterns and more flexibility.

My Pattern Designer is aimed at the person who is at home making clothing for him- or herself, although it will work just as well for the costumer. It is easier to use than Dress Shop. As it was designed with the home seamstress in mind, you can get started with as few as five key measurements. Combining different pieces from styles within a large library creates customized patterns.

Patternmaker has three versions that successively increase the patterning options you have. Patternmaker allows you to work from standard sizing or from your own measurements. The three versions are Home, Expert, and Marker. The Home version works with basic garments. Expert adds the capability to use a digitizer, and Marker helps with cost estimates.

Software is available that does very specific tasks to aid our jobs in the theatre. Other packages are available that are generic to our industry; these break down into four basic categories of graphics software: 2D graphic creation and manipulation, 3D graphic creation, video editing, and compositing. Many software packages are available in each of these categories. Before we get into the different options available, let's discuss a subject that influences the whole conversation. Intrigued? Read on.

Have you heard the terms *raster* and *vector*? The software is divided between these types of processing for the images. Let me explain. **Vector**-based images are created using mathematical formulas to locate each point. Lines are then drawn to connect the dots. **Raster**, on the other hand, is a pixel-based technology. Now, here is the important part. If you need to enlarge a part of the image, vector can scale infinitely larger without losing resolution. Raster, on the other hand, becomes lower resolution instantly on changing the size. Keep this in mind when you are creating images. Choose your software depending on what you will eventually need to do with it. If you need to work in raster, work at the size you will need when you are done. Otherwise you waste a lot of time and have to recreate things.

So, let us talk about 2D graphic software. The king of the raster hill is Adobe's Photoshop® (Fig. 5.24). Another option that performs slightly differently is Corel's Painter®. Both are awesome and powerful software that are raster-based programs. Adobe has a vector-based product named Illustrator®. It is also the king of the hill for what it does. Adobe has kept up with the needs of the market. All these programs are available for both Windows and Macintosh platforms. So, check them out if you do not already know them.

Three-dimensional creation offers a wider range of programs. Cinema 4D® by Maxon and SoftImage® and Maya® (both by Autodesk) are a few that come to mind quickly. LightWave® by NewTek is another that focuses primarily on lighting but also does modeling. Vectorworks by Nemetschek is a 2D CAD program that also has a 3D

■ **Fig. 5.23** Computer drafted elevation of portal for *Ain't Misbehavin* at Long Wharf Theatre, designed by John Lee Beatty.

■ **Fig. 5.24** Photoshop rendering, designed by George Allison.

component. It is nicely integrated. You can go back and forth between each module seamlessly.

There is easy access to digital video now. Many designers hope to incorporate video, either prerecorded or live, into their designs. Video editing software becomes critical for pre-recorded footage. The last thing an audience wants to see is the rough cut of a video thrown in over the top of an ongoing performance. Video should highlight, accent, extend—not run over. Two main programs work on standard computers, Apple's Final Cut Pro® and Adobe Premier®. Both work well and perform exactly like the bigger cousins that run on proprietary hardware. Editing, timeline, trimming, effects, color correction, audio, and fonts are all available tools to you.

Last, let's discuss compositing. Your stills and your video are all ready. Do you think you're finished? Well, you are not. Perhaps the most critical step is left to do. Now, you have to put it together and pray it all fits the way you hope and dream. The one leader in this particular part of the pack *is* Adobe After Effects®.

Perhaps, the most important thing to ask yourself is, What will my playback machine be? After Effects can produce professional output to film, video, DVD, and the Web. It contains powerful masking tools, keying and matte tools, expert visual effects, and text animation and titling

effects. Keep in mind, it's an Adobe product. Any graphics you created in another Adobe product easily integrate.

This is just the tip of the iceberg in terms of software. Many more options are available to you. I can't list them all here, as there isn't enough room and the list is ever changing. The Internet is truly your friend on this subject. Search around and see what you can find. Keep looking for newer versions and better options. The more we expect, the more the developers will give us.

PERSPECTIVE DRAWING

OK, now that we've really gone through drawing and the potential tools, let's approach it from a slightly more technical side. Let's talk about perspective drawing and projection. First, we define the terms. **Perspective** projection is a type of drawing that uses a 2D technique to approximate a 3D object. Now, we look at how to do this from a very technical point of view. Many factors go into a good perspective drawing. Let's start to break it down.

The three main concepts to understand before we go much further are vanishing points, the horizon line, and foreshortening. We start with vanishing points. The most common forms of perspective are one-point, two-point, and three-point

Fig. 5.25 One-point perspective photo with a bit of a twist.

The **horizon line** is usually defined as the line that separates the earth from the sky (Fig. 5.26). In our usage, it is the horizontal line that comes closest to the height of your eye. It divides the entire drawing into two parts. Choosing where to put the horizon line determines a great deal about what your drawing looks like. The horizon line tells us where we, the viewers, are standing to view the object that has been drawn. Are we below it or above it or right in the middle of it? This affects not only the outcome of the drawing but also the feel of it.

The last term I mentioned earlier is **foreshortening** (Fig. 5.27). So far, we have been talking about placing the object to be drawn directly in front of us. It might possibly be above or below our line of sight, but it is centered on us. What happens if we move it off to the side? Instead of standing on the railroad tracks and looking straight down the rails, what happens if you stand off to the side and look down the rails? The rails appear shorter. This is obviously an optical illusion. The rails did not get shorter simply because we moved our position over. This is foreshortening.

OK, now that we have some background to work from, let's dive into one-point perspective. This is the traditional railroad or street photo. The viewer is usually standing in the middle of the road or rail, looking straight ahead. There is one vanishing point in the distance, centered between two parallel lines. As the lines move toward the vanishing point, they are drawn closer together. Keep in mind that this is an illusion. The lines don't actually converge. The point (if you pardon the pun) is to draw something on paper and give it the illusion of three dimensions. It is that simple to create on paper, making the illusion of distance where none actually exists.

Two-point perspective can be used to draw rails or roads as well as many other options. Think about a house for a second. If you stand at the corner of the house, there is a side on your left and a side on your right. Both sides go back to opposing vanishing points. Now here is the cool part. The walls on the back side that we don't see are also drawn with the same vanishing points. Check it out in Figure 5.28.

Three-point perspective is next. It is the most complicated form that I address in this book. Keep in mind that there is much more to learn about perspective drawing. This is just a short introduction. Three-point usually has the effect of making the object appear over our heads or below our feet. Always keep in mind that the further the vanishing points are from your object, the gentler the angles of perspective will be.

perspective (Fig. 5.25). The name refers to the number of vanishing points used to construct the drawing. **Vanishing point** refers to the point in space where two parallel lines "seem" to converge. Think of railroad tracks. We know in reality they never touch, but they sure look like they do in photographs.

Every set of parallel lines can have its own vanishing point. Most often, however, sets of lines share a vanishing point. The most common scenarios for theatre, as I said, are the one-, two-, and three-point drawings. Think for a second about an architect's sketch for a new building. How many parallel lines do they have? Lots! You can keep adding more vanishing points to a drawing, as long as it helps to further the clarity of the drawing. If it just makes it more confusing, you might want to consider limiting yourself. Now consider this: What if you are drawing a landscape with lots of nature, such as trees, flowers, and birds? If there are no parallel lines, there are no vanishing points. This is often referred to as *zero-point perspective*.

■ **Fig. 5.26** The Mid-Hudson Bridge across the Hudson River in Poughkeepsie, NY, showing a clear horizon line.

■ **Fig. 5.27** Foreshortening of a tree limb.

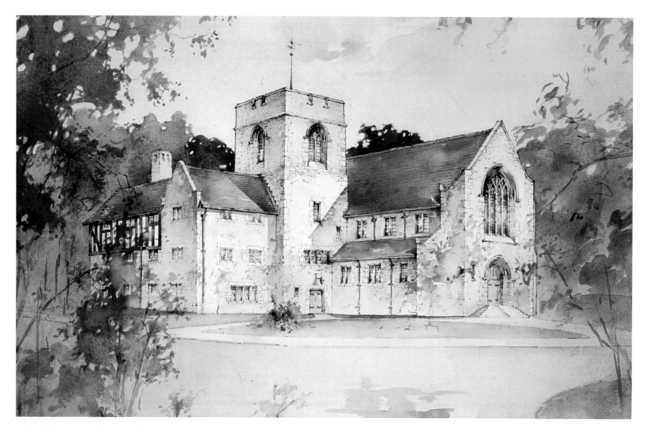

■ **Fig. 5.28** A perspective sketch, circa 1913.

There are several ways to create a perspective drawing. As we have already done, you can draw it completely freehand with no drawing tools other than paper and pencil. When drawing perspective by hand, I find it easiest to work on paper with a preprinted grid. The grid gives me an instant reference as I begin to draw. Add some grid paper and a straight edge, and you can become a little more mechanically accurate. Computers can also simulate this technique. Now, here is the funny part. Sometimes, and only sometimes, you can ignore the rules I just laid out and create a "different" version of perspective. The important thing to remember is that you have to know and understand the rules before you can change them. Oliver Smith knew how to use the rules—then broke them for his purpose. We call it *Oliver perspective*. But, nobody can do this at first.

For now, let's go back to the rules. We look at the development of a two-point perspective, step by step. Figure 5.29 shows a simplistic ground plan from a show. When you look at a ground plan, the next step is to figure out what it will look like standing up. This is the basis for a sketch. Let's get started. We first have to determine the floor line of the existing ground plan as well as the horizon line and base

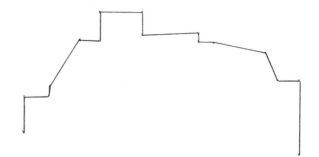

■ **Fig. 5.29** Two-point perspective, step 1.

line for the sketch. The next thing to do is determine what vanishing points you want to use. For sketches like this, we often use a vanishing point close to what our eye line would be if we were standing in the drawing, the average person being about 6-feet tall. Then, we have to draw leader lines to correspond with the different walls on the ground plan and where they intersect in the new sketch.

Now, you are ready to start drawing. All you need are paper, a pencil, and a straight edge. Start on the far left or right. Determine how tall your walls will be and mark that height on your paper (Fig. 5.30). This is why grid paper comes in handy. I marked out 12 grid spaces to make my

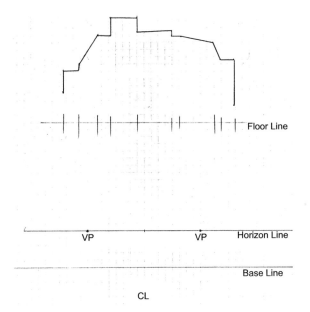

Fig. 5.30 Two-point perspective, step 2.

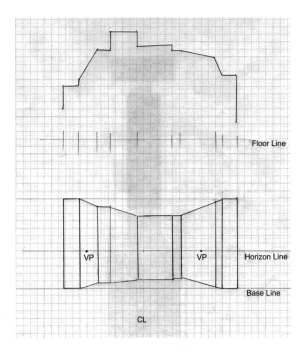

Fig. 5.31 Two-point perspective, step 3.

walls 12 feet tall. Once you determined the height, draw your outside wall line. If the top or bottom of a wall is parallel to the top of your paper, draw the top and bottom of the first wall straight across to the next leader line. If the wall is angled or you moved on to the next wall, use the vanishing point on the far side of the drawing from your wall to connect the top and bottom of the next wall to the first.

The vertical lines on the walls stay vertical. The angled lines drawn from the vanishing point to the last wall determine their length (Fig. 5.31). Continue drawing each wall until you reach the middle of the sketch. Now, start again from the other side, using the opposite vanishing point. When you reach the middle again, your sketch should be almost done. The only thing left to do is to add any openings: doors, windows, arches. If they are square you follow the same rules. The vertical lines stay vertical and the horizontal lines still reference the vanishing point on the opposite side of the stage.

Perspective drawing can be as simple or complicated as you choose or need it to be. I've gone over the basics. Feel free to experiment from here and play around with it. Keep in mind that the placement of the vanishing point(s) determines how distorted the final sketch is. Try making several sketches based on different vanishing points and horizon lines to see how very different they look. Now, here is the important part. Which of your three sketches most "correctly" represents the scenery?

The answer is all or none. What? Well, the vanishing point changes make the perspective more extreme, which may or may not be accurate. Changing the horizon line means the audience is moving around the theatre. One obvious note, if you moved the horizon line up into the ceiling, obviously, the audience won't be sitting there! Keep in mind a very important fact. Anything you can draw can be built exactly as it was drawn. It might take a big budget or a very long schedule, but it can be done. So be careful what you draw and make sure it shows what has been bouncing around in your head. Otherwise, you mislead the director, and everyone is in for a big surprise when the load-in starts.

Your sketch looks great, except the stage is empty. Now, you have to add furniture, props, and people. Once your line drawing of a sketch is populated, it is time to add tone (light and shadow) to the sketch. This makes the black-and-white drawing come to life. Before you can begin, you have to think about how the set will be lit. Lighting becomes critical to making the scenery sketch look real and alive. More important, lighting is critical to make the scenery look at least similar to how it will appear in the theatre.

RENDERING

Our next topic is rendering (Fig. 5.32). This is the step where you definitely are showing your work to the director

■ **Fig. 5.32** *My Fair Lady*, Higgins's study, watercolor rendering, by Oliver Smith. © Rosaria Sinisi.

and other designers and potentially adding color as well. The initial perspective sketch may just be your way of working, which eventually turns into a rendering. It may never be for others to see. But, at some point, you, as the set designer, have to show some representation of the scenery to the director. Otherwise, your budget will never get approved. So, on to the rendering step.

So the sketch turns into the rendering. Is there a difference between a sketch and a rendering? It can be just semantics, but here is how I approach it. The color sketch is part of your process prior to the rendering (Fig. 5.33). Sketching is traditionally known as being a quicker, more relaxed process. Keep in mind that when you show the director and other designers your drawing, sketch, or rendering, one of the first things they react to is the "feel" of it.

When you are working on a sketch, sometimes, you have to back away from it for a little while. When you come back to it fresh, you may see something that you didn't see before. You may choose to keep this new "feature" or get rid of it. Just keep in mind that designing is not an accident waiting to happen. It should be considered. Then, if, as I call it, a "happy accident" occurs, you are ready to decide if you want to keep it or not.

The term *rendering* is usually used for a full-color, finished sketch, finished being the key word. You should now have the furniture, props, and actors on the set. You should have chosen a specific moment in time from the play. The actors should be in place, the light cue should be evident. Your entire design team will look at this rendering for clues as to how you envision the final production.

Keep in mind, now you've finished your rendering, that there is another way to work. You can skip the perspective sketch and rendering completely. What? Why didn't I tell you that before? Well, if you skip these two very important steps, they are replaced most likely with a model. A model is a 3D representation of the scenery instead of a 2D sketch.

■ **Fig. 5.33** Sketch by George Allison for a Berkshire Opera production of *The Rape of Lucretia,* by Benjamin Britten.

DRAFTING

Let me start by saying that drafting is drafting. What do I mean? Well, drafting is meant to convey information, not an emotion. Certain things have to be in a pack of draftings to give all the information needed to build the set. Now, here is the key. Are you ready? It doesn't matter whether you are hand drafting or using a CAD program (Fig. 5.34). How can that be? Well, it actually doesn't matter if you do your sketch by hand or in a program like Photoshop either. What matters, and the only thing that matters, is that you give out the information needed in a way it can be used. The techniques, concepts, and ideas are all the same. Remember in Chapter 3 when we talked about focus? Well, it's the same thing here. You want the drafting to have a focus, so people know where to look first, where to look second, and so forth.

We begin by drafting an orthographic projection. **Orthographic projection** is a way of representing a 3D objection in two dimensions using multiple views. Have you ever taken a flat piece of cardboard and turned it into a box? Well that is the idea (Fig. 5.35). Say, we are going to build a table. We first need to visualize the table inside a box. We then project each side of the table onto the surrounding box. Then we unfold the box, laying it flat. This creates two **plan views**, top and bottom, as well as four **side views**.

The carpenter or scene shop needs the information from each of these views to build the table. This is the basis for all the information you generate in your own drawings. If you are not the designer, it is the basis for all the information you need to create the design. We started this chapter by talking about using drawing to get the ideas out of your head and onto paper. Once the sketch is approved, you need to break down each part of the set into smaller pieces so the scene shop can build it.

Let's talk about some of the standardized conventions. The first thing you are going to do, most likely, is draw a line. Well, what kind of line? A line is not just a line. Are you drawing the centerline of the theatre, a leg, a border, or scenery? It makes a difference. Each of these types of lines has a convention for how it should be drawn. USITT's (U.S. Institute for Theatre Technology) Graphic Standards Board established all of the conventions we discuss next. If you don't follow the conventions, your drawings will be confusing at best and unreadable at worst.

We discussed line weight in Chapter 3. It comes back now. You have to combine the correct line weight with the correct line style to follow the established conventions. Take a look at the examples that follow. These are a few of the many examples you need. A drafting class goes into much more detail, but this should give you a start. If you've ever seen a ground plan or section, I bet these examples will look pretty familiar.

- Border—a thick double line.
- Plaster line—a thin dashed line.
- Centerline—a thin line of long-short-long lines with note of *CL* near lower edge.
- Section—uniform hatching on diagonal lines.
- Leader line—a thin solid line with or without an arrow at the end.
- Dimension/extension lines—a thin line.
- Break line—a thin line that extends beyond the edges of the break.

Next, we talk about lettering and labeling. Drawing is one thing; writing is a whole other thing. This is one area where hand drafting and CAD drafting differ. I talk about each separately. There is one simple piece of advice to follow for lettering. Make it simple and legible. Remember the goal is to convey information. If you try to get to fancy, no one will be able to read what you've written. Most people feel that a straight, clean sans serif typeface is best. My feeling is to add a little style if you want, just don't let it get in the way of the main goal: conveying information.

When most people first start to hand draft, they are okay with the drawing but totally stress out when it comes to the lettering. Lettering takes practice, but a couple of hints will help you do a better job right away. First, remember, earlier in this chapter, I talked about the Ames Lettering Guide? Well, get one. The most important thing to know about lettering, and how to make it look good, is *consistency*. Use a triangle to keep the vertical part of the letters vertical. Use a parallel or T square to keep the horizontal parts of the letters horizontal. This is a good start. Most drafting-style letters use true verticals while changing the horizontals into angles for a little extra flair.

CAD drafting and lettering is a whole different thing. It's easier for the most part but you still have to pay attention to details. So, you're in your CAD program, you type in the text, and you think, "No problem, I'm done, what is so hard?" Well, you have to choose a font, a size, the attributes—there are many more choices. The good

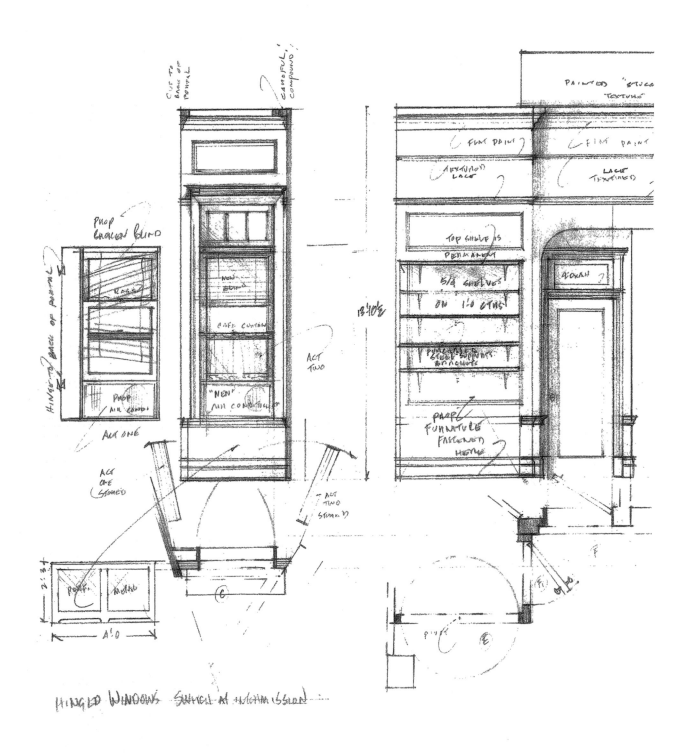

■ **Fig. 5.34** John Lee Beatty hand draftings for a production of Neil Simon's *The Odd Couple.*

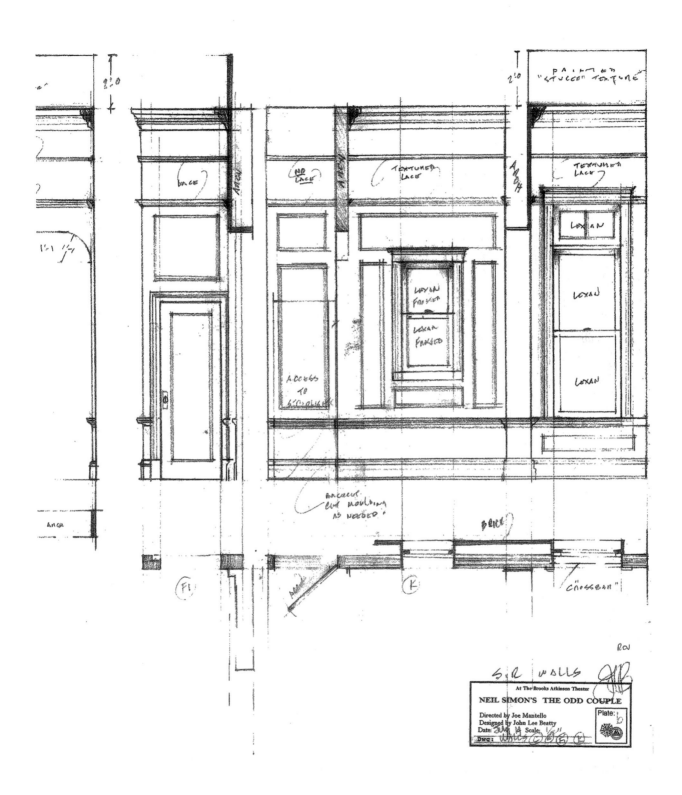

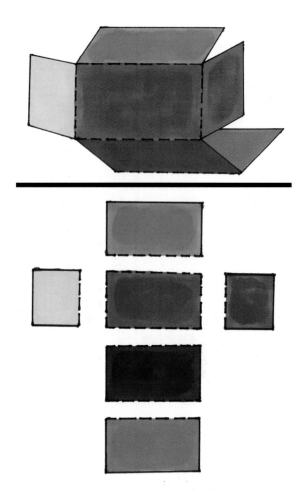

Fig. 5.35 To begin an orthographic projection you must identify the different sides and begin to see how they are connected, as shown on the top. The final orthographic projection on the bottom shows each side lying flat to each other.

news is that a number of fonts are available now that actually look like hand-drafted lettering. Once you pick a font, you have to choose the size. Most important, you then have to stick with that font—remember, consistency. With hand drafting, we're usually lucky if we can get three sizes of lettering on the paper. You can choose 10 point or 11 point or whatever looks good. This is an option the hand drafter lacks. So, use your tools well. Vary the font options and the size to help give focus to what is most important.

Our next topic is dimensioning. Dimensions are used to confirm actual drawn sizes. Whoever reads your drafting will most likely have a scale rule at hand. A quick glance at your dimensioning lets that person know if the drawing is accurate. The scale rule confirms it. Dimensions are usually read when looking at the drafting from the bottom side. If you need to rotate a dimension based on the object or other spacing, make sure it reads from the right side. This is a convention that works well as long as you are consistent.

There are three different styles of dimensions (Fig. 5.36): **Linear dimensions** are used when you are measuring in a straight line; **arc dimensions** are used if you are measuring some kind of angle or radius; and the **multiple dimension** style is used when you are measuring several things in a row from the same starting point.

Certain conventions already have been established for drafting common objects. This makes your job easier. Somebody else already figured out how to draw a wall, floors, and curtains. You just need to use their symbols as a guide. This is like learning another language. But, after you've drawn them once, they will be second nature to you. In fact, most designers' doodles use these same conventions, because it is a common language we all understand.

Walls on a set are divided into small, manageable parts called *flats*. When you are drawing a ground plan, you want to show the flats and where they are joined. There are two ways to do this. Solid walls are usually not the whole set. Usually, there are going to be openings in the walls for doors, arches, and windows, all of which have specific ways of being drawn. More on this in Chapter 7.

The scenic floor has become much more complicated in past years. It used to be that, unless there was a second level, like a balcony, the floor was just painted. Now full-stage decks are constructed to aid in automation of moving scenic units. Stairs and ramps are also used more frequently. So much information must be conveyed about the flooring that there is usually an entire drawing dedicated to the floor (Fig. 5.37). More on this in Chapter 7.

Curtains are the next topics. We are not talking about window curtains here. In the theatre, all fabric items are called **soft goods**. All the fabric that hangs over and around the stage has different names depending on its function. Depending on what it does and how it hangs, each is also drawn differently. Some curtains are meant to touch the stage at all times, some are meant to never touch the stage, and some move around, sometimes touching and sometimes not. More on this in Chapter 7.

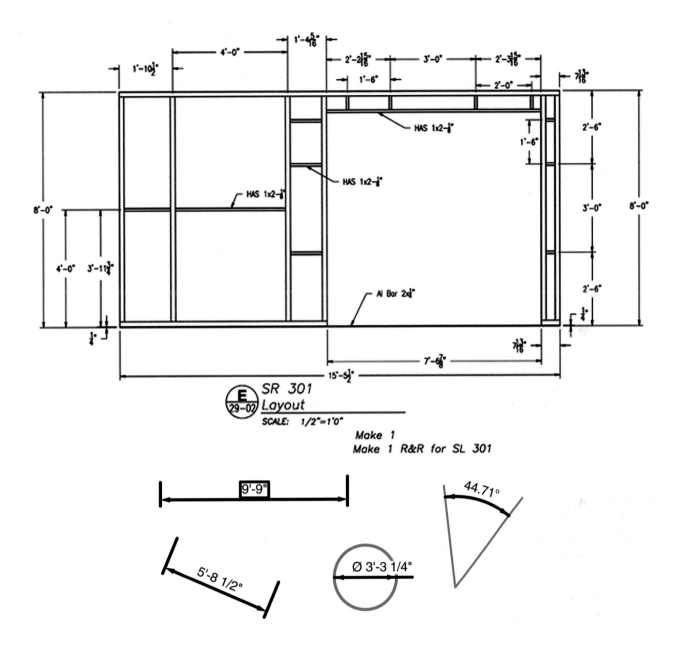

Fig 5.36 Above, an elevation for a wall, fully dimensioned. Below, different styles of dimensioning for all occasions.

Our next convention is one of the finishing touches to a drafting. It is the title block (Fig. 5.38). A **title block** must be placed on every drafting. It also needs to be placed in the same place on each drawing—remember, consistency. The placement varies depending on the type of title block. If you use a floating title block, it should be placed in the lower right corner of the drawing. If you use a docked title block, meaning it runs along an entire side of the drawing, it is usually placed on the right edge or bottom edge of the drawing. The most important thing is to keep it consistent from one drawing to the next within a pack of draftings.

Regardless of the type of block you choose to use or its placement, it contains very important information (Fig. 5.39). The following information should be included:

- Name of producing organization.
- Name of production.
- Drawing title.
- Drawing number.

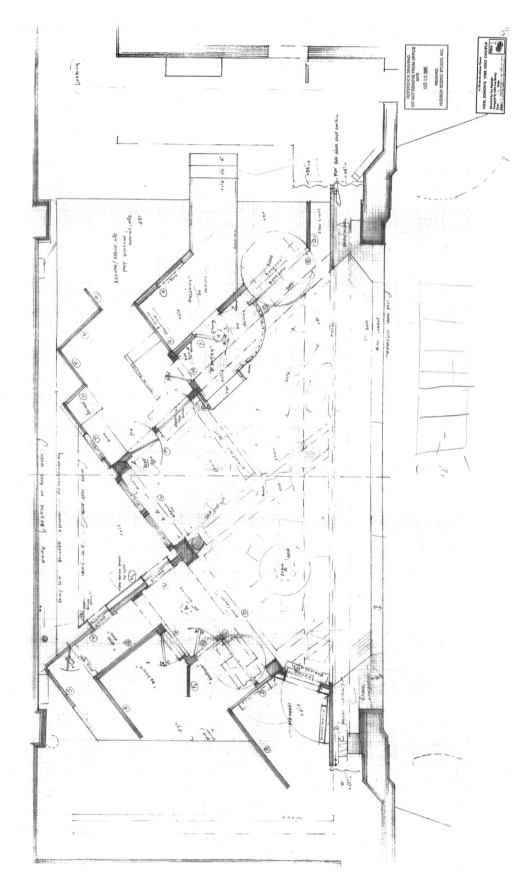

■ **Fig. 5.37** John Lee Beatty hand drafting for a production of Neil Simon's *The Odd Couple*.

Fig. 5.38 Scott Pask sample title block.

Fig. 5.39 Hudson Scenic sample title block.

- Predominant scale of the drawing.
- Date the drawing was drafted.
- Designer of the production.
- Drafter, if different from the designer.
- Drawing approval, if applicable.
- Revisions, if applicable.
- Union stamp, if applicable.
- If it is a digital drafting, the file name can be put in the title block for reference.

If there is a logo for the producer or production, feel free to put that in the title block instead of plain text. It helps make the drawing unique and easily recognizable. Any other information that you think is appropriate to all drawings can be added at your discretion. The following is additional information you may want to include:

- Location of the venue.
- Director of the production.
- Other members of the production team.
- Lighting assistant and/or master electrician.

- Contact information (telephone and fax numbers, email addresses).
- Liability disclaimer (see box).

Sample Liability Disclaimer

This drawing and the ideas, arrangement, design, and plans indicated hereon or represented hereby are owned by and remain the exclusive property of the designer. They have been created and developed for the use on and in connection with the specified project. Written dimensions on drawings shall have authority over scaled. Contractors and manufacturers shall verify and be responsible for all dimensions and the conditions on the job site. Any variations from the drawings are to be reported to the designer prior to performing work. These drawings represent visual concepts and construction and rigging suggestions only. The designer is unqualified to determine the structural appropriateness of this design and will not assume responsibility for improper engineering, construction, rigging, handling, or use of this lighting. All materials must comply with the most stringent applicable federal and local fire and safety codes.

Visually tied into the title block is the border. The border should be a thick double line. It serves two purposes, one visual and one practical. The visual purpose is that the border acts like a frame and visually ends the drawing. From a practical point of view, the border is very important. Anyone who looks at your drawing and sees a border on three sides will rightly assume they are missing part of the drawing. It alerts the viewers to the true edges of the drawing. That way, if something is missing, the next thing they do should be to call for another copy of the drawing.

The next item is the **key to symbols** (Fig. 5.40). This is a common element specifically on a light plot, but let's discuss it now. Think of a street map for a second. There is always a legend on it. It's a little box with different symbols to help you figure out the difference between a town road and a state highway. Our key is the same thing. On a light

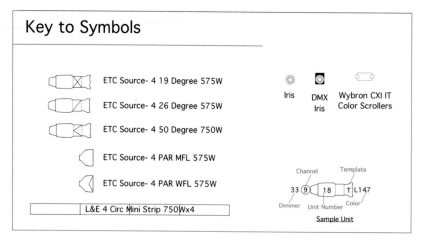

Key to Symbols

ETC Source- 4 19 Degree 575W

ETC Source- 4 26 Degree 575W

ETC Source- 4 50 Degree 750W

ETC Source- 4 PAR MFL 575W

ETC Source- 4 PAR WFL 575W

L&E 4 Circ Mini Strip 750Wx4

Iris   DMX   Wybron CXI IT
       Iris   Color Scrollers

Channel   Template

33 (9) 18   T L147

Dimmer Unit Number Color

Sample Unit

■ **Fig. 5.40** A sample key. Remember the key can have as much or as little information as is needed to convey the information.

plot, the key shows each of the lighting instruments used for the production and some of the accessories and attributes. Information may include

- Graphical symbol as well as verbal description of the fixture.

- Wattage of the lamp.

- Color manufacturer designation (i.e., R = Roscolux®, L = Lee, G = GAM, A = Apollo, etc.).

- Template manufacturer designation, when applicable (R = Rosco, G = GAM, A = Apollo, S = SFX, etc.).

- Accessories such as templates, irises, color scrollers, top hats, barn doors, and so forth.

USITT developed symbol guidelines for hand drafting. Vectorworks with Spotlight has its own set of symbols. Many of the manufacturers have developed CAD symbols for their fixtures. Independent programmers have symbols you can get as well. All this can be a little confusing. Here is the key (no pun intended). As long the symbols on your light plot match the symbols in your key, everything will work out okay. Is it better to use something standardized? It help others to understand what you want a little quicker. If they just finished working in a show with the USITT standard symbols, they are already used to them and know what they mean. If you use other symbols, they can still figure them out. It may just take a little longer initially.

Notes are an important part of every drafting. Scenic drawings tend to place the notes around the drawing as

needed. Light plots tend to use a note box, where all the notes are located. Most lighting notes are applicable to the whole light plot, not just one light. Scenery notes are usually very specific to one piece of scenery. That is the difference.

When you began reading this book, you expected there to be a table of contents, individual chapters, and an index at the very least, right? You use these things to find what you want within the book. Well, drafting is the same way! A complete pack of scenic drafting should include

- Sketch (scenery only).

- Ground plan or Light plot.

- Section.

- Deck plan.

- Elevations.

- Detail drawings.

Let's go through them briefly one at a time. More detail will follow in the individual chapters and through illustrations. I think it is important to include the sketch as the first plate of drafting in a scenery pack (Fig. 5.41). It gives everyone who will look at the drawings a context from which to compare all the individual pieces. Whenever I get a pack of drafting with the sketch attached, it always makes me relax knowing I have all the information in one place.

The ground plan and the light plot are similar drawings (Fig. 5.42). Both are a plan view of the stage. Both show

Fig. 5.41 Hanging in Hudson Scenic's office is a complete pack of draftings for a show.

the theatre architecture, which can include the proscenium arch, plaster line, smoke pocket, and other architectural details needed. The most important thing on either of these drawings is the centerline. Let me say that again. The most important thing on either of these drawings is the centerline! Got it? Why, you might ask? Well, we know where the plaster line is and that it is our reference for all upstage and downstage measurements. Our only reference for left and right measurements is the centerline. Here is the twist. Sometimes the center of the stage is not the center of the auditorium. Sometimes, the set designer moves the center of the set to a different angle. So, how do you know which one to use? It's easy; the set designer selects the one that is the most critical to the set. The lighting designer then needs to use the same centerline. Otherwise, nothing will line up, things will have to be redone, and the schedule will go out the window. Let me just say one more thing. The most important thing on either of these drawings is the centerline!

The scenic ground plan should show all the scenic elements, assembled and in their positions, as this is the primary focus of the drawing. Major scenic elements should be identified through notes. Overhead items, whether static or moving, should be indicated with dotted lines. All curtains, backings, and masking should be shown in position relative to the sightlines.

Also on the ground plan is the line set inventory (Fig. 5.43). This may be one of the most important things to be drawn. The line set inventory is a list of pipes overhead that can be flown in and out. The inventory numbers the pipes beginning at the plaster line and moving upstage as the numbers get higher. The distance upstage from the plaster line to the center of the pipe is shown. The set designer provides a description for what will be hung from this pipe. Last, the designer estimates how high the pipe will be in its playing and storage positions.

The light plot is similar to the ground plan and contains many of the same things (Fig. 5.44). The light plot shows the scenic elements, although usually in less detail than on the ground plan. The focus of the light plot is to show the lighting equipment for the show, in relation to the scenery and masking. The light plot, by its nature, becomes a composite drawing. The scenic designer's ground plan is the base. Lighting is drawn over the top. The line set inventory is altered with the addition of the overhead electrics.

The section drawing, whether for scenery or lighting, is essential (Fig. 5.45). Picture that the theatre has been cut in half along the centerline and split wide open. If you stand between the two halves and look in the stage left wing, that is a "center section looking left." You can make the split anywhere that benefits showing the information you need, and you can look in either direction. The key is to show a cut through the middle of important details, so that we can see how other parts of the show relate.

The deck plan is a drawing of the floor (Fig. 5.47). That sounds simple. But it's really not in today's theatre. Decks have often become the most complicated part of the design. The floor of the theatre is often covered completely with platforms, called a show deck. The reason for this is that much more scenery moves now than ever before and the deck can contain pieces of the automation package for doing this movement. There can also be multiple levels to create more interesting acting areas. That means stairs will

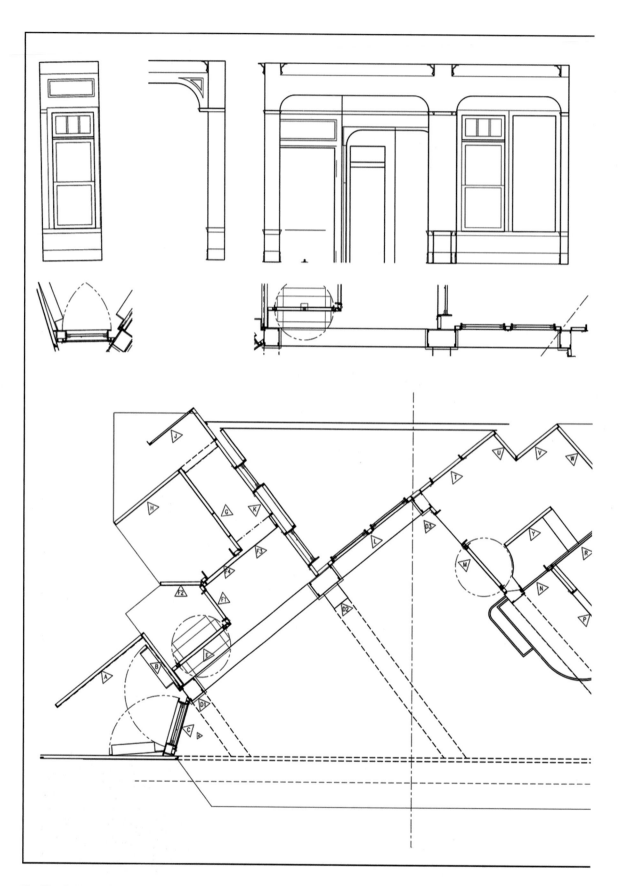

Fig. 5.42 Hudson Scenic's ground plan showing the breakdown of walls.

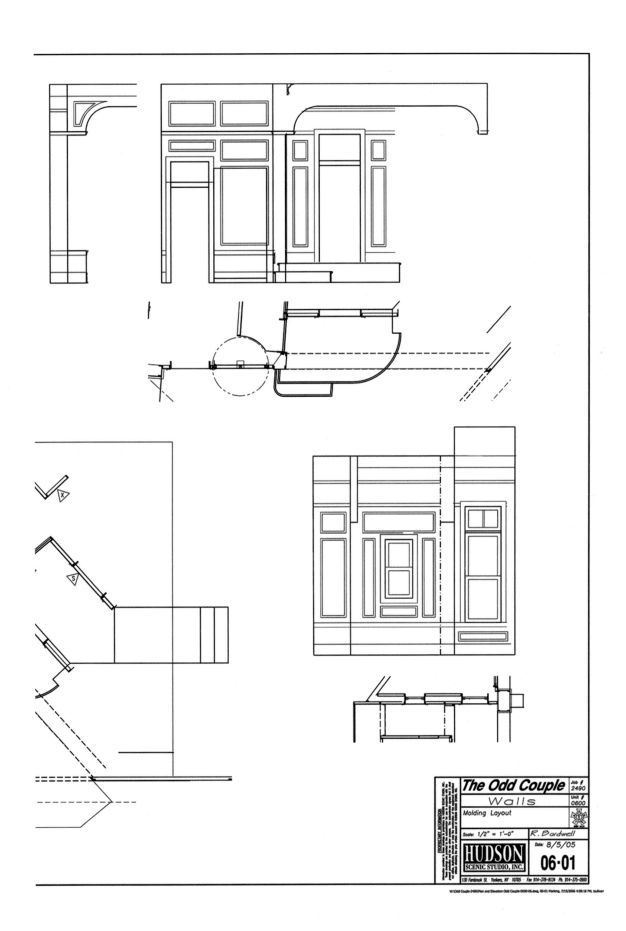

The Odd Couple

Job # 2490
Unit # 0600

Walls

Molding Layout

Scale: 1/2" = 1'-0"   R. Bardwell

HUDSON
SCENIC STUDIO, INC.

Date: 8/5/05

06·01

130 Fernbrook St · Yonkers, NY 10705 · Fax 914-378-9134 Ph. 914-375-0900

W:\Odd Couple-2490\Plan and Elevation Odd Couple-0600-05.dwg, 06-01 Marking, 7/15/2006 4:08:18 PM, bullhorl be needed, both onstage to get the actors up and potentially offstage to get the actors back down. More on that entire idea later, but let's just say that a floor is not just a floor anymore.

Our next topic is the **elevation**. An elevation takes the ground plan and stands it up in three dimensions, one element at a time. This allows the scene shop and carpenters to see each individual piece as it is intended to be built. Measurements are critical at this stage, as building is about to begin. The elevation can go into much more detail than the ground plan because there is more room on the drawing for it. The ground plan is expanded so each piece stands by itself. Studying the elevations is one of the best ways to get to know the set and catch parts that may have been too crowded to see on the ground plan. Elevations are often drawn in the same scale as the ground plan.

Where the elevation leaves off, the **detail drawings** begin (Fig. 5.48). Often, parts of the set require a much closer look. Let's say the scale of the ground plan was ¼ inch or ½ inch; the detail drawings could be 3 inches or full scale (Fig. 5.49). Take a look at your scale rule and think about the difference between these scales. This allows for the detail to almost explode into view. It makes the dimensioning not only easier but doable. Detail drawings also include practicals. Practicals are scenic elements or props that plug into some form of electricity. These items must be planned out in great detail to make sure that they work properly and are safe.

By the way, in case you were wondering, I once asked my professor to take his own drawing test (Fig. 5.46). Remember the cube, chair, rabbit, and human?

Line Set Schedule

Line Set	Position	Standard		Comment	Weight
	0	Plasterline		56' by 23'	
	5"	Fire Curtain		Not Used	
	11"	#1 Border/Legs		Arbor	
1	2' 8"	1st Elec.		42' Batten	350 lbs
	3' 4"	Water Pipe		Obstruction	
	3' 8"	Traveler		Dead Hung	a lot
2	4' 6"	Blackout			
3	5'	Border		55' by 8'	200 lbs
	6' - 7' 3"	Screen		56' by 23'	Winch
4	7' 9"			42' Batten	15 lbs
5	8' 4"	#2 Border		55' by 8'	150 lbs
	9' 6"	#2 Legs	2 - 2 Line	21' 3" Off Center	75 lbs
6	10'	Blackout		(2) 22' by 23'	200 lbs
7	11'	2nd Elec.		42' Batten	250 lbs
8	13'			2 - 21' Battens	50 lbs
9	14' 6"			42' Batten	100 lbs
10	16'	#3 Border		55' by 8'	150 lbs
	16' 6"	#3 Legs	2 - 2 Line	20' Off Center	75 lbs
11	17'			42' Batten	50 lbs
12	18' 6"			42' Batten	
13	19' 6"	3rd Elec.		42' Batten	300 lbs
14	21'			42' Batten	75lbs
15	22'	#4 Border		48' by 20'	200 lbs
16	23' 6"	Blackout		(2) 21' by 22'	200 lbs

Fig. 5.43 Sample line set inventory.

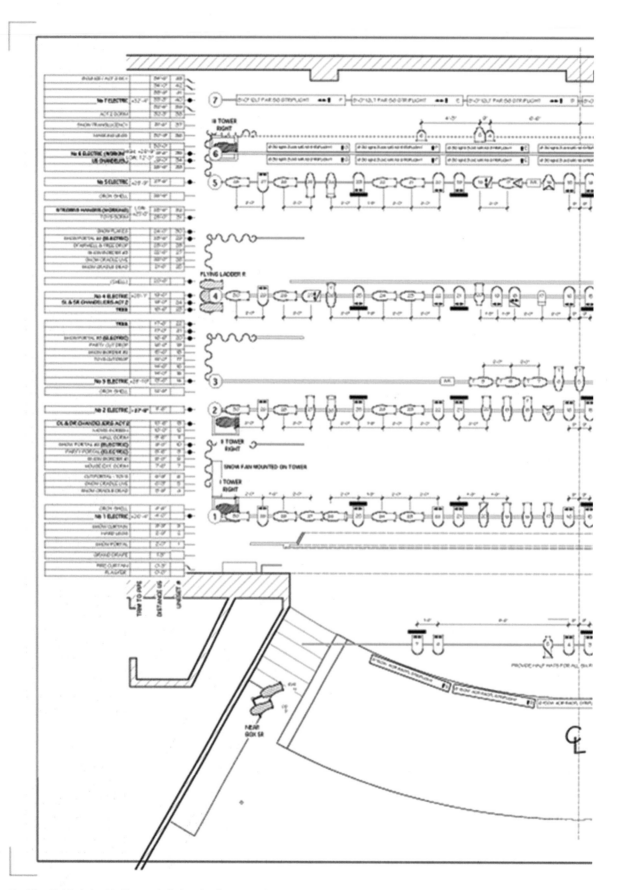

Fig. 5.44 John McKernon's light plot for a production of *The Nutcracker*.

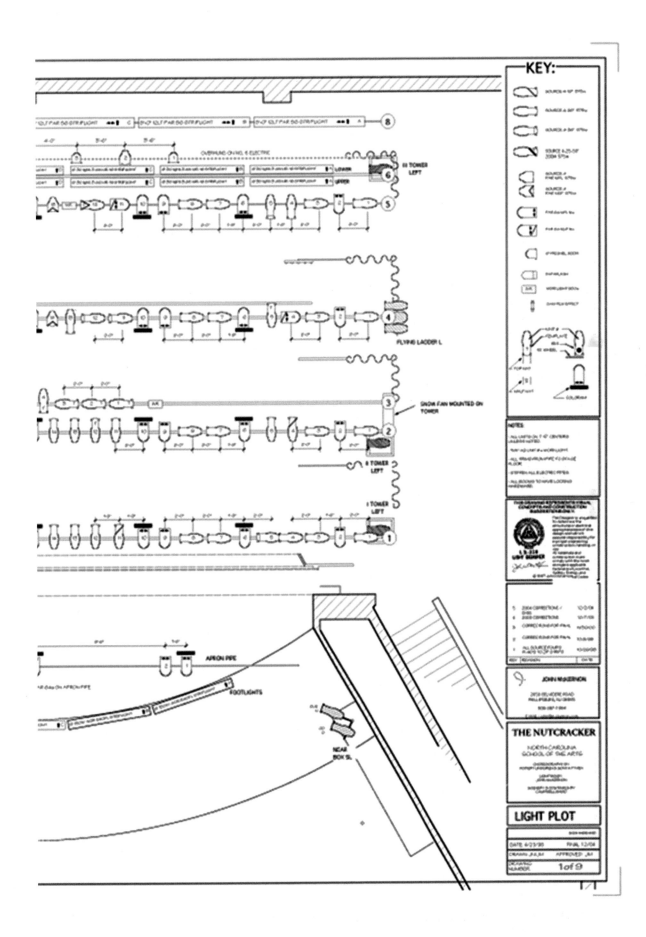

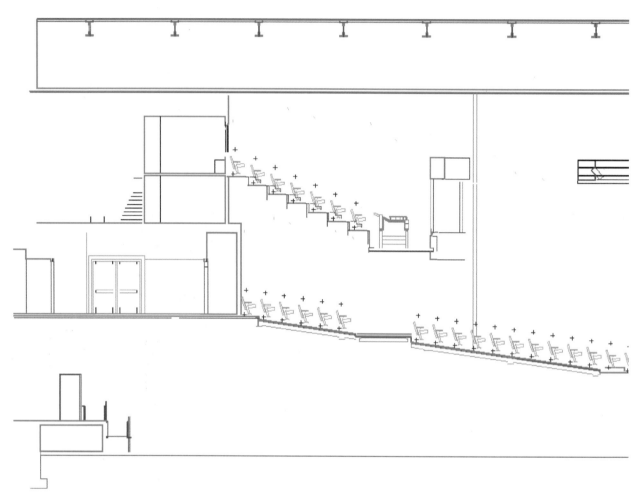

■ **Fig. 5.45** Section for a high school auditorium during new construction.

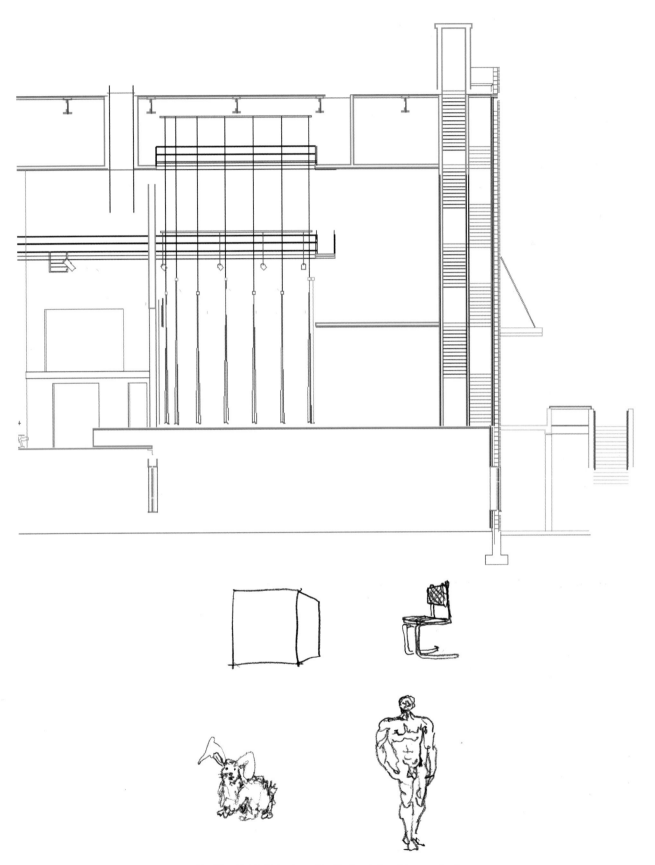

■ **Fig. 5.46** Salvatore Tagliarino takes his own test.

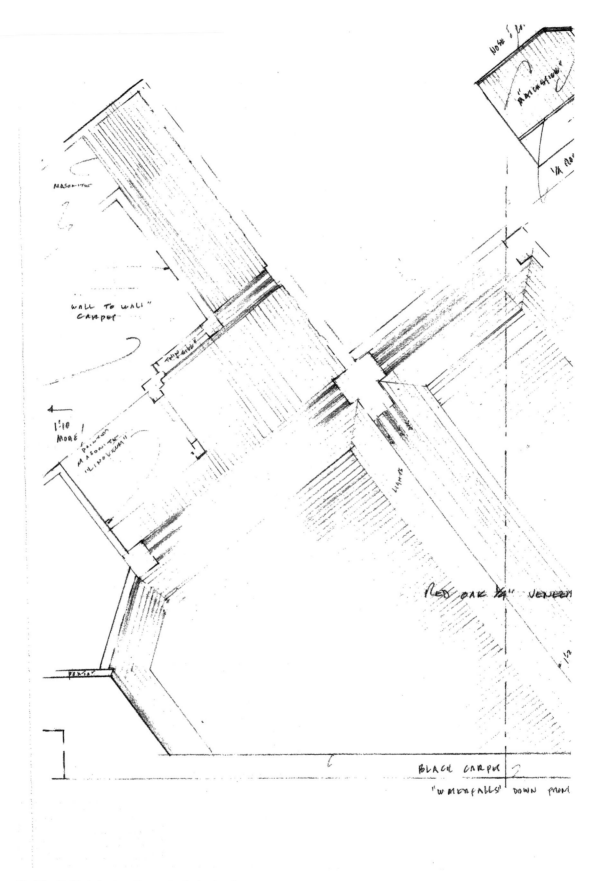

■ **Fig. 5.47** John Lee Beatty's deck plan for Neil Simon's *The Odd Couple*.

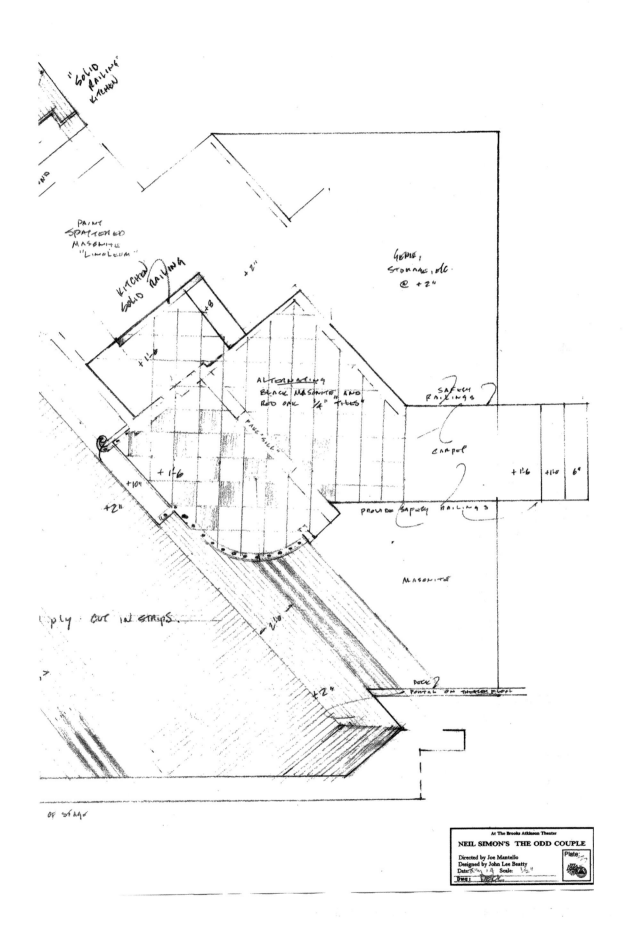

"SOLID RAILING KITCHEN"

PAINT SPATTERED MASONITE "LINOLEUM"

KITCHEN SOLID RAILING

+2"

+8"

+1'6"

GENIE, STORAGE, etc. @ +2"

ALTERNATING BLACK MASONITE AND RED OAK 1/4" "TILES"

PAVE + GILL

SAFETY RAILINGS

CHAPEL

+1'6" +1'0" 6"

+10"

+1'6"

+2"

PROVIDE SAFETY RAILINGS

MASONITE

...PLY CUT IN STRIPS

1'0"

+2"

DECK

PORTAL ON THEATER FLOOR

...OF STAGE

At The Brooks Atkinson Theater
NEIL SIMON'S THE ODD COUPLE
Directed by Joe Mantello
Designed by John Lee Beatty
Date: _____ Scale: 1/2"
Dwg: DECK
Plate:

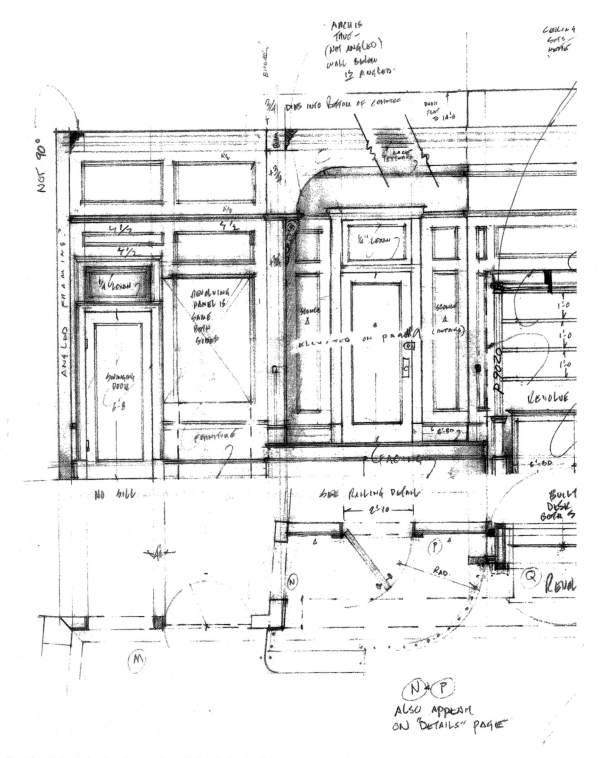

Fig. 5.48 John Lee Beatty's wall details for Neil Simon's *The Odd Couple*.

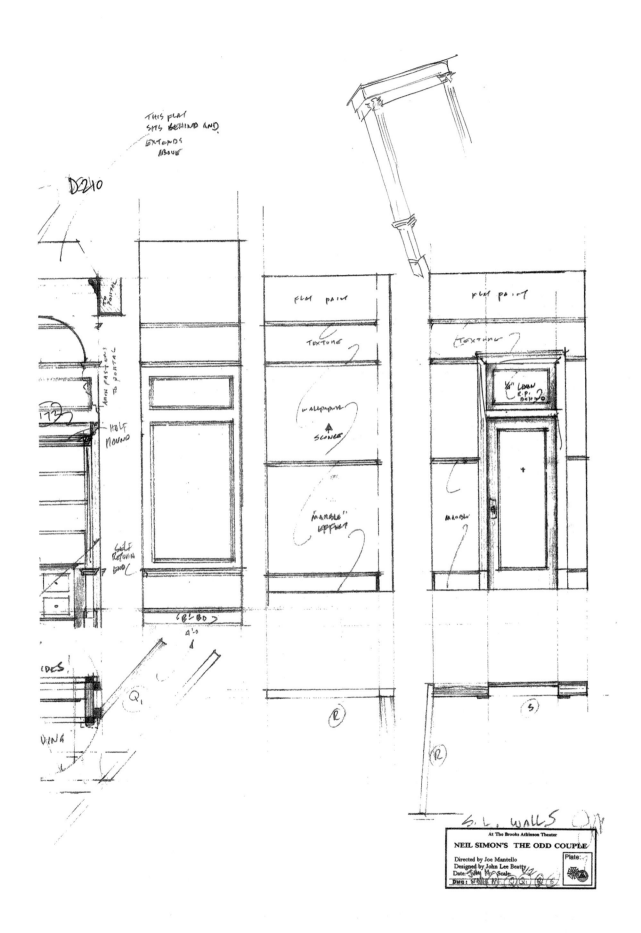

THIS FLAT
SITS BEHIND AND
EXTENDS ABOUT

D210

FLAT PAINT

FLAT PAINT

TEXTURE

TEXTURE

WALLPAPER

SCONCE

MARBLE EFFECT

MARBLE

ARM FASTENS TO PORTAL

HALF ROUND

SELF RETURN END

(8'-BD)

4'-0

Q

R

R

S

S.L. WALLS

At The Brooks Atkinson Theater
NEIL SIMON'S THE ODD COUPLE
Directed by Joe Mantello
Designed by John Lee Beatty
Date: July   Scale:
Dwg:

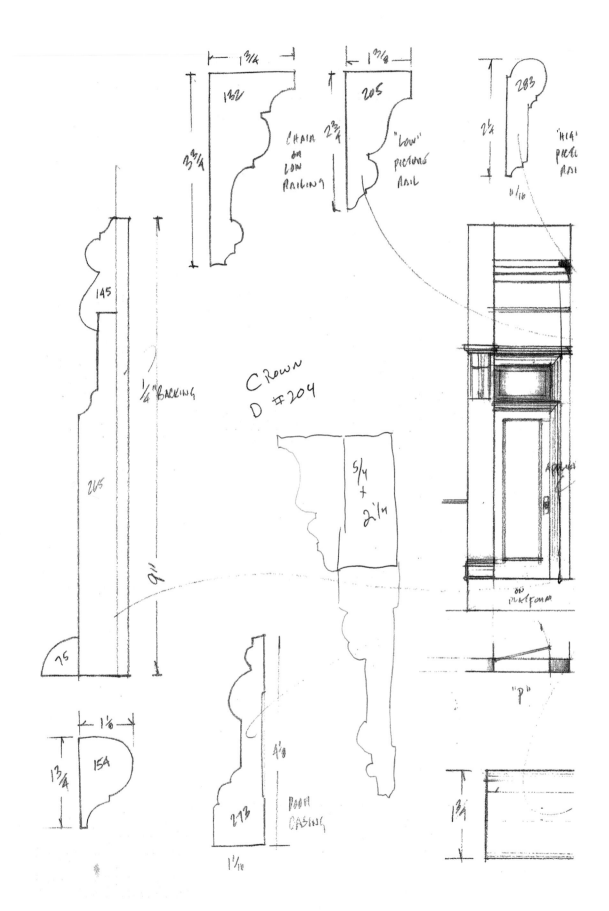

■ **Fig. 5.49** John Lee Beatty's full-scale details for Neil Simon's *The Odd Couple*.

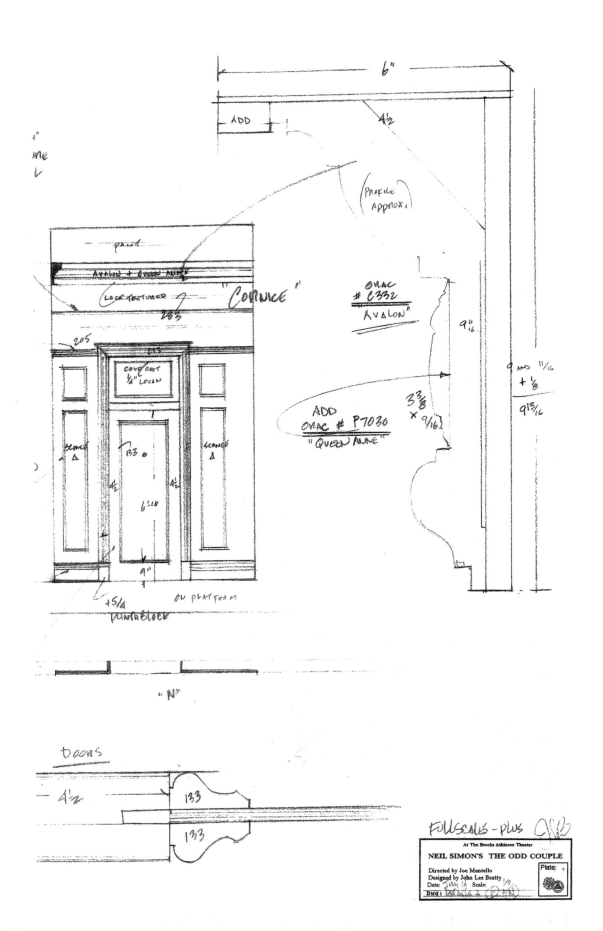

NEIL SIMON'S THE ODD COUPLE

At The Brooks Atkinson Theater

Directed by Joe Mantello
Designed by John Lee Beatty

Arc dimensions
CAD
Centerline
Deck plan
Detail drawing
Drafting
Drafting stool
Drafting table
Drafting tape
Drawing
Elevation
Erasing shield
Foreshortening
French Curve
Ground plan
Horizon line
Insight
Key to symbols
Lettering guide
Light plot
Linear
   dimensions
Line set
   inventory
Multiple
   dimension
Orthographic
   projection
Parallel rule
Perspective

Plan view
Plaster line
Previsualization
Raster
Rendering
Scale rule
Section
Show deck
Side view
Sketch
Soft goods
Title block
Triangle
T square
Vanishing point
Vector

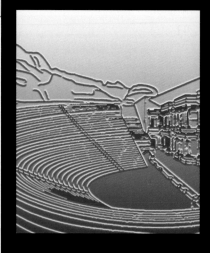

CHAPTER FIVE

Study Words

PART
TWO
Safety and Scenery

Scene Shop

You can have it:
Better - Cheaper - Faster
Please pick two!!!

Safety First!
Safety

My students all know that my favorite saying is, "*I've never had to call 911 for a student, and you're not going to break my record.*" That phrase doesn't mean there are bleeding students all over New England. It means I teach my students the correct procedures to keep them safe. This chapter talks about safety, both backstage in the theatre and in the various shops related to the implementation of all the designs. Safety also is addressed in other chapters while we discuss specific techniques and tools.

There are established standards for safety, and they are practiced for a reason. The theatre can be a dangerous place. We are always trying to accomplish things that simply aren't supposed to be done inside a building, never mind in the dark! If you follow some basic safety rules, you will stay safe. But you've got to think. And, let's face it, most of us got into the theatre because it looked like fun. Let's keep it that way.

> Safety is just danger, out of place.
> **—Harry Connick, Jr.**

Let me warn you. This chapter deals with a lot of information that doesn't seem like the "fun" theatre stuff I've been referring to. The only way to keep theatre fun is to keep it safe. I feel *very* strongly about this. Even with a hectic schedule, there is always time to slow down and do it the right way. If you do it the wrong

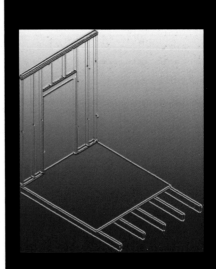

CHAPTER SIX

In this chapter

- Personal Safety
- Fire Safety
- Material Safety Data Sheets
- Examples of Panic
- Study Words

way, because you are in a hurry, think about how much time you waste while you wait for the ambulance to come!

> Don't learn safety rules simply by accident.
>
> —Unknown

Many safety measures are often ignored for a few simple reasons. They are thought to be a bother, take too much time, or are "unnecessary." Well, let me tell you, none of the safety guidelines are created in a void just to frustrate you. Their basis was created when someone was injured—then we realized there needed to be safety procedures to keep us safe. There is a reason why you should never scream "Fire!" in a crowded theatre. More on that later. But it is downright dangerous. Theatre should be—and when done safely is—fun. Danger is a possibility in many practices in the theatre. If you follow the guidelines in this chapter and any that get updated from here on out, you will find yourself in a much safer position.

PERSONAL SAFETY

I absolutely love the theatre and I have fun doing it. Safety is a very personal thing for all of us. You want to keep yourself safe. I have little tolerance for people being unsafe, because it puts everybody at risk. You want to keep your coworkers safe as well as the audience. So let's get started and I'll try not to use too many gory examples.

Let's start with the basics. You. Yes, you. You can be the most dangerous person in the theatre if you don't keep safety in mind—let's hope you never get injured. That is the point of this chapter—to give you the information so you can keep yourself safe. Any situation can turn from safe to dangerous quickly. The best prevention from injury and danger is to be informed. Most people in theatre know that things go wrong in ways we'd least expect and the last thing anyone wants is to cause someone harm through carelessness.

The two main categories of possible hazards are health and safety. They really go hand in hand, but we address each of these separately, using examples from OSHA and others for perspective. **OSHA**, the Occupational Safety and Health Administration, is an agency of the U.S. government's Department of Labor. OSHA's mission is to "assure the safety and health of America's workers by setting and enforcing standards; providing training, outreach, and education; establishing partnerships; and encouraging continual improvement in workplace safety and health." No discussion of safety would be complete, or could even begin, without discussing OSHA. Its mission statement takes on a great deal with extreme consequences. OSHA is discussed periodically throughout this chapter.

We continue by discussing some basic personal safety topics. Let's talk about your clothing first (Fig. 6.1). Clothing that is too baggy can get caught in power tools. Clothes that are too tight restrict your movement, meaning you can't operate tools properly or move out of the way quickly in an emergency. Clothing that doesn't cover you properly won't protect you. Does this mean you can't dress in your own style? No, of course not. There is no stagehand uniform. Pants are better than shorts for protecting your legs. In the scene shop, wood splinters can go flying around. Pants protect your legs from getting splinters, for example. Now, you may say, What is the big deal with a splinter? Well, say you can't find the splinter and it gets infected, or you turn out to be allergic to something the splinter has in or on it. Well, that can stink—now you're off to the nurse. Does"t sound like fun, does it?

OK, let's move on to your jewelry. Guys or girls, it doesn't matter. Chains, bracelets, earrings, or any body jewelry and rings—you all wear it and that is fine to a point. But, look at it a little closer (Fig. 6.2). Chains hanging loosely from your neck can get caught in a machine and pull you toward the blade or cutting edge. Bracelets can do the same thing. Dangling earrings can get caught in more ways than I can list. And trust me when I say it's not too pleasant to have the earring pulled from your ear, never mind any other body jewelry. My father worked with machinery his whole life, and never wore his wedding ring at work to be safe. He knew better. And that knowledge helped him keep all 10 of his fingers! Say there is an accident and your hand gets hurt. The first thing the doctors do is cut off your ring, so why wear it to begin with? Worst-case scenario is the ring can do more damage than the original accident.

Shoes are next and a very important part of your wardrobe for technical work. One of my pet peeves is that flip-flops are for the beach, not the scene shop (Fig. 6.3). But, you also don't need to buy steel-toe work boots.

■ **Fig. 6.1** Take a look at the highlighted areas to see the good choices on the bottom and the not-so-good choices on the top for clothing in the shop.

■ **Fig. 6.2** Notice the jewelry choices on the top that are bad. Also notice that there are no really good jewelry choices. On the bottom, we see a stagehand with no jewelry.

■ **Fig. 6.3** It might seem like a no brainer, but I've had students show up to work in the scene shop in flip-flops. They were sent home for the day!

In fact, opinions are varied on whether steel-toe boots are good or bad in the theatre. For minor incidents, they can help. But if your foot starts to get crushed, the steel toe can actually do more damage than protection. What you want is a good sturdy-soled shoe. Take your shoe off and hold it sole down with one hand near the toe and one hand near the heel. Try to bend the shoe in half. If it bends too easily, it won't protect your foot very well. The goal should be that, if you step on a nail, staple, or screw, it should not go straight through to your foot. The sole should slow it down enough that you notice something is wrong and stop to check.

OK, we've gotten to the last topic of personal safety: hair (Fig. 6.4). Yes, hair. Long hair can be as dangerous as dangling jewelry or baggy clothes. Hair can obscure your vision, it can get caught in machines, and yes, it can catch on fire. I've had all these things happen, because I thought it would take too long to pull my hair back. Now I don't even walk into the shop without already having my hair pulled back or put up. You can also cover your hair with a bandana.

Does all this mean that you have to take out all your jewelry, shave your head, and walk into the shop naked? No! In fact, please don't. Here is the right way to do it:

• Clothing should fit and cover your body.

• Jewelry should be small if not removed completely.

• Shoes should be sturdy.

• Hair should be pulled back.

It all sounds simple, and it is. It's better to be safe from the beginning than to try to fix the problem later. Keep these simple personal safety rules in your mind every time you know you are going to work in the theatre. Take a look at the photos on the next few pages for examples of these rules.

Think of it this way: When put under a lot of pressure, wood will usually break and metal will crush whatever gets caught in the way. Flesh and bone, well, let's just say they are the weakest of all. We also deal with sharp tools meant to cut or shape something. Those same tools don't care if they are cutting wire or skin. So, we have to be careful. If my students show up for class wearing something inappropriate for the shop, I send them home, and they are considered absent from class that day! That is how strongly I feel about safety. My father taught me all these lessons, and one more: don't fear tools, respect what they can do.

■ **Fig. 6.4** Hair is one of the most overlooked safety concerns. Long hair on the left can easily get caught in a motor, and it's not a pretty picture. Hair pulled back into a pony tail or braid, like on the right, will keep you safe.

Let's go through some basics. Take everything I say here as a guideline. Your teacher or the technical director knows more about the specific projects you are working on. Keep in mind that you should aim for at least the minimum amount of safety protection, but sometimes the maximum amount is better, and more appropriate.

When you go out in the sun, you put on sunglasses, right? Well, when you work in the theatre on certain jobs, you need to wear **goggles**. Even if you wear eyeglasses, you need to wear goggles over your eyeglasses. Regular glasses do not protect your eyes should an accident happen. The lenses in eyeglasses break or shatter. This allows for the possibility of getting glass in your eye, causing more damage. In fact, when you are working on certain tasks and with certain tools, you need a **face shield**, not just a pair of goggles (Fig. 6.5).

Protecting your eyesight is very important, as I pointed out. Wearing safety goggles is the first line of defense for your eyes. Accidental exposure of your eyes to chemical substances can result in irritation (temporary or permanent), vision impairment, or blindness. This is not something to joke around about. Since we work with a variety of eye hazards in the theatre, **eyecups** and **eyewash stations** are the next line of defense when something gets past the goggles or shield (Figs. 6.6 and 6.7). We all know accidents can

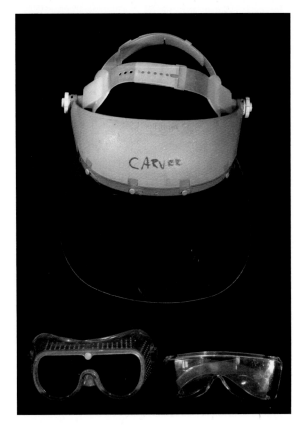

■ **Fig. 6.5** A face shield and two styles of goggles, many of which fit easily over standard eyeglass frames.

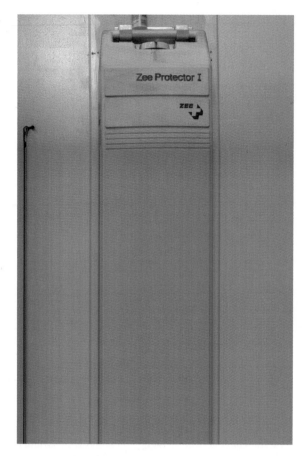

Fig. 6.6 The eyewash station, when closed, mounted to the wall.

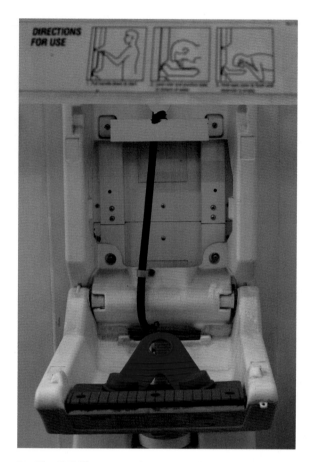

Fig. 6.7 The eyewash station, when opened for use and showing its instructions.

happen and eyewash stations provide an effective means of washing your eyes to minimize the time an irritant comes in contact with them. The first 15 seconds following exposure are the best time to properly cleanse your eyes to minimize further injury.

Let's talk about your hearing next. You will be working with many different types of power tools. All these make noise, to differing levels. Anybody exposed to excessive noise must use appropriate ear protection! Loss of hearing and possible deafness are nothing to play around with. Protection can include **earplugs** (Fig. 6.8), **earmuffs**, or both.

It is often not possible to reduce the amount of noise we are exposed to in the theatre. The best way to deal with this is to use ear protection. Potential sources of noise hazards can include the following list, but keep in mind that any repetitive sound can ultimately affect you:

- Air compressors.
- Power saws.

- Power drills.
- Grinders.
- Welders.

Now that we dealt with your eyes and ears, let's deal with your nose. Or, a better way to say it is this: We are now going to talk about your entire respiratory system and how to keep it safe. If you breathe in the dust or spray from an irritant, it can quickly move from nose to throat to lungs. We start simple and easy. The **dust mask** is the first line of defense to keep you breathing normally (Fig. 6.9). In the theatre, we deal with many small particles: Dust and powdered dyes that are micro fine and prone to suspend in the air are just one example. Your basic dust mask can protect you from inhaling these.

Keep in mind that some of the most dangerous chemicals have no smell, so you may have little advance warning. Always follow the safety instructions for the product you are using (Fig. 6.10). To move on to things of greater risk,

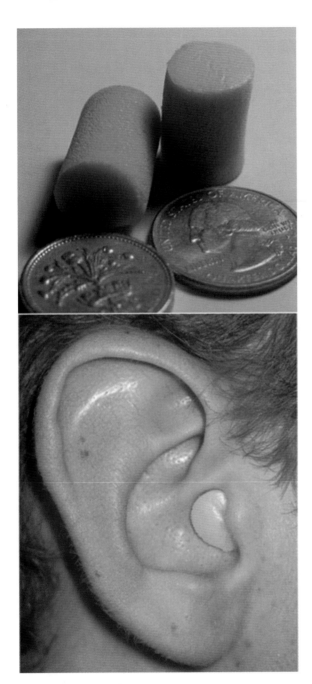

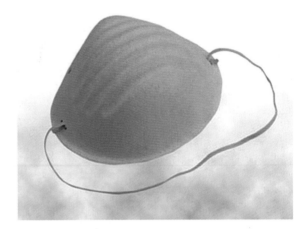

Fig. 6.9 Dust masks come in handy in a number of situations, everything from keeping particles away from you to keeping you from spreading germs.

Fig. 6.8 Earplugs, shown for scale, and how to wear them. The key is to be safe while still being aware of your surroundings.

filter before it reaches you. By the time the air gets to you, it has been "cleaned." Atmosphere-supplying respirators, on the other hand, supply clean air directly to you from an oxygen canister or other source rather than the air surrounding you.

The respirator to use really depends on what environment you are in and what might be floating around in the air. A good guide to what type of protector you need are the **Material safety data sheets**, referred to as *MSDS*. These are discussed later in the chapter. Just keep in mind you need not guess at safety. Guidelines and recommendations are in place because lots of people have studied the situations and figured out the best way to keep you safe. All you have to do is follow the established protocol.

Next, let's address your hands. You may be thinking, my hands—so what? Work gloves are an important part of every stagehand's tool kit (Fig. 6.11). This is not about vanity and the perfect manicure. It's about keeping your hands intact and other people safe. First off, wearing gloves protects your hands from splinters, cuts, and worse. Second, gloves give you a better grip when holding heavy objects or carrying them. The better your grip, the less likely you are to drop something on either yourself or someone else.

Gloves come in a number of styles, fabrics, and of course costs. These combine to make a glove appropriate for one job and not another. Some jobs require a thinner glove,

and therefore more needed protection, we use **respirators**. There are two types of respirators, air-purifying and atmosphere-supplying respirators. The names of these pretty much describe how they work. The air-purifying type has filters, cartridges, or canisters that remove irritants and contaminants from the air by passing the air through a

■ **Fig. 6.10** You need special training to use a respirator properly. These are used when a regular dust mask won't keep you safe from airborne chemicals.

so that your sense of touch is still able to function. Some jobs require heavier gloves, insulated gloves, waterproof gloves, and so forth. You get the idea. It's all about using the proper tool for the job, and that is a theme we discuss throughout the book.

> He that's secure is not safe.
>
> —Benjamin Franklin

Let's change our discussion now to reaching higher places. To do this we need to use one of a couple of devices. First, we talk about ladders (Fig. 6.12). The three basic styles of ladders are step, A-frame, and extension. The first two are self-supporting. That means they can stand up all by themselves. Extension ladders are considered non-self-supporting. I think you get it, but that means they have to lean against something. A hybrid to these is the Little Giant and Gorilla brand of ladders. They are convertible, meaning the same ladder can be used as either a stepladder or an extension ladder.

OSHA developed strict rules for the proper and safe use of ladders. Even though we've all seen the little sticker that says the top rung is not a step, how many

of us have used it as a step when something was just out of our reach and we needed the extra height? Well, this is not safe—there is a reason that sticker is there. Stepladders must have a metal spreader or locking device to hold the front and back sections in an open position when the ladder is in use. Make sure this is engaged before beginning to climb. Dollies are often created for ladders so that the ladders can roll around. OSHA *does not* approve of this.

So, the ladder won't get you high enough, especially since you can't stand on the top step anymore! Well, the next option is a bigger ladder if possible or a personnel lift. The personnel lift is a motorized lift with a bucket or platform (Fig. 6.13). Common brand names are JLG®, Genie®, Condor®, and Snorkel®. Again, OSHA has strict guidelines for safe use of this equipment. Each piece of equipment has specific rules for use and, more specifically, safe use. One piece of safety equipment that is required for most of the nondrivable personnel lifts is outriggers. **Outriggers** are stabilizing legs that attach to the base of the lift. If the lift comes equipped with outriggers, the outriggers must be in place prior to raising or lowering the basket that you stand in. Many of today's lifts have a safety cutoff switch that will not allow the basket to rise

■ **Fig. 6.11** (1) Canvas and leather gloves, (2) cotton gloves with rubber nubs, (3) lined leather gloves, (4) leather gloves, (5) Setwear fingerless gloves, and (6) Setwear full-finger gloves. Find a pair that fits you well and is suited for your job.

without the proper placement of the outriggers. This may be frustrating, but if you've ever seen a lift that tipped over, you understand the need!

Keep in mind the basket around the platform is there for your safety. Leaning over the basket takes your balance out of the center and makes for a more dangerous situation. There are exceptions to rules, but they usually have a counterpart. If you need to lean out of the basket, consider repositioning the lift, if possible. Otherwise, make sure to use a harness or lanyard as a safety precaution to keep you from falling. Also make sure to use a tool leash on all tools you take up in the air.

> Safety means first aid to the uninjured.
> —**Unknown**

No location should be without a first aid kit (Fig. 6.14). This includes your home, your car, your school, and your workplace. Accidents can happen anywhere, at any time. Check the kit regularly. Make sure the flashlight batteries work. Check the expiration dates and replace any used or out-of-date contents. The contents of a first aid kit can be

■ **Fig. 6.13** Motorized lifts come in a variety of types. These require special training before you try to use them.

- Cold pack.
- Disinfectant pads.
- Antiseptic ointment.
- Antihistamine cream, such as Benadryl.
- Calamine lotion.
- Aloe vera gel.
- Band-aids (butterflies, knuckles, fingertips, assorted sizes).
- Eyecup.
- Saline.
- Adhesive tape.
- Gauze pads and roller gauze (assorted sizes).
- Triangular bandage.
- Elastic bandages.
- Plastic bags.
- Scissors and tweezers.
- Small flashlight and extra batteries.

■ **Fig. 6.12** Ladders come in a range of styles and heights. Make sure you are comfortable going up and down a ladder before you try to do it on your own.

dangerous in the hands of young children, so store the kit safely and securely. Here are suggestions for the contents of a basic first aid kit. Your first aid kit may vary slightly depending on your actual needs.

- Hand sanitizer.
- Disposable gloves.

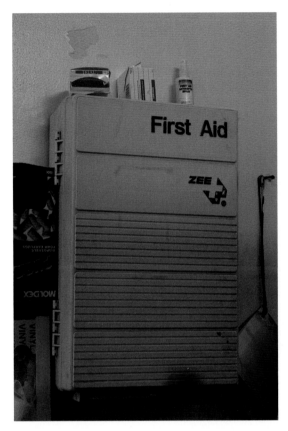

■ **Fig. 6.14** Every shop should have a first aid kit. The person in charge determines the type of kit and where it is located.

FIRE SAFETY

OK, now that we've gotten you safe, let's look at the work environment for other ways to stay safe. The first thing to do whenever you walk into a new theatre or any place you've never been to before is to look around and find out where the exits are. Think about it! What is the first thing a flight attendant points out in the safety speech? The exits are over the wings, in the back, or in the front. Always look for the exit, it's that easy!

Our next topic is fire protection. There are several ways to prevent fires and several ways to put them out once they begin. We start with preventing them. This is really common sense. If you are using a candle on stage, make sure it stays away from any surfaces that can catch on fire. You do this at home, why not do it in the theatre? If you are going to use a candle on stage, the local fire department may require that a licensed person be in attendance whenever the candle is lit. This trained person

may be a firefighter or someone else with training. Either way, having someone like this in attendance makes the show, the theatre, and all the people in attendance safer as well. Make sure to check all local regulations before your production.

Another thing that can get very hot and possibly cause fires are the lighting instruments. And lights are almost always near curtains and scenery. A piece of safety equipment that can be used in this situation is called **Zetex®**. Zetex is used in the theatre as a **thermal barrier** to protect objects from heating up too much (Fig. 6.15). Zetex is manufactured, among other things, into a fabric that can be hung on the pipes between the lights and other objects to protect them. Its use replaced asbestos when we finally figured out that asbestos was really bad for you. Zetex is also manufactured into gloves and other helpful items. Zetex is further used in a number of products that are rated to protect for various degrees of heat.

Let's talk for a minute about the terms *fireproof* and *fire retardant*. These terms are sometimes used interchangeably and they shouldn't be. **Fireproof** implies that an item will not burn, smoke, or flame. **Fire retardant** implies that the item will burn, smoke, and flame although it will do all of these slower than other materials. Every state has its own specific rules governing fire retardancy. Make sure to check what is required in your area. All materials in theatre are susceptible to heat and fire damage when exposed to high temperatures for extended periods of time. With enough heat even metal will melt. A fire-retardant material is one that is designed to resist burning and withstand heat for a certain amount of time. Many fabrics are treated with a flame-retardant chemical, either before or after painting (Fig. 6.16). Keep in mind that any kind of laundering or dry cleaning means that costume or curtain has to be treated again. Scenery coming out of a scene shop is almost always flame proofed.

One hundred percent of all scenery should be flame retardant. Scenic painters treat the curtains, and they need to be tested by someone who has a Supervision of Flame Retardancy certificate from the local fire department. All hard scenery is back painted with latex mixed with one of several different products to make it flame retardant. Certain materials provide resistance to high temperatures for limited periods of time. Safes, for example, properly

■ **Fig. 6.15** Zetex usually comes in black and is a very good thermal barrier. We used asbestos until we found out it can be very bad for us!

constructed with these materials can be classified as fire resistant. Depending on the materials used and the methods of construction, safes can provide varying degrees of fire resistance.

> When you're safe at home you wish you were having an adventure; when you're having an adventure you wish you were safe at home.
>
> —Thornton Wilder

There are several ways to put out fires once they start. In addition to handheld fire extinguishers that may be used for smaller fires, most theatres are equipped with one of three options:

1. Fire curtain.
2. Sprinkler system.
3. Deluge system.

Let's go into detail about each of these.

The **fire curtain** is the oldest of the three options listed and its main purpose is to keep the audience safe from a fire on stage (Fig. 6.17). It is used primarily in proscenium theatres. A fire curtain is a piece of fabric fiberglass or some other type of thermal barrier. These curtains were originally made of asbestos. They get hung between the audience and the stage, usually just upstage of the proscenium arch. Safety and health regulations say that the curtain must be able to "resist" fire and therefore prevent or at least slow fires starting on the stage from spreading into the auditorium and the rest of the theatre.

Fig. 6.16 Hudson Scenic's shelves are full with various flame-proofing products. Products vary depending on what you are treating.

The curtain travels up and down inside a guide called a **smoke pocket**. Traditionally, a piece of rope held the curtain up in the air. In case of a fire, the rope is cut by a stage manager or stagehand, the curtain comes down to the stage and contains the fire, keeping the audience safe. Modern-day technology substituted the rope and knife for a lever release. Just turn or pull the lever and the curtain comes down! Much easier.

A **sprinkler system** is the next option (Fig. 6.18). Most of you are used to seeing sprinkler heads in the ceiling of various rooms and buildings as you enter a classroom at school. They are also in hotels and office buildings. Fire sprinklers are considered an active fire protection measure and are connected to a fire-suppression system that consists of overhead pipes fitted with sprinkler heads throughout the stage and auditorium. These pipes are continuously connected to a water source and can be used at a moment's notice.

Automatic fire sprinklers are individually heat activated and tied into a network of piping with water under pressure.

When the heat of a fire raises the sprinkler temperature to its operating point (usually, 165 °F), a solder link melts or a liquid-filled glass bulb shatters to open that single sprinkler, releasing water directly over the source of the heat. Sprinklers operate automatically in the area of fire origin, preventing a fire from growing undetected to a dangerous size, while simultaneously sounding an alarm. Automatic fire sprinklers keep fires small. Only one or two sprinklers handle the majority of fires in buildings with sprinkler systems.

The last option we discuss is the deluge system. A **deluge** system is similar to a sprinkler system, except the sprinkler heads are open and the pipe is not pressurized with air (Fig. 6.19). Deluge systems are connected to a water supply through a deluge valve that is opened by the operation of a smoke- or heat-detection system. The detection system is installed in the same area as the sprinklers. When the detection system is activated, water discharges through all the sprinkler heads in the system simultaneously. Deluge systems are used in places that are considered high-hazard areas, such as power plants, aircraft hangars, and chemical storage or processing facilities. Deluge systems are needed where high-velocity suppression is necessary to prevent fire spread.

A fire extinguisher is an active fire protection device to put out fires, often in emergency situations (Figs. 6.20 and 6.21). Fire extinguishers consist of pressurized containers of chemicals that, when discharged, can put out fires. It is important for everyone working in the theatre to be familiar with the different types and safe use of fire extinguishers.

A smoke detector or smoke alarm is an active fire protection device that detects airborne smoke and issues an audible alarm, thereby alerting anyone nearby to the danger of fire (Fig. 6.22). Most smoke detectors work either by optical detection or ionization, but some of them use both detection methods to increase sensitivity to smoke. If you are working on a production that uses any kind of smoke, fog, haze, or dry ice, make sure to ask the theatre's technical director what type of smoke detector he or she uses. If he or she uses ionization detectors, your effects will set them off and call the fire department! There are ways to use these effects and still be safe. Check with the technical director to see if the detectors are wired in zones. You might be able to shut off one or two without disabling the whole system.

■ **Fig. 6.17** In Europe, it is still the tradition to lower and raise the curtain before each performance to show the audience it is working. This photo is from the Vienna Opera House.

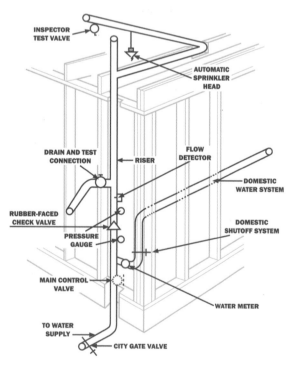

■ **Fig. 6.18** Sprinkler systems in the theatre are critical to everyone's safety. Never try to disable the sensors for your convenience!

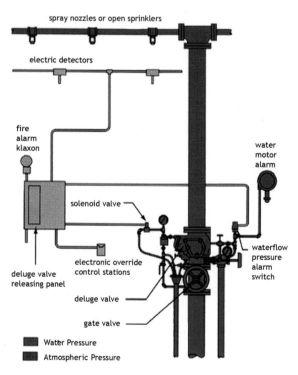

■ **Fig. 6.19** A deluge system will flood the entire theatre. This is one of the least-used systems for fire protection today.

Fig. 6.20 It is important to know how to use a fire extinguisher *before* the fire starts.

Smoke detectors may operate alone, be interconnected to cause all detectors in the premises to sound an alarm if one is triggered, or be integrated into a fire alarm or security system. Smoke detectors with flashing lights are available for the hearing impaired. A smoke detector cannot detect carbon monoxide to prevent carbon monoxide poisoning, unless it has an integrated carbon monoxide detector. There are also carbon monoxide detectors that operate separately.

In addition to possible carbon monoxide poisoning, we are all aware of allergies much more than we used to be. And there seem to be more things than ever before to be allergic to. Allergies and carbon monoxide poisoning can manifest in many different ways. There are several things to watch out for as you begin your career in the theatre:

- Breathing difficulties that can range from shortness of breath to wheezing to coughing.

- Swelling of your hands, arms, feet, or legs.

- Discoloration of your skin.

- Bumps or hives that may or may not itch.

If you notice any of these symptoms, go *immediately* to your teacher. The last thing any of us want is to come

Choose The Right Fire Extinguisher

Class	Symbol	Type of Fire	Examples	ABC DRY CHEMICAL	BC DRY CHEMICAL	DRY POWDER	WATER	FOAM	WET CHEMICAL	HALOGENATED	CARBON DIOXIDE
A		Common Combustables	Wood, Paper, Fabric, etc.	■			■	■		■	
B		Flammable liquids & gases	Gasoline, propane, solvents	■	■			■		■	■
C		Electrical	tools, lights, electronic equipment	■	■					■	■

■ **Fig. 6.21** There are different types of extinguishers; each is appropriate for different kinds of fires.

■ **Fig. 6.22** Smoke detectors are in our homes, as well as in our theatres. They are often the first line of defense should a fire start.

across a student who has passed out. Our goal is always to keep you safe!

I sometimes work with latex sponges or gloves. Before ever handing one to someone, I always ask if they have any known allergy to latex. Most often people say no. But I don't let it end there. I always keep an eye on the students who are using these products. At least once every year,

I find a student with an allergy to latex who had never had a reaction before. Safety should never be taken lightly, never.

MATERIAL SAFETY DATA SHEETS

You may have heard about **material safety data sheets** or as they often are referred to, MSDS (Fig. 6.23). I mentioned them before, but let me go into some detail now. These data sheets provide detailed hazard and precautionary information for hazardous materials. What the heck does that mean? Well, OK, *hazardous* you get, right? Anytime you are dealing with chemical compounds, such as paint, solvents, dyes, adhesives, or even fogger juice, there is no good way to know how these items (which are all chemical based by the way) might interact with other chemicals. And this could cause a possibly dangerous situation. Based on all of this, OSHA originally established these data sheets. Now, the manufacturers are responsible for providing them as an informational document regarding the safety and handling procedures and precautions for materials used in the workplace.

EXAMPLES OF PANIC

I don't want to turn this chapter into a list of horror stories for all the things that can, and sometimes do, go wrong.

Rosco Laboratories Inc.
52 Harbor View Avenue
Stamford, CT, USA, 06902
Phone: (203) 708 8900

ROSCO STAGE & STUDIO FLUID

MSDS Preparation Date: January 17, 2007

MSDS No.:ROS007

MATERIAL SAFETY DATA SHEET

SECTION 1 - PRODUCT AND COMPANY IDENTIFICATION

Product Name	: **ROSCO STAGE & STUDIO FLUID**
Product Use	: Fog fluid
Chemical Family	: Aqueous glycol solution
Supplier's name and address:	

Rosco Laboratories Inc.

52 Harbor View Avenue
Stamford, CT, United States
06902

24 Hr. Emergency Tel # : (800) 424-9300

HMIS Rating : ★- Chronic hazard   0 - Minimal   1 - Slight   2 - Moderate   3 - Serious   4 - Severe

Health: 1   *Flammability:* 0   *Reactivity:* 0

WHMIS Classes:

Unregulated

SECTION 2 - COMPOSITION/INFORMATION ON INGREDIENTS

Ingredients	CAS #	% (weight)	ACGIH TLV		OSHA PEL	
			TWA	STEL	PEL	STEL
Propylene glycol	57-55-6	N/Av	10 mg/m3	N/Av	50 ppm(total) ; 10 mg/m3 (aerosol)	N/Av
Deionized water	N/Av	N/Av	N/Av	N/Av	N/Av	N/Av

* Note: The ACGIH TLV listed above for the following ingredient(s) is an AIHA WEEL: Propylene glycol.

SECTION 3 - HAZARDS IDENTIFICATION

EMERGENCY OVERVIEW

Clear, colorless liquid. Faint odor. No special hazards exist with this product. As with any chemical substance, caution and care will prevent unnecessary accidents and safety problems. Read instructions on label before use. **HEALTH CAUTION: Vapor from this fluid, like any other common material in an aerosolized state, may be irritating to or cause allergic symptoms in some persons with allergenic sensitivity. Do not fog in the presence of known asthmatics.**

POTENTIAL HEALTH EFFECTS

Target organs	: None reported by the manufacturer.
Routes of exposure	: *Inhalation:* YES *Skin Absorption:* NO *Skin & Eyes:* YES *Ingestion:* YES
Potential acute health effects	:

Eyes:	May cause mild transient irritation.
Skin:	Not a hazard under normal conditions of use.
Inhalation:	Inhalation problems are not anticipated. Persons suffering from asthma or reactive airway disorders may experience asthma-like effects from exposure to this material.
Ingestion:	Not an expected route of entry. Ingestion of large amounts may cause nausea, vomiting, diarrhea, as well as depression of the central nervous system.

■ **Fig. 6.23** Material data safety sheets are key to knowing how to safely use and clean up different materials.

However, I think it's good to get an idea of what can happen. The most dangerous times are during the load-in and strike of a production. People are often rushing to get things done, and they may take a few shortcuts. Safety is often the thing that is compromised when we take shortcuts. Here are a couple of "horror stories" just to give you an idea of what can happen even with the best of all intentions.

> Better a thousand times careful than once dead.
>
> **—Proverb**

It was the first day of stagecraft class and we were walking around getting orientated with the theatre and the scene shop. Since it was the first day, I didn't know the students by name yet. I just kept taking a head count trying to make sure everyone was still there. Well, I always seemed to be missing at least one person, and I saw people going in and out the door to the restroom, in theory. Well, I found out after the class ended that one of my students had started to feel lightheaded. So she headed back to the theatre to get her backpack and a piece of fruit. Good idea? Well, not really. She almost passed out in the theatre, all by herself. Luckily she was found, had something to eat, and started to feel better. The moral of the story: If you are ill or injured, don't go off by yourself. Find someone to tell, so he or she can get you help or at least check in on you.

Here is a story you may have already heard. It comes from the movies, specifically the making of the *Wizard of Oz*. An actor by the name of Buddy Ebsen was originally cast as the Tin Man. The makeup they were using to make him look like tin was an aluminum powder. It was applied directly to his skin. It turned out to be toxic and it made him very ill. He ended up in the hospital for 2 weeks. A different actor had to play the part in the movie, using different makeup of course.

Another story comes from my days of assisting. I was working as the associate lighting designer on an opera. The designer and I ran up onto the stage from the house to do one last check before rehearsal started. While we were walking back toward the house, the electrician took the house lights out. I suddenly heard a "thud." Now, let me tell you, this is not a sound you want to hear in a dark theatre. I screamed for house lights. As the lights came on, I looked down into the orchestra pit in horror. The designer was

lying where she had fallen, about 15 feet below the stage level. Luckily, she recovered and was OK.

Two brief versions of stories involving fire follow.

The Hartford Circus Fire happened in 1944 in Hartford, Connecticut. Ushers spotted the flame and threw buckets of water on it, but to no avail. Seconds later, the fire reached the roof. At the top of the center pole, the fire split in three directions. Because the big top had been coated with 1800 lbs (816 kg) of paraffin and 6000 U.S. gallons (23 m^3) of gasoline (some sources say kerosene), which was a common waterproofing method of the time, the flames spread rapidly. Obviously we don't waterproof with flammable materials any longer!

Now, here is one that you will probably remember. In 2003, 100 people died and over 200 were injured in a Rhode Island nightclub. The fire started just seconds into the headlining band's opening song, when pyrotechnics were set off. They inadvertently lit flammable soundproofing foam behind the stage. The flames were first thought to be part of the act; only as the fire reached the ceiling and smoke began to billow did people realize it was uncontrolled. In less than a minute, the entire stage was engulfed in flames. An investigation of the fire, using computer simulations and a mockup of the stage area and dance floor, concluded that a sprinkler system would have successfully contained the fire and allowed everyone to get out safely.

Useless Factoid: "Stars and Stripes Forever"

In show business, particularly theatre and the circus, this hymn is called the "Disaster March." It is a traditional code signaling a life-threatening emergency. This helps theatre personnel handle things and organize the audience's exit without panic. One example of its use was at the Hartford Circus Fire in July 1944.

One last word of caution. Being trained in the safe procedures for all of this doesn't necessarily make you safe. There are still variables. You might forget some of the rules. Or, you might be working with someone who doesn't know how to be safe. Do not allow yourself to settle into a false sense of security. Be aware of not only what you are doing, but also of your surroundings.

Deluge
Dust mask
Earmuffs
Earplugs
Eyecup
Eyewash station
Face shield
Fire curtain
Fireproof
Fire retardant
Goggles
Material Safety Data Sheets
OSHA
Outrigger
Respirator
Smoke Pocket
Sprinkler system
Thermal barrier
Zetex

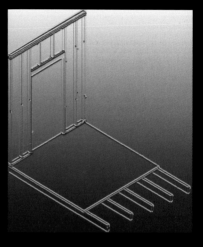

CHAPTER
SIX
Study Words

Setting It All Up

Scenic Tools and Materials

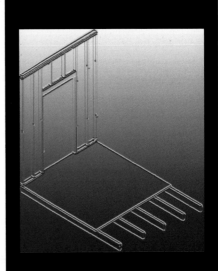

OK, enough with all this theory stuff. Are you ready to dive in and learn about tools? And, yes, I know you may already know what some of them are. This book is all about theatre, so we look at tools from that specific perspective. There are many variations on the basic tools. We take a look at the most common ones you find in a scene shop, and keep in mind, this is by no means a comprehensive list of every tool ever made. I put them into four main categories that follow the schedule for building. That means we explore tools that measure and mark first. Second, we look at tools that cut. And, third, we look at tools that assemble. Last, we look at pneumatic, or air powered tools. Are you ready? Let's get started.

TOOLS

The first and most important thing we need to talk about before we look at any individual tool is its safe use. The manufacturer for each tool issues some kind of a manual with operating instructions. This manual includes not only the safe and intended use for the specific tool, but also any safety precautions you need to take to operate the tool in the manner the manufacturer intended. Please continue to reference the safety chapter (Chapter 6) as well as any available manuals. Safety first!

Each of the three categories includes many tools. Every tool has an intended purpose. The key is to match up the right tool with the right job. As you go through this list, there will be tools that are appropriate for more than one job. Keep in mind that each job is specific; you have to know how to pick the right tool for the right job. This is the only way to get the job done safely. We look into this idea more within each category. As you go through the rest of this chapter, you'll see many photos of tools. Keep in mind that every style of tool can have many manufacturers. I can show only one version of each tool, so if you see more than one tool in a certain brand, realize I am not showing a preference for that brand.

> Measure twice and cut once!
>
> —Al Kogler, my dad

So, you walk into the scene shop and are given a drawing of a flat to build. On the side of the drawing is a list of the wood you will need to cut. You walk over to the lumber rack and pull out a piece of wood. What is the first tool you are going to reach for? Well you have to measure the wood to know where to cut it, right? Measuring and marking tools come with a wide range of options. Let's look at them one at a time. We start with one more kind of pencil that we haven't discussed before.

MEASURING AND MARKING

In addition to the pencils we already discussed, there is such a thing as a **carpenter pencil**. This is different from a regular pencil in its shape and graphite. Its shape is a flattened octagon that prevents it from rolling. The graphite is thicker and stronger than a regular pencil, which comes in handy when writing on wood instead of paper. You cannot sharpen this in a pencil sharpener; most people just use their pocketknife.

The **tape measure** we are most used to seeing these days is the self-retracting pocket tape measure (Fig. 7.1). Its flexibility allows you to measure long lengths while still allowing it to be easily carried in your pocket. Now you've probably all seen a tape measure, right? The tape measure is easy to read. A tape measure blade is usually marked both in inches and in feet. At the end of the blade is a metal edge called a tang. This tang is intentionally left loose to compensate for measuring outside dimensions versus inside dimensions of objects. Also, the case of the tape measure is usually labeled with its length, so that if you are measuring an inside dimension, you will know how much to add for an accurate measurement.

Well, before we had today's version of a tape measure, there was the **folding rule**. The folding rule is sort of a

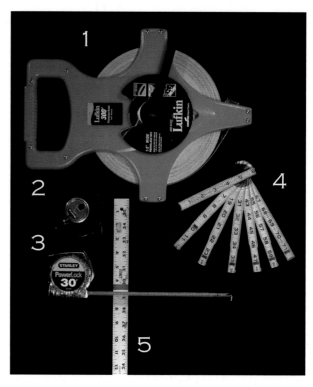

Fig. 7.1 (1) 300-foot tape measure, (2) 50-foot tape measure, (3) 30-foot tape measure, (4) folding ruler, and (5) metal ruler.

combination of a regular ruler and a yardstick. It is made up of small sections in 6-inch increments connected by a pivot point. This allows for the whole length of the rule to compress and make it small enough to easily fit in your pocket or bag. The folding rule is the granddaddy of today's tape measure. You still see these occasionally in the shop, and every once in a while they are still the perfect tool!

The latest development in tape measuring is the **laser measure**. This is a totally amazing piece of equipment. Laser measuring can be more accurate than a traditional tape measure. Human error is all but eliminated. In most cases, you just press a button, the laser emits its beam until it hits a solid surface, then a digital display shows the distance measured. You can usually measure indoors and outdoors. The key to a laser measure is that you can measure in those hard-to-reach places.

Sometimes a tape measure won't quite do everything you need. Perhaps you are not doing a simple measurement, but more of a layout, drawing square shapes and so forth. The next line of tools that can help with this is the framing square, combination square, speed square, and sliding bevel gauge. Let's take a look at these one at a time.

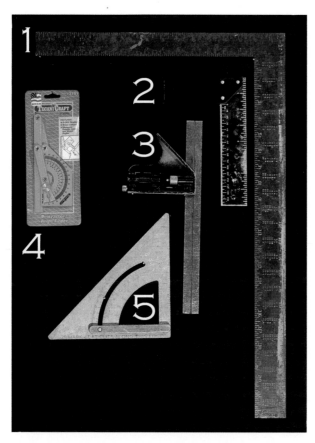

Fig. 7.2 (1) Framing square, (2) tri-square, (3) combination square, (4) speed square, and (5) protractor.

Next is the **speed square**. This is a metal triangle containing both 90-degree and 45-degree angles. There are measurement markings along the sides. The important difference between the speed square and other types of squares is that the speed square has a flange on one side that you can use to hold it square against the edge of your material.

When you are working with angles, you will need to measure an angle from a drawing or sample piece of research or scenery. The sliding **bevel gauge** is used to check or copy the angle of an existing unit or drawing. It consists of a handle or stock and a blade or tongue, connected by a wing nut. You place the handle against a straight edge, and by rotating the blade, you can match the angle of what you are trying to copy. A wing nut is loosened so that the blade can rotate to a variety of angles. This nut is then tightened to hold this new angle. It can then be used to copy an angle from one part of a unit to the next. Please note that this tool *does not* measure an angle. It simply copies the angle from something that already exists.

The compass is another tool for measuring (Fig. 7.3). I think most of you have seen a compass. It consists of two pointed arms joined at the top by a pivot point. The end of each arm can contain a sharpened metal point. A pencil can replace these points, or other writing device as needed. A compass can have two purposes. The primary purpose is to draw a circle. The secondary use is to measure a given distance and then copy that distance in equal-length segments.

Levels are the next kind of tool. There are spirit or bubble levels, string levels, plumb bob, and laser levels (Fig. 7.4). They all measure whether a surface is level or plumb, but they all do it in a slightly different way. The **spirit level** is so named because the little vial containing liquid is actually partially filled with ethanol. There is enough room left in the vial to create a bubble and this bubble is what we use to determine plumb. By placing the level on either a horizontal or vertical surface, the bubble will line up with one of the calibration marks on the vial.

A **string level** is fairly accurate for basic stuff. You use a string that is pulled fairly taut between two points in the area you are trying to measure. The string can't sag. This is the key. You hang the string level onto the string and watch to see where the bubble lands with the vial. It's the same basic idea as a regular spirit level.

Framing squares are very versatile (Fig. 7.2). They can vary in size, but the average looks like a big L with the long side being 24 inches long and the shorter side being 16 inches long. They are made of metal. They are the most accurate of our squares because they have a fixed angle; you can make no adjustments. If you need to draw or measure a 90-degree angle, then this is your tool. A great deal of our initial layout in theatrical design is based on the 90-degree angle. This is the best tool to start with.

The **combination square** is the next tool to discuss. As the name implies, this differs from the framing square in that it is adjustable. Not only can the combination square handle 90-degree angles, it can also help you draw 45-degree angles. Another benefit is that you can loosen a knob and slide the square's head along the ruler, then tighten it down at a different location on the rule. This allows you to transfer measurements from one place to another. The sliding head of the square contains a level. This can be very useful for certain types of measuring.

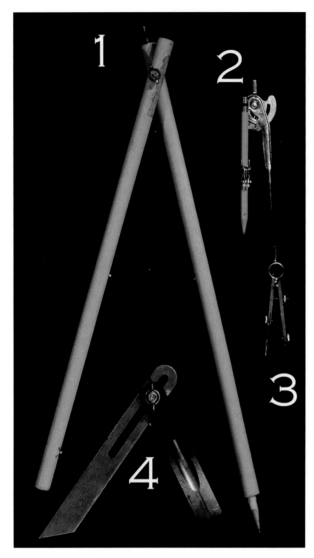

Fig. 7.3 (1) Large homemade compass, (2) compass with pencil, (3) compass with lead, and (4) bevel guide.

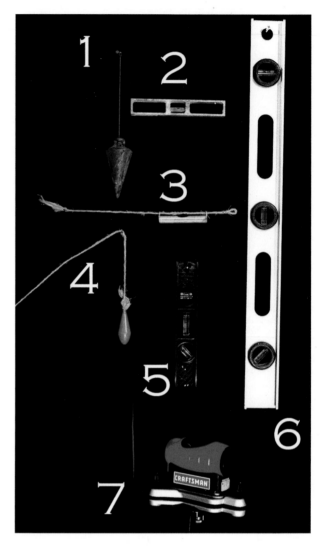

Fig. 7.4 (1) Plumb bob, (2) small spirit level, (3) string level, (4) plumb bob, (5) spirit level, (6) large spirit level, and (7) laser level.

A **plumb bob** can be used if you are trying to determine a level line from one point only. That means you can attach a string to the top of a wall. Let the string drop down with a plumb bob attached to the bottom. The plumb bob is a weight and will stop swinging at the point of making the string level. You then adjust the angle of the wall until everything lines up.

The **laser level** is similar to the laser tape measure in how it works. Some laser products are self-leveling, via a spinning sensor. Others are done manually, and you're responsible for getting it set up. Once the setup is complete, you push the button and a laser emits its beam. The cool part is that the beam remains level as it goes into the

distance. This is a great tool if you need to line up several items along the same line across a distance.

The **chalk line** is the last tool we will discuss in this category. A chalk line is an almost diamond-shaped container containing a very long string and powdered chalk (Fig. 7.5). It is used to mark a straight line between two points. You must measure and mark where you want the line to be. Shake the chalk line to make sure the chalk inside has coated the string. Then, you stretch the string, holding it taut at both ends. Make sure you are lined up with your measurements. Snap the line once by pulling it up away from your surface about 5 to 6 inches and letting it go. When it snaps back down, it will hit the surface with enough force to transfer the powdered chalk along

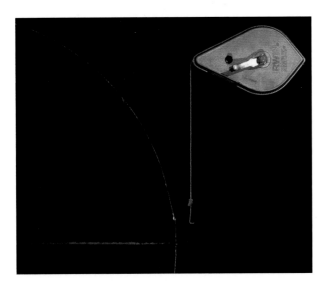

■ **Fig. 7.5** A chalk line with evidence of its use!

the string to your scenery. You now have a line of chalk that can be used as a guide for cutting, painting, nailing, or pretty much anything.

CUTTING AND SHAPING

Now that you are all measured and marked, what is next? Cutting. We break cutting up into several smaller categories. There are hand tools, which you hold in your hand when there is no power source other than your own muscles. Then, we discuss power hand tools and power stationary tools as they relate to cutting. Keep in mind that many of the tools we discuss can cut wood or metal, depending on the blade you put into the tool. Our last topic is welding torches that specifically cut metal.

All these tools are meant to cut. Some are meant to cut wood, some metal. All cutting tools cut a variety of things indiscriminately. They aren't designed to cut one thing and not another. Does that mean you can use a utility knife to cut a piece of wood. Yes, but it's not a smart choice and I don't recommend it. Keep in mind that the tool can't tell what it is cutting. This means that if skin, tendon, muscle, and bone get in the way, the tool will most likely keep cutting. So choose the right tool for the job and use it safely. My father told me something a long time ago that I have always remembered. He said, "Don't fear tools, respect them." This basically means know what the tool can do, but more important, know what the tool can't do. Choose the right tool for the right job!

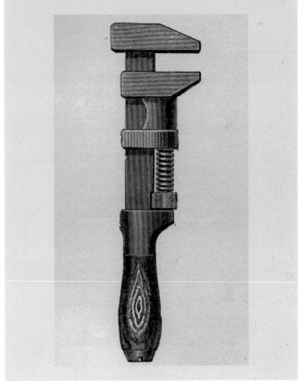

CUTTING TOOLS AND SAWS

The most basic cutting tool we have is the pocketknife. You may have one of these in your pocket right now. They are simply designed. There is a blade that rotates out from inside the handle. When fully closed you can't see the blade, and more important, there is nothing sharp sticking out to hurt you.

The **utility knife** or mat knife is next (Fig. 7.6). This type of knife comes in a metal or plastic handle. The blade is retractable, meaning it stores completely in the handle. It uses a two-sided blade. This means when the blade gets dull you can open the handle, pull out the blade, turn it around, and put it back in. Now you have a brand new sharp edge to cut with.

Scissors or shears can be used for a lot of cutting. We all know about scissors. It's a tool with blades on two opposing

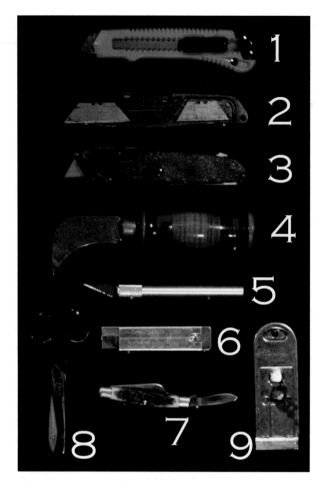

Fig. 7.6 (1) Snap-off utility knife, (2) open utility knife showing blades, (3) utility knife, (4) carpet or linoleum knife, (5) Xacto knife, (6) box cutter, (7) pocketknife, (8) scissors, and (9) razor scraper. Don't take these to the airport!

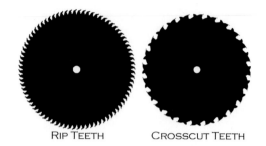

RIP TEETH   CROSSCUT TEETH

Fig. 7.7 Notice the difference in the teeth patterns between the rip and crosscut saw blade teeth.

The different materials the blade can be made out of also affect its use. High-speed steel blades are usually used for wood and the occasional light metal. Cobalt steel blades are harder and last longer, also holding the sharp edge better. Carbide blades are generally used for masonry board. Scrolling blades are typically the narrowest of this type and are appropriate for tight turns while cutting. Keep in mind, you should never plan to stop a saw blade in the middle of a piece of wood. Always finish the cut before turning off a saw. The various people-powered saws we discuss are the hand saws, miter saws, coping saws, flush cut saw, and keyhole saw.

Hand saws first. There are two basic kinds. I bet you've guessed why. There is one style for crosscutting wood and another style for ripping wood. The handle and the metal blade can be identical. The difference between the two is the teeth on the blade. Always look at a hand saw when you first pick it up so that you know which saw you have and, more important, whether or not it is the right tool for the job you are about to do.

Mitering is making a joint, or corner, by combining two angled pieces of wood to make a third angle. It takes two separate pieces of wood with 45-degree angles that combine to make a 90-degree angle. A **miter saw** uses crosscut teeth (Fig. 7.8). Miter saws are often used in conjunction with a **miter box**. A miter box has precut slots in it to guide the saw into a certain angle. This precision is critical or the miter won't turn into the correct angle needed for the project.

The next saw is the **coping saw**. The coping saw has a handle with a U-shaped steel frame. The very thin blade is held between the arms of the U. Turning the handle tightens or loosens the tension on the blade. Holders at either end of the blade can also be pivoted so that you can adjust the angle of the cut. Coping is similar to mitering. It is fitting two pieces of wood together when both pieces have

sides, one facing up, the other facing down, joined at a pivot point somewhere between the blades and the handles. The scene shop often has to cut paper or fabric as a beginning preparatory step to other parts of the process. It's not all about wood. But, now that we've mentioned wood, none of the tools we talked about so far works very well on wood. So let's start exploring.

Before we get into the individual saws, let's discuss the different kinds of saw blades. Blades for cutting wood come in one of two varieties of teeth: crosscut and rip. The basic idea is that **rip blades** cut parallel to the grain and **crosscut blades** cut across the grain (Fig. 7.7). It sounds easy but take a look at the difference between the blades visually. The crosscut blade has a much harder job to do. It should look much more fierce … and it does!

an irregular surface. This usually refers to molding, whether on the wall or a picture frame. The coping saw allows you to make these kinds of cuts in very tight spaces, especially since there tend to be inside corner joints.

The **flush cut saw** has a handle with the blade coming straight out of one end. The blade is very flexible, cuts flush with the bottom surface, and has a very fine set of teeth that cut in one direction. That means the saw will not cut on both the push and pull. It cuts only as you pull the saw toward you. This is used for detail finishing. Another benefit of the flush cut saw is that you rarely have to sand the wood afterwards due to the fine teeth.

Fig. 7.8 (1) Coping saw, (2) keyhole saw, (3) miter saw, and (4) hand saw.

The **keyhole saw**, or drywall saw, is a long, narrow saw used for cutting small awkward holes into a variety of building materials. The blade is secured into the handle by one or two screws. One recent modification to the keyhole saw is the addition of a sharpened point on the tip of the blade. This allows for jabbing the saw through soft materials such as dry wall to begin your cut.

Metal-Cutting Saws

We now change from saws that cut wood to saws that cut metal. Metal cuts very differently than wood. The blades on these saws have teeth much closer together and much sharper. Keep in mind, we are still talking about hand tools with no power source other than you and me. OK, let's talk about hacksaws, tin snips, pipe cutters, tube cutters, pipe reamers, and pipe threaders. A quick safety note: Metal, especially the newly cut edges, can be very sharp. Be sure to wear goggles and work gloves when handling or cutting it.

Hacksaws are the one metal-cutting saw that most of you are already familiar with. It is a metal handle shaped in an arch with two places to attach the blade. The blade is both narrow and rigid. The teeth are angled, and the blade can be installed in the handle in either direction. This allows you to choose whether you will cut on the push or the pull motion. The replaceable blades come in a variety of types depending on your exact purpose.

Tin snips are used to cut thin sheets of metal (Fig. 7.9). They work under the same premise as scissors, two opposing blades coming together. Tin snips come with different blade designs: straight cutting, left cutting, and right cutting. Your individual project and material will inform your decision as to which is the correct tool. Use tin snips as you would use scissors on heavy cardboard. As you cut, open the jaws of the snips fully, and make cuts as long as possible. Avoid snapping the jaws closed completely at the end of the cut, as this will nick the edges of the metal.

Pipe and tube cutters are very similar. Some look like a big pair of bolt cutters. You put the pipe or tube between the blades and squeeze the handles together. The other style is shaped like a C with a handle coming out of the bottom. You twist the handle, which tightens the pressure into the pipe. This forces the sharp blade into the pipe while wheels around the clamp continuously rotate the pipe. The pressure from the rotation is much stronger than you could possibly do on your own! **Pipe cutters** are rated by the type and size of pipe they can cut.

Fig. 7.9 (1) Pipe cutter, (2) PVC cutter, (3) reamer, (4) conduit cutter, (5) threader, (6) tin snips, and (7) hacksaw.

Pipe reamers are used whenever a pipe is cut. Both the inside and outside of the cut edge may retain burrs, little pieces of sharp metal that can block the pipe from fitting to another piece of pipe. To remove the burrs from the inside of the pipe, use a reamer. Reamers are usually cone shaped with some sort of ratcheting handle. They have many cutting edges that remove the burrs on contact. Reamers are as sharp as the burrs, so be very careful! Now that your pipe is cut and free of burrs, you need a **pipe threader**. Your newly fabricated pipe may need to screw into a coupling or flange or some other type of mounting hardware. To do this you need to create threads that screw into the other piece of hardware.

> Toys can turn into tools. The difference is usability.
>
> —Curt Ostermann

Powered Hand Tools

Next we talk about hand tools for cutting that have an external power source, either a battery or a plug to go into an outlet. We discuss jigsaws, spiral saws, reciprocating saws, circular saws, router, grinder, and drills. Before we go any further, remember that power tools require steps taken to ensure safety. Always wear eye and ear protection when using these tools! Also, keep in mind that the blades can get bound up in the wood as the tools cut. If this happens, the saw will most likely want to kick back toward you. A good firm hold on the tool goes a long way to controlling this, should it happen. Being aware of this will keep you safe!

The **jigsaw**, also known as a *saber saw*, has a small straight blade that cuts with an up and down motion (Fig. 7.10). Because of its small blade, it is great for cutting curves and not as good for cutting straight lines. Cutting a straight line requires some kind of guide. The guide is often called a **fence**. Different blades are available for cutting ceramic, leather, linoleum, plastic, wallboard, metal, and hardwood. Variable-speed blades and an adjustable foot for cutting at different angles are options that are important to have. You can think of the jigsaw as a powered version of the keyhole saw.

Reciprocating saws have a straight blade mounted at one end of the body (Fig. 7.11). The blade moves back and forth (that is where they get their name), much like the action of a jigsaw. Reciprocating saws are much more powerful and versatile than jigsaws. A variety of blade options means they can cut through almost anything. The brand name Sawzall® by Milwaukee Tool has become synonymous with this type of saw. This saw is perfect for big rough cuts that might then be followed up with a jigsaw to refine the final look.

A **circular saw** is one of the more popular portable tools in the shop. It gets its name from the circular saw blade it uses. It is designed to make long, straight cuts. This saw can crosscut or rip wood. The bottom foot can be angled to allow for a consistent angled cut. As with most of the tools in this category, circular tools can be corded or run from batteries. If your saw has a cord, please, please, make sure to always know where the cord is. Running over the cord is a very bad thing!

Routers are tools that typically cut grooves or decorative trims along the edge of a piece of wood. Think picture frame. Instead of a blade, like most of the saws we've been talking about, a router has a bit. This bit is shaped just like the shape you will be cutting out, and is sharp on all edges. The shapes you can cut out are limited only by the number of router bits you have. To route a straight line you use a straight fence. Routers typically rotate their bit in a clockwise motion. That means it is best, and safest, to cut from left to right. If you are left handed, like me, this

Fig. 7.10 On the left is a jigsaw and on the right is a spiral saw.

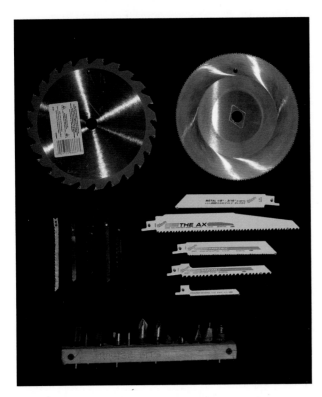

Fig. 7.11 A variety of circular blades and straight blades for saws, also router bits.

means you have to adjust your normal hold on the tool to operate it safely. Experiment with this idea before using the tool for the first time.

A **grinder** is a tool that drives an abrasive disc mounted to a geared head. The abrasive disc can be replaced when it becomes worn. Different discs can be used for a variety of tasks, such as cutting, sawing, and even buffing. These discs are intended primarily for metalworking. This particular tool requires different safety protocols. A face shield should always be worn and gloves, respirators, earmuffs, long sleeves, and hard hats are highly suggested, depending on what you are grinding.

Powered Stationary Tools

Our next category is powered stationary tools. Stationary power tools differ from what we've been discussing by the fact that they are built into a table or stand of some sort. You bring your materials to the tool, not the other way around. The same safety precautions for eyes and ears that we already discussed are to be used here as well. We discuss table saws, radial-arm saws, panel saws, band saws, scroll saws, and the chop saw/compound miter saw.

The **table saw** is possibly the most-used tool in the whole scene shop. It works similarly to the circular saw in the last section. It is mounted in a table, which gives it more stability and allows for a more powerful engine. A rip saw blade is usually installed. The tabletop gives stability to the wood you are cutting, allowing you to cut bigger pieces of wood more easily. A fence helps you line up your wood and keep it straight. A blade guard keeps you physically separated from the blade—a very good idea! The table saw has many other custom accessories that you can check into for helping with various types of cuts. This is a powerful and very useful tool.

Radial-arm saws work similarly to circular saws (Fig. 7.12). A crosscut saw blade is usually installed. The blade head is suspended from a long arm, hence the name, in a yoke that allows for selectable degrees of rotation. There is a handle for moving the blade head forward and back while cutting the wood. If you need to cut many pieces of wood to the same length, you can set up a **jig**, or guide, at the correctly measured distance. The table saw and radial-arm saw complement each other perfectly.

Panel saws were originally used primarily by cabinet-makers. However, their use is also perfect for the scene shop. A panel saw is basically a circular saw with a big bracket on it to allow for movement across a large-scale prede-termined grid. They can be either horizontal or vertical, although most scene shops prefer the vertical one to save space. Cutting sheets of plywood into smaller pieces is this tool's specialty. Today, there are even computer-controlled

■ **Fig. 7.12** (a) Panel saw, (b) scroll saw, (c) table saw, (d) radial-arm saw.

■ **Fig. 7.12** cont. (e) band saw, (f) compound miter, and (g) drill press.

panel saws that can make multiple cuts and repeat them from one piece of wood to another with amazing accuracy. For repeated 90-degree cuts, this is the fastest way to do it.

Band saws are useful for cutting wood or metal into nonlinear shapes. A band saw is a unique tool in that the blade is one continuous loop, or band, stretched over two pulleys. The blade operates by moving in one direction continuously. It has teeth on only one side of the band. You move the material through the saw to create your design. Different bands are available for wood and metal as well as with coarser and finer teeth. Keep in mind, there is no blade guard so safety is more of a concern here. However, the designs you can achieve are unique to the band saw.

Scroll saws are used for freehand cutting of intricate shapes in fairly thin wood. The scroll saw uses thin blades, similar to a jigsaw, to allow for the small radius needed to complete these designs. The band saw can do many of the same things, just not in as fine a degree of detail. This is the right tool if you need to create delicate inlaid designs. Scroll saws have size designations that are determined by the distance between the blade and the back arm. Like the band saw, there is no blade guard, so be careful! The band saw and the scroll saw complement each other very well.

The chop saw/compound miter saw is a very versatile tool. You can probably guess that just from its name. **Chop saws** have a circular saw blade just like a circular saw. Originally, chop saws worked by having a pivoting arm containing the blade. The arm came down and cut, then went back up to its resting location, similar to a radial-arm saw but in the other direction. Newer chop saws still do this, and much more. They now also pivot around to become a miter saw. The newest addition to this tool is an arm that turns the saw into a radial-arm saw as well. Just remember that the more a tool can do, the more you have to be aware of its proper use to keep safe.

A new advance in the development of cutting tools is the table router. This is a very expensive piece of machinery. Remember the hand router? Well picture that on a huge horizontal table. Then picture that it is computer controlled. You can now upload a CAD file to the router's memory, and it will cut the exact design that has been drawn! This is not only amazing to watch, but also an unrivaled advancement in using technology in the scene shop.

> Just because you can, doesn't mean you should!
>
> **—Curt Ostermann**

There is another type of cutting we haven't addressed at all yet. **Oxyacetylene** welding, commonly referred to as *gas welding*, is a process that relies on the proper combination of oxygen and acetylene. This usually is a very specialized department, but I touch on it briefly. The equipment needed for oxyacetylene cutting and welding is very portable and easy to use once you have been thoroughly trained. Oxygen and acetylene gases are stored under pressure in steel cylinders. These cylinders are fitted with regulators and flexible hoses. The gases are then mixed together in the correct proportions to create a hot flame that can cut through metal. When welding, the operator must wear protective clothing and tinted colored goggles. This is nothing to play around with, but can be a very good tool in the right hands.

> When people describe rockets and wheels and a universe that is spinning through space, the mind spins.
>
> **—Eugene Lee**

ASSEMBLY

We now segue from cutting and shaping tools to a category I call *assembly*. Once all your materials are cut out into the proper sizes and shapes, the next step is to put it all together into something that resembles the original drawing. We break these tools into the same basic categories as the cutting tools: hand tools, power hand tools, and power stationary tools.

Hand Tools

Hand tools for assembly include the claw hammer, framing hammer, ball peen hammer, mallet, tack hammer, deadblow hammer, nail set, center punch, stapler, and pry bar. Then, we move on to all kinds of wrenches. We're still talking about hand tools. Keep that in mind. Here is the list of wrenches: adjustable wrench, open-ended wrench, box wrench, speed wrench, pipe wrench, nut driver, socket and ratchet, Allen keys, Yankee screwdriver, and screwdriver (flat versus Phillips).

Let's deal with all the hammers at once, since they all do a similar job. At their simplest, hammers are intended to push things together or take things apart. Keep in mind that the metal head of the hammer not only pushes a nail into wood, but it also can dent the wood. If you are concerned about damaging the wood, make sure to use some kind of buffer between the tool and the wood. Hammers can also be used for many jobs that were not intended for them. Be aware that the hammer's main job is pushing nails into wood and pulling them back out.

The **claw hammer** is most common and standard of all the hammers (Fig. 7.13). This is the hammer you see the most in the scene shop. It has a metal head for striking a nail, or whatever else you need to hit, and a curved claw for ripping nails back out of the wood. The head usually weighs about 16 ounces but can vary quite a bit. **Framing hammers**, on the other hand, are much heavier and are meant for larger nails and harder woods. Carpenters putting up the framing of a house originally used them, so that is where they get their name. The claw is not as curved, as on a claw hammer, and the head usually weighs about 22–28 ounces. A **tack hammer** is a much smaller hammer, usually used for the detail work on finishing projects. Small nails and tacks with very small heads are the perfect use for this tool. The head usually weighs between 5–8 ounces, much smaller than what we've been discussing so far.

The **ball peen hammer** has a much harder head than other hammers. Because of this, it is used mainly on metal instead of wood. *Peen* in the dictionary definition talks about drawing, bending, or flattening. The ball end of the hammer is used for shaping. So think about it. You have a hammer to bend, flatten, or shape metal. Sounds pretty handy, huh?

Dead-blow hammers may sound dangerous, but they are actually pretty cool (Fig. 7.14). They are unique in that the head is filled with metal shot. This gives the hammer extra force on impact and very little recoil or bounce back. What does that really mean? Well, when you swing the hammer

to hit something, the metal shot in the head sort of swings with your swing, adding momentum. It also means that, when the hammer hits something, the metal shot helps it to stay in contact with the object. All this adds up to a much more forceful strike with less effort! They also have a soft head that won't damage your project.

Mallets are another type of hammer, with a soft head that helps avoid damaging delicate surfaces. The head of a mallet is also substantially larger than a regular hammer, and this helps to spread out the force of the hit. If you are hammering into a finished surface, a mallet may be the better choice than a claw hammer, as it is less marring to the surface.

A **nail set** is often used in conjunction with a tack hammer. It is made of metal with a flat surface on either end. The nail set is used for driving the head of a nail either flush or just below the finished surface. Line up the nail set with the nail head; use a hammer to hit the nail set forcing the nail head into the wood. This gives you a smooth surface for painting or other finishes. The **center punch** is used in

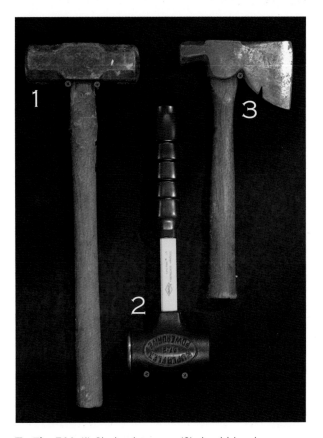

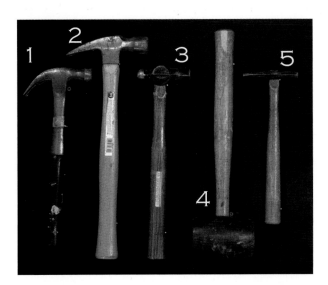

■ **Fig. 7.13** (1) Claw hammer, (2) framing hammer, (3) ball peen hammer, (4) mallet, and (5) tack hammer.

■ **Fig. 7.14** (1) Sledge hammer, (2) dead-blow hammer, and (3) hatchet.

a similar way to the nail set. The difference is that it has a sharp, pointy end. It is used, primarily on metal, to mark a starting point for drilling into the material. Once you have used the center punch, it is much easier to begin drilling into metal without the drill slipping.

We all know what a stapler is, right? Well this type is a little different than what you probably have sitting on your desk. A **stapler** binds things together by forcing thin metal staples into the material with pressure. But, you already knew that. What you may not know is that staples come in a variety of sizes, and you must make sure to choose the right size for your job. What you may also not know is that there are a variety of staplers. They vary in size, similar to the actual staples, but they also vary in how you load them, how you hold them, and what they look like. Always make sure the staples and stapler are meant to work together. Otherwise, the stapler will jam and cause you many headaches. We discuss this later in the chapter.

There are many kinds of **pry bars** (Fig. 7.15). Pry bars are made of metal and both ends are designed to be used for different purposes. Some pry bars have unique names, like *wonderbar*, and are made only by certain manufacturers. They are used as leverage for separating objects. Some pry bars are meant to remove nails and do minor lifting. Some are bulky enough to be able to perform demolition. Your scene shop most likely has several types. Be aware of the capabilities of each to choose the right tool for the right job.

The **adjustable wrench** is often called a *crescent wrench* and with good cause (Fig. 7.16). We are talking about an open-ended wrench with one fixed jaw and one adjustable

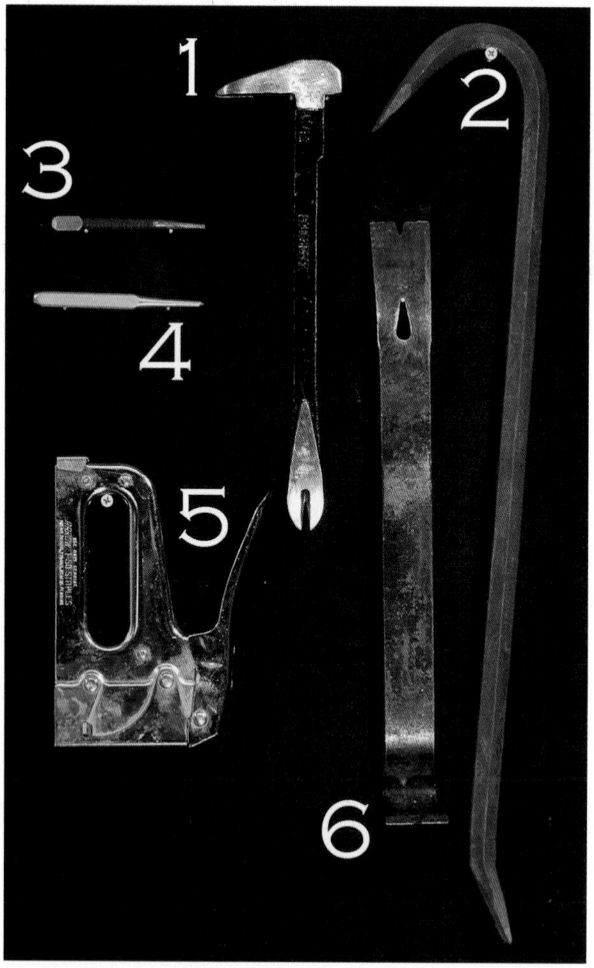

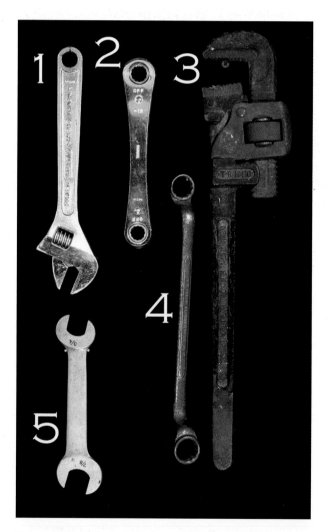

■ **Fig. 7.15** (1) "Catspaw" pry bar, (2) large pry bar, (3) nail set, (4) center punch, (5) stapler, and (6) flat pry bar.

■ **Fig. 7.16** (1) Adjustable wrench, (2) speed wrench, (3) pipe wrench, (4) box wrench, and (5) open-ended wrench.

jaw. The adjustment works by a screw positioned within the handle. This allows you to grasp any size nut or piece of hardware to loosen or tighten it. Although the wrench is shaped like a crescent, that is not where it gets its name. Its name actually comes from the original manufacturer, Crescent Tool Company, which began production in upstate New York in the early 1900s. Crescent® is a brand name, but it is used interchangeably for an adjustable wrench, as is the phrase C-wrench. Nowadays, adjustable wrenches are made by a wide variety of manufacturers and they are indispensable to the theatre technician!

The nonadjustable type of wrench is called an **open-ended wrench**. The open-ended wrench fits a specific size of hardware and has an open end usually at a 30-degree angle away from the handle. This allows a greater range of motion when trying to tighten or loosen a nut. A **box wrench** has a closed end and fits only one size of hardware. The box often has between 6 and 12 points of contact to the hardware, which makes for a much more secure hold as you are trying to move the hardware.

A **speed wrench** is similar to a box wrench with one major exception. It contains a ratchet on both ends. This "speeds" up your usage and is how the wrench gets its name. A ratchet is a device used to restrict motion to one direction. This happens by the use of a gear inside the head of the wrench that engages in one direction to tighten or loosen hardware as required. On the backswing of the handle, the gear disengages, which allows it to reset with the moved hardware. Ratchets often have a lever that allows motion to be either clockwise or counterclockwise.

The **pipe wrench** is meant for gripping round objects like, well, pipe, so its design is a little different. Primarily it is used for metal pipes, hence its name. It has an adjustable jaw similar to the adjustable wrench. It closes and opens by screwing itself tighter as the wrench clamps down on the pipe. When putting two pieces of pipe together or putting a pipe into a base, the pipe wrench is the essential tool.

There is a range of tools for tightening and loosening small fasteners. Keep in mind, as always, that, although several tools may actually be able to do what you want, they are not all appropriate for the job. In this category, using the wrong tool can actually damage or destroy the fastener! Let's look at each of the tools in this small category.

Sockets and nut drivers work in similar ways. A **socket set** is a handle and a series of replaceable heads. Each head has an opening on one side; each opening is a different size to correspond to different sizes of bolt heads and nuts. Sockets work with a ratcheting technology that allows you to loosen or tighten the bolt or nut quickly (Fig. 7.17). A **nut driver**, on the other hand, is a single tool, handle, and head in one that does not ratchet. These normally come in a set with various sizes.

Allen key is a brand name having a hexagonal head for adjusting nuts with a recessed six-sided opening. You may have used one of these if you ever purchased self-assembly furniture. Allen keys can be bought as a single key, as a

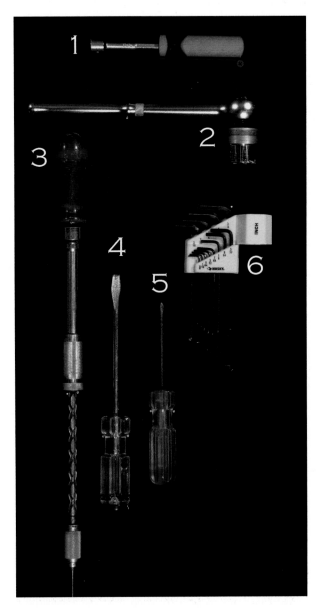

Fig. 7.17 (1) Nut driver, (2) socket wrench, (3) Yankee screwdriver, (4) slotted screwdriver, (5) Phillips screwdriver, and (6) Allen key set.

loose set, or as a full set packaged together within a shared handle. **Torx**® is also a brand name for a type of screw with a six-pointed star on the end. You may have heard of a star screwdriver—that is what this refers to. The Torx has better points of contact and therefore you tend to damage the screw and your tool less than with an Allen key.

Now that we've gone through all of these "modern" tools, let's go back to the basics, the screwdriver. First, let's take a quick look at the **Yankee screwdriver**. It is also referred to as the *push screwdriver* and is an older style. This screwdriver has a spiral center so that when you press down on the handle the head turns the spiral center so you can drive in or back out a screw by just pushing down on the handle. They have become less popular over time, but they are still out there.

Screwdrivers, as we know them today, have either a slotted or Phillips head. **Slotted screws** have a single straight indent in the top. **Phillips screws** have an X indented into the top. Slotted and Phillips screws come in different sizes, which we talk about later in this chapter. Just be aware that you must fit the driver to the screw. Stripped screw heads are the biggest problem to overcome, but most of the time it's the driver you choose and not the screw that creates the problem. Avoid the whole mess by choosing the right screwdriver for your projects. Using a driver that is too small or too large strips the screw head or damages the driver. Both are bad. Stripping a screw head means rounding out the slot or Phillips indentation. If this happens you won't be able to easily tighten the screw or get the screw out again.

Let's continue with hand tools in a slightly different direction, by discussing ways to hold things during the assembly process. We will discuss linesman's pliers, slip-joint pliers, needle-nose pliers, vise grips, hand-screw clamp, bar clamp, spring clamp, carriage or carpenter clamp, and vises.

Linesman's pliers are your basic, average, all-around great pair of pliers (Fig. 7.18). Linesman's pliers are very strong. They are great for holding, bending, and forming. Linesman's pliers' jaw surfaces are slightly toothed for better gripping. The jaws also have a built-in side-cutter tool. **Slip-joint pliers** are similar to linesman's pliers with one major difference. The joint that holds the two sides together is keyed so that the jaws can be opened wider as needed for certain jobs. **Needle-nose pliers** are good for smaller jobs. They are basic pliers, like the rest that we talked about so far. The difference in their design is that the gripping end is

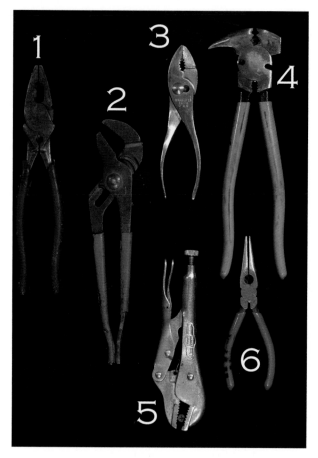

■ **Fig. 7.18** (1) Linesman's pliers, (2) tongue and groove pliers, (3) slip-joint pliers, (4) fence pliers, (5) vice grips, and (6) needle-nose pliers.

not flat but comes to a small narrow point. This makes them great for holding much smaller items with more precision.

Vise grips have an adjustable locking mechanism. If you are trying to loosen or tighten hardware where you will be using two tools, one to hold something in place and one to do the bulk of the work, vise grips lock their grip and hold it tightly for you, freeing up one of your hands to do the rest of the job. They come in a variety of sizes and shapes that makes them applicable for many jobs.

The **hand-screw clamp** is an older style of clamp still used today (Fig. 7.19). It is great when you need to be careful not to destroy your surface. This clamp is easy to recognize by its two heavy, broad wooden jaws. Passing through the jaws are screws with reverse threads at the ends so the jaws come together rapidly. Hand screws are available with jaw lengths from 4 to 16 inches. **Bar clamps** have a fixed jaw and a sliding jaw, which makes them easily adjustable to different lengths. The determining factor of

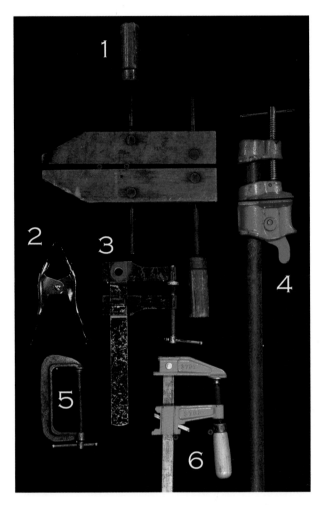

Fig. 7.19 (1) Hand-screw clamp, (2) squeeze clamp, (3) small flat bar clamp, (4) round bar clamp, (5) carpenter clamp, and (6) flat bar clamp.

a screw, the jaws are brought together, thereby holding whatever has been caught inside. The screw can be loosened to reposition the object being held and retightened. The vise can be closed quite tightly so that your work can be held very firmly.

There are also various shaping tools to choose from during the assembly process for fitting and detailing. These are primarily chisels, planes, rasps, and files. Each has differences not only in how they are used but also in their shapes and way of working. Let's look at each group separately.

A **chisel** is a tool with a cutting edge on its end. It is used primarily for carving and cutting hard materials like wood, stone, or metal. The sharp edge of the chisel is forced into the material, usually with a hammer or mallet. Chisels can have different shapes on their cutting edge. Some shapes are straight while others are more U shaped and meant to gouge out pieces of the object.

A **plane** is used to flatten, reduce the thickness of, and smooth a surface to a generally rough piece of lumber. Planes usually have a cutting edge on the bottom that is attached to the solid body of the plane. You move it back and forth over the wooden surface while the cutting edge removes uniform shavings a little at a time. This is a slow process, where all the pieces of the wood (usually at a joint) eventually become level.

A **rasp** is another woodworking tool for shaping the wood. It is made up of a long, narrow steel bar (Fig. 7.20). There is a handle on one end while the rest of the rasp has triangular teeth cut into it. When drawn across a piece of wood, it will shave away parts of the wood, very coarsely. A **file** is very similar to a rasp. The major difference is that a file has much finer teeth. The amount of wood removed is much smaller, and it is, overall, a gentler process.

Powered Hand Tools

We move on to electric assembly tools with the same purposes as those hand tools we just discussed. We have the main tools and one big group of accessories: drills, drill presses, hammer drills, and drill bits. Since this whole section is about drilling, let"s talk about the basics of drilling for a second. A **drill** is a tool for making holes. The drill is a motor that can rotate the drill bit forward or in reverse. The size of the hole is determined by the size of the drill bit that does the cutting. The drill bit is held in place on the front of the drill by a chuck. The chuck is a hole in front of

their usage is the bar they are attached to—the longer the bar, the bigger an object they can clamp!

Spring clamps are identified by the size their jaws can open. They are clamps that are strong and lightweight. They differ from the hand-screw and the bar clamps in that they tighten and loosen based on a spring's tension. These clamps usually feature soft, durable pads to protect fine finishes. They can be used on everything from wood to fabric. The last style of clamps is the **carpenter** or **carriage clamps**. They are the basic clamps you find in a scene shop. They are shaped like a C with a screw that tightens and loosens. They can leave marks on wood, so they are usually used when that is not a factor.

Vises are made from metal and are usually attached to a shop bench for stability. There are two jaws on the top that are usually fairly wide and smooth. By turning

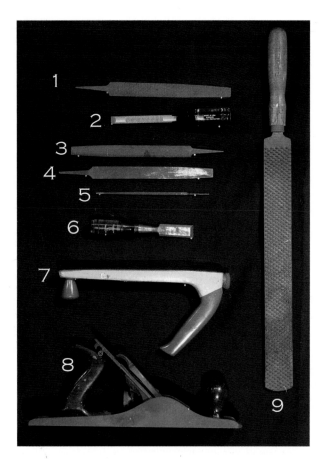

Fig. 7.20 (1) Course rasp, (2) combination rasp/chisel, (3) half-round file, (4) flat file, (5) triangular needle file, (6) wood chisel, (7) hand rasp, (8) hand plane, and (9) ultracoarse rasp.

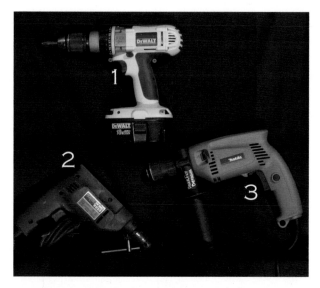

Fig. 7.21 (1) Cordless drill, (2) corded drill, and (3) hammer drill.

Fig. 7.22 (1) Belt sander, (2) palm sander, and (3) detail sander.

the motor. You insert the drill bit into the chuck and then tighten it, using a chuck key.

Electric drills have many different options and capabilities (Fig. 7.21). The chuck size can vary for holding larger drill bits, they may have variable speed motors for both forward and reverse, and the newest addition is torque control. Drills operate on either battery or regular electricity. All of these options make this a versatile tool for the scene shop. Cordless, battery-powered drills are most popular, as they are more flexible and need not be tethered to an extension cord.

A **hammer drill** looks similar to the electric drills we discussed previously. It works in a similar way, with a drill bit that does the cutting. The added option in a hammer drill is that the chuck creates a short, rapid hammer-type action to break through hard or brittle material. This significantly speeds up the drilling process. Hammer drills are used mostly when working with masonry or stone.

The **drill press** is a stationary tool that does the same job as a regular drill. It has the added advantage of being mounted over a tabletop. There is usually a large handle on the side that moves the drill bit up and down into the material you are drilling. Since the drill is at a fixed angle and so is your material, you are guaranteed to drill exactly the same hole every time. This works out great for making multiple holes when working on a large project.

OK, on to drill bits. Drill bits come in many sizes, as you can imagine, but they also come in different shape styles (Fig. 7.24). The bigger the hole you need to make, the stronger the drill bit needs to be! To choose the right bit, you need to know what material you will be drilling into as well as the size of the hole you need to make.

The basic drill bit you are most accustomed to seeing is the **twist bit**. This bit is a straight bit with spiral twists

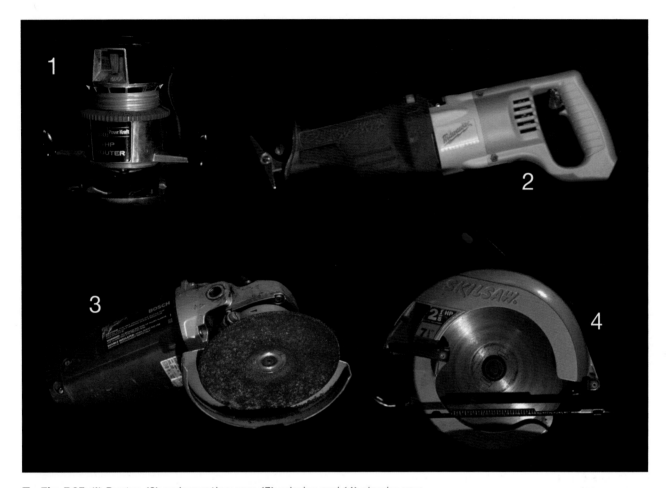

■ **Fig. 7.23** (1) Router, (2) reciprocating saw, (3) grinder, and (4) circular saw.

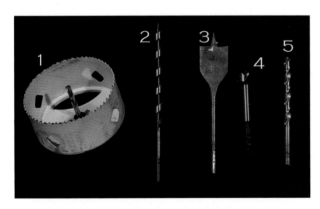

■ **Fig. 7.24** (1) Hole saw, (2) auger bit, (3) spade bit, (4) forstner bit, and (5) twist bit.

down its length. The front edge of each spiral is a cutting edge. The spiral design helps to remove the debris from the hole as you drill. These bits are usually made from high-speed steel, carbon steel, or tungsten carbide, and can be used on wood, metal, or plastics. Titanium nitride is a coating sometimes used to increase the bit's hardness. But that is way too much chemistry stuff. All bits are marked in their packaging so just look for the info! Different manufacturers have different size ranges, but twist bits are usually available in a variety of sizes from $1/_{64}$ inch to 1 inch. See Figure 7.24, numbers 2 and 5.

Spade bits are the next category. See figure 7.24, number 3. They come in larger diameters as well as longer lengths than regular twist bits, allowing for larger holes to be made. Spade bits are designed differently than twist bits. They have a straight shaft with a rectangular bottom that comes to a point. Think of a shovel (a.k.a. *spade*), and you get the visual. Spade bits are usually available in sizes ranging from $3/_8$ inch to 1 inch. Forstner bits are starting to be used as an alternative to spade bits. See figure 7.24, number 4. They are sharper due to their design. They also have a rim instead of a center point, which makes for easier positioning. All of this combines to make a cleaner hole and makes the bits safer to use.

Need to make an even bigger hole? **Hole saws** make even larger holes. See figure 7.24, number 1. These are no longer constructed in the same manner as a single drill bit. Think of a band saw blade, then make it smaller in diameter and you'll be close to what a hole saw looks like. A piece of thin metal wrapped in a circle with teeth added on one side. These are awesome to work with. There is usually a small twist bit in the center of the hole saw. This allows you to get the hole started in the exact place you want it. Then the hole saw starts working! Sizes for hole saws usually range from ⅞ inch to 5¾ inches.

The last bit we talk about is not a drill bit but a screw bit. These are one of the most important items in the scene shop. Before their invention, all screwing was done by hand. I'm sure you've all used these. They come with slotted and Phillips heads and in different sizes. Sometimes, you can even find ones that are magnetic, which can be very helpful when you are working in tight spaces and the screw tends to drop off the screwdriver before you get it started! This is also really handy for keeping the screw on the end of the bit to begin with.

Our last tool fits into many categories and no categories all at the same time. It is the **hot-glue gun** (Fig. 7.25). Hot glue is an amazing thing and has changed how we do many things in the theatre. You've probably seen these in craft stores, stationery stores, hardware stores, and maybe even grocery stores. They are very handy for a number of reasons. The basic idea is that you plug in the hot-glue gun and it begins to get hot. Hot glue is a plastic material that is solid at room temperature but melts into a sticky fluid when heated. You insert a stick of solid hot glue into the gun. When you pull the trigger or push the glue in, the glue

stick advances and begins to melt. Use it as you would any other adhesive, since all the glue has to do is cool down to produce a fast bond. Keep in mind that if it gets heated up again, it will lose its holding power. Big safety note: Hot glue is really, really *hot*! You can burn yourself, so be careful.

Pneumatic Tools

So far we discussed hand tools and electrically powered tools. Now we move on to **pneumatic** tools, specifically nailers and staplers. However, a big disclaimer, almost all tools that are electric also come as pneumatic. Nailers and staplers are two used frequently in most shops. However, many, many pneumatic tools can be useful. Chisels, ratchets, grinders, and jigsaws are just a few of the options. Learn the technology first and the tools will follow!

Pneumatic tools require a compressor to generate air pressure. Compressors have regulators on them that allow you to set the pressure your tool requires. The compressor then manufactures a high pressure, sending the air down the hose to the tool at the end. Think of holding a garden hose and putting your finger over part of the opening. Remember how the water pressure increases? It's not exactly the same, but it is similar.

This higher air pressure forces the nail or staple out of the gun and into whatever material you are working with. This is one of the fastest ways to work, once you are properly trained on the equipment. Keep in mind that there are different safety guidelines for this type of equipment. Make sure to follow the manufacturer's guidelines for safe use. Also make sure you are trained properly before beginning!

Pneumatic tools come in a wide variety of types with differing styles and features (Fig. 7.26). Nailers are specifically designed to take certain lengths and weights of nails. Staplers are the same way. You load a "clip" or a "cartridge," which contains varying amounts of nails or staples. Make sure that you have the right clip for the tool! This is really important. If you use the wrong nails or staples, it won't just jam; there is the possibility of the nails shooting out at the wrong angle and hurting you or someone else!

When working with metal we need slightly different ways of joining pieces together. Please keep in mind that working with metals requires a completely different set of tools and skills than working with wood. Certain things about working with metal are much more dangerous than wood. If your shop has a metal working area, make sure

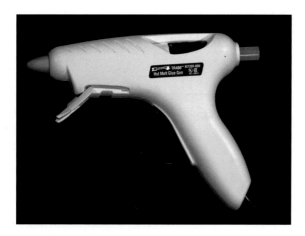

■ **Fig. 7.25** Hot-glue gun.

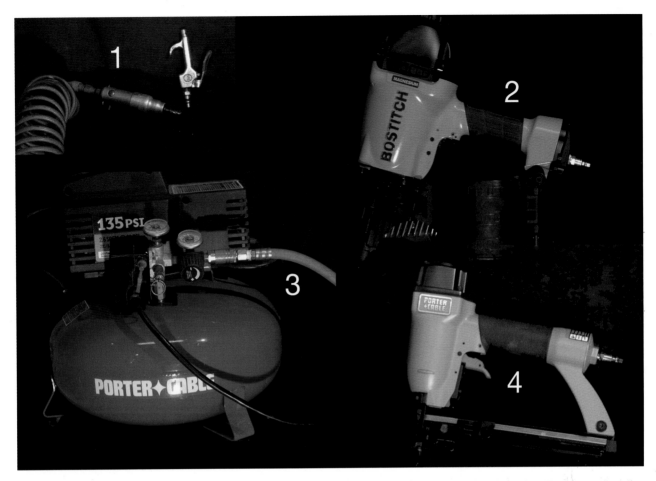

■ **Fig. 7.26** Pneumatic tools: (1) pneumatic grinder on the left and pneumatic air nozzle on the right, (2) pneumatic coil nailer, (3) air compressor, and (4) pneumatic brad nailer.

you are fully checked out on the equipment before even attempting to make a project.

Earlier, we discussed the use of oxyacetylene for cutting metal. Now, we look briefly at the variety of ways to join metals together. Welding is the most common way of permanently joining metal parts. A generic description of this process is heat applied to metal pieces, melting and fusing them to form a permanent bond. There are many types of welding.

Welding Tools

Arc welding is the most common type. Standard arc welding involves two large metal alligator clips that carry a strong electrical current. One clip is attached to any part of the project being welded. The second clip is connected to a thin welding rod. When the rod touches the project, a powerful electrical circuit is created. The massive heat created by the electrical current causes both the project and

the steel core of the rod to melt together, cooling quickly to form a solid bond.

Two common, but advanced, types of arc welding are tungsten inert gas (**TIG**) and metal inert gas (**MIG**) welding (Fig. 7.27). TIG welding is used with stainless steel or aluminum. While TIG uses welding rods, MIG uses a spool of continuously fed wire, which allows the welder to join longer stretches of metal without stopping to replace the rod. In TIG welding, the welder holds the welding rod in one hand and an electric torch in the other hand. The torch is used to simultaneously melt the rod and a portion of the project's material. In MIG welding, the welder holds the wire feeder, which functions like the alligator clip in arc welding.

Like arc welding, **soldering** and **brazing** use molten metal to join two pieces of metal. The main difference between them is that the metal added during the process has a melting point lower than that of the material, so only the added metal is melted, not the material. Soldering

Fig. 7.27 Various gas tanks, gauges, and hoses for welding setups.

uses metals with a melting point below 800° Fahrenheit; brazing uses metals with a higher melting point. Because soldering and brazing do not melt the material, these processes normally do not create the distortions or weaknesses in the project that can occur with welding. Soldering commonly is used to join electrical, electronic, and other small metal parts. Brazing produces a stronger joint than soldering and often is used to join metals other than steel, such as brass.

CLEANING UP

OK, so the set is finally built. You're ready to move on to the next project. What is the first thing you should think about at this very moment? Clean up! That's right. If you don't clean up, you will be making your next project in the middle of a mess. You'll also suddenly realize you can't find any of your tools. And, wait a minute—there is no room to lay anything out. Have I made my point? At the end of every scheduled shop time, there should be a clean-up period before people

head home. If everyone works together, it should take only about 15 minutes.

There is one tool left to talk about. It's for cleanup. It is technically referred to as the **wet/dry vacuum**. I'm sure you've all seen one, but just in case, let me describe it. It is a vacuum cleaner with a substantial tank for collecting whatever you're cleaning up. And when I say *whatever*, I mean it. They are called wet/dry for a reason. With the flick of a switch, depending on the brand, you can go from vacuuming sawdust to water! They are rated based on how much liquid the canister holds. Some models also change from vacuuming to blowing. This can be very handy in all sorts of circumstances.

We are now at the end of our tool discussion. Keep in mind what I said at the beginning of this chapter. This is only a small sampling of what is out there. Keep on the lookout for other tools that may make a certain job easier. Many tools may be able to do a similar job, but it depends on the individual situation as to which one is *right* for the job. Also, always keep in mind the safe way to use these tools. I stress

> When I sit alone in a theatre and gaze into the dark space of its empty stage, I'm frequently seized by fear that this time I won't manage to penetrate it, and I always hope that this fear will never desert me. Without an unending search for the key to the secret of creativity, there is no creation. It's necessary always to begin again. And that is beautiful.
>
> —Josef Svoboda

■ **Fig. 7.28** A lumberyard showing outdoor storage.

this all the way through the book, which is the same thing I do when I'm teaching. It's amazing how quickly a situation can turn from being fun as soon as someone gets hurt.

SUPPLIES

We're going to leave the tools behind for a little bit and explore some of the supplies that are out there. Once you are familiar with all the different options for materials and hardware out there, we go on to the next chapter, where we put it all together and start talking about building techniques. So, let's begin with wood.

WOOD

Wood is probably the most commonly used building material in theatre. Even with the advent of new technologies, there is still a huge amount of building and fabrication out of wood. Let's deal with some basic information about wood. There are hardwoods and softwoods. Hardwoods come from deciduous trees or trees that lose their leaves in the fall. Hardwoods are from trees like cherry and maple as well as trees like oak, ash, or poplar. Softwoods come from evergreen trees. The most popular of these is the pine, cedar, fir, and spruce. For theatre, we tend to stick mostly to softwoods for our projects. They are most often affordable and available.

Dimensional Lumber

We use two cuts of wood: dimensional lumber and sheet lumber. Dimensional lumber refers to solid wood that

has been milled into standardized sizes, which are then used primarily for framing (Fig. 7.28). Examples of this are probably common to you. Ever heard of a 2 × 4? That is only one example of dimensional lumber (Fig. 7.29). Sheet lumber on the other hand is a composite of wood and glue that dries under pressure, sometimes with a hardwood veneer, sometimes not. As the name suggests, sheet lumber comes in large sheets, usually 4 × 8 feet. There are also different thicknesses, anything from ⅛ to ¼ to ½ to ¾ inches.

Dimensional lumber uses grading categories to describe its attributes:

- *Clear* wood is free of structural defects (warps, knots, etc.) though it may have minor imperfections (grain variations).
- *Select* wood is almost "clear" but has some natural characteristics such as knots and color variations.
- *Common* wood has many more natural characteristics showing than either clear or select.

Each of these three categories can be broken down with ratings of first, second, or third:

- *First*-grade wood has the best appearance, with minimal color variations and limited marking.
- *Second*-grade wood is more variegated in appearance both in color and texture.
- *Third*-grade wood is very rustic in appearance allowing all the wood's qualities to come through.

Dimensional lumber comes in a variety of sizes as well as grades (Fig. 7.30). Let's talk about the different sizes now. Many sizes of milled lumber are available. As with

Fig. 7.29 *As You Like It* at NYU Department of Graduate Acting/Department of Design for Stage and Film in February 2005. Director, David Hammond; scenic designer, Arthur R. Rotch; costume designer, Courtney McClain; lighting designer, Joshua Benghiat.

Fig. 7.30 Dimensional lumber, clearly labeled and organized by size, in storage.

the tools, I discuss only the most common sizes used in theatrical building. Now, here is the confusing part, what we call a 2 × 4, is not actually 2 inches × 4 inches. Also notice that I didn't use the inches on the first usage of 2 × 4. That is technically a name, and doesn't refer to the actual dimensions. The following compares the nominal size (what we call it) against the actual size:

NOMINAL SIZE	ACTUAL SIZE
1 × 3	¾" × 2½"
1 × 4	¾" × 3½"
1 × 6	¾" × 5½"
1 × 8	¾" × 7½"
1 × 10	¾" × 9½"
1 × 12	¾" × 11½"
⁵⁄₄ × 4	1 × 3½"
⁵⁄₄ × 6	1 × 5½"
⁵⁄₄ × 8	1 × 7½"
⁵⁄₄ × 10	1 × 9½"
⁵⁄₄ × 12	1 × 11½"
2 × 4	1½" × 3½"
2 × 6	1½" × 5½"
2 × 8	1½" × 7½"
2 × 10	1½" × 9½"
2 × 12	1½" × 11½"
4 × 4	3½" × 3½"

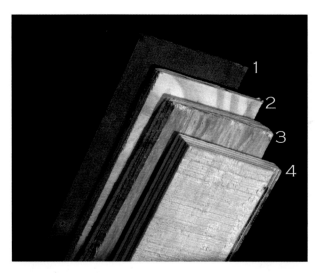

Fig. 7.31 (1) ⅛-inch masonite, (2) ¼-inch plywood, (3) ⅜-inch plywood, and (4) ⅝-inch plywood.

Sheet Lumber

We've gotten to sheets of wood. We use several kinds in theatrical construction: plywood, lauan, homosote, masonite, and MDF. What is wrong with that last sentence? One of the examples is not actually wood—read on to find out more! Let's look at a brief explanation of each and a listing of in what thicknesses they are available (Fig. 7.31).

Plywood is graded differently than dimensional lumber. With plywood, the front and back of the sheet are graded separately. The front is graded with letters A, B, C, or D. A shows an excellent appearance, similar to the clear-grade dimensional lumber. B allows for minor natural characteristics to show through, similar to the select grade in dimensional lumber. C and D allow for unlimited color variations, knots, and repairs. In some ways, this is similar but somewhat poorer quality than the common grade for dimensional lumber.

The back of plywood is rated using a slightly different system. Numbers 1–4 are used. Numbers 1 and 2 provide for surfaces with all openings and/or repairs to be smaller than $1/16$ inch. Number 3 provides for some open defects, meaning not repaired. This could include knotholes or splits and joints. Number 4 allows for open defects up to 4 inches in diameter. Plywood is commonly available in 4"-0" × 8"-0" sheets. It is also occasionally available in 4"-0" × 9"-0" and 4"-0" × 10"-0". Common thicknesses are ¼, ⅜, ½, ⅝, ¾, and 1 inches. You get the idea. There is a lot of flexibility in ordering plywood.

Lauan is a tropical hardwood plywood product and is pronounced *loo-on*. The name *lauan* comes from trees found in the Philippines but has become a generic term in the United States for imported tropical plywood. As this is a tropical wood, it comes mostly from the destruction of rainforests. Whenever possible, try to substitute another wood! If you must use lauan, it comes in 4" × 8" sheets in thicknesses of ⅛, ¼, ½, and ¾ inches.

Homasote is a type of wallboard made from recycled paper that is compressed under high temperature and pressure and held together with glue. Its primary use in the theatre is as sound proofing, either on top of platforms or as part of walls. Homasote is commonly available in 4"-0" × 8"-0" sheets, and occasionally in 4"-0" × 10"-0". Common thicknesses are ½, ⅝, and ¾ inches.

Masonite is a wood by-product formed by taking wooden chips, blasting them into long fibers using steam, and then forming them into boards (Fig. 7.32). These boards are then pressed and heated to create the finished product. The long fibers give masonite a very high strength and stability. All of this combines to make a great product, which is incredibly heavy. Masonite is commonly available in 4"-0" × 8"-0" sheets, and occasionally in 4"-0" × 9"-0" and 4"-0" × 12"-0". Common thicknesses are ⅛ and $3/16$ inches.

MDF, otherwise known as *medium-density fiberboard*, is made from wood fibers glued under heat and pressure, similar to masonite. The main difference between the two is that masonite is very dense, and the MDF is medium dense. This affects the weight and the cost! There are a number of reasons why MDF may be used instead of plywood. It is dense, flat, stiff, has no knots, and is easily machined. Because it is made up of fine particles, it does not have an easily recognizable surface grain. MDF can be painted to produce a smooth quality surface. However, MDF can be dangerous to use if the correct safety precautions are not taken. MDF contains a substance called *urea formaldehyde*, which may be released from the material through cutting and sanding. This can cause irritation to the eyes and lungs. Proper ventilation is required when using it; masks and goggles should always be worn at all times. MDF is commonly available in 4"-0" × 8"-0" sheets, and occasionally in 4"-0" × 9"-0" and 4"-0" × 12"-0" sheets. Common thicknesses range from 1 to 2½ inches.

Fig. 7.32 *Pelleas et Melisande* at the Metropolitan Opera. Director, Jonathan Miller; scenic designer, John Conklin; costume designer, Clare Mitchell; and lighting designer, Duane Schuler.

Molding

That pretty much wraps up the typical wood types. Let's talk about molding for a little while. Although molding is primarily made of wood, it is also made from other material, which is why I saved it until the end of this part of our discussion. Molding falls into five basic categories: baseboard, paneling, chair rail, picture rail, and crown or cornice. From ceiling to floor there are a number of places for the use of molding on walls. Typical placement for molding on walls is the cornice, picture rail, chair rail, and baseboard.

Moldings can be made from any number of types of woods, as well as MDF and even a flexible resin. The really great thing about moldings is that separate pieces can be joined to form a totally unique piece of finished molding. You can also combine bought molding with other pieces you have made from dimension lumber with the use of a router. Take a look at Figure 7.33 showing molding pieces sold by Dykes Lumber, and you will see the variety of what is available.

METAL

We move from wood to metal next. This is going to be somewhat short and to the point. Metal is much more dangerous to work with than wood. Most school shops don't have a metal working area. Here is the basic idea from the professional shops. They have a whole separate area of the shop, and separate personnel, dedicated to metalworking. Steel and aluminum are most commonly used. Steel is less expensive. Aluminum is much lighter but also more difficult to work with.

As I said throughout this chapter, look at all the choices for materials that are available, then decide which is the more appropriate for your design! Metals can be fabricated into any shape you need (Fig. 7.34). The potential for "custom" needs is much higher with metal than wood. Always defer to metal fabricators for advice and consultation before beginning any project of this type.

Fig. 7.33 Molding stored horizontally by style. All ends are labeled with the design number.

There is one metal I will address, as it is not necessary to have advanced skills in metalworking to use it. It is a personal favorite of mine: chicken wire! Chicken wire is a wire mesh that is usually used for making fences to keep in, you guessed it, chickens. It is fairly thin wire, very flexible, and easy to cut with the proper tool. When you need to make organic shapes, like trees, rocks, and mountains, chicken wire can be bent and twisted to form the basic shape. It can then be stuffed or covered, and finally painted. It is an old-fashioned way of doing this type of building—it is inexpensive, supplies are easily available, and almost any skill level can do it!

FABRIC

Enough of this wood and metal stuff, let's move on to the softer side of scenery (Fig. 7.35). Although any kind of fabric you can imagine can be used in the theatre, there are a few "standard" fabrics used commonly in the scenic realm (Fig. 7.36). They are, in no particular order, velour, duvetyn,

muslin, and scrim. Let's discuss each one's characteristics and uses.

Velour

Velour is a very plush fabric with a feel similar to velvet. It comes in a variety of colors and thicknesses. The thickness of velour, or any fabric, is measured in ounces per linear yard. Velour is made in different ways. It can be 100 percent cotton to 100 percent polyester to anything in-between. The average width is 60 inches. The plushness is due to velour having a "nap." Think of nap in the same way as you think of wood grain. It doesn't really matter which way you use it, unless you are putting panels side by side. The nap has to all run the same way.

Duvetyn

Duvetyn has a brushed matte finish and is therefore very different in feel than velour. It is 100 percent cotton, usually 54 inches wide, and comes in many colors. The most popular color is black. Duvetyn is much less expensive than velour and is used as a cheaper substitute for masking. Duvetyn is sometimes called *commando cloth*. Although they are similar, there is a difference. Duvetyn tends to be lighter weight, 8 ounces. Commando is heavier, starting at 10 ounces and can be as heavy as 16 ounces.

Muslin

Muslin has many uses in the theatre. It is a 100 percent plain-woven fabric and is used primarily as a base for other things. In costumes, muslin is used to make samples from patterns or as base layers that fancier fabrics are put on top of. In scenery, muslin is used to cover flats as well as for drops. More on flats and drops later. Muslin comes in widths from 44 inches to 39 feet. Yes, feet! It is an inexpensive fabric in regular widths but can become quite expensive in the much wider widths. It is available in three general weights: light, medium, and heavy. As opposed to other fabrics, it is not classified by ounces.

Scrim

Last, let's talk about scrim. Scrim is something of a specialty fabric, but it is so commonly used that I want to include it here. It is an open-weave netting, which means there is more open space than fabric. There are several styles of scrim. The most common is called *shark's tooth scrim*. There is also bobbinette, filled scrim, and netting. They vary by the

■ **Fig. 7.34** *Les Troyens* at the Metropolitan Opera. Director, Francisco Zambello; scenic designer, Maria Bjornson; costume designer, Anita Yavich; and lighting designer, James Ingalls.

■ **Fig. 7.35** The 2005 Theatre de la Jeune Lune production of *The Little Prince*, directed by Dominique Serrand.

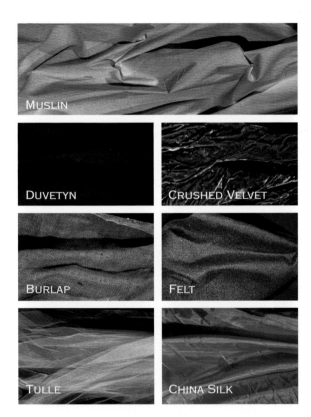

Fig. 7.36 Many different fabrics are used in the theatre. These are just a few of the samples.

openness of the weave as well as the pattern of the weave. The really cool thing about scrim is that depending on the lighting, you can either see through it or make it appear opaque. It is great for doing big reveals or for making things look like they are very far in the distance.

> The first show where I noticed this is what I wanted to do with my life was a Broadway revival of *West Side Story* in the early 1980s. I'd never seen a scrim before; I thought it was remarkable. Mind-blowing, like a movie special effect.
> —David Gallo

FOAMS AND PLASTICS

Styrofoam®—you know what it is. You've seen it. It comes in shipping boxes to keep fragile things safe. Then, you throw it away, right? Technically, Styrofoam is a trademark name. The actual name is extruded polystyrene—not near as fun, but accurate!

Foams

Well, the white Styrofoam you are used to seeing is actually called *bead foam*, because it is made up of tiny beads compressed together. It has great insulating properties and also resists moisture. Have you ever noticed that if you break off a piece, you can see the little beads? The beads are always the drawback, as you couldn't easily get a smooth edge. It is also hard to paint! Well, this foam used to be used all the time for creating various 3D designs. Any design ideas that require organic shapes have to be fabricated using a number of materials that allow for that kind of freedom.

Enter the wonders of pink and blue foam (Fig. 7.37). Both are denser than bead foam. The different colors have different densities and different insulation factors. Neither of those means anything to those of us in the theatre. We can pretty much use them interchangeably. These foams can be cut, joined, and carved to create almost any shape. However, a word of caution: If these foams are heated or even sanded vigorously, they can give off toxic and noxious fumes. Even breathing in the powder after sanding is a hazard. Make sure to use a respirator as needed when working with this material.

Ethafoam rods are another form of foam that we use. This is round and comes in a variety of diameters and lengths. It is bendable and easily cut and shaped. It is made through a different process than the other foams we discussed, making it much safer to work with and use.

Plastics

A wide variety of plastics, silicones, and other materials are also used for scenic and prop fabrication. Most come in similar sizes and shapes similar to what we already discussed. The key differences to look for between similar materials are

- Sizes and shapes.
- Weight.
- Strength and weight bearing ability.
- Tools and skills required.

■ **Fig. 7.37** Blue sheet foam on the left with white bead Styrofoam on the top right and ethafoam rods on the bottom right.

- Price.

- Availability.

HARDWARE

Let's move on to hardware, starting with fasteners. Once you've have the material, cut it to size, and shaped it, you are ready to put things together. One of the most important things to remember is that you want the fastener to penetrate at least three quarters of the way through your material. Halfway isn't strong enough to hold well, and all the way leaves the possibility of a sharp tip sticking out and hurting someone. Three parts can help to identify all nails, screws, and bolts: head, shank, and tip. We discuss the differences next.

Nails

Nails—we all know what they are. We know what they look like. We all used them. But, are you aware of how many different kinds there are? *Nails, pins, tacks, brads,* and *spikes* are all names for nails. The head style of nails varies from round to nonexistent. Some nails have two heads so that once you have hammered it into wood, another head is sticking out, which makes it easier to remove later. Shanks, for the most part, are smooth and round. Tips are pointed and sharp. Variations are all based on individual combinations of size, length (table follows), and diameter, as well as the head style (Fig. 7.38).

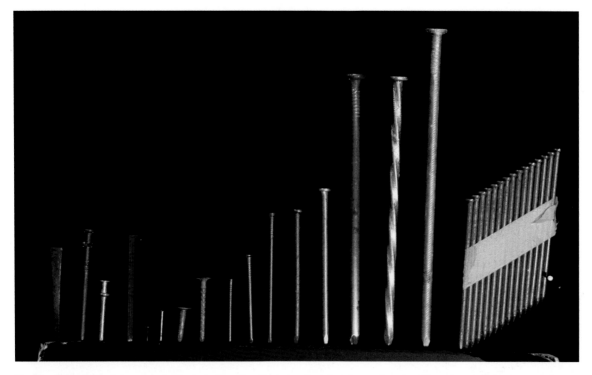

■ **Fig. 7.38** Nail styles vary to include length, diameter, head style, and so on. There is a nail for every job, so make sure to use the correct one for yours!

PENNY SIZE	LENGTH (IN.)	LENGTH (MM)
2d	1	25
3d	1¼	32
4d	1½	38
6d	2	51
7d	2¼	57
8d	2½	65
9d	2¾	70
10d	3	76
12d	3¼	83
16d	3½	89
20d	4	102
30d	4½	115
40d	5	127
50d	5½	140
60d	6	152

On a side note, nail sizes are designated by the word *penny*, which is indicated by the *d* after the size. This is based on a very old custom of selling nails in quantities of 100. The cost of the nails—6 penny, 10 penny, 20 penny—is how we now refer to that size of nail.

Screws and Bolts

Screws and bolts, we all know them as well (Fig. 7.39). And we all used them. Head styles vary from pan, to round, to button, to truss, to flat. Another part of the head is the provision for turning the screw. There are various styles for this as well: slotted, Phillips, Torx, and hex. The shank has a thread formed on the surface that either partially or fully covers the shaft, and also varies, depending on the individual screw and the material for which it is intended. Screws are identified using three numbers: the first is the diameter of the screw or bolt, the second number is the dimension between the threads, and the third is the overall length of the screw.

The tip can also vary. Tips that are pointed are tapping screws and their shaft tends to be tapered. These types of screws include wood screws, lag screws, sheet metal screws, drywall screws (probably the most popular in the theatre), and screw eyes. Tips that are flat require predrilling and usually have shafts that are not tapered. These types include bolts, hex bolts, machine screws, eyebolts, carriage bolts, and thumb screws.

Washers and Nuts

Screws work great by themselves. But bolts need a little extra help to stay put.! A washer is a thin disk with a hole in the

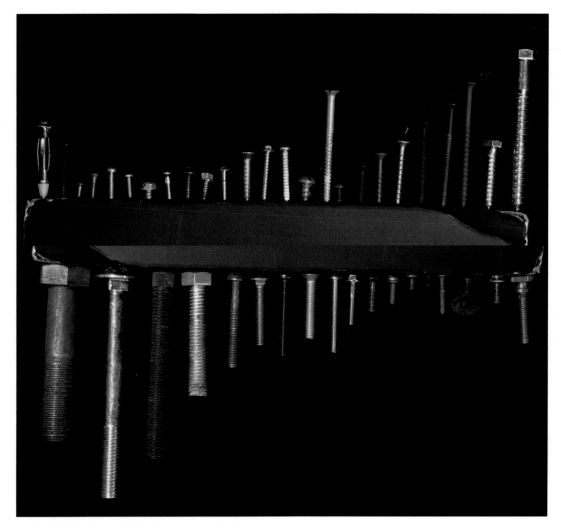

■ **Fig. 7.39** There are so many types of bolts it is amazing. They vary in length, width, screw thread, and head type.

middle (think donut) used as a spacer between the bolt and the nut. Nuts come in various outside shapes, but the insides are round, threaded, and sized to match the bolt with which they are used. The bolt is put into the material from one side, washers can be used at either or both sides, and the nut is put on the other side from the bolt. As the nut is tightened, the material and hardware compress into a tight fit.

As with everything else, there are a variety of washers and nuts depending on the job you are doing (Fig. 7.40). Washers can be plain, toothed, or cupped. Nut styles are hex nut, square nut, wind nut, cap nut, and T-nut. All work slightly differently, and it is important to know the different kinds. The actual use comes from learning from others and experience. Just keep your eyes and ears open, as it is easy information to pick up.

Staples

Staples—again we all use them to hold paper together. The same basic design works in the scene shop as well with some minor modifications. First, let's talk about the parts of the staple. We can break it down into the crown, the leg, and the teeth (Fig. 7.41).

Staples come in a wide range of sizes and are much easier to produce than nails, screws, or bolts. Since they don't go into the material as far, they are not structural. But they are good for attaching thinner materials like fabric. The sizes vary in both the crown and the leg dimensions (Fig. 7.42).

Adhesives

Several kinds of adhesives are used in theatre. Drying adhesives are glues that, as they dry, the solvent they are made

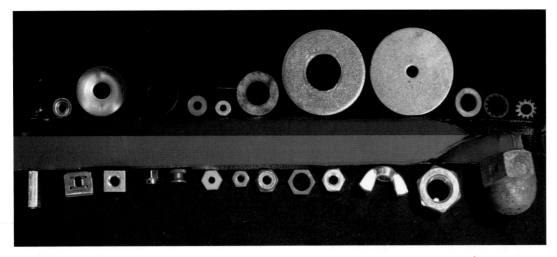

■ **Fig. 7.40** There are as many types of washers and nuts as there are bolts, maybe even more. Here is a small sampling.

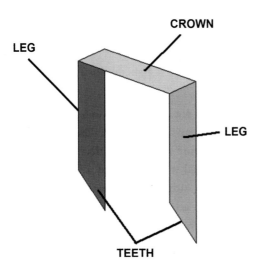

■ **Fig. 7.41** Each part of the staple has a name. The different dimensions for these parts determine which staple to use for a job.

with evaporates. These are white glue, wood glue, Gorilla® glue, and Sobo®. Another adhesive group is contact adhesives. This group is applied to both pieces of material and allowed to dry a bit before joining the two items. These are rubber cement and contact cement among others. Reactive adhesives are those where you mix two compounds together and they change each other to form an adhesive. Epoxy is an example of this. Let's talk about each one in a little detail.

White glue is your basic school glue (Fig. 7.43). You all used it. It works well, dries clear, and has a medium strength. Wood glue is very similar but much stronger. Sobo and Gorilla glues are both brand names. Sobo is white craft glue. It dries faster than regular white glue, can be frozen

and thawed repeatedly, and is water soluble. Gorilla glues are strong like wood glue; they are 100 percent waterproof and easy to sand or paint.

Rubber cement—we all used it in elementary school. Remember, it was fun to play with once it dried. You could roll over it with your finger and play with it? Yeah, that is the stuff! Well, it is a very good adhesive even if you don't play with it. Use the brush in the cap of the can, spread rubber cement on both pieces of material, and wait for it to dry a bit, then put the items together. Contact cement works in a similar way.

Epoxy is the last adhesive we discuss. Epoxy is a two-part adhesive. By mixing together equal quantities of each part, you create a chemical reaction that forms epoxy. The two parts individually are fairly inert. When combined they form a very strong adhesive.

Hinges

The next topic is hinges. The most common usage for a hinge that you have seen is most likely for a door. Hinges allow for something to pivot on a given point for a specific degree of rotation. Sound complicated? Not really. Let's talk about the different kinds of hinges, with examples, to make it easier to understand.

One of the most basic "options" with any hinge is the pin. Do you want the pin, or pivot point, to be fixed with the hinge or removable? There are reasons for each choice. Obviously, a fixed-pin hinge is very sturdy and strong as it is manufactured together. A loose-pin hinge does not

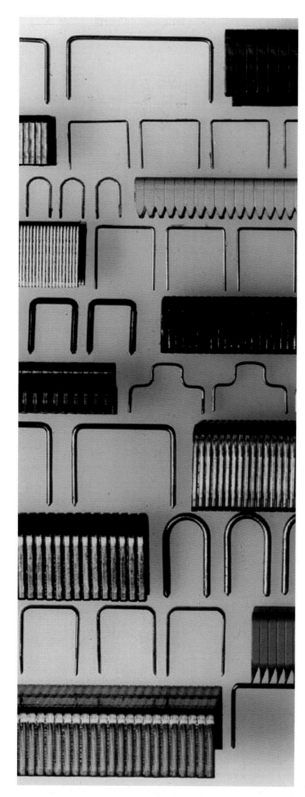

Fig. 7.42 Staples come in a variety of sizes and shapes depending on what type of stapler you will be using. Putting the wrong staples in the stapler will cause it to jam and cause a potentially dangerous situation.

make as rigid a pivot point. However, once each side of the hinge is attached to scenery, the loose pin can be removed and the one big item can become two smaller items. This is very handy for shipping, storage, and the general running of the show. Keep this concept in mind as we go on to the specific kinds and shapes of hinges.

Strap hinges are an older style of hinge (Fig. 7.44). They are most often used on large doors, like on a barn. When laid flat they look like two H triangles joined by a pivot. The design of these hinges makes them incredibly strong. T-hinges are similar to strap hinges. A T-hinge has one side shaped like a triangle while the other side is rectangular. Sort of makes it look like a T!

A back flap hinge is one of the most commonly used hinges in theatre. Each side of the hinge is roughly square and there are usually three holes in each side for screwing into. A broad butt hinge is slightly smaller than a back flap. A broad butt hinge is rectangular in shape, about half the size of a back flap, and usually has two screw holes.

Piano hinges are named for—well—pianos. Think of the top lid on a piano. It has a long, skinny, thin hinge with lots and lots of tiny screws. Well, that is a piano hinge. It is the perfect tool when you need a long uninterrupted length of hinge, either for the aesthetic of it or for the stability. Double-acting hinges can swing their door both in and out, which makes them very unique. Think of old Western movies. Remember the doors on the saloons? Now you have the image!

Casters

Our last topic in this chapter is casters. Yes, that is right, we've finally gotten to the end! A caster is a wheel within a mounting assembly and makes movement of heavy pieces of scenery much easier. So you're going grocery shopping, and you always seem to get the shopping cart that won't steer properly? Blame it on the caster!

There are a wide variety of types and styles of casters (Fig. 7.45). Let's address the two basic differences and the one thing you have to decide first when selecting a caster. Will your piece of scenery travel in a straight line? Or, does it need to turn a corner or move in different directions? If you need movement in only one direction, a fixed caster is for you. If you need multiple directions of movement, then choose the swivel caster. Swivel casters

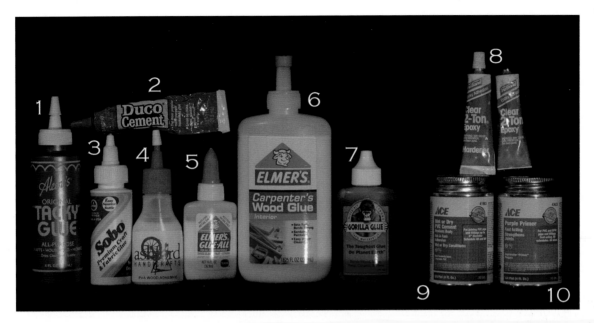

Fig. 7.43 (1) All-purpose tacky glue, (2) Duco® cement, (3) Sobo craft glue, (4) wood adhesive, (5) Elmer's glue, (6) Elmer's wood glue, (7) Gorilla glue, (8) two-part clear epoxy, (9) PVC cement, and (10) PVC primer.

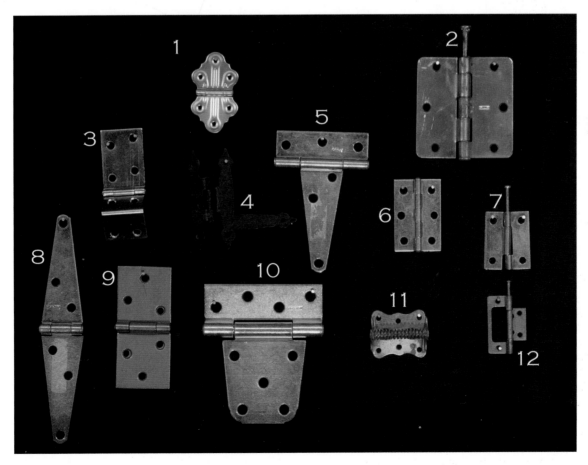

Fig. 7.44 (1) Cabinet hinge, (2) loose-pin broad butt hinge, (3) chest hinge, (4) decorative cabinet hinge, (5) T-hinge, (6) fixed-pin broad butt hinge, (7) small loose-pin broad butt hinge, (8) strap hinge, (9) back-flap hinge, (10) gate hinge, (11) spring hinge, and (12) nonmortised loose-pin hinge.

can rotate 360 degrees, but keep in mind, there is always a turning radius, or the amount of time and space the wheel needs to rotate.

The size of the mounting plate and the size of wheel are two of the determining factors when choosing a caster for a job. Another factor is the material the wheel is made from. Wheels can be made from metal, plastic, rubber, or wood.

The last factor that should be considered when choosing a caster is whether or not you need it to lock. When you combine these four factors, you can roll almost anything, almost anywhere. Overall weight and sound are major factors with these choices. As with any hardware, know your application and choose what will work best, within your budget, of course.

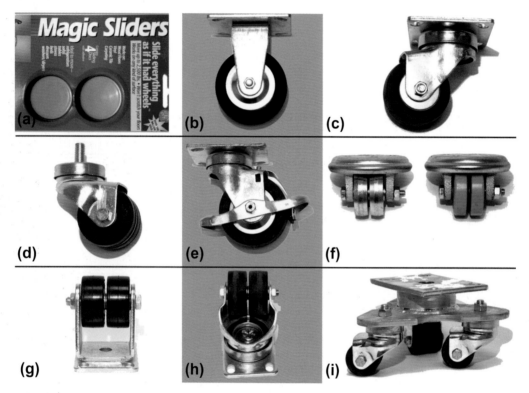

■ **Fig. 7.45** (a) Furniture slides, (b) rigid caster, (c) swivel caster, (d) swivel caster with screw mount, (e) swivel caster with brake, (f) heavy-duty low-level casters, (g) low-profile double-fixed caster, (h) low-profile double-swivel caster, and (i) tri-way swivel turtle.

Adjustable wrench
Allen keys
Arc welding
Ball peen hammer
Band saw
Bar clamp
Bevel gauge
Box wrench
Brazing
Carpenter or carriage
    clamp
Carpenter pencil
Center punch
Chalk line
Chisel
Chop saw
Circular saw
Claw hammer
Combination square
Coping saw
Crosscut blade
Drill
Drill press
Fence
File
Flush cut saw
Folding rule
Framing hammer
Framing square
Grinder
Hammer drill
Hand-screw clamp
Hole saw
Hot-glue gun
Jig
Jigsaw
Keyhole saw
Laser level
Laser measure
Linesman's pliers
Mallet
MIG
Miter box
Miter saw

Nail set
Needle-nose pliers
Nut driver
Open-ended wrench
Oxyacetylene
Panel saw
Phillips screws
Pipe cutter
Pipe reamer
Pipe threader
Pipe wrench
Plane
Plumb bob
Pneumatic
Pry bar
Radial-arm saw
Rasp
Reciprocating saw
Rip blade
Router
Scroll saw
Slip-Joint pliers
Slotted screw
Socket set
Soldering
Spade bit
Speed square
Speed wrench
Spirit level
Spring clamp
Stapler
String level
Table saw
Tack hammer
Tape measure
TIG
Tin snips
Torx
Twist bit
Utility knife
Vise grips
Vises
Wet/dry vacuum
Yankee screwdriver

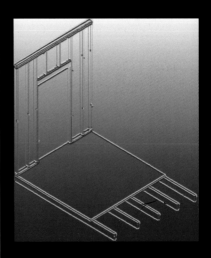

CHAPTER SEVEN
Study Words

Macbeth

By:
Francis Bacon

How to Get It Done

Scenery Standard Techniques and Practices

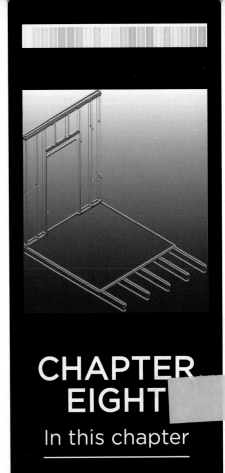

This chapter is all about scenery. Yes, finally we're going to talk about scenery. Did you think that scenery was going to be Chapter 1? Well, you have to lay the groundwork before jumping in. As we get into the "down and dirty" of implementing scenic ideas you'll see how the first seven chapters have given you a background you didn't think you'd need but is now going to come in very handy. This chapter gives you a background in the traditional scenic techniques as well as how they developed over time. As always, we are honoring the theatre's past before moving into the future. And, keep in mind that, when the budget is tight, you will need this information to come up with a well-rounded solution to whatever "challenges" might arise. Once we get the basics in hand, we discuss some of the new technologies available today.

SCENIC TECHNIQUES DEVELOP THROUGH HISTORY

We continue our discussion from Chapter 1 (remember Chapter 1?) about history and catch up to when scenery started to really take off and come into its own. Playwrights and audiences always wanted more, and the theatre rose to the challenge. We discussed in Chapter 1 the use of the backdrop as it developed during the Greek genre. The Greeks also started to develop a back wall that contained doors for entrances and exits. The next set of scenic developments needed to wait until theatre was indoors or at least partially covered from changes in the weather.

This brings us to developments that happened primarily between the 16th and 19th centuries. This time in theatre saw many developments to scenery. To create more of an illusion, the idea of the backdrop was expanded and continued further downstage. Each of the **wings** now had a **leg** on either side that was painted to continue the design of the backdrop. Overhead, to simulate the heavens, painted **borders** were added to complete the visual effect. The wings and borders also became known as **masking**, which had the added benefit that they blocked the backstage area from the audience's view. This style of scenery came to be known as the **wing and drop**, a term still used today.

Another element that had been used in the past but came into much popularity was the periaktoi. **Periaktoi** are triangular columns that revolve to reveal other sides and sets. Multiple periaktoi are usually used in each wing or across the upstage side of the stage, replacing the backdrop. Picture a backdrop cut vertically into five pieces. Each piece is then put onto one side of one periaktos. A piece of another backdrop is put on the second side, and a piece of a third backdrop is put on the third side. The five periaktoi line up across the upstage wall and they create a backdrop. They all rotate so another side faces the audience, and like magic, the backdrop has changed. This can be used for wings to create an extra sense of depth. It doesn't have to be used just for the backdrop. The rotation of the periaktoi was done originally with stagehands pulling on ropes. Later, it was automated with the use of the early winches.

Primitive flying effects had existed since the Greek genre came up with the idea of **deux ex machina**. They were only slightly more advanced here. Flying could indeed happen inside, which is an advance in and of itself. The designers were still concerned with masking the machinery and used 2D clouds to mask the machinery as it was raised and lowered. This technology often required a vertical track to be secured to a piece of scenery or the actual building. A horizontal beam or platform was then attached to the track. A scenic cloud was attached to the downstage side of the mechanism, so that it moved with the platform, as if to hide it. Of course, the track was in full view above and below the platform, and nobody seemed to mind that!

The next advance used was the predecessor to our current tracking decks. During the 17th century, banks of trolleys were installed under the stage to facilitate scenery moving within a predictable path. *Predictable* is the key here; the scenery had to go from point A to point B, moving along the same path, every time. These trolleys connected to scenery, usually the hard legs, through a series of ropes. Using a sandbag for a counterweight, a central shaft was rotated, pulling the ropes and moving the trolleys. Suddenly, the two legs had changed positions in the wing and the scene change was complete.

These trolleys evolved into what we know today as a **traveler** track. Just like a curtain track in your house, only bigger and sturdier, the traveler can hold a very heavy curtain and allow it to move. This usually happens in front of the audience's view, with the curtain splitting at center or moving from one side of the stage to the other.

Another addition to the scenic inventory at this point is the trap. A **trap** is a hole in the floor with a replaceable plug. When the plug is in place, the floor looks complete, and it is usually hard to detect where the plug may be. With the plug removed, you have direct access to below the stage floor. This idea can work great for surprise entrances or exits. Depending on the amount of room below the stage, ladders, scaffolding, and elevators were all used to convey actors and scenery up and down. The elevators were primitive, using traditional counterweighted sandbags. But, hey, it worked!

The 18th century brought with it a variety of ways to change the set. We are still dealing primarily with wing and drop changes. The wing change techniques advanced from the 17th-century device to eliminate the counterweight and add a winch—a primitive winch with a crank handle but a winch! The borders and backdrops were now rolled around a tube that allowed them to be brought up and down. This combination of technologies allowed the whole set to be changed quickly, and apparently by magic.

The use of traps was also expanded during this time. Traps became much more popular, with many being built into an individual stage, instead of the original one, two, or three. There were now several ways to open a trap. The trap could be hinged, either up or down. There were sliding traps that were not as obvious to the audience. The trap opened by sliding the cover to the side and basically was stored inside the stage floor.

Useless Factoid: Evil Curtains

Even the drop curtain contributes its share of stage superstitions, as nearly every actor and manager believes it is bad luck to look out at the audience from the wrong side of it when it is down. Some say it is the prompt side that casts the evil spell, while others contend it is the opposite side. The management, not being sure from which side the bad luck is likely to accrue, places a peephole directly in the center.

Toward the end of the 19th century, the audience started to want more realism. This led to the elimination of the wing and drop sets. What developed is called the box set. A **box set** usually contained three walls and perhaps a ceiling. It was, and still is, used to represent interiors. Striving for realism led to other changes in scene design as well.

The raked stage was done away with in favor of a level stage floor. To ease the floor into the backdrop, a **scenic ground row** was added to the design. This ground row was two-dimensional and usually had a cutout design on the top to help the transition to the drop. Flying was curtailed, as this didn't fit in with the new "realism" mandate.

It was alright to put scenery on casters; this was not considered supernatural. So rolling platforms and revolving stages became very popular. The revolving stage allowed for another kind of set change. You could set up three box sets on the stage, with their backs all touching. Then revolve the stage from one to the next to the next—a complete set change in mere seconds. This had never been seen before and became the newest kind of theatre magic!

The box set brought about an interesting development in the acting style of the day, which in turn influenced future design as well. The **fourth wall** became a convention of acting within a box set, where you create an imaginary wall to complete the room. There is no recognition that the audience is in attendance. As a result, the act curtain began being used to close off the stage from the audience prior to the show. This created an atmosphere of catching the action in progress, making the audience a nonparticipating observer.

As theatre buildings became more technically able, variations in the normal way things are done started to pop up in standard use. One example of this is the tab curtain. Picture a normal masking leg in the wings. Now, take that leg and turn it 90 degrees so it hangs upstage to downstage. This, called a **tab**, is used to mask the wings from the audience. Many other variations are created as needed. Don't feel the need to be locked in by what you see in this book or any other!

SCENIC DESIGN PROCESS

Now that we have this perspective on a bit more of scenery history, let's talk about the scenic design process a little more in depth. We discussed, in Chapter 2, the phone call, meetings, research, and sketching. Part of this process is for the designer to complete color renderings or models. Keep in mind that, depending on the situation, time frame, and complexity of the design, parts of the process may be expanded or cut completely.

At some point, the director, producer, or someone who controls the aesthetics or money will approve the design. This is the point when the designer and however many assistants are hired get to work on the pack of drawings. Let's break down the pack of drawings, as this will be essential to ultimately getting the show built. A pack of draftings consists of the following, as appropriate, since productions vary so much:

- Cover sheet with index of drawings.
- Sketch or model photos.
- Ground plan.
- Section.
- Deck plan.
- Elevations.
- Details.

Each of these drawings, or groups of drawings, can be expanded as needed by the design. If there is a complicated deck with a lot of automation, there may be several drawings of the deck alone. It is for the designer to decide what drawings are needed to communicate with the scene shop.

What we have been talking about are designer drawings. Let me explain.

Designer drawings are drawn, as you would expect, by the designer. They are meant to convey the artistic vision of the designer. They are critical to informing the shop what the designer's ideas and goals are. The shop must look at these drawings to determine a price and, more important, to begin building the set. Often a scene shop will not get a full pack of drawings. Sometimes, they get a list of the units that make up the set; sometimes, they get a partial pack of draftings; sometimes, they get a model and only a model (Figs. 8.1–8.3). Obviously, the more information they have the better chance they have to properly evaluate the design.

Let's talk about models for a second. A scenic model is a 3D miniature version of the completed set design. The model is in scale, usually ¼ or ½ inch, depending on the size of the theatre. Making the model this small allows for easier portability to meetings. Some designers prefer to work in three dimensions instead of two. If the design is more sculptural than painterly, it can often give the director

a better sense of the finished design. Remember, in Chapter 5, I talked about semantics and the need to put ideas into a visual form so that everyone could understand it better and more accurately? Well, the bottom line is that any tool at your disposal can be used to convey ideas. Quick pencil sketches on a napkin are as valid as a sketch, rendering, or model. The only mandate is that visual ideas are conveyed in a nonverbal way.

> Just because you can, doesn't mean you should!
>
> **—Anonymous**

Before any building can be done, the shop must evaluate the designer drawings and determine the best way to interpret the drawings and translate them into wood, metal, paint, and whatever other materials are called for. Before the shop workers can begin to build the set, they must first create their own set of drawings. These are known as **construction drawings** (Figs. 8.4–8.6). Construction

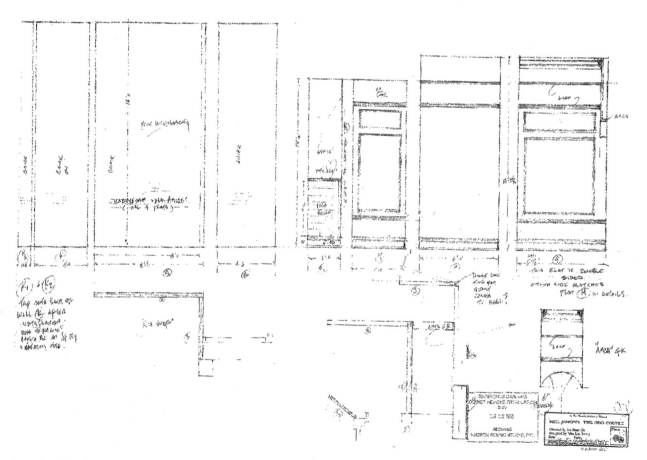

■ **Fig. 8.1** John Lee Beatty's backing wall drafting for Neil Simon's *The Odd Couple*.

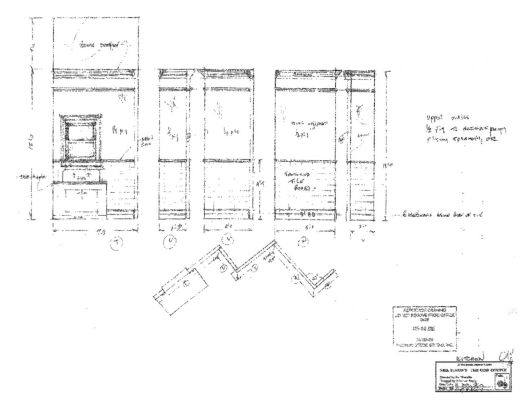

Fig. 8.2 John Lee Beatty's drafting for the kitchen walls of Neil Simon's *The Odd Couple*.

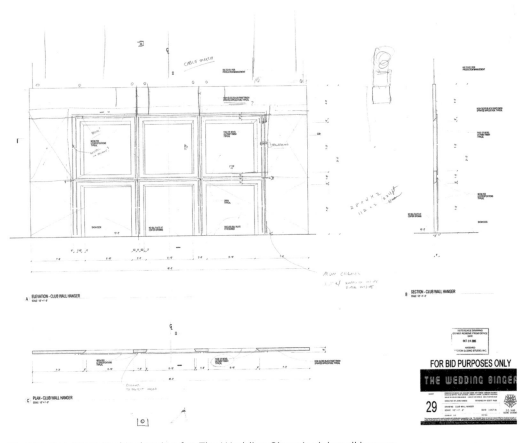

Fig. 8.3 Scott Pask's drawing for *The Wedding Singer*'s club wall hanger.

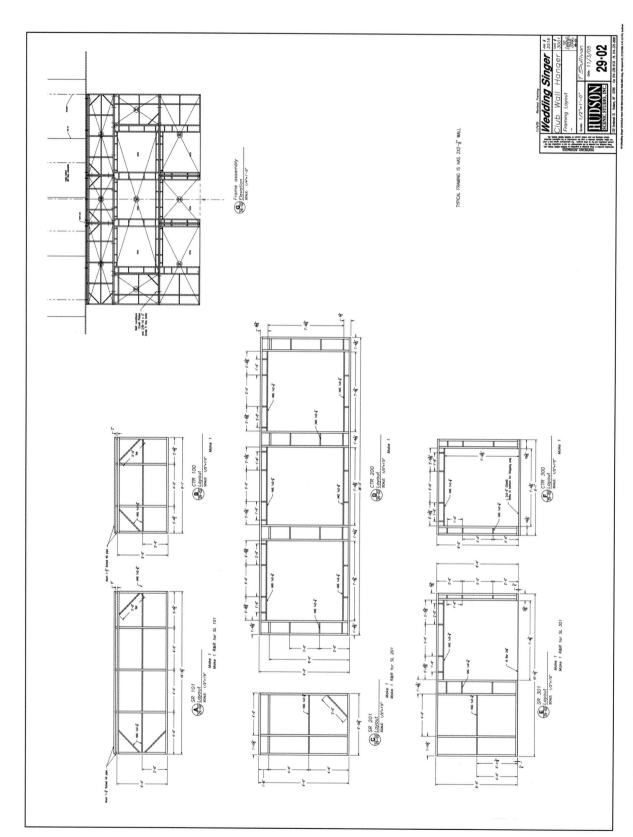

Fig. 8.4 Hudson Scenic's shop drawing for *The Wedding Singer*'s club wall hanger.

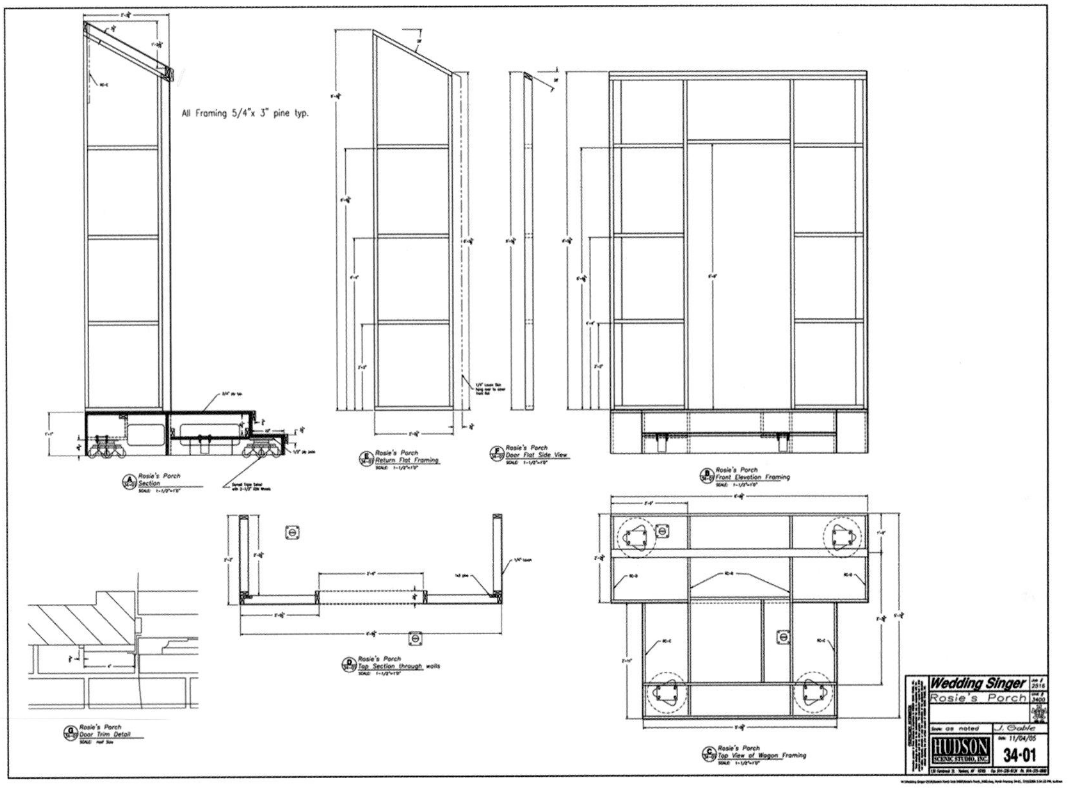

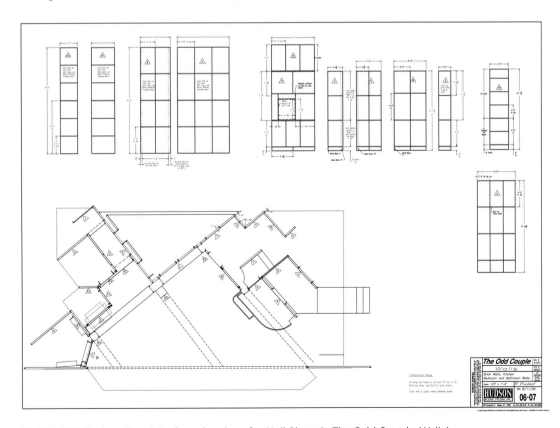

Fig. 8.5 Hudson Scenic's shop drawings for *The Wedding Singer*'s Rosie's porch framing.

Fig. 8.6 Hudson Scenic's shop drawings for Neil Simon's *The Odd Couple*, Wall A.

drawings differ from designer drawings in that they are much more technical. For example, a designer drawing of a deck may show the outside shape and dimensions and materials choices. The construction drawing breaks the deck into manageable pieces to be built separately and put together during the load-in. This is a critical phase, as pieces of scenery need to fit out the door of the shop, into a truck, and in the door at the theatre. These doors are all different sizes. Materials then are identified and lists made of what is required for each piece.

A professional scene shop can vary greatly in its organization from a college scene shop. Professional shops usually have more people and are broken up into smaller departments. Let's look at Hudson Scenic Studio, Inc., for a moment, as they were kind enough to give me access to their shop during my research for this book. I am grateful to everyone there for their willingness to share their time, energy, and craft with me.

Hudson is one of the largest full-service production and scenic fabrication companies serving the professional entertainment community. The company prides itself on providing support from preproduction planning and budgeting to installation with in-house engineering, fabrication, scenic art, and automation departments performing all the related services needed to make any project a success. Its clients include producers of theatre, touring productions, television, casino, themed environments, corporate presentations, live advertising, commercials, theme parks, industrial theatre, theme restaurants, and various special projects that involve many types of specialty construction.

Services that Hudson Scenic Studio, Inc., can provide include

- Production design planning and budgeting.
- Project management.
- Technical supervision and installation.
- Design engineering services.
- Custom scenic fabrication: Carpentry and stage craft.
- Metal fabrication.
- Scenic and backdrop painting.
- Sculpting.
- Automation, motion control, and mechanization.
- CNC router design and fabrication.

- Set electrics.
- Soft goods and traveler track systems.
- Rigging system design and installation.

The process at Hudson can be broken up into very clear steps. The first step is of course to get the job. A designer presents documentation, as we discussed earlier. Hudson assigns a project manager, who will evaluate the design and begin assigning dollar amounts to the different parts of the scenery. A proposal is put together for the client, showing a total price to execute the design. This may be approved right away, or more likely, there may be alterations or cuts to the design to fit within budget. Eventually, everyone will agree and the proposal turns into an actual job!

The project manager then creates a job order; this is internal paperwork for use at the scene shop, so that all those working on the job have a frame of reference for the entire job, not just the piece they are working on. A **kick-off meeting** is scheduled. This is one of the most important parts of the process. From the production team, the designer and the technical supervisor are present at this meeting. The technical supervisor is responsible for everything technical on the production. This includes scenery, lighting, rigging, etc. This person is with the show from the first meetings through opening night.

Hudson will now assign an internal production manager to the project. This person will create a flowchart for all departments to use, which includes assignments of different units as well as a timeline from the very first day through trucking the scenery to the theatre (Fig. 8.7). These flowcharts are updated continuously, as schedules may need to shift within the shop. Details that go into the flowchart are which departments are needed for any given unit, when the department is available to work on the unit, and when materials are arriving. Also of importance are the scenic pieces that need more than one department's attention. If this is the case, scheduling may be even tighter. Materials have to be ordered and the crew has to be hired. The goal, obviously, is to have the materials arrive before the crew!

Let's talk about the departments within a scene shop. Now, remember, in smaller shops, jobs can get combined. This doesn't mean that the task goes away, it just means that one person is doing lots more work! At its most spread out and organized the departments of the scene shop are broken down into eight categories: engineering, carpentry,

The Drowsy Chaperone
10/5/05
Job #2502-Prepared by Mark O'Brien - Ver. 1

Unit #	Unit	Draft	Drafting Complete	Router Start	Router End	Metal Start	Metal End	Carpentry Start	Carpentry End	Automation Start	Automation End	Electrics Start	Electrics End	Paint Start	Paint End	Tech Start	Tech End	Load-out	Load-in	Notes
	Scenery																			
0300	Show Deck	RB	10/4			10/3	10/12	10/3	10/13					10/14	10/18			Wed 10/19	Sun 10/23	Sanding deck 10/13am
0400	Show Portal	JG	10/5					10/6	10/15					10/17	10/20	10/14	10/15	Fri 10/21		
0500	DS Plaster Arch	JG	10/5					10/6	10/15			10/14	1/2 day	10/17	10/20	10/14	10/15	Fri 10/21		
0600	US Plaster Arch	JG	10/6					10/6	10/15			10/14	1/2 day	10/17	10/20	10/14	10/15	Fri 10/21		Add jacks for door. Purchase drop box fabric and paint
0700	Apartment Walls		10/3			10/4	10/7	10/4	10/12					10/14	10/18	10/12	10/12	Thu 10/20		
0700	US Apartment Walls	JG	9/29			10/3	10/7	10/3	10/11					10/14	10/18	10/12	10/12	Thu 10/20		
0700	US Apartment Fiber Optics	DSR										10/19	10/20					Thu 10/20		
1000	SR and SL Windows	JG	10/7					10/12	10/17					10/18	10/21			Sat 10/22		
1200	Bridal Suite	CL	10/5	10/3	10/5			10/5	10/14			1 day		10/17	10/21			Sat 10/22		
1250	Flying Mirrors (2)	CL/JG	10/6	10/5	10/6			10/11	10/14			1/2 day		10/19	10/21			Sat 10/22		Flex Moulding due by 10/13
1600	French Doors	CL	10/3	10/3	10/5			10/3	10/12					10/17	10/20			Sat 10/22		
1700	Globe																	Sat 10/22		By Scenic Arts Studios and Costume Armour
1800	Swag Hanger with Chandelier																	Fri 10/21		Need to make paint sample
1900	Stairs (2)	RB	10/6			10/6	10/18	10/8	10/15					10/20	10/26			Wed 10/26		
2000	Murphy Bed Frame and Flats	DK	10/6			10/6												Wed 10/26		
2100	Beds (3)	DK	10/10															Wed 10/26		Beds go out to be upholstered
2200	Airplane	AG												10/17	10/25	10/22	10/24	Thu 10/20		
2300	Palace Portal Drop	TS				10/17	10/18							10/11				Thu 10/20		Need rendering
2400	Palace Backing Drop	TS				10/17	10/18											Thu 10/20		
2500	Vaudeville Drop	TS				10/17	10/18											TBD		
2600	Country Drop	TS																TBD		By Scenic Art Studios
2700	Fountain/Sunset Drop	TS				10/17	10/18					1 day						Thu 10/20		By Scenic Art Studios - Piece will drop ship from fiber optic vendor
2800	Cityscape Drop	TS				10/17	10/18							10/11				Fri 10/21		
2900	Palettes	RB	10/13															Fri 10/14		
3000	US Masking Portal	TS				9/30												Fri 10/14		
3100	Black Serge Masking	TS						10/3	10/11									Fri 10/14		
3400	Ballet Drop	TS				10/17	10/18	10/3	10/12									Fri 10/14		
3500	Bounce Drop	TS				10/17	10/18											Fri 10/14		
3800	Serge Window Inserts w/fiber																	Wed 10/26		
1300	Garden units SR and SL																	Fri 10/21		By Scenic Art Studios
1400	Foliage Hanger	RB	10/11									1-1/2 days						Wed 10/26		By Scenic Art Studios
1500	Finale Trees									10/5	10/13							Wed 10/26		Hudson builds the wagons and tree frame. Scenic Art studios provides the foliage
	Automation																			
	Rigging package	AG																Fri 10/14		
	Deck Track 1	AG																Wed 10/19		
	Deck Track 2	AG																Wed 10/19		
	Deck Track 3 - Tandem Split Ctr	AG																Wed 10/19		
	Deck Track 4 - Tandem Split Ctr	AG																Wed 10/19		
	Main Trap Lift	AG						10/3	10/11									Fri 10/14		
	DS Flying Walls	AG						10/3	10/12									Fri 10/14		
	US Flying Walls	AG																Fri 10/14		
	Airplane Fly Winch	AG								10/5	10/13							Wed 10/26		
	Airplane Propeller	AG																Wed 10/19		
	Fountain Sunset Fly Winch	AG																Fri 10/14		
	Murphy Bed Manual Rigging	AG																Fri 10/14		
	Automation control package	AG																Wed 10/19		

Fig. 8.7 Hudson Scenic's production flowchart for *The Drowsy Chaperone*.

iron, automation, electrics, rentals, scenic artists, and trucking. There are plenty of blurry lines between the different departments based on the fact that it is rare for a piece of scenery to be fully fabricated within one department. Let's go through the departments, one by one, to see what each does.

Engineering is the first department to begin work on a job. Let me interrupt by saying that there used to be a position called the *layout man*. This person would look at the drafting and sketch out the design in full scale on the actual wood to be used. Then, he or she would cut out the wood. It was that easy. This way of working has changed, and the position has evolved into that of an engineer. The engineer drafts the construction drawings and much, much more! The engineer drafts any automation and plans out the control for it. This often entails a custom control system, where software programming is required. The engineer also develops and plans the set electrics. Research of new products is another function of the engineering department.

The carpentry shop is filled with—carpenters. What a surprise! They deal with everything made of wood—measuring, layout, cutting, fabrication, everything. A fairly new addition to the shop is a CNC router. This is a very cool piece of machinery. It is a router, which we talk about later in the chapter. Basically, routers cut using different size and shape bits. Molding can be created with a router. Got the idea? Well, this router is huge and computer driven. So, basically, the carpenters make a CAD file, load it into the router, and the cutting begins. The best part is that the level of accuracy is amazing.

The iron department is the same as the carpentry department, only instead of using wood it uses metal. Steel and aluminum are two metals used in the shop. Welding becomes an important skill, and there are major differences between welding these two metals. Measuring, lay out, cutting, and fabrication are all dealt with. Today's designs seem to call for more metal and less wood. This has to do with the current aesthetic as well as the structural needs for these designs.

The automation department is next in line. Automation deals with anything that moves. That may sound simple, but in today's theatre, it is anything but! The deck is not the only part of the set that may contain automation. There may very likely be flying elements. Any of these ideas may require automation. And, here is the key: All of the automation today is customized. There is no such thing as a standard deck with standardized automation. Often pieces and parts need to be fabricated for a specific situation. A full machine shop can be a handy thing for just this reason. This is what the automation department specializes in.

THE ROAD TO VALHALLA
Das Rheingold commences the Metropolitan Opera's stunning new Ring Cycle

David Barbour

Excerpt 1

The opera world loves a controversial new production, and this season the Metropolitan Opera has given it a real beauty in Das Rheingold, the opener in its new staging of Wagner's Ring Cycle. All the elements were in place for a potential scandal: An internationally famous director, an ambitious set design that tested the limits of the venue, interactive projections, and a staging that makes use of acrobatic feats and body doubles. Oh, and a budget that reportedly reached $16 million dollars.

Usually, the pre-opening publicity for a new Met Opera production focuses first on the stars, secondly on the director, and, if there is any time or interest left, on the production. In the case of the Ring Cycle, the design concept became a major talking point months before the curtain rose on Das Rheingold. The New York Times sent a reporter to cover the load-in. The New York Post offered a detailed guide to the set and how it functions. As the premiere approached, the level of chatter became deafening. Many questions lingered: In this economy, could the Met afford it? Would the design overwhelm the opera? Would the set function as required? And how would the worldwide audience of Wagner fans—an eccentric lot not known for being shy about their opinions—react?

The answers are not yet final—there is no way to judge the whole cycle until all four operas have been staged—but the early signs are promising. Das Rheingold opened to raves for the cast and James Levine's handling of the score. The production garnered a broad range of opinions, most of them ranging from respectful to favorable. At the very least, everyone seems to agree that it is a fascinating combination of complex technology and aesthetic simplicity, a design that, above all, means to serve Wagner's sprawling epic drama of gods and humans locked in a struggle over a magic ring—a struggle that will mark the end of one world and the beginning of another.

Source: Originally published in *Lighting and Sound America*, January 2011.

Next is the electrical department. All set electrics are wired at the scene shop. That means anything that lights up and is built into the set is dealt with in the scene shop. This doesn't include the simple table lamp. The props department handles that, which often ends up as a subdepartment. If a piece of scenery lights from within, lighting fixtures are built into it, then the electrical department is responsible for all the wiring to make it work. If a unit requires dimmers or ballasts (more on both of those in Chapter 11) to travel with the scenery, this is also handled here. Now, here is something you might not have thought of: If the automation department needs to control a piece of scenery or put a control unit into a piece of scenery, it's going to need power. You guessed it! The electrical department handles that as well.

Here is the interesting twist: the rental department. It's a scene shop, why do they have a rental inventory? Hudson rents some soft goods (legs, borders, curtains) as well as personnel lifts and some lighting equipment. In addition to straight rentals, the shop also rents some of the automation to shows it is constructing. Shows basically have two options: They can buy all the equipment for the automation design or they can rent certain portions of the equipment that may be more expensive to purchase. Shows can rent the automation equipment whether or not their scenery is being built at Hudson.

Next, we move on to the scenic artists. Scenic artists paint, right? Well, they do paint and so much more. Scenic artists begin by sketching on paper what they will draw. It is then transferred to the actual scenic element before they begin to texture, sculpt, and paint. They create a sample for certain techniques to show the designer before completing the real piece.

The last department is trucking. You may think that this shouldn't be listed as a department. Well, without trucking, the audience would have to come to the scene shop! So, yes, trucking is important. The trucking department loads the trucks and drives them to the theatre. This department is also utilized during the overnight shifts to help move large units into a position where they can be worked on.

THE ROAD TO VALHALLA
Das Rheingold commences the Metropolitan Opera's stunning new Ring Cycle

David Barbour

Excerpt 2

According to Robert Lepage, who is staging the operas at the Met, "The Ring is a revolutionary work of art. You're not the same person once you've done it." By the time Wagner's cycle has been completed, one has the feeling that the Metropolitan Opera may never be the same.

The Valhalla Machine

The lion's share of attention has been focused on Carl Fillion's set, or what the Times, in its feature story, called "The Valhalla machine." Interestingly, it is meant to serve all four operas. If that seems like an unworkable idea, rest assured that this is no ordinary set. As described by Daniel J. Wakin in the Times, it "consists of two 26'-tall towers holding an axis, which can move up and down driven by hydraulics. Twenty-four planks, actually in the rough form of severely elongated triangles, are attached to the axis at their thickest point, like seesaws. When at rest, they create a platform that fills out most of the stage. But the planks can revolve around the axis together or independently, producing myriad shapes, and they serve as both stage architecture and a canvas for projections. The planks, driven by an old-fashioned spindle system, ripple like water or form giant hands for Fasolt and Fafner [the giants] to stand on.

Source: Originally published in *Lighting and Sound America*, January 2011.

BUILDING TECHNIQUES

This section is all about the building techniques currently in use today for the standard scenic elements. What do I mean by *standard*? Well, there are so many variations in today's designs that the best we can do is to learn the basic pieces. Once we have those established, you can combine them, or abstract from them, to create the specific design you need to accomplish. The three basic divisions are floors, walls, and ceilings. Sounds simple, right? Well, here goes!

The disclaimer: I am not an engineer; I am a designer. I draw pictures and then give those drawings to someone with specific training in rigging and engineering. The techniques I describe here are the "standard" practices in use today. Just remember, always, always consult a technical director to confirm all projects!

Scenic floors have a wide range in today's theatre productions. The simplest design is to use the actual floor of the theatre as it exists. The next step up is to paint that floor with a design appropriate to the show. This kind of painting is dealt with in Chapter 9. Anything beyond these two examples requires building platforms, ramps, and stairs or possibly complete decks. Let's take a look at these one at a time.

> Sometimes it's hard to get back to building a basic platform out of wood. No need to always have a full deck made out of steel with automation.
>
> **—Carrie Silverstein**

Platforms are a mainstay in design. They've been around for a long time, and there always will be a use for them. **Platforms** are small sections of flooring that add height to the existing stage. A standard size for a platform is based on the sizes of sheet lumber. So think of a 4 × 8" platform

as a stock size. A stock size is one that can be used many times in different shows (Fig. 8.8). It is good to build up an inventory of stock size platforms to be available for quick build schedules.

The framing lumber used for a platform is determined by the overall size of the platform as well as how it will be used. Common choices are 1 × 6 or 2 × 4 dimensional lumber. Always check with the technical director to confirm what type of lumber should be used. Once you have cut the lumber to the proper sizes, the frame is glued and either screwed or nailed together (Fig. 8.9). The difference between screwing and nailing has to do with overall strength. Gluing can be eliminated, if you have plans to take the platform apart and save the lumber after your show. Make sure to keep it square as you go, using a framing square! A plywood top, usually ¾ inch, is then glued and screwed or nailed to the frame. Ramps are framed out the same way; the difference is when you attach legs (Fig. 8.10).

Legs for platforms and ramps have a couple of different styles. Older-style legs are made from 2 × 4s. Newer styles use 2 × 4 or 2 × 6 lumber, two pieces making a right angle. This is a very strong configuration. Legs are either screwed, nailed, or bolted onto the platforms. They are usually not glued, since the legs can then be removed to make storage easier.

Stairs are more complicated (Fig. 8.11). The first thing that has to be determined is the rise, tread, and overall length of the stairs (Fig. 8.12). Then stringers, or the side supports, must be cut out of wood. The easier solution is to buy a precut stringer from the hardware store. If that isn't an option for whatever reason, the usual stringer is cut from 2 × 12s. You need one stringer for each side. If the width of the stairs is wider than usual or needs to support very heavy weights, you should also consider adding center stringers.

The next step is to cut the treads and risers, if they are also a part of the design, to the correct length. Lumber for these are often 1 × whatever size is appropriate for the

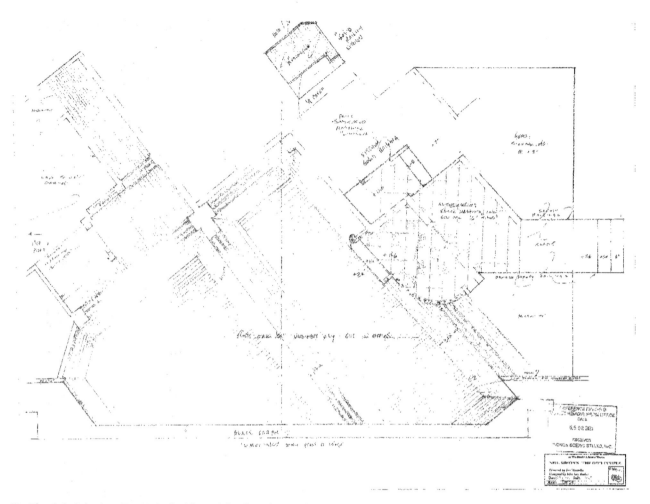

Fig. 8.8 John Lee Beatty's drafting of the floor layout for Neil Simon's *The Odd Couple*.

design. Assembly is relatively simple. The treads and risers are glued and screwed or nailed onto the stringers. The tricky part is that you can't lay the stairs flat until you are done, so extra hands are a must!

I mentioned a complete deck. Let's talk about that for a moment. Think of the **deck** as a complete replacement for the existing stage floor. The stage is completely covered by a series of platforms that interlock to form a new surface. Built within the deck is often machinery for moving large scenic elements, electrics as required, and any other elements that contribute to the overall design, which we want to hide from the audience's view (Fig. 8.13).

Walls, doors, **arches**, and windows form our next discussion. As always, there are huge variables based on the style and design. Let's address the simple ideas with the knowledge that you can add things like molding and decorative items as required.

Look around the room you are sitting in. Really look. What do you see? Start to break it down into smaller elements, as if you had to build a duplicate copy. Walls are vertical surfaces that usually start at the floor and go up to the ceiling, or at least the perceived ceiling. In the theatre, walls are divided up into manageable sizes. These wall pieces are called *flats*. The framing for flats is a bit different than for platforms (Fig. 8.14). And, to complicate things further, there are two different kinds of flats: soft flats and hard flats. We discuss the differences as we learn how to build them.

Soft flats, which are the traditional theatre type, have stiles and rails to form the outside frame (Fig. 8.15). **Rails** are on the top and bottom, and **stiles** are on the sides. This frame is traditionally made from 1 × 3 lumber. The rails and stiles are laid flat, edge to side. **Corner blocks**, which are triangular, and **keystones**, which are rectangular, are the

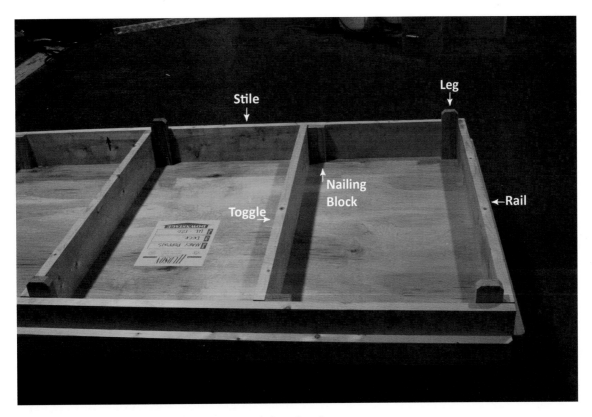

Fig. 8.9 A platform under construction at Hudson Scenic.

Fig. 8.10 A closeup of a platform leg under construction at Hudson Scenic.

next step. They are made of ¼" sheet lumber. Traditionally, the wood has been Lauan. This is a generic term for tropical wood that comes from Southeast Asia (see Chapter 7). These forests are now endangered, so more and more regular plywood is being used as a replacement.

Corner blocks and keystones are used to connect the rails and stiles. Use glue and screw or nail the frame together as shown in Figure 8.16. Make sure the wood grain of the corner block and keystones runs in the opposite direction

of the joint between the rails and styles. Also note the pattern for nailing, as it is very important to make a good tight bond while the glue dries.

The last step for a soft flat is to cover it. Use either lightweight or medium-weight muslin. Cut a piece that is approximately 2 feet larger than the frame, both in height and width. Lay down a drop cloth. Then, put the frame on the drop cloth with the corner blocks and keystones facing down. From here on, have all your supplies ready, as the next steps need to be accomplished very quickly. Brush glue onto the frame's styles and rails. Now, lay the muslin over the glued frame. Begin at the top or bottom and staple the muslin to the frame, starting in the center, while pulling gently to eliminate any fullness. Do the same on the other end. Then, work the two sides simultaneously.

You want the muslin to be tight, but not taut. Why? Because the next step will add even more tension to the fabric, and you don't want it to rip. Next, mix a small bucket of glue with water in a ratio of 1:5. Brush the glue/water mixture everywhere on the muslin. Make sure to use a figure-eight stroke to get the glue into all parts of the fabric's weave. The flat must now dry completely. And I mean, completely! Once the flat is dry, use a utility knife to cut off the excess muslin, using the rails and styles as guides.

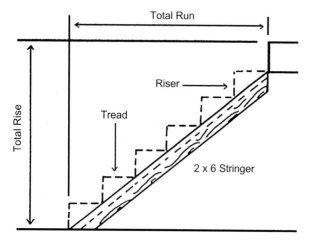

Fig. 8.11 Stair diagram showing all the different parts' names.

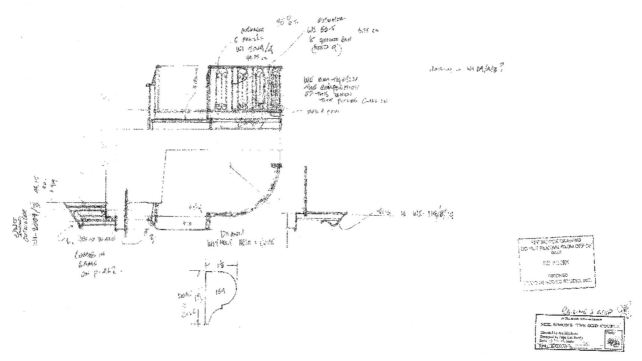

Fig. 8.12 John Lee Beatty's drawing of stair and railing details for Neil Simon's *The Odd Couple*.

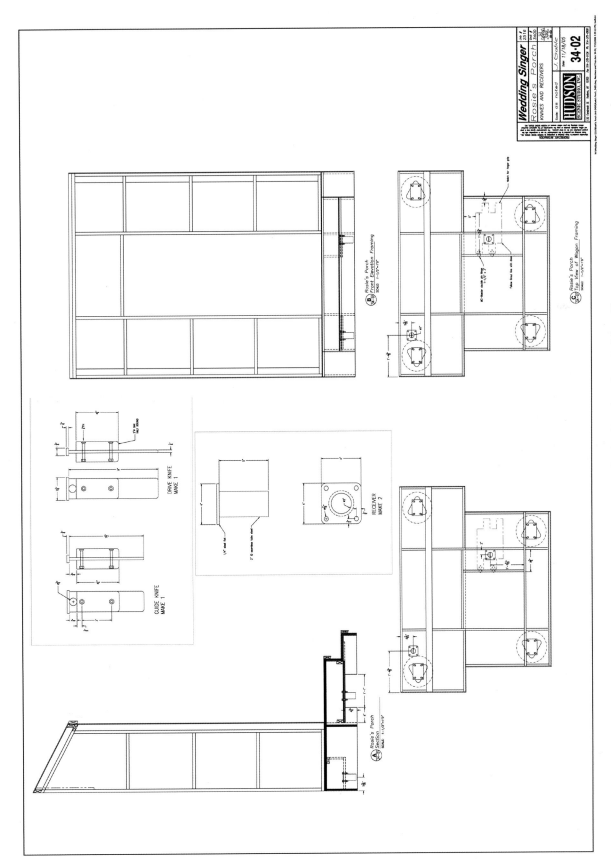

Fig. 8.13 Hudson Scenic's shop drawing of Rosie's porch receivers and trap door for *The Wedding Singer*.

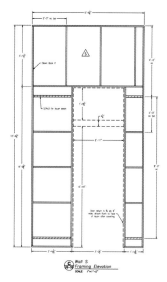

Hard flats, sometimes called *Hollywood flats*, are traditional in television but becoming more standard in theatre and have styles and rails just like a soft flat. This frame is traditionally made from 1 × 3 lumber, the difference being that the wood is laid on edge to assemble it. Corner blocks and keystones are not needed. Use glue and screw or nail the frame together as shown in Figure 8.17. Again, make sure to use the pattern for nailing, as it is very important to make a good tight bond while the glue dries.

The last step for a hard flat is to cover it. Use ¼" sheet lumber, trying to avoid the use of Lauan, as we discussed before. Glue the top of the frame before proceeding. Lay the sheet of wood on top of the frame, squaring the wood and frame to each other. Nail or staple the sheet to the frame. That is it. Your hard flat is done!

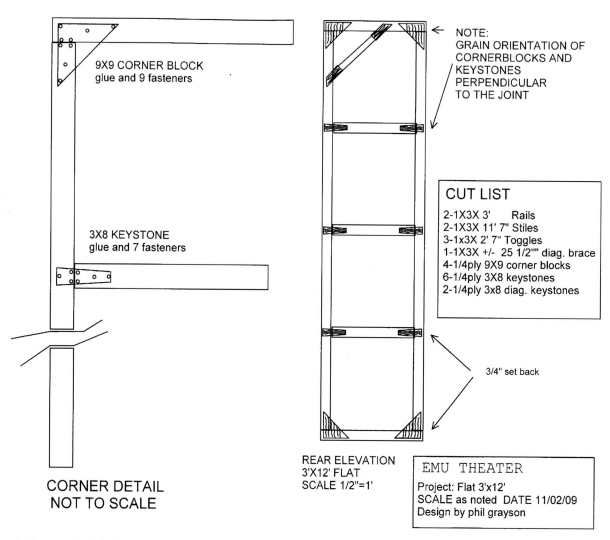

■ **Fig. 8.15** Detailed construction drawing for flats, thanks to Phil Grayson.

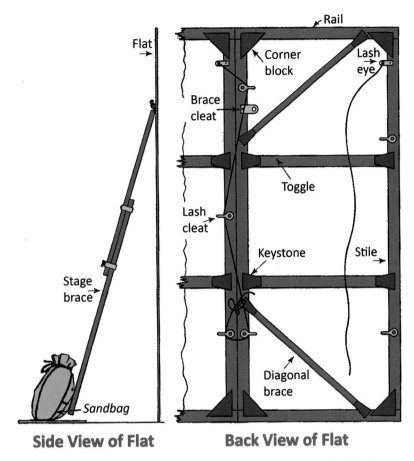

Labels on diagram:
Flat
Rail
Corner block
Lash eye
Brace cleat
Toggle
Lash cleat
Keystone
Stile
Stage brace
Diagonal brace
Sandbag

Side View of Flat   **Back View of Flat**

■ **Fig. 8.16** Soft flat diagram showing all the parts and names you need to know to build and use a soft flat.

There is a hybrid style of flat, where you frame as if you are making a soft flat but cover it as a hard flat (Fig. 8.18). This style can be used when space is at a premium or if the design simply requires this style.

Doors, arches, and windows are the next possibility to consider. Obviously, all of this is guided by the design and drawings. Now, here is the scoop. It's easy to put in an opening, as long as you have a good frame to start with. You need to add crosspieces with the outside frame to create the opening as required by the design. Use the same type of lumber and attachment as we did in the outside frame. It's really that easy. Take a look at Figures 8.19 and 8.20.

One quick note about the arch. There are many different styles of arches: Roman, Tudor, and Gothic, just to name a few. Make sure to follow the designer's drawings to create the correct shape for the arch (Figs. 8.21 and 8.22).

Let's talk briefly about ceilings. OK, so they are overhead and they connect the walls. Sometimes, in theatrical design, a ceiling or part of a ceiling is required. Depending on the design, often the ceiling is divided into smaller pieces and built as either soft or hard flats. The only difference is in how they are hung. That is discussed in Chapter 10.

Useless Factoid: Baby Dolls

When baby dolls are off stage during performance, set them face down on the props table instead of face up. This superstition comes from China. It is believed that if a baby doll is left face up, its spirit (kind of like a poltergeist) will emerge from its eyes and do poltergeistlike things in the theatre.

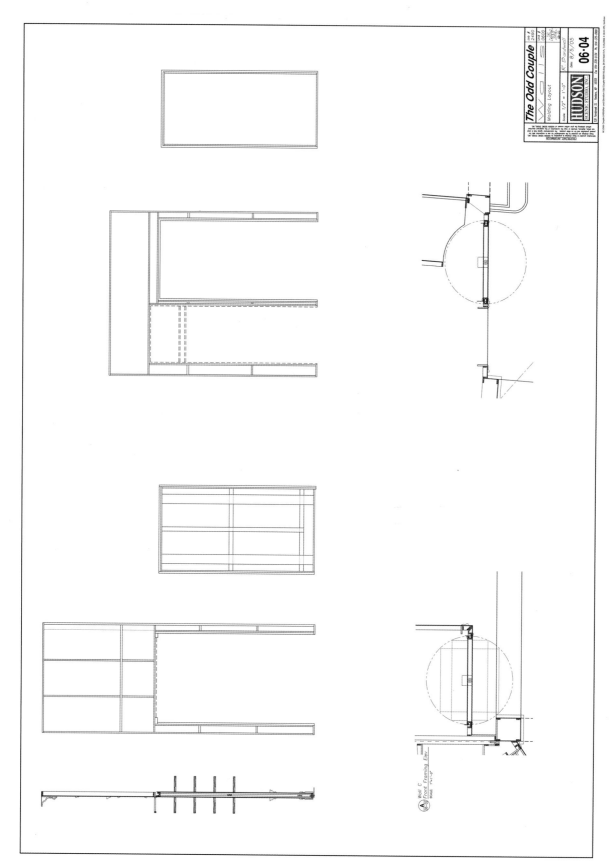

■ **Fig. 8.17** Hudson Scenic's shop drawing of hard flats for Neil Simon's *The Odd Couple.*

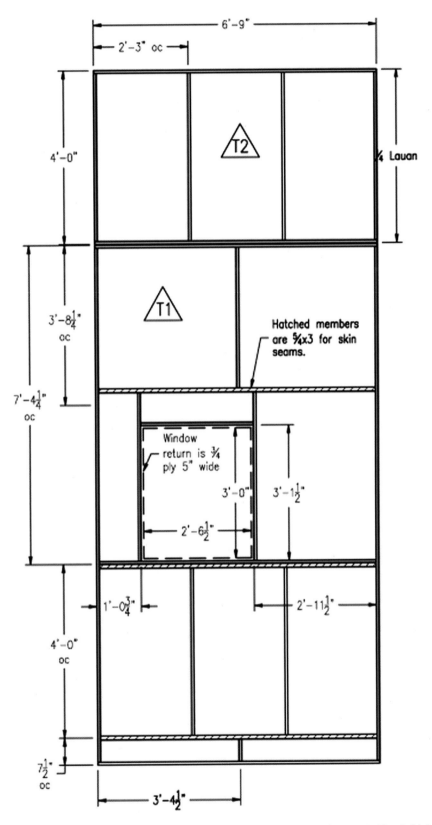

■ **Fig. 8.18** Hudson Scenic's shop drawing of window for Neil Simon's *The Odd Couple.*

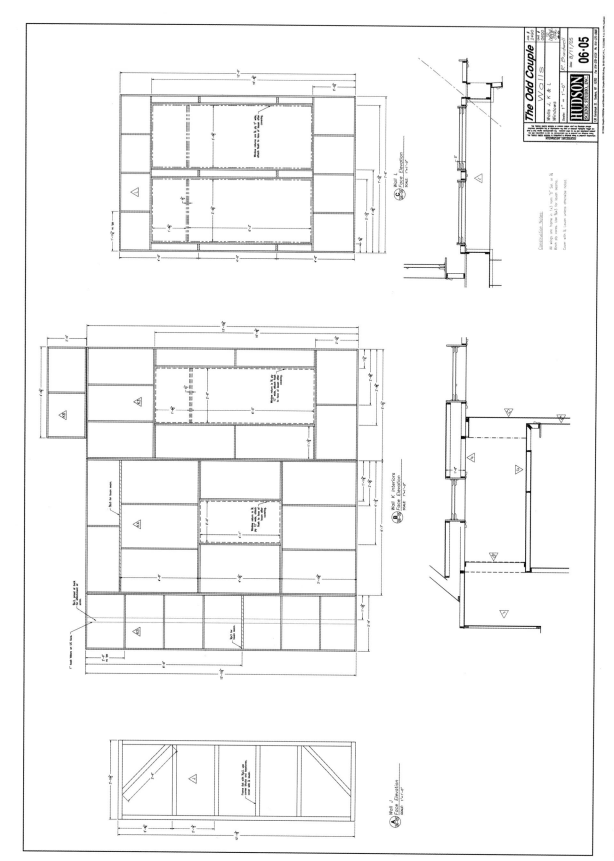

Fig. 8.19 Hudson Scenic's shop drawing of wall J for Neil Simon's *The Odd Couple*.

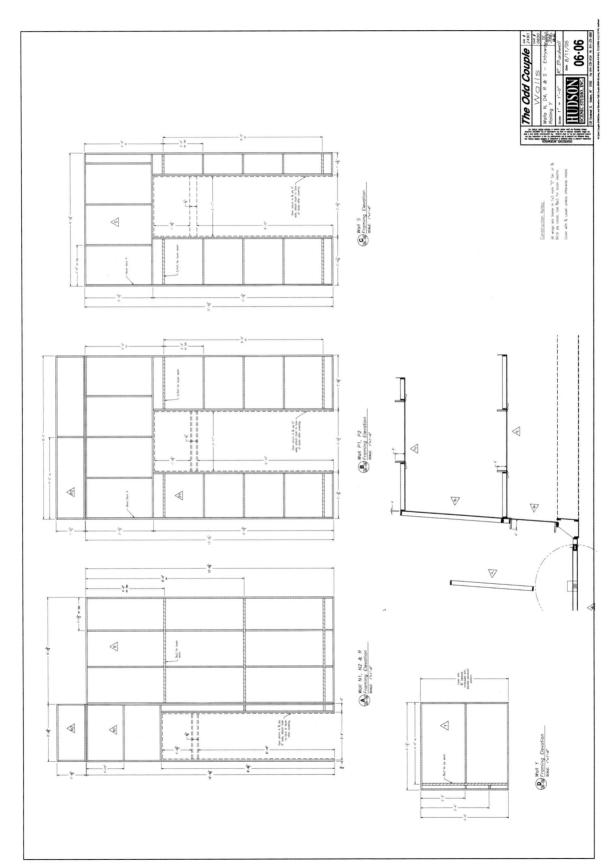

Fig. 8.20 Hudson Scenic's shop drawing of wall N for Neil Simon's *The Odd Couple*.

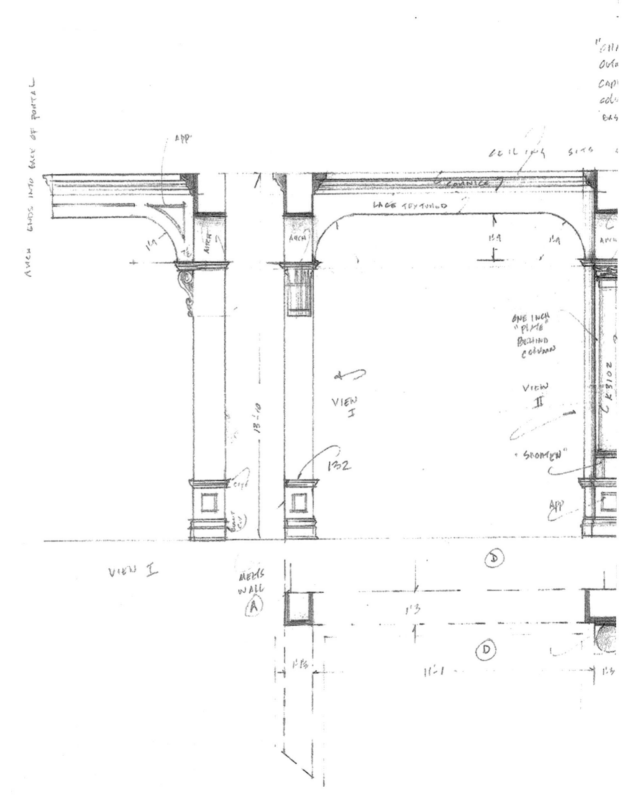

■ **Fig. 8.21** John Lee Beatty's drafting of the wall arches for Neil Simon's *The Odd Couple*.

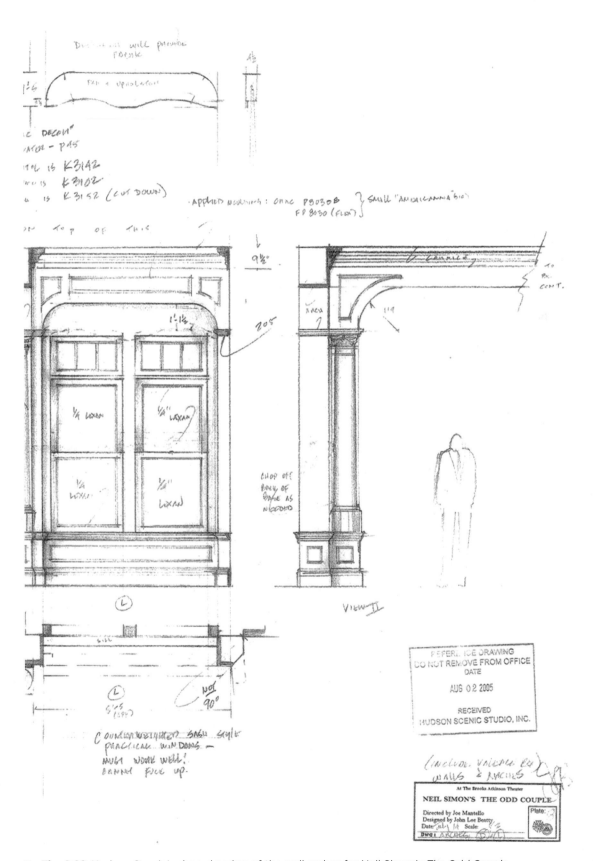

■ **Fig. 8.22** Hudson Scenic's shop drawing of the wall arches for Neil Simon's *The Odd Couple*.

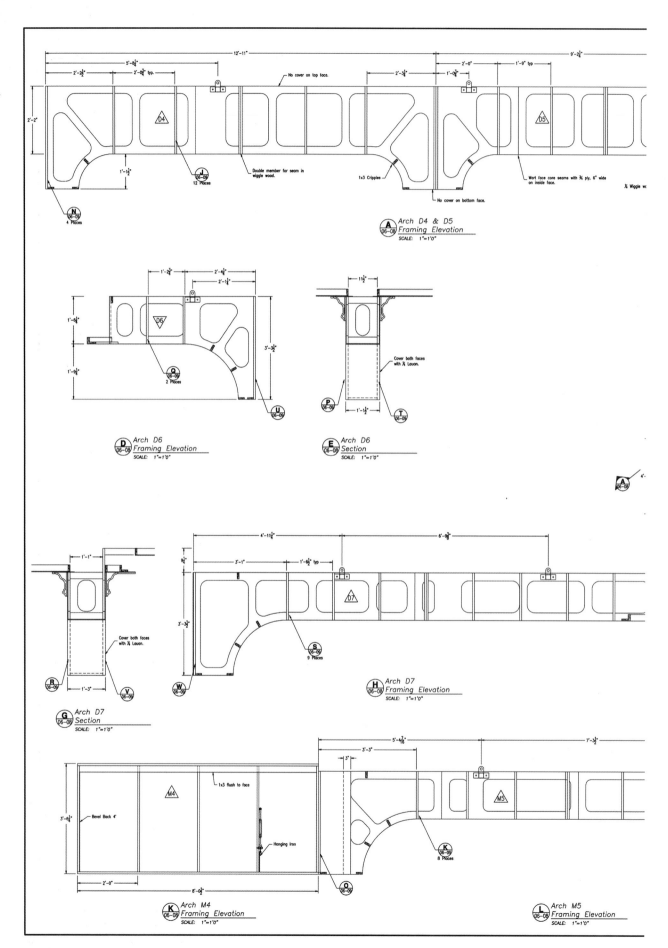

Fig. 8.23 More drawings from Hudson Scenic's design for Neil Simon's *The Odd Couple*.

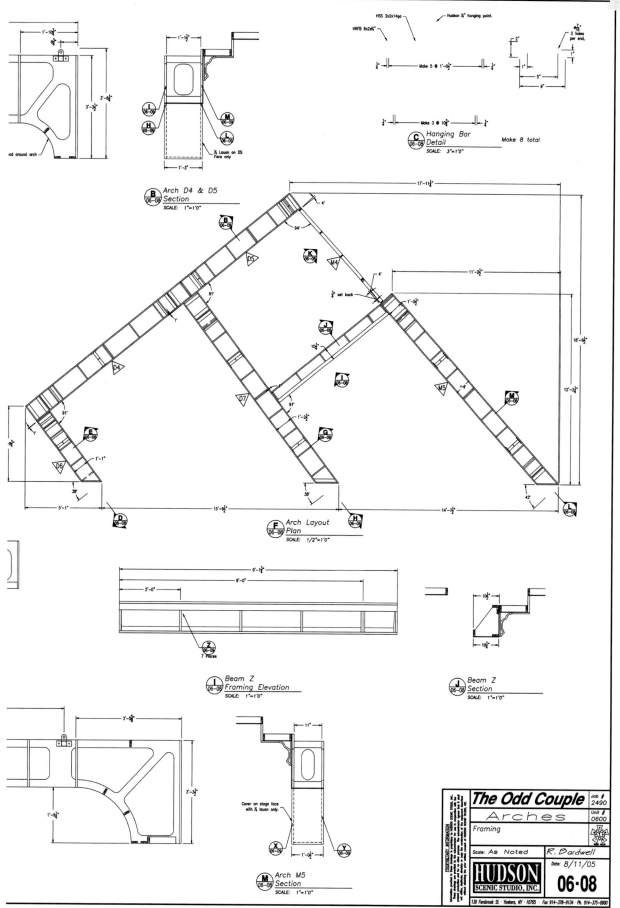

B 06-08 Arch D4 & D5 Section
SCALE: 1"=1'0"

C 06-08 Hanging Bar Detail   Make 8 total
SCALE: 3"=1'0"

HSS 2x2x14ga
HRFB 6x2x¼
Hudson ¾" hanging point.

Make 5 @ 1'-0¾"
Make 3 @ 10½"

2 holes per end,

F 06-08 Arch Layout Plan
SCALE: 1/2"=1'0"

I 06-08 Beam Z Framing Elevation
SCALE: 1"=1'0"

J 06-08 Beam Z Section
SCALE: 1"=1'0"

M 06-08 Arch M5 Section
SCALE: 1"=1'0"

Cover on stage face with ¼ lauan only.

¼ Lauan on DS Face only

The Odd Couple   Job # 2490
Arches   Unit # 0600
Framing

Scale: As Noted   R. Bardwell

HUDSON SCENIC STUDIO, INC.   Date: 8/11/05
130 Fernbrook St · Yonkers, NY · 10705 · Fax 914-378-9134 · Ph. 914-375-0600

06·08

Arch

Borders

Box set

Corner block

Construction drawings

Deck

Designer drawings

Deux ex machina

Fourth wall

Hard flat

Keystone

Kick-off meeting

Leg

Masking

Periaktoi

Platform

Rail

Scenic ground row

Soft flat

Stile

Tab

Trap

Traveler

Wing and drop

Wings

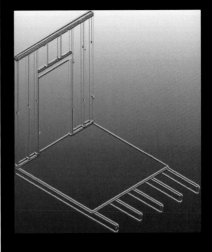

CHAPTER EIGHT

Study Words

A Little Dab Will Do Ya

Paint

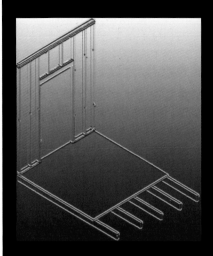
The next logical topic is a discussion on paint. This chapter first addresses the paint shop and its tools. Then, we talk about the range of paint techniques in use for centuries and still in use. You might wonder how painting has changed or what new technologies there are. It's just a paintbrush and some paint, right? Wrong! There are many new developments in this area. Some changes are small, some are large, but all are important. There has been a resurgence of painted faux finishes both in the theatre and in homes. These techniques help complete our picture of what is possible from a scenic point of view as well as how to use these techniques in a nontheatrical way at home!

OVERVIEW

Let's start with a little background on getting a job as a scenic artist. What kind of training is needed to become a scenic artist? You need a good understanding of and background in architecture, including the orders of architecture and architectural styles. Your training must obviously include drawing and, very specifically, perspective. Expect as a matter of course to know the basic techniques that include wood, marble, and the like. You need that kind of groundwork, since it is the basis of many other techniques. Specialty techniques are great, but only if you can also have a handle on everything else, including the basics. Perhaps most difficult yet important, you need to be able to look at a rendering and envision what the designer intends.

> It is a huge help to have all scenic departments under one roof in the shop. Someone is always watching your back. The whole vision is evident. There is always camaraderie. You work better as a team.
>
> —Grace Brandt

Obviously, to paint something, it needs to be built first. The scene shops organize all the different departments' schedules so that there is a smooth process following each element from the first meeting all the way through to it being loaded on a truck. Almost every painted element in the show needs a sample created by the charge painter. The first week or two is usually for these samples, and there is no limit to the size of the samples (Fig. 9.1). They can be large or small, whatever size is needed to show the color and texture properly. The samples are primarily for internal use but are also shown to the designer or client. This is the time when the final look for each technique is controlled and determined. The "recipe" for the paint color and texture as well as the technique are determined and documented, so that other scenic artists can share projects seamlessly (Fig. 9.2). This is a crucial step as everyone in a paint shop needs to be able to work on each piece and have it look like one person did everything. Communication is key here.

Backdrops are the one exception to this rule, as they can be started right away. The backdrop design is first cartooned onto kraft paper with vine charcoal. **Cartooning** refers to drawing the basic design at full scale using a **grid** to enlarge it. The **kraft paper**, also known as *brown butcher paper*, is then pounced. A **pounce** wheel is a small tool with sharp teeth around the wheel. Think of a small pizza cutter and you have the right idea. You use the pounce

■ **Fig. 9.1** Hudson Scenic's paint bay, empty and waiting for the next job.

■ **Fig. 9.2** Hudson Scenic's paint bay, in full swing with several projects and workers.

wheel to trace the cartoon, punching holes in the paper as you go. To transfer the design to the drop's fabric, lay the kraft paper on the fabric and use a pounce bag filled with either chalk or charcoal to transfer the design through the pounced holes. A newer technology to help this process along is the electronic pouncer (Fig. 9.3). It is much easier on your hand, taking less strength and doing the job much faster. However, training and technique with this new tool becomes more crucial (Figs. 9.4–9.8).

SAFETY

Let's address some safety concerns in the paint shop before going further. First and most important, research all products before buying them to check for safe use practices. MSDSs (which we discussed in the safety chapter) are available for almost all products, and you

■ **Fig. 9.3** Hudson Scenic painter Kyle Higgins using the electronic pouncer.

can download this to make sure your shop is properly set up to use the product. You should always keep a copy of the MSDSs in the paint shop in case of an accident! Latex gloves used to be the standard in a paint shop, but they are now being replaced completely by vinyl gloves. The reason for this is that latex allergies are becoming a bigger and bigger issue.

Solvents and sprays must be stored in a metal cabinet, as they are combustible. Theatre, as an industry, is getting away from the use of metal flake for safety reasons. Ingredients in the metal flake and other types of these products have been shown to be fire accelerants. That is a bad thing, discussed more fully later in this chapter. There is really nothing you can do to change it. So just don't use them, find a substitute. There is an OSHA requirement that, when you are mixing different products together, you have to create a label for the container that states all the various elements you put into the mixture. Think about it for a second. You made a new chemical compound, whether you think of it that way or not. Labels are important to identify what type of paints went into the mixture, in case you need to make more of it, but also as a safety concern, since you might not be the only one to use it.

TOOLS AND SUPPLIES

OK, let's move on to the tools of painting. We all used a paintbrush, but it isn't the only tool of the trade. And, there isn't just one kind of brush. Before we go into the different types and styles, let's look at the anatomy of a brush. Every brush can be divided into three different parts: the bristles,

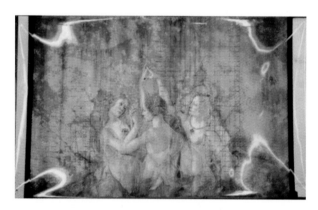

■ **Fig. 9.4** Painter's elevation by Scott Pask for *Nine*.

■ **Fig. 9.5** Full-color model by Scott Pask for *Nine*.

■ **Fig. 9.6** Backdrop in the process of being painted at Hudson Scenic for *Nine*.

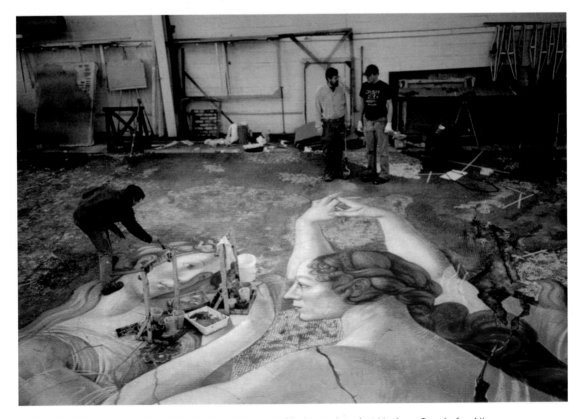

■ **Fig. 9.7** Backdrop further through the process of being painted at Hudson Scenic for *Nine*.

Fig. 9.8 Finished painted backdrop for *Nine* at Hudson Scenic.

ferrule, and handle (Fig. 9.9). The bristles are what you dip into the paint. They can be made from a variety of materials and in many shapes, depending mostly on what kind of paint you are going to use and how you will use the brush. The handle is what you hold and can also come in a variety of different shapes and sizes. The word you are probably least familiar with is *ferrule*. The job of the ferrule is to hold the bristles in the proper shape and attach them to the handle. Like bristles and handles, they can be made in a variety of ways to match the brush they are creating. This is the "weak" spot of the brush. What I mean by that is, if the brush is left soaking in liquid before cleaning, the ferrule can loosen its hold on the bristles and handle. Once the bristles are loose, they fall out. This is the main way that brushes are ruined!

The different styles and shapes of brushes have different names (Fig. 9.10). The standard brush you are most used to using has no special name. It is a good rectangular utility paintbrush for many general uses. They come in a variety of sizes, including ¼, ½, ¾, 1, 1¼, 1½, 2, 3, and 4 inches. **Lining** brushes, also known as **fitch** brushes, have a much

more defined shape. They are usually better made and much more expensive. The ferrule is seamless, which helps to keep its shape, and the bristles are natural not synthetic. They also come in a range of sizes, including ¼, ½, ¾, 1, 1¼, 1½, and 2 inches.

Chip and **foam** brushes, as well as pads, are now popular as inexpensive alternatives to standard brushes. Chip brushes are a very inexpensive alternative to the standard paintbrush. They are less durable and considered to be disposable. They come in the same standard sizes as better quality brushes. Foam brushes and pads come in a variety of sizes and are mostly rectangular or round. Instead of bristles, these brushes have a foam block that comes to a wedge at the tip. These are great for cutting in and keeping a straight line. Once the foam has been saturated for a while it tends to become limp. Although these brushes can be washed and, when completely dried, return to almost their original condition, they are considered to be disposable by some.

The **lay-in** brush is a specialty brush used specifically for painting large areas, such as a drop or a large expanse

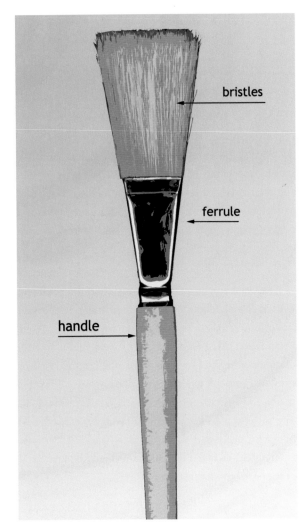

Fig. 9.9 Diagram of scenic brush with the parts labeled.

Fig. 9.10 Various lengths of bamboo at Hudson Scenic.

of scenery. They are larger than most other brush types, with typical sizes of 5 and 6 inches. Due to their large size they can hold a lot more paint, so painting goes faster. That is good, but it also makes the brush heavier and properly cleaning them more difficult.

When you need to create a wood grain, **graining** brushes and tools come in a wide range of choices. Brushes typically look like a standard brush with the bristle end varying in length and density to create the grain texture. These can even be created in the shop as a last minute substitute for store-bought ones. Rubber rollers and rockers are another way to create wood grain. The rubber surface has the texture raised to grab the paint. As the tool is rolled or dragged along the painted surface it can leave, or remove, paint to create the effect.

Another type of specialty brush is called a **flogger**. Think of a regular paintbrush with really, really long bristles. The flogger can be used for creating textures in wet paint or removing cartooned chalk and charcoal from the material's surface. It is very versatile but also expensive. Be careful when using it, as the longer bristles can bend and break. Also, make sure to clean it out fully when you are done.

OK, so brushes are cool and you now understand the differing kinds and their purposes. But how on earth do you paint something that is bigger than you can reach? With a piece of **bamboo**, of course! Bamboo sticks come in a variety of lengths and diameters (Fig. 9.11). Since bamboo is hollow, you can put your paintbrush handle into the center and tape it in place. This lengthens the span of your arm, which means you can reach more surface, and save your back from having to bend over at the same time. With all these wonderful tools, you will still have to occasionally paint a straight line. A **lining stick** is a beveled straight edge that allows you to run your brush along the side, using it as a guide for creating precise lines. It usually has a handle to make holding it easier when working from a distance with a paintbrush in bamboo.

Paint rollers, similar to paintbrushes, are something you've seen and probably used many times. But, did you know that both the frames and the covers come in many sizes and textures? Well, they do! The frames come in different widths and most have a female receiver at the end of the handle to accept an extension. This allows you to add an extension pole to paint further away than your arm can reach. The covers come in differing widths as well. They also come in different materials, from wool, to a synthetic

version of wool, to microfiber. Differing surfaces include smooth, semi-smooth, semi-rough, rough, and extra rough. Textures can include anything from generalized texture to carpet stipple and custom-cut rollers. The sky is the limit with the custom rollers. You can even cut these yourself to make a design specifically for your show.

Sponges, plastic wrap, rags, and anything else that will hold paint and create a pattern are all viable choices for texturing the paint. Most of these are messy techniques, so be aware and use gloves. These "tools" are easy to use. Load them with paint by dunking, dipping, or whatever. The way you apply the paint to the wall controls the final look. Testing these options and creating samples becomes critical, as so much variation can happen.

Flame retarding is an important step in the paint shop. You can use a variety of products, depending on the scenic element that needs to be treated. These chemicals require caution when using, and you *must* follow the instructions that come with the products. Someone certified in flame testing will come in to check your scenery once everything is ready. This certification process is very important, as it is the only way to know whether you have applied the product properly and the product is working the way it was intended. Your flame certificate should be kept on file for as long as you use the scenery.

Fig. 9.11 Scenic brush storage at Hudson Scenic.

Useless Factoid: Church Key

Church key—the monks made their own ale. To keep the recipes secret, the monasteries were locked. Since the new bottle opener looked a bit like a skeleton key, it was referred to as a *church key*.

There are a number of other general supplies that the paint shop needs (Fig. 9.12). These can include blue painter's tape in a couple of sizes and frisket. The painter's tape you may have seen and used at home. It is good for covering molding when you are painting a wall. **Frisket** is a plastic sheet with an adhesive back. It is used when you need to mask a specific part of a design (Fig. 9.13). You lay it down and cut a design out to reveal the portion you need to work on, leaving everything else masked and therefore safe from the new paint (Figs. 9.14–9.16).

Fig. 9.12 More scenic tools in storage at Hudson Scenic.

Fig. 9.14 Removing the frisket at Hudson Scenic.

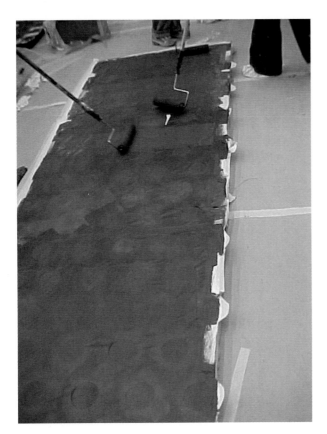

Fig. 9.13 Painting over a frisket at Hudson Scenic.

Fig. 9.15 Finished drop after frisket removal at Hudson Scenic.

■ **Fig. 9.16** *Romeo Et Juliette* at the Metropolitan Opera, November 2005. Director, Guy Joosten; scenic designer, Johannes Leiacker; costume designer, Jorge Jara; and lighting designer, Peter Cunningham.

Another very handy tool is the **Hudson® sprayer**. The brand name Hudson has become synonymous with the canister type of compression sprayer. The **Floretta®** is a smaller, handheld version of the compression sprayer. These are the most popular brands. A sprayer allows you to put paint into a canister, put the top on, and then pump air into the paint. A nozzle allows you to release the paint/air mixture. You can also use the sprayers with water to help stretch a backdrop that has wrinkles or creases in it. This is a great tool for many, many uses.

PAINTS AND GLAZES

OK, let me give a generic disclaimer for this whole chapter. Whenever I say *paint*, I mean anything you might apply to change the color of a surface. There are many different compounds that will do this, and I get into that shortly. It is easier as we go on if we all agree to a simple shorthand.

Scenic paint started out as powdered pigment. We used to start out by mixing different powdered pigments together until we achieved the color we needed. Then, we would need to make a binder and a medium that, when mixed together, became the sizing. Be happy you don't have to still do this! Here are the details. The binder was originally made from flake or ground glues. The glue was made from parts of a horse or ox—I'm not going into any more detail. So anyway, you melted the glue in a double boiler, added water, stirring constantly as your product is sizing. Slowly mixing the sizing into the pigment, stirring constantly, created scenic paint. It smelled nasty, never mind the fact that it wasn't exactly animal friendly. So we don't do that anymore.

Now, there are a variety of manufacturers for theatrical paints, such as Rosco, Artist's Choice, Wild Fire, Spectral, and Mixol. By far, Rosco is the unrivaled leader. Rosco offers the biggest variety for these kinds of paint, suited to any type of product. These include Off-Broadway®, Super Saturated®, Iddings Deep®, and a variety of clear glazes.

Special Effects paints from Rosco include fluorescent, Vivid FX®, Clear Color®, and Rosco Glo®. All these are water soluble, meaning you can clean your tools in water. It also means these paints can all be thinned with water for varying effects.

> The concept of economics in using scene paint is one subject that completely gets overlooked. The basis for this idea would be using paint that has been formulated for scenic materials and scenic situations—i.e., flats that flex because they are handled and set up every night versus house paint that goes on a flat, hard wall surface and never moves. Scenic paint still has bright colors even though it has been thinned out 2 to 1 or more. This is not possible with house paint. Plus, you just made three gallons of paint for the cost of one gallon. Compare that to the price of one gallon of house paint. Muslin drops can be painted more than one time with scenic paint but not house paint. House paint would add tons to the weight put on the fly rail and on the fibers of the fabric causing them to have stress tears or the paint is so thick it becomes crunchy.
>
> **—Jenny Knott, Rosco**

You are probably wondering what the difference is between paint and glaze. Well, I'm just getting to that. Paint is what you are most familiar with. It is usually opaque, meaning it completely covers the surface below it. I say *usually*. When you are painting, sometimes, it will take several coats of paint to cover, but eventually it will cover. **Glazes** are used differently. Glazes are thinner than paint and they are transparent or translucent instead of opaque. Glazes are used for a variety of effects that we talk about shortly. The key with glazes is to make sure the first layer of paint is dry, to put them on thinly, and let them dry completely before you disturb them. Otherwise you end up with an ugly mush of colors.

All of the paints listed can be mixed within their type to achieve the exact color you are trying for. Remember the color wheel from Chapter 4? Now is the time to use that knowledge. Easy to mix, easy to use, easy to clean up. Easy! Don't forget, you can experiment (a.k.a. play) and create your own techniques. Nothing is truly set in stone, except of course Excalibur.

Many other products are on the market for varying effects. What about metallics, you might ask? You want silver, gold, or copper? Well, some of the best metallic paints and powders on the market are from Europe via Benjamin Moore's Metallics series. Metallic paints are used the same as regular paints. If you get metallic powders, they need to be mixed into a glaze of some sort to be used. Keep in mind that metallics, by their nature, have a higher possibility of being volatile. That means they can be unstable and must be used and stored according to the directions that come with them. Always read the MSDS about a product before using it to make sure you are safe.

Here is a little trick that can be good to know. Whatever the color you are going for, if it is intense it might be good to add a little ultraviolet (UV) paint. This makes the color pop out a bit. Of course, you can't do this if there will be UV lights used in the productions. If you add UV paint by accident to a mixture, there is no way to cover it up. So be careful, and be sure of yourself before you try this.

The last thing to discuss regarding paints and tools is their care (Figs. 9.17–9.20). Paints must always be sealed tightly when you are done using it for the day. Otherwise a skin will form across the top and eventually the paint will completely dry out or get rancid, depending on the type of paint. Good brushes and roller covers can cost a lot of money. While cheaper ones are meant to be disposable, not all are. Take care of your tools and they will last a long, long time!

Brushes and rollers require a good cleaning after each use. What you use to clean the brush depends on the type of paint you were using. Water-soluble compounds can be cleaned in good old-fashioned soap and water. The key to cleaning is to make sure to remove all the paint that is possible. Tools have been specifically designed for cleaning brushes and roller covers. The brush cleaner looks like a metal hair comb. After wetting the bristles, insert it at the bottom of the ferrule/top of the bristle and gently pull down toward the end of the bristles. Roller

■ **Fig. 9.17** Paint storage at Hudson Scenic.

covers can be cleaned using a five-in-one paint tool. This has been specifically designed for cleaning rollers and roller covers in a variety of ways to get the longest life from your tools.

Now that we know the tools and paints available, let's put them together (Fig. 9.21). You can just dip the brush in the paint, or you can dry brush, scumble, rag roll, spatter, sponge, wet blend, or stencil. Let's look at these simple textures before we move on to the techniques that use them. Here is an idea that will mess with your mind. Any of the tools we discussed for applying paint can also be used to remove paint. Huh?! Well, think about it. You lay in the **base** color, then you apply another color. While that color is wet, you can remove some of it to create the texture!

TEXTURING

There are many methods for adding texture (Fig. 9.22). **Dry brushing** is when you keep your brush as dry as possible, using only a minor amount of paint or using a brush with no paint, to move around or remove paint that has already been applied to the surface.

Scumbling is putting a small amount of paint on your brush and lightly dragging it across a dry surface. This is often used as an overlay to a background image, for example, to create sunbeams coming out of clouds.

Fig. 9.18 Scenic tool storage at Hudson Scenic.

Wet blending is just what it sounds like. You apply one layer of paint, and while it is still wet, you apply a second coat that blends partially or completely with the first.

Fig. 9.19 More scenic tool storage at Hudson Scenic.

Rag rolling can be done in two ways. You can use a roller and paint a surface, then take a cotton rag that has been bunched into a loose ball and roll the rag ball across the paint to remove paint while also making a texture. You can also do the reverse by applying paint to the rag and rolling it onto the surface, adding paint and texture at the same time.

Spattering is a messy texture, so be sure to use plenty of drop cloths. To spatter, you load a brush with a small amount of paint and then basically shake the brush at the surface without allowing them to touch. If you use too much paint all at once, it will just make big ugly blobs of paint. And, the paint for spattering is often thinned to avoid the blob idea. You can also spatter using a Hudson sprayer to make it a little neater and get more coverage quickly.

> I found I could say things with color and shapes that I couldn't say any other way—things I had no words for.
>
> **—Georgia O'Keeffe**

Sponging is fun and can provide a great variety to the texture. Sea sponges are often used, as they are more natural in appearance than a kitchen sponge. However, any sponge can be used to apply paint. Just dip the sponge in paint then dab it at the surface. You can vary the amount of texture and paint you use to create each part of a design. You can also take a sponge and a pair of scissors and cut a design into the sponge. This will create your own custom texture that is fun while making your design even more custom.

A texture I won't go into much detail on is distressing. **Distressing** is used in the theatre all the time. So why don't I want to talk about it? Because there are so many different kinds and ways, it could fill a whole book. Let me just say distressing is a way to make something new look like something old. So the best way to distress anything is to get some research of the same item when it is old and copy that. Experience is great on this texturing idea because everyone you talk to has different thoughts on how to do it. Keep a list of your favorites!

> Creativity is allowing yourself to make mistakes. Art is knowing which ones to keep.
>
> **—Scott Adams**

Three-dimensional texture can be created in any number of ways (Fig. 9.23). I like to combine 2D and 3D techniques for the best result. If you want to add 3D texture, there are a variety of options. You can use joint compound, cheesecloth, sawdust, newspaper, chicken wire, or almost anything that adheres to the surface and is paintable in one fashion or another. The sky is really the limit here.

Before you do any of these techniques, one basic thing has to happen. You must **prime** your surface. Priming is a way to make the surface ready to accept your design. Raw wood or fabric soaks in a great deal of the first layer of paint. This is the basis for priming. It is better to use a neutral

■ **Fig. 9.21** *Romeo et Juliette* at the Metropolitan Opera, November 2005. Director, Guy Joosten; Scenic Designer, Johannes Leiacker; Costume Designer, Jorge Jara; and Lighting Designer, Peter Cunningham.

■ **Fig. 9.22** Kyle Higgins, scenic painter, applies texture at Hudson Scenic.

■ **Fig. 9.23** Hudson Scenic scenic artist working on a 3D texture project.

color and a less-expensive paint for this part of the process, since it won't be visible in the final product.

STEP-BY-STEP TECHNIQUES

The following are the basic scenic painting techniques that create a base for all other techniques (Fig. 9.24). You should practice these and become familiar with each step. Then, and only then, you can begin to experiment with your own variations to create different images. Let me give you a couple of basic disclaimers before going into the step-by-step instructions. Most important, do not rush the drying time (Fig. 9.25). If you start the next step before the paint is dry, you will not end up with a good, recognizable effect. You will, instead, end up with a murky mess. Don't skip the glazing either. Glazing is what helps to separate the differing layers of paint from each other, giving the visual effect of a 3D object.

> It doesn't make sense to have painters searching through a pile to find the brush they want. Organization is key.
>
> **—Grace Brandt**

Research becomes your last important phase before beginning to paint. You may have the designer's **paint elevations** (Figs. 9.26 and 9.27). You may also have a sample that was created and approved. Or, you may have none of these and it is all up to you. However the process goes for you, it is important to do your own research. How many different kinds of marble, brick, and wood do you think there are? You'll be amazed. Each different kind is slightly different. The more specific you are when researching, the more realistic you will be when painting. Last, remember that each step is a part of the process and *not* the finished product. Have faith, keep your research nearby, and here we go!

MARBLE

Marble comes in many colors and textures, depending on where it comes from. Water and pressure are the major forces in marble's formation. Use puddling and spattering with clean water during the following steps to achieve the best results. Since this is such a wet technique, make sure to work it flat on the floor. Drips from working on a vertical surface ruin the effect. The traditional method of veining marble is to use a feather instead of a brush. I find that using a combination of different feathers and brushes

■ **Fig. 9.24** *Pride and Prejudice* at the Guthrie Theatre in 2003.

■ **Fig. 9.25** Floor fans at Hudson Scenic.

gives me the range I want and need to make the most successful marble.

Step 1—*Lay in the base coat.* Using a wet-blend technique, lay in the base colors based on your visual research. Blend a contrasting color over the base to lay in some texture as a part of the base. This coat may then be sprayed lightly with water to soften, if desired. Allow to dry. Apply a complimentary colored glaze selectively over the surface to vary color of textured areas (Fig. 9.28). Allow to dry.

Step 2—*Establish veining.* Select two different vein colors within the same color family, one lighter and one darker. Lay in major vein areas in the lighter color (Fig. 9.29). Assure that no pattern emerges in this part of the process, as marble is very random. Next, lay in the minor veins with your other vein color. You may want to wet the surface before laying in the veins so that they are softened as they are applied. Or, you may apply the veins and then spatter with water to soften afterwards.

Step 3—*Glazing.* Apply glaze colors as appropriate for your marble. Glazes tend to make colors look richer (Fig. 9.30). They also add depth to marble. Both of these are good, but be careful not to overdo it.

Step 4—*Veining detail.* Apply additional veining detail as needed using a variety of colors, if appropriate (Fig. 9.31). Wetting the surface lightly will enhance your results, enhancing the blending and making everything

Fig. 9.26 *"The Sound of Music" Outside the Trapp Villa*, watercolor rendering by Oliver Smith. © Rosario Sinisi.

Fig. 9.27 *"Hello Dolly" Harmonia Gardens*, watercolor rendering by Oliver Smith. © Rosario Sinisi.

Fig. 9.28 Rosco scenic finishes: marble, step 1.

Fig. 9.30 Rosco scenic finishes: marble, step 3.

Fig. 9.29 Rosco scenic finishes: marble, step 2.

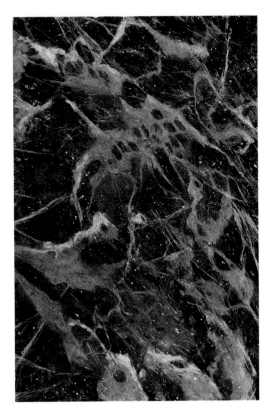

Fig. 9.31 Rosco scenic finishes: marble, steps 4 and 5.

pull together. Apply glaze colors on select veins to add more interest and depth. Allow to dry thoroughly.

Step 5—*Final glaze.* Apply a final coat of clear acrylic gloss to the entire surface for added depth. This is the only time to use a clear glaze. It seals the layers of paint to make everything unified.

BRICK

Bricks come in many sizes, shapes, and colors. Some brick is very old and worn while others look brand new—and everything in-between. The following technique is a basic guide for a common brick wall that can be adapted to suit many types of brick. These can also be suited to many types of stone as well. Remember what I said earlier: Follow the steps, and once you are comfortable with them, you can begin to put in your own variations.

Step 1—*Mortar as your base coat.* Mix the base coat mortar colors based on your research. Your mortar colors should be light in value with some gray/brown components, as this is the most common mortar color (Fig. 9.32). If your research shows something else, feel free to go with it. Cover the entire surface using a scumble technique with your base coat colors. This will make sure you have variety throughout the entire surface.

Step 2—*Prepare your stencil.* Prepare your stencil based on your research. The most important thing to consider when cutting your stencil is the proportion of the bricks. Lie out and cut desired sizes from craft paper or regular poster board. There are two ways to line up a stencil for repeating patterns. You can either put registration marks on the edges of your stencil or use an overlay method if your stencil is big enough.

Step 3—*Stencil your base brick colors.* Now, you can mix your brick base color using two colors to add depth (Fig. 9.33). Line up your brick pattern stencil and stipple the brick base color onto the surface using a sea sponge or

■ **Fig. 9.32** Rosco scenic finishes: brick, steps 1 and 2.

■ **Fig. 9.33** Rosco scenic finishes: brick, step 3.

stiff brush. This is one time when the more inconsistent you are, the better it will look. Allow to dry thoroughly.

Step 4—*Adding realism with spatter and glazes.* Look closely at your research. Brick has naturally occurring dings, dents, chips, and other irregularities in the surface. The use of a fine spatter over the entire surface replicates this effect convincingly (Fig. 9.34). Mix two or three glaze colors, light and dark. Experiment with different colors for different looks. Apply the glaze over your dry brick base and notice how it adds dimension, just like it did with the marble. Allow some original base color to show through for more variety in the surface. Allow to dry thoroughly.

Step 5—*Highlight* and *shadow.* The final step is to add highlight and shadow to individual bricks for even more added depth (Fig. 9.35). Mix highlight color based on your research and thin it with water to the consistency of whole milk. Create your shadow color in the same way

as the highlight. The final touch, if you are going for a strong lighting effect, is to add a "cast shadow." Choose a cast shadow color that will work with your research. A cast shadow should be placed below the first shadow.

WOOD GRAIN

Wood, like brick, comes in many types, including differences in color, texture, and grain. Factor in the age of a tree, and the possibilities are endless. The following technique gives you an idea for how to create faux wood grain. Keep in mind that research is still key and you should keep it in front of you as you paint. As always: Follow the steps, and once you are comfortable with them, you can begin to put in your own variations.

Step 1—*Lay in base coat.* Prime your surface with a neutral color (Fig. 9.36). Select several colors for your wood. Do a wet blend of your colors, keeping in mind the grain of your wood. Remember that wood is organic; therefore, it is not perfectly straight. Minor variations will help this

Fig. 9.34 Rosco scenic finishes: brick, step 4.

Fig. 9.35 Rosco scenic finishes: brick, step 5.

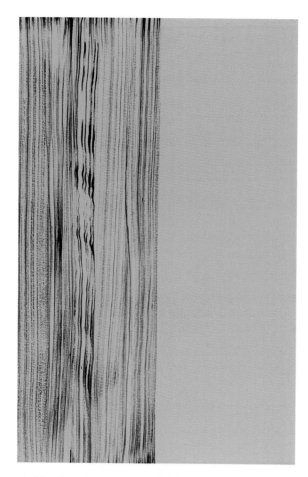

Fig. 9.36 Rosco scenic finishes: wood grain, steps 1 and 2.

Fig. 9.37 Rosco scenic finishes: wood grain, step 3.

look better, especially if you are creating wood made from individual boards.

Step 2—*Graining the surface.* Mix the graining color as a thin glaze. This is a fine balance, because if you make the glaze too thin, it won't show up enough, but if it is too thick, it will look like a cartoon. Use a dry-brush technique with a graining brush. Lightly drag the brush along the surface leaving a "combed" look. Make sure you have enough paint on your brush to do the entire length of the board; if you have to stop and restart, the wood will not look right. Vary your technique including the pressure and amount of paint for more realism. Gently drag a clean, dry brush over the grain to soften.

Step 3—*Create individual boards.* Using the same grain color and a thin fitch brush, paint lines between boards to delineate one from another (Fig. 9.37). Vary the line thickness slightly for added realism. Do a light spatter

over the whole surface to add more depth and tie everything together.

Step 4—*Glazing individual boards.* Mix your glazing colors using one part paint, four parts clear glaze, and four parts water. Check your research to determine if you will need one or two glazing colors. Apply each glaze selectively over the grained surface to achieve your desired result (Fig. 9.38). Glazes allow for variations in color and give depth, as we discussed with previous techniques.

Step 5—*Finish coat.* Your finish coat can be flat, glossy, or somewhere in-between depending on the wood you are simulating. Mix one part clear acrylic (in desired finish) to one part water. Apply the finish in several thin coats, allowing them to dry *thoroughly* between each coat. You can also mix a small amount of your wood color into the glaze to add another level of uniformity.

Now that we have all this information in our heads, let me tell you a little about one of today's design trends.

■ **Fig. 9.38** Rosco scenic finishes: wood grain, steps 4 and 5.

There is a shift to using more and more "real" materials instead of faux painting. There does not seem to be any shyness in ordering expensive materials for the theatre, as some budgets can be extravagant on Broadway. The audiences' expectation has made many modern musicals really costly. Big-money musicals in the 1980s started a trend that continues today. However, academic and amateur theatre still use many of the techniques we've been discussing (Fig. 9.39).

■ **Fig. 9.39** Hudson Scenic scenic artists enjoy their work at the end of the day!

Bamboo

Base

Cartoon

Chip

Distressing

Dry brushing

Fitch

Flogger

Floretta

Foam

Frisket

Glazes

Graining

Grid

Hudson spray

Kraft paper

Lay-in

Lining

Lining stick

Paint elevation

Pounce

Prime

Rag rolling

Scumbling

Spattering

Sponging

Wet blending

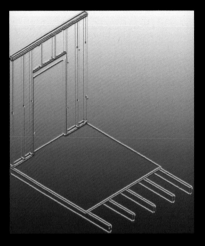

CHAPTER NINE
Study Words

PART THREE
Rigging and Lighting

Hanging by a Thread

Rigging

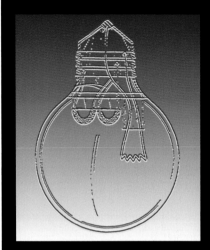

CHAPTER TEN

In this chapter

- **Ropes**
- **Knots**
- **Rigging Systems**
- **Study Words**

Now that the scenery is built, how do you get it into place? How do you get it into its storage position? Does it fly in and out, does it track on and off, or does it just sit there? Once you know the answer to these questions, the solution lies with the rigging department. Rigging is one of the most critical, and therefore dangerous, parts of theatre. We build scenery that is heavy, then we hang it over people's heads. We hang pipes with many lights and cables on them—over people's heads. If any of that weight falls down, it can be disastrous.

Useless Factoid: Whistling

Whistling backstage is a taboo, because it supposedly brings dire results. This superstition quite likely has its roots in the past, when managers hired sailors to run the fly loft, on the premise that the sailors' expertise with knots and raising and lowering sails made them ideal workers. A signal system of whistles cued the sailors. Someone whistling for personal enjoyment could sound like a cue, resulting in a dire event, like a heavy batten falling on actors' heads. Therefore, whistling can be bad luck.

Rigging at its most basic is all about knots. Where do we get these knots? Again, we honor the history of knots, which all come from sailors! Once we learn about the knots that make theatre rigging safe and easy, we move on to more complicated rigging, where new technology has really made a huge impact. Fifty years ago, if you wanted a platform to move across the stage somebody had to push it! It sure is different today, with the advent of mechanization.

The earliest stagehands in history were also sailors. Many of our knots, ways of rigging, and general traditions come from the standard uses on boats (Fig. 10.1). More modern equipment and techniques come from mountain climbers. It is an interesting combination that gives the theatre the capability to fly things into the air (Fig. 10.2).

ROPES

Let's start at the beginning and talk about rope. You can pretty much divide rope into two basic categories: natural and synthetic. Natural ropes are made from a wood pulp fiber that is harvested from plants like jute, hemp, and bamboo. The fibers are then twisted, braided, or both to add strength to the fibers. Watch out for splinters as the rope ages, especially if you might be allergic to hemp! There are no longer any advantages to natural rope (Fig. 10.3). It starts degrading the moment it is made, because it was once alive. It loses its moisture and elasticity; basically it's biodegrading.

Synthetic fibers include nylon and polyester. Synthetic ropes are made through the twisting and braiding process as well (Fig. 10.4). Abrasion, chemicals, heat, and UV (sunlight) all affect synthetic rope and cause it to degrade. Rope can also be made from wire, but we discuss that later in the chapter. Originally, theatre used natural rope, because it was the only option. Natural fibers are subject to changes to heat and humidity, which can make them stretch. Synthetic fibers don't have this problem and therefore can have a longer life. The replacement schedule for natural rope is 5 years, whether it has been used or not.

■ **Fig. 10.1** All of our rigging techniques and traditions come from sailing. Take a look at this fully rigged boat for comparison.

Fig. 10.2 Backstage at the 1869 Bardavon Opera House. Look at the rigging both below the loading floor and above it.

■ **Fig. 10.3** Natural rope made from hemp.

■ **Fig. 10.4** Synthetic rope made from nylon.

There is no replacement schedule for synthetic. It lasts practically forever.

Both types of rope come in a variety of thicknesses and lengths. The material the rope is made from, the thickness, and the manufacturing process all combine to give the rope its strength rating. Always check a rope's rating for how much weight it will hold *before* you use it. The best advice about rigging I can give you is to be cautious and never attempt anything you are unsure of, and always ask for help if you need it. One last thing, wear gloves when working with rope. It will help you to keep a good hold on the rope, and should the rope slip, you will not hurt your hands. Rope burns are a total drag, so avoid them at all cost!

KNOTS

Knots are the basis of rigging. There are many different knots, and a handful of those are critical to theatre. The overhand knot, square knot, bowline, clove hitch, belaying, and coiling are all essential to theatre rigging. The **overhand knot** is the simplest of them all (Fig. 10.5). Hold the rope with both hands parallel to the ground; cross it over to form a loop; wrap the right-hand end through the

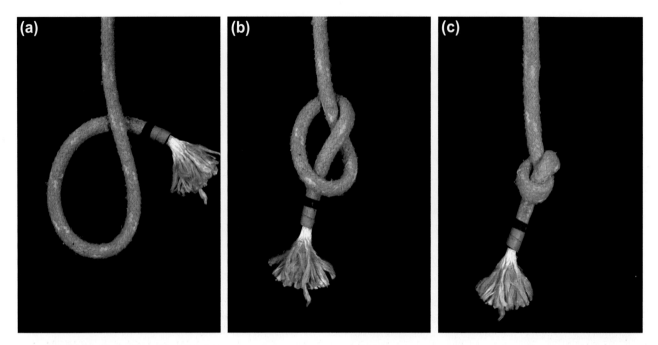

Fig. 10.5 Overhand knot step-by-step.

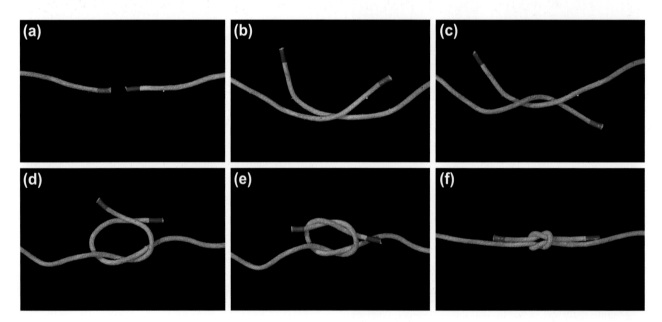

Fig. 10.6 Square knot step-by-step.

loop; and pull! Congratulations, you've learned a knot. Of course, you probably already knew this one—and be careful not to use it too much, since it is the one knot that can destroy rope faster than any other.

The **square knot** is the basis for so much (Fig. 10.6). Almost everyone knows how to tie this knot, or at least has heard of it. Also known as a *reef knot*, the square knot is secure and easy to untie. While holding both ends of the rope, cross the right side over left and wrap around the left, just like when starting to tie your shoes. Then cross the left over the right and wrap. Pull to make the knot tight. To untie, hold both ends and both sides of the loop and push them toward each other.

The **bowline** is my personal favorite (Fig. 10.7). I learned it in Girl Scouts, where we were told to recite the following story while tying the knot: The little bunny comes out of

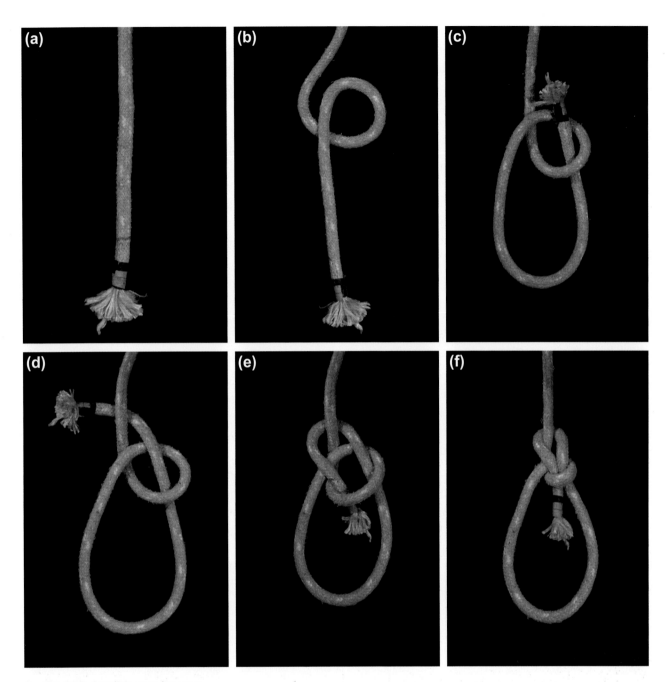

(a)

(b)

(c)

(d)

(e)

(f)

■ **Fig. 10.7** Bowline step-by-step.

the hole, walks around the tree, and goes back in the hole. OK, so you'll understand that better after I describe it more fully. A bowline is one of the most important knots to know. If properly tied, it will not slip and can be used to secure things or lift people. Hold one end of the rope in your left hand. With the portion of rope in your left hand, make a small loop in the rope above your hand with the part going away from you on the underside of the loop. With the piece of rope in your right hand feed it through this small loop

from the bottom. Take it around the piece of rope going away from you. Bring the end back down through the small loop. Pull the end tight.

The **clove hitch** is very important to almost every rigging job in the theatre. Used as a traditional hitch that secures only one end, the clove hitch is liable to slip. It requires a load attached in each direction to be effective. Since the clove hitch is almost always a load-bearing knot, it should not be tied with rope that is thin or very slippery, as it can work itself loose, especially under a swinging or rotating load. However, for this very reason, the knot is useful in situations where the length of the rope ends need to be adjustable. It can also jam and become difficult to untie under some situations, so be aware of this.

To tie a clove hitch, first place a loop around the pipe, with the working end of the rope on top (Fig. 10.8). Run the working end around the pole once more until you meet the place where the ropes cross, then pass the working end under the cross. Pull to tighten. Sounds easy, right? Well, going correctly under the cross can be confusing, and it is the step that makes the clove hitch secure. Practice this repeatedly until you can do it almost without having to think about it.

You can use the clove hitch to join two pieces of pipe or wood together. You can also use it for pulling a straight length of pipe up into the air. To do this you need the **half hitch**. The half hitch is really a cornerstone knot that forms the basis for a multitude of other knots, and so you should take the time to truly master it. By itself, it is not particularly reliable. To tie a half hitch, loop your rope around the pipe. Cross the short end under the long, main length of the rope. Bring the short end over and down through the hole between where the rope crosses and the pole. Push the knot to the pole, and pull to tighten!

Now you can raise straight pipes using a combination of the clove hitch and the half hitch: Grab the pipe, tie a clove hitch at the bottom, flick the rope around the top, and do a half hitch to pull the pipe up without it flailing. Now, you've got the basis for knots in the theatre. Most other knots are based on these. Once these are mastered, all the other ones are easily learned.

Belaying is not technically a knot, but it does have to do with all of our rigging (Fig. 10.9). To belay, you need a cleat or pin. The goal is to secure a rope by winding it in a figure-eight pattern around the cleat. To secure the belay, the final figure-eight wrap gets a 180-degree twist before being put on the cleat. Pull down on the working end of the rope to tighten.

A quick note about working with any kind of rope. Every time you tie a knot in it, you weaken the rope at the point of the knot. Keep this in mind and realize that rope does have a life span. Knowing all of this helps you to properly store rope to extend its life and keep your backstage area as clean and safe as possible. This brings us to the last knot I discuss, and again it is not actually a knot.

Coiling rope is one of the few ways you can safely store rope without putting any bends, kinks, or knots in it. It doesn't take much time to learn or to do on a regular basis. Once you are in the habit, you'll wonder how you continually stepped over piles of rope in the dark for so long. To coil a rope, take one end and make a big loop. The loop size will change depending on the diameter of the rope, but let's say it should be around 18 inches. Continue to loop more

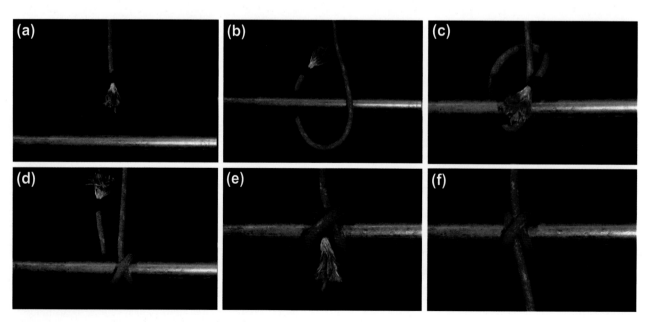

■ **Fig. 10.8** Clove hitch step-by-step.

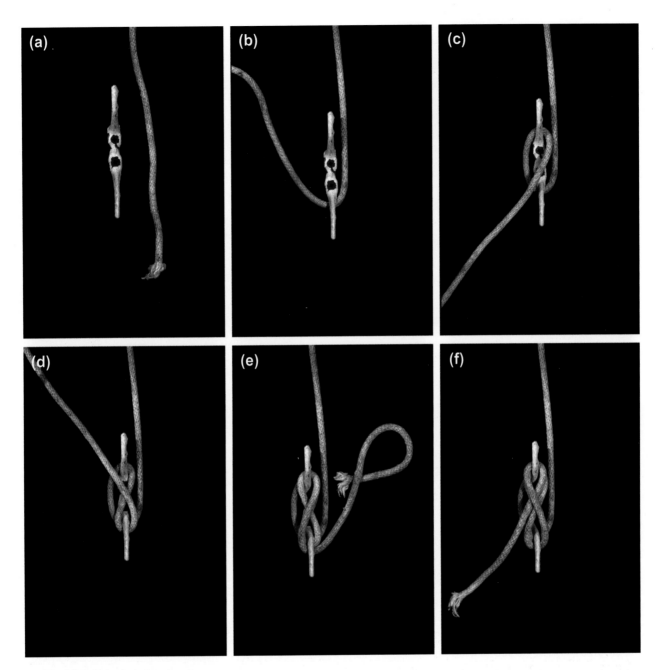

■ **Fig. 10.9** Belaying step-by-step.

and more of the rope in this way until you have about 2 feet left. Hold the looped rope in your left hand and grab the remaining rope in your right. Begin to wrap the remaining rope around the top of the loop; it will probably take five to six wraps. Then, thread the loose end of the rope through the coils and pull tight.

The **monkey's fist** is an interesting knot to know about, based on its history (Fig. 10.10). I won't explain how to tie it, as you will probably never need it. However, there are interesting stories about it, and it is a fun knot to know about. Sailors on boats originally used the monkey's fist. Once the knot is tightened it adds a substantial amount of weight to the end of the rope. This allowed the sailors to throw the rope up into the air, hope to go over something, and have the rope come back down. The extra weight helped that last part. Putting a stone or marble into the fist and tying the knot around it is the original way to do it. This added more weight and made it easier to tighten the knot.

Fig. 10.10 The monkey's fist is a knot that is more about tightening than tying. It's fun to attempt once you are more advanced.

The key with this knot is not tying it, but tightening it. I like to tie it without the stone or marble as more of a challenge.

RIGGING SYSTEMS

OK, now that you've learned the basic knots, let's start looking at the basic rigging system within a theatre. All theatres have parts of the following in common. There are differences, and I point these out along the way. Let's start by talking about line sets. **Line sets** are the individual rigging points for hanging pipes and scenery in the air. It doesn't matter how they are hung, if they are in the air, they are line sets. The **line set inventory** tells everyone where the pipes are in relation to the plaster line (Fig. 10.11). That way everyone has a line that they can all reference. If everyone agrees to the same point of reference, then any information after that is coordinated.

Over time, while working in the theatre, you will be exposed to four basic rigging systems: hemp house, single

Fig. 10.11 Sample line set inventory.

purchase, double purchase, and winch or automated. We look at each system one at a time, explaining the varying reasons for each. All are still in use today at different theatres, and all are viable options for many of the techniques you'll learn, which carry over to other rigging topics we discuss. Don't think that you'll ever run into a hemp house or a double purchase system and just ignore the information. There is something to learn within each style and use elsewhere (Fig. 10.12).

HEMP HOUSE

I spoke with Jason Adams at the 1869 Bardavon Opera House while the stage house was being renovated. Jason said the theatre had evaluated many options before deciding to stay as a hemp house. A **hemp house**, or rope house, is defined as such since the lift lines from the battens are rope, organic or synthetic, not wire. A hemp system is counterweighted with sandbags tied onto the lines. Wow, hang on, what is a counterweight? A **counterweight** is used to offset the weight of what you are trying to lift. Think of a seesaw (Fig. 10.13): There is a pivot point in the middle and a child sits on one end, which makes that side drop to the ground. If a child sits on the other end (providing a counterweight), then the first child can rise into the air.

The locking device to make sure nothing falls down unexpectedly is a **pin rail**. Belaying, which we just learned, is done using the working end of the rope and the pin rail. When you do this, keep in mind you are holding all the weight until you get it tied off. The same is true when you are untying the line. Make sure you have a good hold on the rope above the pin rail. Once the belay is released you will be holding all the weight.

The next step in the rigging progression is to add weight to the working line before belaying to the pin rail. This is the counterweight that helps to balance the weight on the other end of the rope. **Sandbags** are just what they sound like: a bag filled with sand (Fig. 10.14). They come in a variety of shapes and sizes. The difference in the sizes

■ **Fig. 10.12** Even the rigging backstage can look awesome with the right lighting!

changes the amount of sand and therefore the weight of the filled bag. The goal is to add enough sandbags to the working end of the rope to equal the weight on the other end.

For all of this to work properly, a number of pieces or hardware has to be in place. Let's discuss those now, so we can get a bigger view of the rigging system. We look at each type of system individually. Some of the hardware repeats for each

system, so as we go, it will get a little easier. Let's start with a hemp house. Hemp rigging is the simplest of all the rigging systems. Let's get some vocabulary out of the way. A **sheave** is basically a pulley. It has a groove around its circumference to support and contain a rope and a bearing at its center to permit rotation. A block is an assembly that consists of one or more sheaves in a housing. A **spot block** is designed for a temporary and easily movable connection to a gridiron or other theatre structure. A **head block** is a pulley mounted to overhead steel above the fly loft that changes the direction of multiple ropes. A **loft block** is a pulley mounted to the gridiron or support steel that supports and changes the direction of a lift line rope between the load and the head block. Figure 10.15 illustrates how all the parts we've just talked about go together.

The rope attaches to the pipe with a clove hitch. Then, the rope goes straight up to the loft block. The rope could also go to a spot block. All the blocks have pulleys, so the rope goes through it to make a 90-degree change of direction. Due to the width of the rope, the groove is U-shaped. Usually, three or five ropes are attached to the pipe. All

■ **Fig. 10.13** Seesaw with a center pivot point.

■ **Fig. 10.14** Sandbags on the floor backstage, waiting for their next job.

these now go over to the head block, where they go through their individual sheaves and turn direction again. The various blocks have to have enough sheaves to accommodate the number of ropes per pipe. Once the ropes come out of the head block, a sandbag is attached. Then, the ropes continue down to the pin rail, where they are belayed to secure them.

> This hemp system has smells and feels and sounds and it's like a full sensory experience. You can feel flex in the floor . . . and anything that gives you a little weird feeling is to be paid attention to!
>
> **—Jason Adams, 1869 Bardavon Opera House**

If you are dealing with something that is extraordinarily heavy, you can add a block and fall for an additional mechanical advantage. A **block and fall** is a piece of equipment that simulates the standard blocks, allowing multiple ropes to come in through the top. The difference is in the "fall" side, as it reduces the number of ropes coming back out down to one. The ropes coming out of the head block are now tied off to the top of the block and fall. This reduces the number of ropes to one and also the overall weight to make it workable for one stagehand to move the pipe. The bottom of the block and fall is fixed to the pin rail.

Keep in mind the goal is to balance the weight, to keep it in place, and make the pipe lighter, to get it moving. If you have to choose, you always want the pipe to be slightly heavier than the sandbags, so the pipe is more likely to drift down rather than up. This helps when you are flying pipes into the floor and doesn't really affect anything when the pipe is tied off. A **dead lift** is tough, meaning trying to lift the full weight with no help from counterweights. You can't get enough hands around the rope to physically lift heavy items. Plus, the stagehands have to take one hand off the rope to move their hand higher before pulling again.

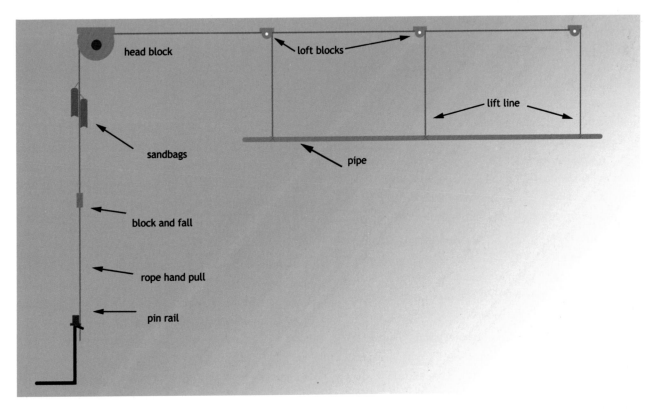

■ **Fig. 10.15** Diagram of a hemp house.

SINGLE PURCHASE

Before we change topics to single and double counterweight systems, let's introduce some more vocabulary. We are now changing from using synthetic rope to using wire rope (Fig. 10.16). **Wire rope** consists of a number of strands twisted on the diagonal around a core. Each strand consists of a number of wires twisted on the diagonal around a core. You can see how strong it can be! A **thimble** is a grooved fitting around which a wire rope is bent to form an eye. It supports the rope and prevents it from kinking and wear. To hold the thimble in place, you use a **wire rope clip**. This is a U-shaped bolt and a pad with two holes for sliding up the bolt. Two small nuts are used for holding the pad in place. The wire rope comes out of the thimble and doubles back on itself. Both pieces of rope go between the bolt and the pad. Once the nuts are tightened, the wire rope stays securely in place.

The **arbor** is a carriage or rack that contains weights, usually cast iron called pig iron. The **loading floor** is where the technicians add and remove counterweights from the arbors. It is usually located so that technicians can change the weights when the pipe is at the lowest level.

In both single and double purchase systems, the rigging overhead is identical. Wire rope goes up to the loft block. Blocks can be shaped differently, depending on how they are to be hung and how many ropes must pass through them. As wire rope is thinner than synthetic rope, it uses a

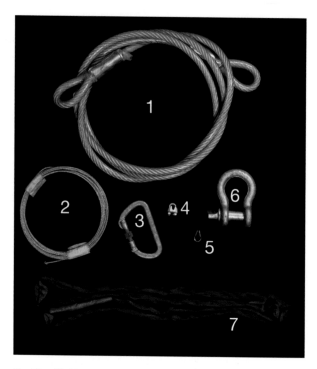

■ **Fig. 10.16** (1) ⅝-inch wire rope sling, (2) ⅛-inch wire rope, (3) locking carabiner, (4) ⅛-inch wire rope clip, (5) $1/16$-inch thimble, (6) ⅝-inch shackle, and (7) 3-foot span set.

V-shaped track in the blocks. The wire rope goes through the head block and down to the arbor. A wire rope then connects directly to the arbor. The **hand pull** is a big, thick, synthetic rope that attaches to the bottom of the arbor and goes around to the head of the block. Pulling on the hand pull raises and lowers the pipe.

In a **single purchase** setup, the loading floor is on the stage floor (Fig. 10.17). This means you lose a lot of stage space in wings to accommodate the arbors. The advantage of the single purchase system is that the counterweight requires a 1:1 ratio. You need to add one pound on the pipe for every one pound of arbor weight.

DOUBLE PURCHASE

A **double purchase** system puts the loading floor halfway between the stage floor and the loft blocks (Fig. 10.18). There is also an extra pulley, both above and below the arbor, to double the wire rope length. This is necessary to make the system work properly. The pipe travels 1 foot for every 2 feet the rope has to travel. You need to use twice the amount of weight of what is hung on the pipe. The advantage is that you lose no floor space. This is often the major deciding factor in which type of system to use.

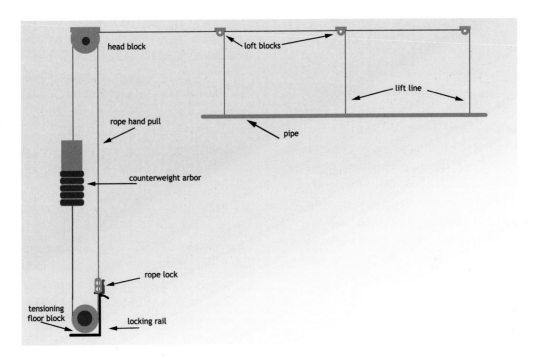

Fig. 10.17 Diagram of a single purchase system.

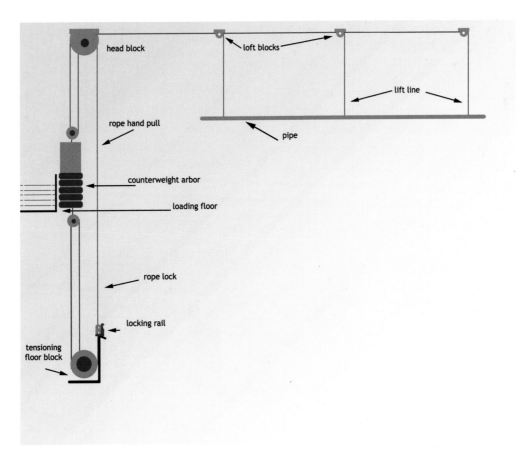

Fig. 10.18 Diagram of a double purchase system.

Let's look at automated systems next. **Winches** are geared mechanisms that can be either hand operated or motorized. They are used to raise or move heavy equipment. The gearing produces a mechanical advantage in both speed and load capacity. As a transition between counterweight and winches, let's look at the counterweight assisted-winch setup. This is a motorized winch that is retrofitted into existing manually operated systems that use counterbalancing weights. The counterbalancing weights are fixed at 50 percent of the maximum capacity of the set. The winch is rated at 50 percent of the maximum capacity of the set. The winch operates the line set at any load from 0 to 100 percent of its rated capacity, without the need to ever adjust the counterbalancing weights.

Fully motorized systems contain one of two types of winches: single drum winches and line shafts. A drum winch system has a head block and loft blocks, just like a regular counterweight system. This is a good way to motorize a system and balance the costs. The line shaft winch has a drum for each lift line, which eliminates the need for blocks. The biggest concern with the line shaft system is the cost. If your system has 30 line sets, you need 150 drums.

TRUSS

A truss is our next concept in the realm of rigging. A **truss** is two or more pieces of pipe fabricated together with cross bracing (Fig. 10.19). This is used in place of standard pipes when you have extremely heavy loads to lift or there are extended distances between lift lines (Figs. 10.20 and 10.21). Trusses come in a variety of shapes and lengths. There are flat trusses, triangular trusses, square trusses, and then any kind of custom shape you can think of (Fig. 10.22).

Let me also explain that there is a major difference in rigging truss for a theatre versus an arena. In a theatre, a truss usually is rigged no higher than a normal pipe. In an arena, that is not the case. Arena rigging can be much higher, and the riggers that do this work are specialists.

A 12" × 12" general purpose truss is manufactured from 2" dia × 0.125" wall and 1" dia × 0.125" wall 6082T6 or 6061T6 aluminum tubing. Bolts are supplied for assembly of truss elements. This truss is ideal for conference, exhibition, and small venue work. By incorporating suitable sleeve blocks and towers, this truss can be used with a ground support system. An 18" × 12" is manufactured the same way as the 12" × 12" but has the added advantage, due to its width of 18", of being able to accommodate two lighting bars back to back (Fig. 10.23). Also, the truss is slightly stronger over longer spans. It is made from 6061T6 or 6082T6 alloy 2" × 0.125" tubes for the main chords and 1" × 0.125" tubes for the diagonals. The truss can be used with a ground support system with suitable sleeve blocks and towers (Fig. 10.24).

The 20.5" × 30" truss is for those ever increasing load requirement situations. The truss is connected together with bolts as standard and can be used with a ground support system by using suitable sleeve blocks and towers. This truss can also be specified with castor wheels. The main chords of the truss are made from 2" × 0.157" and the diagonals are 1" × 0.125". The pre-rig truss is 30" × 26" in size (Fig. 10.25). It is manufactured from aluminum tube 6082-T6 with 2" × 0.125" wall thickness for main tubes and 1" × 0.125" wall tube for the diagonals. Each truss piece has four castor wheels for easy maneuverability and bolts for the connection of truss pieces.

■ **Fig. 10.19** Different styles of truss.

■ **Fig. 10.20** Hick, a rigger for the 1869 Bardavon Opera House, stands next to a 1-ton chain hoist box during a load-in.

Each truss is designed to carry two lighting bars complete with lanterns. The lighting bars are stored internally in the truss and can be lowered to the working position when in use. This design reduces the amount of space required for lighting and rigging in the truck. Each truss is also designed to carry a varying amount of lanterns, the 10' section carries two bars of eight lanterns, the 7' 7" section carries two bars of six lanterns, the 5' section carries two bars of four lanterns, and the 3' 9½" section carries two bars of three lanterns. This feature enables great flexibility in the truss design.

The pre-rig truss accepts a modified lighting bar, which has two sleeved holes in it. The lighting bars are located inside the truss by guide rods. In the storage position the bars are securely held in the truss by shank hooks. The whole system can be used with a ground support system by using suitable sleeve blocks and towers. A revolutionary truss was designed to offer all the advantages of the regular prerigged in a single bar pre-rig layout. The size is 20.5" wide × 20.5" deep × 96" long as standard. The truss features a guide rod. This truss allows the use of pre-rig lighting bars with short nose PAR lanterns. It is ideal for when a small truck pack is required.

The moving light truss has been designed around the prerigged truss size (Fig. 10.26). The truss is 91" × 30" × 26" in size (other sizes are available). It is manufactured from aluminum tube 6082-T6 with a 2" × 0.125" wall thickness for main tubes and a 1" × 0.125" wall tube for the diagonals. Each truss piece has eight castor wheels for easy maneuverability and bolts for the connection of truss pieces.

Each 91" truss is designed to carry three moving light fixtures. The moving lights are stored internally in the truss and can be lowered to the working position when in use. This design reduces the amount of space required for

■ **Fig. 10.21** A box truss with chain hoist attached, waiting to be raised.

■ **Fig. 10.22** A curved box truss at Production Resource Group.

GP 18 x 12

18" x 12" manufactured the same way as 12" x 12", but has an added advantage, due to its width of 18" of being able to accommodate 2 lighting bars back to back. Also the truss is slightly stronger over longer spans. It is made from 6061T6 or 6082T6 alloy 2" x 0.125" tubes for the main chords and 1" x 0.125" tubes for the diagonals. The truss can be used with Ground Support System with suitable sleeve blocks and towers.

PRODUCT CODE	DESCRIPTION	WT lbs
B0600	10' Section	61.5
B0601	8' Section	52.5
B0602	5' Section	37.5
B0603	2' 6" Section	24
B4600	3m Section	61.5
B4601	2.5m Section	53
B4602	2m Section	42
B4603	1.5m Section	37.5
B4604	1m Section	28.5
B4605	0.5m Section	19.5
B4608	4 Way Corner Block	22
B46	5 Way Corner Block	
B4	6 Way Corner Block	

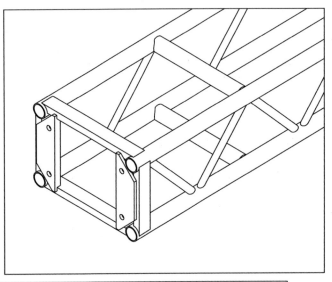

Allowable Load Data	Maximum Allowable Uniform Loads		Maximum Allowable Center Point Loads	
Span feet (meters)	Loads pounds (kgs)	Maximum deflection inches (mm)	Loads pounds (kgs)	Maximum deflection inches (mm)
10 (3.048)	6140 (2785)	0.276 (7)	4497 (2040)	0.20 (8)
20 (6.096)	3100 (1406)	1.10 (28)	1550 (703)	1.10 (28)
30 (9.144)	1726 (783)	2.20 (56)	864 (392)	2.20 (56)
40 (12.192)	855 (388)	2.95 (75)	427 (194)	2.95 (75)
50 (15.24)	425 (193)	3.70 (94)	214 (97)	3.70 (94)

LOADING FIGURES show maximum loads between supports in addition to the self weight of the truss. Information extracted from the structural report by Broadhurst, Goodwin, and Dunn suit maximum shear capacity. All loads include 20% overload factor for dynamic effects.

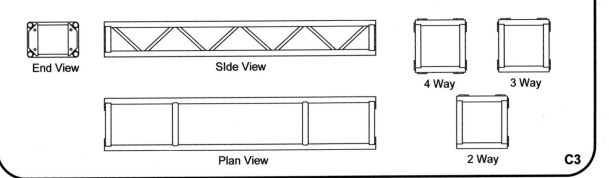

End View   Side View   4 Way   3 Way

Plan View   2 Way   C3

Fig. 10.23 James Thomas Engineering's general purpose 18″ × 12″ truss.

GP TRIANGULAR

ENGINEERING

23 1/4" x 60 degree equilateral triangular truss is designed and manufactured for high strength, in relation to storage space required. The main chords are 2" x 0.125" tube and the diagonals are 1" x 0.125" tube in either 6082T6 or 6061T6. The truss can be used with a Ground Support System with appropriate Sleeve Blocks and Towers. Each section is complete with bolts.

PRODUCT CODE	DESCRIPTION	WT lbs
B0500	10' section	66
B0501	8' section	53
B0502	5' section	35
B4500	3m section	66
B4501	2.5m section	53
B4502	2m section	44
B4503	1.5m section	35
B4504	1m section	26.5
B4505	2 way corner block	35
B4506	3 way corner block	39.5
B4507	4 way corner block	44
B4508	Flat pivot section	39.5

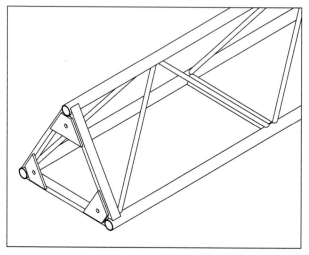

Allowable Load	Maximum Allowable Uniform Loads		Maximum Allowable Center Point Loads	
Span feet (meters)	Loads pounds (kgs)	Maximum deflection inches (mm)	Loads pounds (kgs)	Maximum deflection inches (mm)
10 (3.048)	5600 (2540)+	0.1 (2)	2800 (1270)+	0.1 (2)
15 (4.572)	5600 (2540)+	0.34 (8)	2800 (1270)+	0.34 (8)
20 (6.096)	4700 (2131)	0.70 (17)	2350 (1065)	0.70 (17)
25 (7.62)	3700 (1678)	1.09 (27)	1850 (839)	1.09 (27)
30 (9.144)	3000 (1360)	1.57 (39)	1500 (680)	1.57 (39)
40 (12.192)	2100 (952)	2.8 (71)	1050 (476)	2.8 (71)
50 (15.24)	1300 (589)*	3.75 (95)	650 (294)*	3.75 (95)
60 (18.288)	700 (317)*	4.50 (114)	350 (158)*	4.50 (114)

LOADING FIGURES show maximum loads between supports in addition to self weight of truss. Information extracted from structural report by Jessie Mise. + Denotes load limited to suit maximum shear capacity. *Denotes load limited to a maximum deflection of (span /160). All loads include a 20% overload factor for dynamic effects.

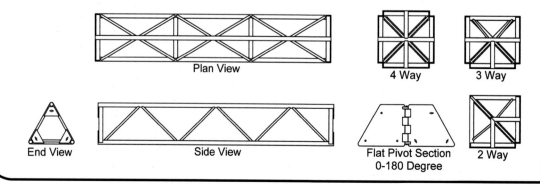

Plan View

4 Way   3 Way

End View   Side View   Flat Pivot Section 0-180 Degree   2 Way

C6

■ **Fig. 10.24** General purpose triangular truss.

PRE-RIG TRUSS

Pre-Rig truss is 30" x 26" in size. It is manufactured from aluminium tube 6082-T6 with 2" x .125" wall thickness for main tubes and 1" x .125" wall tube for the diagonals. Each truss piece has 4 castor wheels for easy maneuverability and bolts for the connection of truss pieces.

Each truss is designed to carry 2 lighting bars complete with lanterns. The lighting bars are stored internally in the truss and can be lowered to the working position when in use. This design reduces the amount of space required for lighting and rigging in the truck. Each truss is also designed to carry a varying amount of lanterns, the 10' section carries 2 bars of 8 lanterns, 7' 7"section carries 2 bars of 6 lanterns, 5' section carries 2 bars of 4 lanterns, and the 3' 9-1/2" section carries 2 bars of 3 lanterns. This feature enables great flexibility in the truss design.

The Pre-Rig truss accepts a modified lighting bar which have 2 sleeved holes in them. The lighting bars are located inside the truss by guide rods. In the storage position the bars are securely held in the truss by shank hooks. The whole system can be used with our Ground Support System by using suitable sleeve blocks and towers.

PRODUCT CODE	DESCRIPTION	WT lbs
B0300	10' section (empty)	111.3
B0301	7' 7" section (empty)	91
B0302	5' section (empty)	77.15
B0303	3' 9 1/2" section (empty)	57.35
B0304	6"-12" make up piece (empty)	-
B4300	2 way corner block	52.9
B4301	4 way corner block	61.75
B4302	Universal pivot section 0-270 degree	59.5
B4303	Universal pivot section 0-90 degree	59.5
B4304	Horizontal load-bearing pivot section	123.5
B4305	Vertical load-bearing pivot section	123.5
B4306	P.R.T. to G.P. adapter	28.65

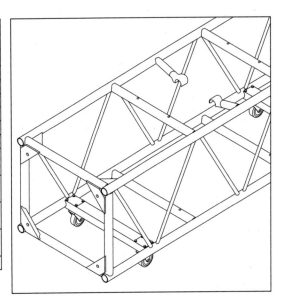

Par 64 lanterns in storage position

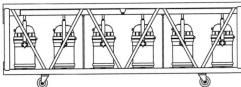

Par 64 lanterns lowered to operating position

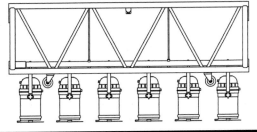

To lower lanterns from storage to operating position, simply pull tab on shank hook with one hand whilst holding the lighting bar with the other hand. Then lower the lanterns into operating position.

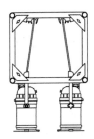

C12

Fig. 10.25 James Thomas Engineering's pre-rig truss.

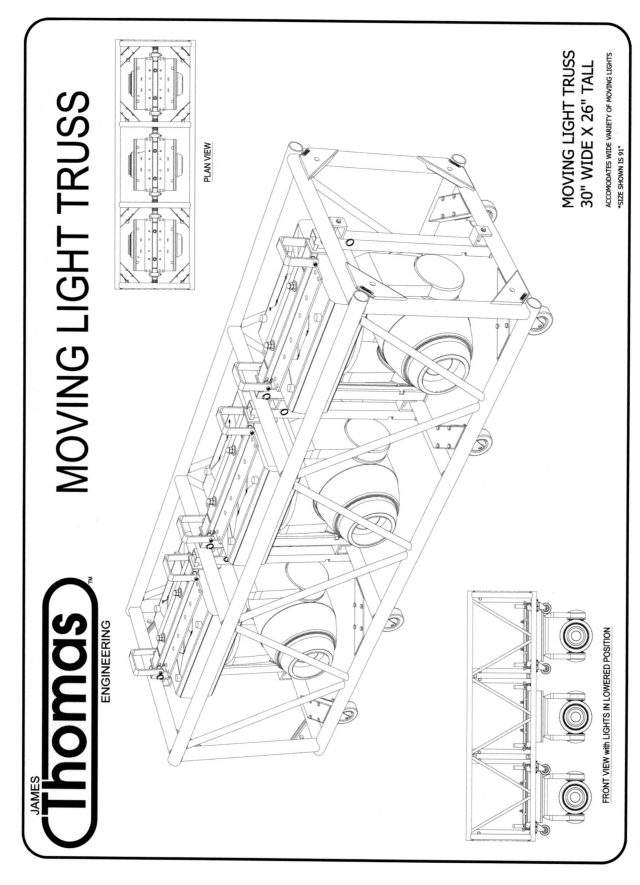

JAMES

Thomas™

ENGINEERING

MOVING LIGHT TRUSS

PLAN VIEW

MOVING LIGHT TRUSS
30" WIDE X 26" TALL

ACCOMODATES WIDE VARIETY OF MOVING LIGHTS
*SIZE SHOWN IS 91"

FRONT VIEW with LIGHTS IN LOWERED POSITION

Fig. 10.26 James Thomas Engineering's moving light truss.

lighting and rigging in the truck. Two handles allow the lowering of each moving light. The whole system can be used with a ground support system by using suitable sleeve blocks and towers.

Supertruss is the revolutionary truss designed to offer all the advantages of the 20.5" supertruss in a 12" × 12" layout (Fig. 10.27). The 12" × 12" supertruss provides a substantial increase in load-bearing capacity over the existing general purpose 12" × 12" truss. The main chords of the truss are made from 2" × 0.157" 6061-T6, and the diagonals are 1" × 0.125" in an 18" × 12" layout. This truss has the advantage of being able to accommodate two lighting bars back to back. The 18" × 12" supertruss provides a substantial increase in load-bearing capacity over the general purpose 18" × 12" truss. It is made from 6061-T6 alloy 2" × 0.157" tubes in the main chords and 1" × 0.125" tubes in the diagonals.

The ProPlus rescue system™ from Sapsis Rigging, Inc., needs to be mentioned as well (Fig. 10.28). The rescue system was designed by and for entertainment industry professionals.

This versatile lifting and lowering system is a cost effective rescue system for people working at heights. The ProPlus rescue system is lightweight, compact, and can be set up quickly. With a 3:1 mechanical advantage, the system can be easily operated by one person. No special tools are needed to install or remove and all components are reusable.

Designed for assisted rescue from the deck or from the truss, the system can be mounted on a grid, on a truss, or in the high steel. It meets or exceeds all applicable industry standards, including OSHA and ANSI Z359-2007.

The ProPlus rescue system consists of

- A manually operated controlled decent device.
- 15' (extended) telescoping rescue pole with rescue clip.
- Carabiner for use with the rescue pole.
- Scaffold hook for system anchorage.
- Synthetic rescue ladder for use in an alternate rescue scenario.
- 100' × ½" Showbraid synthetic rope.
- Rescue 8 with ears.
- Storage bags with attachment straps.
- Utility gloves.
- Operating manual.
- ProPlus T-shirt.

Span sets, generically known as *round slings*, are continuous loops of monofilament or steel-galvanized aircraft cable in a canvaslike (polyester) sheath. The number of loops used determines rating or weight capacity. A wire rope sling is an alternative to the span set. A wire rope sling is made from larger gauge wire rope and is fabricated with a large eye and thimble at each end.

To use the span set or wire rope sling you need a shackle. The shackle is a U-shaped device with holes at each end to accommodate a pin or bolt. There are three different configurations for using a span set with a shackle. The strongest of these is called a *basket*. This is made by creating a U shape out of the span set. It gives you four points of contact. The next configuration is to use the span set straight. This gives you two points of contact. The last is the choke. You wrap one end around and put one through the other. It is not as strong, since a bend weakens the line of the span set. Of course, there are ways to shackle two span sets together for more length and flexibility.

> The only thing that can ever go wrong in a fly rail or rigging system is operator error! Your best friends are in danger of you killing them at any minute!
> —Jason Adams, 1869 Bardavon Opera House

I cannot stress enough how dangerous rigging systems can be if they are not used properly. Regular inspection prevents a lot of problems. The person operating the system needs to pay attention to every part of the system. The initial installation needs to be done properly, of course. Regular inspection should be a continuous process during the use of equipment, as well as one or two times a year for a complete maintenance inspection. With that said, if you do the job well, there will be time to relax between cues (Fig. 10.29).

SUPERTRUSS
12 x 12

The revolutionary truss designed to offer all the advantages of the 20.5" Supertruss in a 12" x 12" layout. The 12" x 12" Supertruss provides a substantial increase in load bearing capacity over the existing GP 12" x 12" truss. The main chords of the truss are made from 2" x 0.157" 6061-T6, and the diagonals are 1" x 0.125".

PRODUCT CODE	DESCRIPTION	WT lbs
B1260A	12' Section	87
B1261	10' Section	72
B1262	8' Section	67
B1263	6' Section	51
B1264	5' Section	42
B1265	2' 6" Section	27
B1200A	60 Degree corner gate	14
B1201	90 Degree corner gate	8
B1203	135 Degree corner gate	5
B1204A	3 Way gate/ 120° gate	8
B1204B	3 Way gate with lifting point	8
B1208	Square support plate	4
B1211	12" Super-truss to GP 12" x 12" adaptor gate	7
G6671A	12" Supertruss pin extraction tool	7

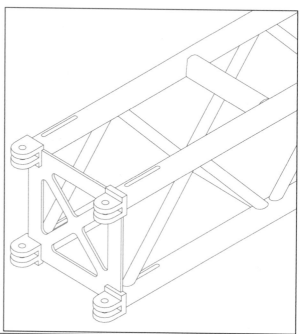

Allowable Load Data	Maximum Allowable Uniform Loads		Maximum Allowable Center Point Loads	
Span feet (meters)	Loads pounds (kgs)	Maximum deflection inches (mm)	Loads pounds (kgs)	Maximum deflection inches (mm)
10 (3.048)	8496 (3854)*	0.20 (5)	7348 (3333)	0.20 (5)
20 (6.096)	7255 (3291)	1.50 (38)	3628 (1646)	1.50 (38)
30 (9.144)	3324(1508)	2.20 (56)	1662 (754)	2.20 (56)
40 (12.192)	1695 (769)	2.95 (75)	848 (385)	2.95 (75)
50 (15.24)	888 (403)	3.70 (94)	445 (202)	3.70 (94)

LOADING FIGURES show maximum loads between supports in addition to self weight of truss. Information extracted from structural report by Broadhurst, Goodwin & Dunn for Super-truss manufactured after November 1993. * Denotes load limited to suit maximum shear capacity. All loads include 20% overload factor for dynamic effects.

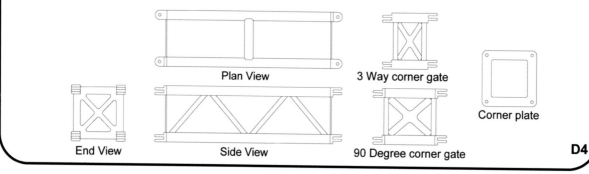

Plan View

3 Way corner gate

Corner plate

End View

Side View

90 Degree corner gate

D4

■ **Fig. 10.27** James Thomas Engineering's supertruss.

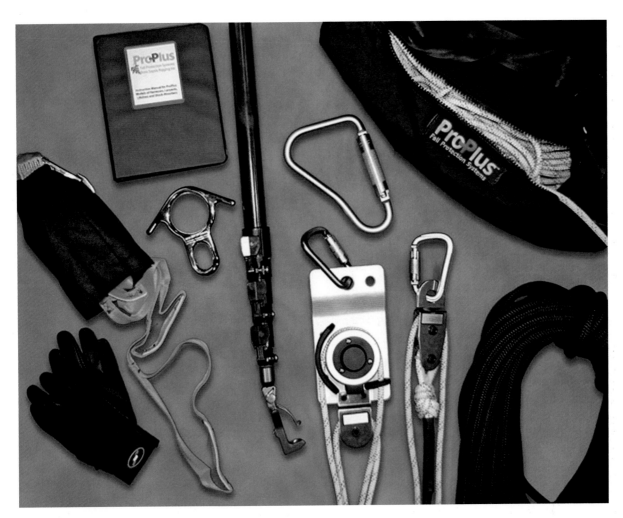

■ **Fig. 10.28** Sapsis Rigging Inc.'s ProPlus rescue system.

■ **Fig. 10.29** At the end of a long call, the riggers get a chance to relax!

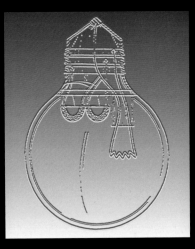

CHAPTER TEN
Study Words

Arbor

Belaying

Block and fall

Bowline

Clove hitch

Coiling

Counterweight

Dead lift

Double purchase

Half hitch

Hand pull

Head block

Hemp house

Line set

Line set inventory

Loading floor

Loft block

Monkey's fist

Overhand knot

Pin rail

Sandbag

Shackle

Sheave

Single purchase

Span set

Spot block

Square knot

Thimble

Truss

Winch

Wire rope

Wire rope clip

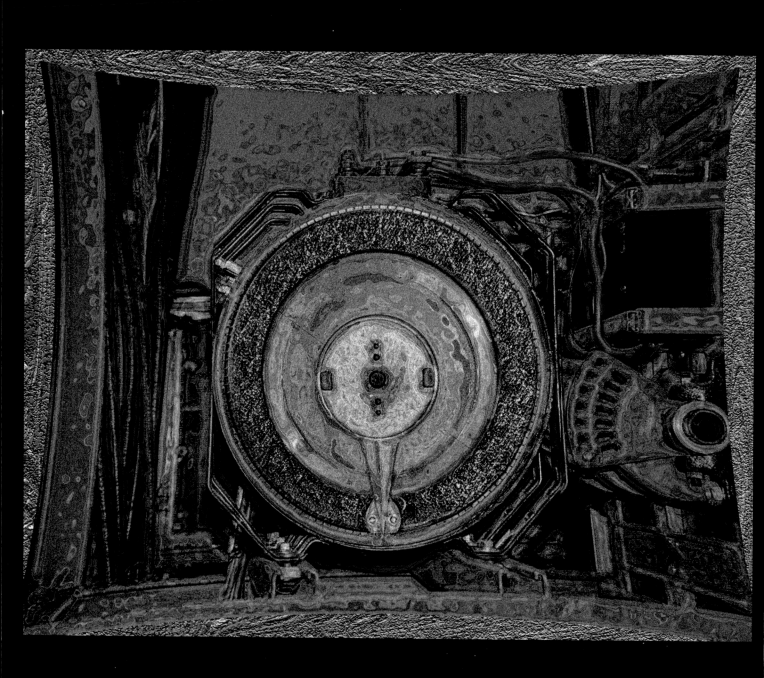

House to Half

Lighting

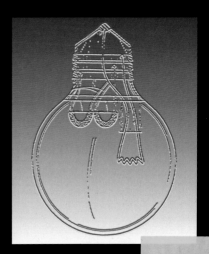

> McCandless . . . he's dead, let's move on!
>
> —M. L. Geiger

From all things scenic to lighting, this chapter discusses lighting. In the same format as other chapters, we discuss some of the history for lighting through a variety of developments straight to today's fixtures. Automation is the biggest overall change the lighting industry has seen since electricity. **Conventional lighting** (meaning nonmoving lights) and **intelligent lighting** (meaning the fixture can move in some way) are both viable options in today's theatre. In some ways, this is one department where both old and new technologies coexist on the stage seamlessly.

As with other chapters, we start by taking a look at theatrical lighting in history. So, I guess, we all know it started with the sun. The Greeks and Romans performed all their shows outside. They based the starting time for the show on the position of the sun. Once the theatre was moved indoors, in Shakespeare's time, the use of candles started to come into play (Fig. 11.1). The candles were used both as props as well as for overall ambience within the theatre.

The first **footlights** were candles. Footlights were named for exactly what they sound like: lights near your feet. Footlights are traditionally located on the downstage edge of the stage or apron (Fig. 11.2). They focus upstage toward the back wall,

Fig. 11.1 Candle, the original indoor light.

pointing up into the actors' faces from below. The "invention" of footlights was a changing point for lighting in the theatre. Suddenly, there was some control over the lighting. Putting candles on the edge of the stage wasn't enough. It was figured out pretty quickly that, if you put some sort of reflector behind the candle (meaning between the audience and the actor), the light would be brighter. It also wouldn't blind the audience. These reflectors became decorative, and that is how we primarily remember them.

A little taste of lighting control wasn't enough. The next step was to put a glass of colored liquid between the footlight and the actors. This changed the color of the light that was projected. Then, of course, the audience wanted it brighter, in different locations—more control, more control, more control.

What a surprise! Enter the wonderful world of gaslight. As gaslight began to be piped into buildings, people working in the theatre suddenly got some great ideas. And, this leads us to the invention of limelight. It was first used at the Convent Garden Theatre in London in 1837. Limelight is an intensely bright light created when a gas flame is directed at a cylinder of calcium oxide (Fig. 11.3). Let's hear it for chemical reactions!

Fig. 11.2 *Vagabond Stars* production using traditional footlights.

Enter Thomas Alva Edison to shed some additional light on the subject. Or rather Joseph Swan. Who, you might ask? Well, Sir Joseph Wilson Swan was a physicist and chemist in England, born in 1828. In 1850, he began working on a lightbulb, using carbonized paper **filaments** in an evacuated glass bulb. By 1860, he was able to demonstrate a working bulb and obtained a U.K. patent covering a partial vacuum, carbon filament **incandescent lightbulb**. However, the lack of a good vacuum and an adequate electric source resulted in an inefficient bulb with a short lifetime.

Fifteen years later, in 1875, Swan returned to consider the problems he had with the lightbulb. The most significant feature of Swan's improved lamp was that there was little residual oxygen in the vacuum tube to ignite the filament. This allowed the filament to glow almost white-hot without catching fire. However, his filament had low resistance, therefore needing heavy copper wires to supply it. Swan received a second British patent in 1878, about a year before Thomas Edison (Fig. 11.4).

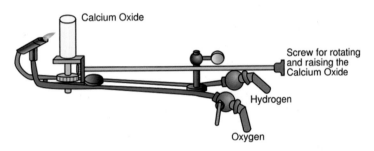

Fig. 11.3 How limelight actually worked.

Fig. 11.4 *Khovanschina* at the Metropolitan Opera. Director, August Everding; scenic designer, Ming Cho Lee; costume designer, John Conklin; and lighting designer, Gil Wechsler.

Fig. 11.5 Thomas Edison's original patent.

In America, Edison worked from copies of the original Swan patent, trying to make them more efficient. Though Swan had received a patent in England, Edison obtained patents in America for a fairly direct copy of the Swan light (Fig. 11.5). In 1878, Edison applied the term filament to the element of glowing wire carrying the current, as had Swan. At this point, Edison's main goal was to improve the longevity of the lamp so that it would have commercial possibilities. Edison took the early features and set his workers to the task of creating longer-lasting bulbs. By 1879, he had produced a new concept: a high-resistance lamp in a very high vacuum, which would burn for hundreds of hours (Fig. 11.6). Edison said, "We will make electricity so cheap that only the rich will burn candles."

Edison then started an advertising campaign claiming that he was the real inventor. Swan, who was less interested in making money from the invention, agreed that Edison

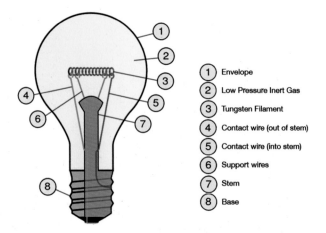

Fig. 11.6 Lightbulb diagram showing individual components.

1. Envelope
2. Low Pressure Inert Gas
3. Tungsten Filament
4. Contact wire (out of stem)
5. Contact wire (into stem)
6. Support wires
7. Stem
8. Base

THE LOVE MACHINE
Usher's OMG Tour is a seductive exercise in pop idol worship

Sharon Stancavage

Excerpt 1

Usher's current tour, entitled OMG, not only reflects the name of a hit single, it's also an accurate representation of the audience's reaction to the production. "We definitely wanted to have a show that would give an experience," explains show director Barry Lather, who also worked on Usher's last tour. The artist himself actively participated in the production. "He was very involved with lighting, wardrobe, set design, content, shoes, sound, microphone stands, and pyro—he understands all production, knows what he wants, and if he's not sure about something, he'll see it, develop, and shape it," notes Lather.

The tour, in support of the album Raymond v. Raymond and the extended mix Versus, is a typical Usher spectacle, with plenty of gags, effects, an elaborate production design, and extremely colorful lighting—all of it designed to woo and win his largely female fan base. Thus the star interacts seductively with his fans—in New York, an onstage romp with one of them ended when she accidentally kicked him in the face—and takes part in some graphic flirtations with his female dancers. According to Entertainment Weekly, "Such was the evening's loosely tied storyline: a thriving playboy trying to walk the straight and narrow path of monogamy."

Working with Lather was scenic designer Butch Allen, of Ugly American Productions. The production consists of Usher and a total of nine dancers as well as the band, so the stage needed to accommodate

could sell the lights in America while he retained the rights in Britain. To avoid a possible court battle with Swan, Edison and Swan formed a joint company called Ediswan, to manufacture and market the invention in Britain. And, you thought it was simple! Well, Edison wasn't done yet, read on.

The next development we talk about is the fluorescent lamp. A **fluorescent** lamp is a gas-discharge lamp that uses electricity to excite mercury vapor. The excited mercury produces shortwave ultraviolet (UV) light that causes a phosphor to fluoresce, producing visible light. Ugh, what a description. But you get enough of the idea, so let's move on. Unlike incandescent lamps, fluorescent lamps always require a **ballast** to start and properly control the flow of power through the lamp. A fluorescent lamp converts electrical power into useful light more efficiently than an incandescent lamp. Compared with incandescent lamps, fluorescent lamps use less power for the same amount of light and last longer.

Thomas Edison briefly pursued fluorescent lighting for its commercial potential. He invented a fluorescent lamp in 1896 that used a coating of calcium tungstate as the fluorescing substance, excited by X rays. It received a patent in 1907, but it was not put into production. Edison had little reason at this point to pursue an alternative means of electrical illumination. Nicola Tesla, from Croatia, made similar experiments in the 1890s, devising high-frequency-powered fluorescent bulbs that gave a bright greenish light, but as with Edison's devices, no commercial success was achieved. Although Edison lost interest in fluorescent lighting, one of his former employees, Daniel Moore, was able to create a gas-based lamp that achieved a measure of

commercial success. In 1895, Moore demonstrated lamps 7–9 feet in length that used carbon dioxide or nitrogen to emit white or pink light, respectively. As with future fluorescent lamps, there are pros and cons to each type of lamp.

After years of work, Moore was able to extend the operating life of the lamps by inventing an electromagnetically controlled valve that maintained a constant gas pressure within the tube. Although Moore's lamp was complicated, expensive to install, and required very high voltages, it was considerably more efficient than incandescent lamps, and it produced a more natural light than incandescent. That is right, fluorescent was more natural than early incandescent! The next development is the **halogen lightbulb**. It is an incandescent lamp with a tungsten filament. The filament is sealed into a compact transparent, **quartz envelope**, filled with an inert gas and a small amount of halogen. The halogen increases the lifetime of the bulb by depositing tungsten from the inside of the bulb back onto the filament. Another benefit is that the halogen lamp can operate at a higher temperature. Thus ends the age-old question: Is it tungsten, halogen, or quartz? Well, actually it's all three!

Today, bulbs come in all sorts of options. The envelope shape has a whole bunch of possibilities and so does the base. Then there is the wattage. When you combine these three parts, you find that bulbs are actually very specific for the fixture you want to put them in. They are also specific for the purpose you have in mind. It is important to know the options so you can properly choose what you want, and also so that if you need to replace a bulb, you know which one to use. Take a look at

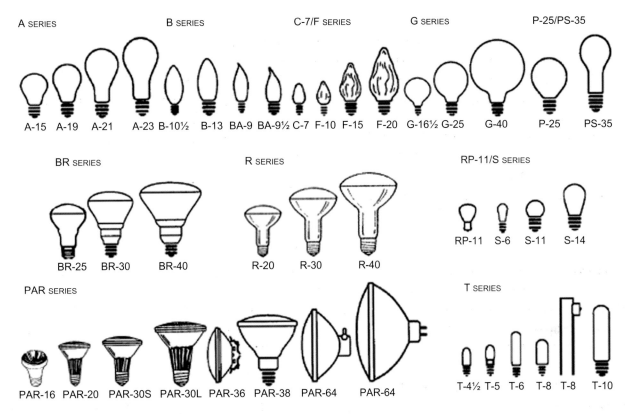

Fig. 11.7 Various envelope shapes.

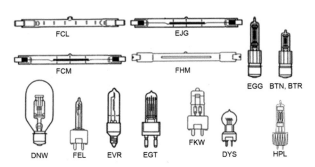

Fig. 11.8 Standard theatre lamp types.

Figures 11.7 and 11.8 to see charts of envelope shapes and base shapes.

The next thing to talk about is the **Kelvin** scale. Color temperature is a part of all visible light (Fig. 11.9). It is important in lighting, photography, film, and other fields. The color temperature of a light source is determined by comparing the quality of the color with that of the perfect black. Yellow-red colors are considered warm, and blue-green colors are considered cool (Fig. 11.10). Well, that is nothing new. Confusingly, higher Kelvin temperatures are considered cool and

lower color temperatures are considered warm. Cool light produces higher contrast. Warm light is considered more flattering to skin tones and clothing. The scale ranges from 1,000 to over 10,000. Some basic benchmarks along the scale follow:

KELVIN TEMPERATURE	BENCHMARK
1700 K	Match flame
1850 K	Candle flame
2800–3300 K	Standard lightbulb
3400 K	Theatre lamps, photofloods
4100 K	Moonlight
5000 K	Horizon daylight
5500–6000 K	Typical daylight
6500 K	Overcast daylight

ELECTRICITY

OK, before we go any further, we have to talk about electricity. I can't put it off any longer. It won't be that bad, so

■ **Fig. 11.9** *Tristan und Isolde* at the Metropolitan Opera. Director, Dieter Dorn; scenic and costume designer, Jurgen Rose; and lighting designer, Max Keller.

■ **Fig. 11.10** *Hedda Gabler* at NYU's Department of Graduate Acting and Department of Design for Stage and Film in 2005. Director, Cigdem Onat; scenic designer, Veronica Ferre; costume designer, Sarah Greene; and lighting designer, Dans Sheehan.

let's just do it and get it out of the way. Let's start with current. There are two kinds: direct and alternating. **Direct current** (DC) is an electric charge that flows in one direction. DC is produced by such sources as batteries and solar cells. DC may flow in a conductor, such as a wire, but can also be through semiconductors and insulators. On the other hand, **alternating current** (AC) is an electric current whose direction reverses cyclically. AC is the most efficient transmission of energy and is the type used in residences and commercial buildings.

The system of three-phase alternating current electrical generation and distribution was invented by a 19th century creative genius named Nicola Tesla. He made many careful calculations and measurements and found out that 60 Hz (Hertz, cycles per second) was the best frequency for alternating current power generating. He preferred 240 volts, which put him at odds with Thomas Edison, whose direct current systems were 110 volts.

Perhaps Edison had a useful point in the safety factor of the lower voltage, but DC couldn't provide the power to a distance that AC could.

When the German company AEG built the first European generating facility, its engineers decided to fix the frequency at 50 Hz, because the number 60 didn't fit the metric standard unit sequence (1, 2, 5). At that time, AEG had a virtual monopoly and their standard spread to the rest of the continent. In Britain, differing frequencies proliferated, and only after World War II was the 50-cycle standard established.

Originally, Europe was 120 V too, just like Japan and the United States today. It was deemed necessary to increase voltage to get more power with less loss and voltage drop from the same copper wire diameter. At the time, the United States also wanted to change, but because of the cost involved to replace all electric appliances, it decided not to. At the time (1950s–1960s), the average U.S. household already had a fridge, a washing-machine, and the like but not in Europe.

The result is that the United States is still evolving from the 1950s and 1960s and—mostly in older buildings—still copes with such problems as lightbulbs that burn out rather quickly when they are close to the transformer (too high a voltage) or, just the other way round, lack enough voltage at the end of the line (105 to 127 volt spread).

Note that, currently, all new American buildings get in fact 240 volts split in two 120s between the neutral and the hot wire. Major appliances, such as virtually all drying machines and ovens, are now connected to 240 volts. Mind, Americans who have European equipment shouldn't connect them to these outlets. Although it may work on some appliances, this will definitely not be the case for all of the equipment.

Electrical power, in general, is defined as the rate at which electrical energy is transferred by an electric circuit. The unit of measurement for this is the wattage (W). Voltage (V) is the difference of electrical potential between two points of a circuit. In the United States, the standard voltage is 120 V and 240 V but can range anywhere from 110 V to 240 V. In Europe, it is almost exclusively 220 V. The ampere (A), usually shortened to *amp*, is a unit of electric current, or amount of electric charge per second. Every theatre has a different amount of amps available for you. It is always good to know what is available before you begin to plug things in. You often have two of these three measurements and need to determine the last one. Consequently, the following three formulas apply to electricity for our needs. They are often referred to as the West Virginia formulas for somewhat obvious reasons.

$$W = VA$$

$$V = W/A$$

$$A = W/V$$

In your travels, you are likely to encounter two power types. First is single-phase power. You probably have this in your home, as it is most often used in residences and in more rural areas. You can tell single-phase power by looking at the main power feed lines coming into the breaker panel. You'll find two hot wires (typically one black and one red), a neutral wire (the white one), and a ground wire (the green one). Each hot wire, when measured with the neutral, equals the two halves of AC, and can be metered around 120 V. If you measure the two hot wires, one to the other, you get around 240 V. When I say around 120 V or around 240 V, this is because, in a perfect world, it would be exact. In actuality, you're likely find between 110 and 120 V and 220 and 240 V, depending on how much power is being used and, well, how the local power company is getting power into the building. The ground wire is there as a safety in case of some sort of short circuit.

Next to discuss in detail is three-phase power. You can tell three-phase power because it has three hot wires (black, red, and blue) along with the neutral and ground. Three-phase power is found more often in urban areas where there is industry or manufacturing. This is because there is a greater likelihood of motors and other equipment that require more overall power, which justifies the extra expense of installation. Each hot wire measured to neutral is around 120 V, while when measured to each other (black to red, red to blue, black to blue) is around 240 V. The neutral and ground wires work the same way here as in the single-phase system. Always be extremely careful around breaker panels since it is possible for *you* to be the short circuit. This would be bad!

There is no standard mains voltage throughout the world and also the frequency, that is, the number of times the current changes direction per second, is not everywhere the same (Fig. 11.11). Moreover, plug shapes, plug holes, plug sizes, and sockets are also different in many countries (Figs. 11.12 and 11.13). Those seemingly unimportant differences, however, have some unpleasant consequences.

Europe and most other countries in the world use a voltage which is twice that of the United States. It is between 220 and 240 volts, whereas in Japan and in most of the Americas the voltage is between 100 and 127 volts.

Let's move on to types of cable or, more specifically, the wire that makes up a cable. Since we chatted about lamps, wattage, voltage, and ampere, now we need to figure out how to plug in this stuff. The AWG, or American wire gauge, is a standardized way of measuring wire and determining how much current it can carry. The following lists the most common wire gauges used in the theatre. When a zero specifies the gauge, it is pronounced "aught." For example, the first line in the chart would be "four aught."

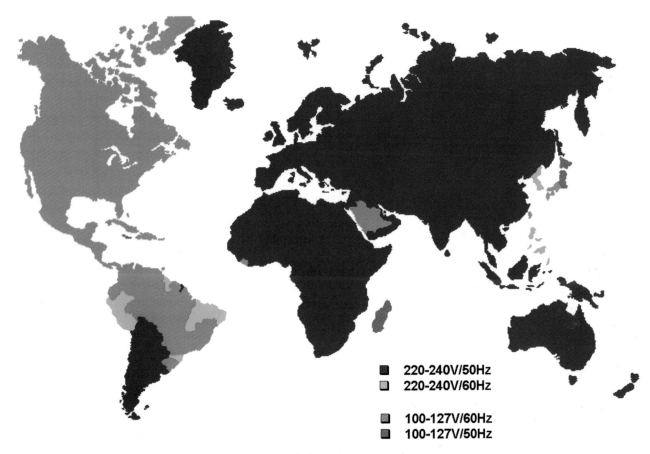

Fig. 11.11 World map showing various voltages and where they are used.

■ 220-240V/50Hz
▢ 220-240V/60Hz

■ 100-127V/60Hz
■ 100-127V/50Hz

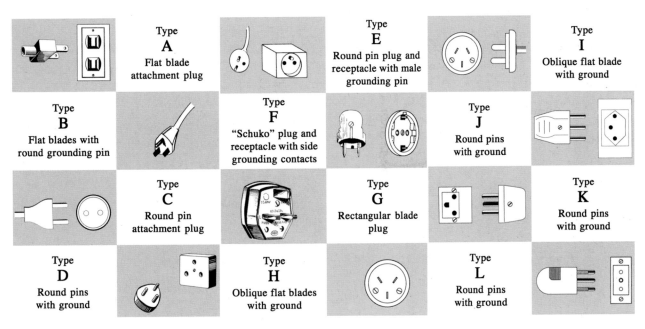

Type **A**
Flat blade attachment plug

Type **B**
Flat blades with round grounding pin

Type **C**
Round pin attachment plug

Type **D**
Round pins with ground

Type **E**
Round pin plug and receptacle with male grounding pin

Type **F**
"Schuko" plug and receptacle with side grounding contacts

Type **G**
Rectangular blade plug

Type **H**
Oblique flat blades with ground

Type **I**
Oblique flat blade with ground

Type **J**
Round pins with ground

Type **K**
Round pins with ground

Type **L**
Round pins with ground

Fig. 11.12 Electrical plug types used around the world.

Type of Plug by Country

Country	Plug Type
Afghanistan	D
Albania	C
Algeria	C, F
Angola	C
Argentina	C, I
Australia	I
Austria	C
Bahamas	A, B
Bahrain	G
Bangladesh	A, C, D
Barbados	A, B, F, H
Belarus	C
Belgium	A, C, E
Belize	A, B, H
Benin	D
Bermuda	A, B
Bolivia	A, C
Botswana	C, D, H
Brazil	A, B, C
Brunei	G
Bulgaria	F
Burkina Faso	B, E
Burma	C, D, F
Burundi	C, E
Cameroon	C, E
Canada	B
Canary Islands	C, E
Cape Verde, Rep. of	C, F
Cayman Islands	A, B
Central African Republic	C, E
Chad	E
Chile	C, F, L
China, Peoples Rep. of	C, D, G, H
Colombia	A, B
Congo, Dem. Rep of (form. Zaire)	E
Congo, Peoples Rep. of	C, E
Costa Rica	A, B
Cyprus	G
Czech Republic	E
Denmark	C, K
Djibouti, Rep. of	C, E
Dominican Republic	A
Ecuador	A, B, C, D
Egypt	C
El Salvador	A, B, C, D, E, F, G, I, J, L
England	A, C, H
Equatorial Guinea	C, E
Eritrea	C
Ethiopia	C
Fiji	I
Finland	C, F
France	E
Gabon	D, E
Gambia, The	G
Germany, Fed. Rep. of	F
Ghana	D, G
Gibraltar	C, G
Greece	C, F
Greenland	C, K
Grenada	G
Guatemala	A, B, G, H, I
Guinea	C, F, K
Guinea-Bissau	C
Guyana	A, H
Haiti	A, B, H
Honduras	A
Hong Kong	H
Hungary	C, F
Iceland	B
India	C, D, G
Indonesia	C, E, F
Ireland	G
Israel	C, H
Italy	L
Ivory Coast	C, E
Jamaica	A, B, C, D
Japan	A, B, I
Jordan	C, F, G, L
Pakistan	B, C, D
Lesotho	D
Liberia	A, B
Luxembourg	F
Macedonia	C, F
Madagascar	C, D, E, J, K
Malawi	G
Malaysia	G
Mali, Rep. of	C, E
Malta	G
Mauritania	C
Mauritius	G
Mexico	A, B
Monaco	C, D, E, F
Morocco	C, E
Mozambique	C, D, F
Namibia	C
Nepal	C, D
Netherlands	F
New Zealand	H
Nicaragua	A
Niger	A, C, E
Nigeria	C, D, H
Northern Ireland	A, C, H
Norway	C, F
Oman	H
Qatar	D, G
Romania	C, F
Russia	C
Rwanda	C, J
Saudi Arabia	A, B, G
Scotland	A, C, H
Senegal	C, D, E, K
Serbia-Montenegro	F
Seychelles	D,
Sierra Leone	D, G
Singapore	B, H
Slovak Republic	E
Somalia	C
South Africa	D
Spain	C, F
Sri Lanka	D
Sudan	C, D
Suriname	C, F
Swaziland	D
Sweden	C, F
Switzerland	C, E, J
Syria	C
Tajikistan	C, I
Tahiti	A
Taiwan	A, B
Tanzania	D, G
Thailand	A, B, C, D, E, G, J, K
Togo	C
Trinidad and Tobago	A, B
Tunisia	C, E
Turkey	C, F
Turkmenistan	B, F
Uganda	G
Ukraine	C
United Arab Emirates	C, D, G
Uruguay	C, F, I, L
Uzbekistan	C, I
Venezuela	A, B, H
Wales	A, C, H
Western Samoa	H
Yemen, Rep. of	A, D, G
Zambia	C, D, G
Zimbabwe	D, G

■ **Fig. 11.13** Alphabetical list of countries and what plug type they use.

AWG GAUGE	MAX AMPS AT 120 V
0000 (4/0)	400
00 (2/0)	200
0	175
1	150
2	125
4	100
6	80
8	50
10	30
12	20
14	15
16	10

FIXTURES

Now that we laid the groundwork with all this background information, we can move on to fixtures (Fig. 11.14). Let's do just one more thing first, but don't worry, it will be much easier than electricity was. Let's talk about the basic parts of a fixture so that we can reference them throughout our next discussion (Fig. 11.15). At the front of the fixture, is an accessory holder. Directly behind that there may be a lens. Similar to the lens on a camera, the lens on a fixture helps to focus the light coming out. Each style of lens is a little different, and some fixtures don't even have them.

The main body of the fixture is next. It may be completely open and be the only way the light gets shaped. Or, it may have additional lenses to help shape the beam. The middle of the fixture has mounting hardware attached, either a yoke for hanging or a grunion for sitting on the floor. This is the place in the fixture where most of the locking bolts exist, which you need when you focus. Focus is the process aiming the lights to the place the designer wants. This can include a number of different adjustments, depending on the type of light involved.

If there is a yoke, it will have a pipe clamp bolted on that allows you to hang the fixture on a pipe. Continuing further back, there is a reflector. Again, shapes change but the premise is the same. The reflector bounces the light from the lamp around, gaining brightness, until it comes out the front of the fixture. At the very back of the fixture is the lamp housing. The lightbulb, or lamp as it is called in the theatre, obviously lives here, so does the socket for the lamp. On the outside is a power cable with a plug on it.

There are some basic categories of fixtures based on their individual qualities. I do have to put in one more bit of techno-speak before we go on. When you are looking at the product specification sheets supplied by manufacturers about their fixtures, you'll see the phrases *beam angle*, *field angle*, and *beam spread*. If this sounds confusing, don't worry, it is actually pretty simple. First, the easiest part: Field angle and beam spread are the same thing. Every

Fig. 11.14 Lighting load-in.

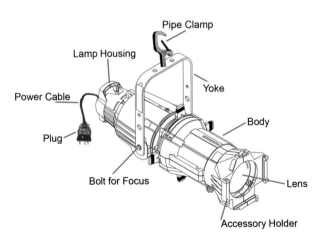

Pipe Clamp

Lamp Housing

Power Cable

Yoke

Plug

Body

Bolt for Focus

Lens

Accessory Holder

Fig. 11.15 Diagram showing fixture parts.

light fixture has a beam of light that comes from it. It is shaped as the light comes from the front of the fixture. These terms are based on a percentage of the maximum intensity of the beam at its center. The **beam angle**, where you get the best quality of light, is measured at a level of 50 percent of the maximum intensity of the beam. The beam spread (wider than the beam angle) is measured where you get down to 10 percent of the maximum intensity of the beam. In the case of an Altman Lighting, 20-degree Shakespeare®, the beam angle is 13 degrees while the beam spread is considered to be 20 degrees. Keep in mind that there is usually some light beyond the measured beam spread (that last 10 percent). The quality of the remaining light is unpredictable at best, so just ignore it for now.

Now, back to lighting fixtures. The beam projector is still one of my favorite fixtures even though it is not in common use today (Fig. 11.16). A **beam projector** is an open-face fixture that produces a narrow beam of light. It does this through the use of two reflectors. The primary reflector in the back of the fixture is a flattened parabolic reflector. In front of the lamp is a secondary reflector that is spherical. The spherical reflector reflects light from the lamp toward the parabolic reflector in the back. The parabolic reflector organizes the light into nearly parallel beams. The result is an intense shaft of light. Beam projectors have a history of creating a "fingers of God" effect. They are made in two sizes, both of which are defined by the size of the front opening.

The scoop light is our next fixture. **Scoops** are open-face units, meaning they have no lens (Fig. 11.17). The housing

Fig. 11.16 Beam projector.

Fig. 11.18 Fresnel.

Fig. 11.17 Scoop.

for the light has an ellipsoidal shape. There is no reflector in a scoop, however the inside of the housing is usually painted white to help reflect the light forward. The lamp, as it is called in the theatre, enters at the narrow end of the ellipsoidal. To focus the scoop, you have only two options: You can pan the scoop, and you can tilt the scoop. The quality of the light from a scoop is very soft and gentle, creating an even wash. It has often been used as a work

light. Scoops come in a number of different sizes from 10 to 18 inches.

The **Fresnel** is a soft-edge light (Fig. 11.18). It can create an even wash or a small, focused spot. The Fresnel has a spherical reflector in the back that is attached to a slide in the bottom of the fixture. Also attached to the slide is the socket and lamp. This slide is what allows the Fresnel to be focused. By adjusting the slide forward and back, you change the relationship of the reflector and lamp to the lens. And speaking of lens, the **Fresnel lens** is what makes this fixture special (Fig. 11.19). A French physicist by the name of Augustin-Jean Fresnel invented the lens that carries his name. He was trying to make a thinner lens that would be lighter and less expensive. He divided the lens into a series of concentric circles that step in toward each other. Take a look at Figure 11.19. This design achieved his purpose, making the lens much lighter while light output is not sacrificed. The original use for this lens was in lighthouses. Fresnels come in a wide range of sizes from as small as 3 inches all the way to 24 inches!

Our next fixture has an "official name" that almost nobody uses any more. It is the **ellipsoidal reflector spotlight** (ERS). But, like I said, almost nobody calls it that. Everybody calls it a **leko**, more on that later. Its official

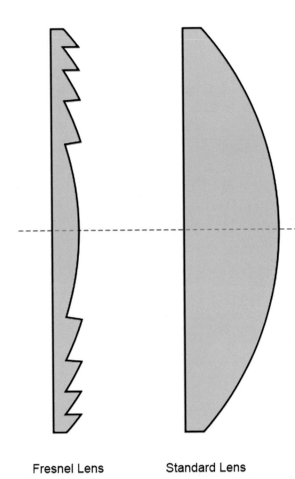

Fresnel Lens   Standard Lens

Fig. 11.19 Fresnel lens diagram.

name tells you a bit about it. For starters, the leko has an ellipsoidal reflector. This fixture also has something new for us to talk about. It has two lenses. Yes, two lenses! This means you can focus the beam by changing the distance between the two lenses, just like changing the focal length on a camera's lens. Depending on this focus, the light coming out of the leko can have a hard edge or a soft edge. This feature makes this fixture one of the most flexible in our inventories. It is probably the most-used fixture in all of theatre.

Lekos come in a range of focal length possibilities, including zooms that have an adjustable range. There are differences between manufacturers and between newer and older styles. But the basic idea and workings of the leko remain the same. Lekos are capable of projecting various designs, known as *templates* or *gobos*. We talk about these later in the chapter, but just remember this great option when you use them. Another feature that makes the leko unique is that it has shutters. **Shutters** are shaped pieces of metal inside the leko with a handle attached on the outside. By pushing the shutter into the leko, you can mask a portion of the light that comes through the lens (Fig. 11.20). This allows you to frame objects or people. Some of the newer lekos have a lens barrel that rotates. This is awesome for getting the perfect shutter cut at a truly weird angle.

Fig. 11.20 Old and new style lekos.

■ **Fig. 11.21** Old and new PAR cans.

Bear with me through a little more history. Century Lighting opened in New York by Edward F. Kook and his partners, Joseph Levy, Saul Levy, and Irving Levy. Century Lighting created their version of the ERS in 1933. By taking the first two initials from the last names of the founders you get LE-KO. Who knew it was an acronym? Pretty cool!

The PAR is a fixture named for its lamp. Actually, this is the first fixture with a very different kind of lamp. The PAR fixture takes a PAR lamp. Duh! **PAR** stands for parabolic aluminized reflector. The lamp and the reflector are sealed together with a lens. Think car headlight. This combination is then inserted into the back of a tube, or "can," to help shape the beam of light (Fig. 11.21). The lamps come in a variety of configurations with different lenses, from very narrow to very wide, meaning that simply by changing the lamp you can get a variety of beam sizes from the same fixture. Most PAR beams have an oval shape that can be rotated to change the direction of each beam's axis. This makes them very useful for creating alleys of light on stage. These fixtures have been around for a long time but are still used extensively today. Some newer varieties separate the lamp from the lens, making it very similar to the other fixtures we discussed so far. This means you can now change

the lamp independently from the lens. The optics on these newer fixtures are much more efficient than their older cousins, and by having to keep only thin lenses around, they save you a ton of space. It's also way more convenient and a better quality of light!

It used to be that, if you wanted to light a large area like a cyc, you'd have to use a whole bunch of fixtures and a boatload of cables. Well, someone clever figured out that, if you take several fixtures and build them together into one fixture, you could save a lot of time and cost in your setup. This led initially to fixtures called *far cycs*, but they were huge and very bulky. They required a lot of space to hang them. Next, the **strip light** is invented. Think of one long fixture with several lamps in it (Fig. 11.22). Most strip lights come in one, two, three, or four circuit. They can be hung with clamps on a pipe over the stage or put on the floor using **trunnions**. In the multiple-circuit fixtures, you can have access to several colors from one fixture. Cool! Strip lights are great for creating large swaths of color and wonderful for color mixing, too. Since it's one fixture with several lamps, you know they're all going to be on the same angle, making your focus way faster, too! You have many lamp options here, too. Depending on what strip lights you

■ **Fig. 11.22** Old and new strip lights.

use, they could vary from 20 watts per lamp up to 2000 watts per lamp. *Wow!*

So, now that we've gone through the conventional fixtures, are you ready to have some real fun? Over the years folks have said, "Wouldn't it be cool if I could only . . . ?" To answer this question, manufacturers have come up with a variety of specialty fixtures. We discuss some of them next to get your creativity flowing.

UV lights get a lot of use in the theatre. They make things glow. You've probably seen this in use many times. UV gives a special glow to white gloves or other garments on what looks like a dark stage or adds an extra punch to a lit stage where costumes or set pieces have been treated with UV-sensitive paints or dyes. There is even special UV makeup. If you've ever seen any of The Blue Man Group© shows or commercials, you know what I mean. *Very* cool! UV fixtures come in a wide variety of sizes and shapes to provide many different uses. UV can be a small or large fluorescent or a high-intensity discharge type to be used in larger areas. They are made in flood styles and spot styles. UV lekos can do all of the things a regular leko can do but with the added benefit of being UV. Fresnels can be made as UV fixtures as well giving you a variable-size beam of light from one specialty fixture. I've even seen follow spots with UV filters on them, so you can move the effect from place to place on the stage.

Fluorescent lights, when they're not being UV lights, are more versatile than many people give them credit for. They can be used to fill in tight areas on a set, such as behind windows and doors or maybe on Juliet's balcony. Modern fluorescents can be dimmable for added flexibility. They can be lamped with different color-temperature lamps to make the light cooler or warmer. They can also be gelled to make them even more useful.

LED fixtures have become the wave of the future. Although LED (light-emitting diode) technology has been around since the early 20th century, building them into theatrical fixtures is fairly new. These fixtures come in a single color or several colors. The most common type today is the three-color fixture. The three colors are—and this should be familiar—red, green, and blue. If you recall the color wheel we discussed earlier, you can mix these three colors and get pretty much any color. The math tells us that you can get approximately 16.7 million, yes, million, colors. How is that for a versatile fixture? Some companies are also adding amber for more mixing options and so you can alter the color temperature.

> So much modern scenery is about how you light it. Many plays are written with 20-40 scenes and you really can't make all those places with hard physical scenery so you're dependent upon creating a lot of those places with light and color and shapes.
>
> —Derek McLane

LED fixtures can come in a variety of sizes and shapes—from small fixtures, to hideaway fixtures in very tight places, to strip-light versions that are incredible for color washing cycs (Figs. 11.23–11.28). There are even some companies building them into automated fixtures. Some are even flexible so you can go around curves on a set. Some can be set up to run on their own, but most are controlled through your light board. Possibly one of the coolest things about LED fixtures is that they are very low wattage, which means that you can put a lot onto one circuit. They operate at a low temperature because of the wattage, making them perfect for use where heat may be a problem for people, scenery, or soft goods. LEDs don't eat up dimmers, since all the dimming is digitally controlled. The only drawback, sort of, is that they are fairly expensive these days. However, what they save in electricity and dimmers makes up for that.

■ **Fig. 11.23** Robert Juliat Fresnel (left) and Robert Juliat LED Fresnel (right).

■ **Fig. 11.24** Altman Spectra (LED) PAR.

■ **Fig. 11.25** Robert Juliat Plano-Convex Wash fixture.

■ **Fig. 11.26** Robert Juliat Profile fixtures.

Fig. 11.27 Robert Juliat cyc light (left), Altman's Spectra (LED) cyc (right).

Fig. 11.28 Selador X7 LED strip light.

LED fixtures are shown in Figures 11.23 and 11.27 with their incandescent comparable fixtures. As always, keep in mind that the fixture and the light source are two separate items. When choosing a lighting unit, you now have many more options than ever before (Fig. 11.29).

Another fairly expensive but versatile and fun fixture is the automated light or moving light. These fixtures come in a wide variety of styles for particular purposes. The two main types are spot versus wash fixtures. This means pretty much what it sounds like. Spot fixtures are focusable fixtures that can produce a hard-edge beam like a leko, while the wash fixture is designed to cover an area in a soft-edge beam (Figs. 11.30–11.37). If you've ever been to a rock concert you've certainly seen these in use. The main differences in these fixtures are in their features. They can be as simple as a leko or PAR mounted into a moving yoke, like City Theatrical's **Auto Yoke**® (Fig. 11.38), or they can have so many bells and whistles that it would make your head (and the light) spin.

Some of the fixtures have color mixing built in, so you can achieve virtually any color (similar to LEDs) as well

■ **Fig. 11.29** Shakespeare's *Romeo and Juliet* at NYU's Department of Graduate Acting and Department of Design for Stage and Film in 2005. Director, Michael Sexton; scenic designer, Matthew Allar; costume designer, Arnulfo Maldonado; and lighting designer, Stacey Boggs. Four photos from the production *and* a photo of the empty space!

Fig. 11.31 Strong's Super Trouper follow spot.

■ **Fig. 11.30** Altman's AltSpot follow spot.

as a bunch of **gobos** to project different patterns. You can even spin the gobos for some great motion effects. All the fixtures pan and tilt remotely. They can be programmed to do all sorts of movements. Some designers keep them moving almost all the time (usually with a whole bunch

■ **Fig. 11.32** Lycian's M2 follow spot.

of fog flying around so the audience can see the light beams), while others use them to create specific looks on the stage. Think of it this way. Scene 1 takes place in a castle, so you use the gobos in the fixture to create the look of stone on the stage floor and maybe the walls as well. Then, you go to Scene 2, which takes place out in the forest. Simple. You take the next cue and the fixtures readjust focus and change their beam size and color. The gobos change to a leaf pattern slightly out of focus, and there you are in the middle of the forest. The possibilities are endless.

DIMMERS

Now that we covered the basics of lighting fixtures, we have to talk about what you plug those fixtures into. I am talking about dimmers. Dimmers come in almost as many configurations as light fixtures. Their essential function is to raise and lower the brightness level of a fixture. Modern-day dimmers are rated by their capacity. This capacity can range from 600 watts to 12,000 watts, but the most common ones you find in a theatre are 1,200 and 2,400 watts. The number of dimmers in the system can be as few as one or as many as several hundred, up to well over 1000.

Fig. 11.34 Robert Juliat's Super Korrigan follow spot.

Fig. 11.33 Lycian's 1275 follow spot.

Fig. 11.35 Martin MAC 2000® wash moving light.

> It's exciting that the computer age is allowing us to realize the kind of movement in light and the flexibility we want to achieve. We can make light move in ways we never could before. And we haven't even begun to tap what computers can do.
>
> **—Tharon Musser**

Dimmers, like light fixtures, have a history. The first dimmers were mechanical devices that were lowered in front of candles to dim them. By 1900, saltwater dimmers were developed. These worked by increasing or decreasing the salinity in a vat of water to increase or decrease the conductivity and thereby raise or lower the light level. Be glad you don't have to do this anymore. It was inexact and could be pretty messy, not to mention the whole water and electricity not mixing thing. Then, around 1910, resistance dimmers were developed. They were huge Frankenstein-looking things that worked by changing the resistance on the wires using a big lever.

> Any monkey can light a show with 900 lights all individually controlled. That's not doing your work.
>
> **—M. L. Geiger**

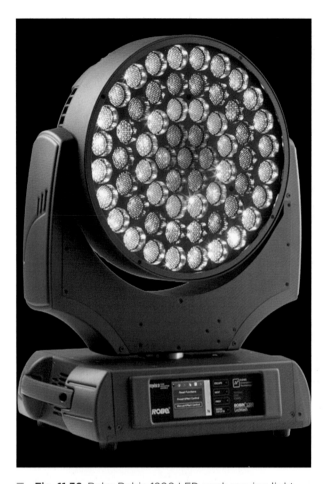

Fig. 11.36 Robe Robin 1200 LED wash moving light.

Fig. 11.38 City Theatrical's Auto Yoke.

Fig. 11.37 Martin MAC 2000® profile moving light.

Ring in 1933 and ring in the advent of autotransformers. **Autotransformer** dimmers, which really aren't much different (in concept, anyway) from the wall dimmer you may have at home that works by turning a knob, came in different capacities and configurations. When you move the handle on an autotransformer, inside it moves a brush along a coil varying the amount of electricity getting through to the lamp. On a larger system, which could be 24–30 dimmers, you sometimes needed several people to run a show and move all the handles (Fig. 11.39). There are still some places today that are using autotransformers. They're pretty tough to kill.

In 1958, we got the **SCR**, or silicon controlled rectifier. This innovation allowed manufacturers to make things much smaller and lighter by comparison. The big difference is that this required a separate controller. We talk about these soon. SCR is basically the same technology used today. Today's dimmers have gotten even smaller and much

■ **Fig. 11.39** Very scary old circuit panel.

CONTROL

more clever. Actually, the dimmer itself isn't necessarily all that smart. It is the way it is controlled. The newer dimmer racks have electronics installed in them that can do all sorts of things from turning on an individual dimmer to giving you readings on exactly how many volts are coming into it and exactly how much is going out and so on (Fig. 11.40). The long and the short of it is that, when you ask the dimmer to raise the brightness of the light, it should do it, no matter what type of dimmer it is.

CONTROL

Controlling dimmers has changed over the years. The concept, however, has always been the same. The first dimmers were manual, meaning that you had to raise and lower a handle to raise and lower the brightness of a light. Eventually that handle evolved into a signal cable and a separate controller. These controllers used a low-voltage DC signal to tell the SCRs what to do (Fig. 11.41). The DC signal was raised and lowered by moving a potentiometer (pot). Sometimes, these were moved in a circle; sometimes they were straight. With the straight ones, and these are still used today, you would literally raise and lower the handle to raise and lower the level on the light. In the 1970s, the DC signal was changed to a multiplexed signal called AMX, or analog multiplex. This was essentially a computer signal. Modern controllers use DMX, or digital multiplex. While DMX is pretty much the standard control signal today, some manufacturers have started using Ethernet for controlling dimmers and lights.

While we were getting upgrades in control signals, the complexity of the lighting controllers grew by leaps and bounds. Early control boards could control only the pots. Granted, this was a huge improvement over several types of controllers, since the complexity of each can be so great.

PERISHABLES

Even the best set up theatre needs to replenish its supply of **gel** and other things on a regular basis. These things are officially called *perishables*. Perishables are any of the items that are used for one show, then discarded. This can be gel, gobos, tapes, tie line, batteries, and so on. Some theatres have a supply house they work with to order perishables or they may purchase them from a lighting rental shop when they get rental equipment for the next show.

> It's been very exciting to see that happen. It's exciting to see that lighting is becoming known as an art form and not just a director saying to an electrician, "Can I have some moonlight through that window?"
>
> —Tharon Musser

ACCESSORIES

We discussed all sorts of fixtures, both old and new. Designers have a tendency to first see their designs in their heads. Thankfully, many manufacturers are out there who make a good living from translating those visions onto the stage. As Gary Fails of City Theatrical says, "It's all about the accessories."

Each of the following accessories is great in its own right. There may be other ways of accomplishing the effect, usually higher-end ways, but sometimes the simpler ways are best. Let's start small. Many products made to add onto or into light fixtures help us do fun things with the light beam. First is the color frame. Simply put, this is a metal or cardboard frame that holds gel in place. It goes into the **accessory slot** on the front of a fixture. The next is a donut, a piece of metal the same size as a color frame with a hole. It is designed to help a sharp leko look even sharper. The **top hat**, or high hat, gets its name because it looks like an old-fashioned gentleman's top hat with the exception of being open at the top. It helps reduce flare and cut out some of the excess light, such as the light beyond the beam spread.

■ **Fig. 11.40** ETC Sensor+® installation dimmer rack.

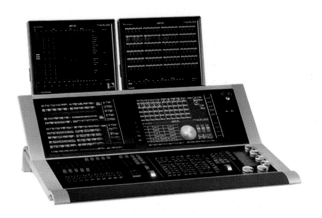

■ **Fig. 11.41** ETC Eos® lighting console.

people wielding 2 × 4s and using both arms and a leg to be able to move multiple autotransformers at one time. Today, controllers are computers capable of anything you can think of. These newer controllers have really opened up possibilities for designers (Figs. 11.42–11.44). Ideas that designers could only imagine before can now be accomplished with the push of a button. Keep in mind that a whole lot of programming needs to happen first, though. There are technicians that specialize in certain

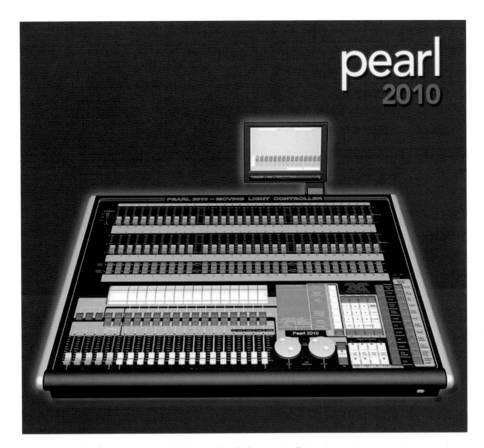

Fig. 11.42 Avolites Pearl 2010 moving light controller.

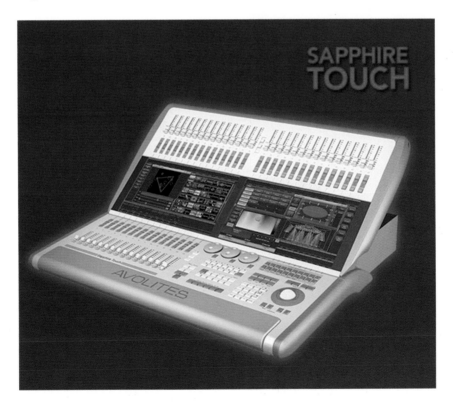

Fig. 11.43 Avolites Sapphire Touch moving light controller.

The Beam Bender® and the Image Multiplexer® are pretty cool tools. The beam bender goes in front of a fixture and has an adjustable mirror on it. The idea is to light some of those hard-to-reach spots by focusing the light into the mirror. The mirror then bounces the light out at a 90-degree angle, making it seem like you can light around corners! The image multiplexer goes in the accessory slot of a leko. It splits the light beam into several beams, sort of like a kaleidoscope. Just add a gobo to the multiplexer and see what happens!

Barn doors go in front of soft-edge fixtures, like Fresnels or PARs, to allow you to block parts of the light beam. This works great when you have a Fresnel or a PAR that is spilling onto a border and you want to block a little of the light without having to lose what that light is doing on stage. This works sort of like a leko shutter, it's not as crisp, but it works in a pinch. Another great product that goes on the front of

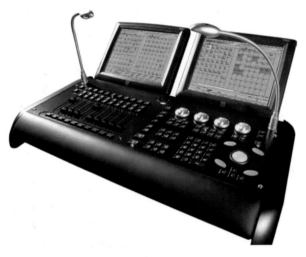

the fixture is the color scroller. This is a machine that holds a long string of gel in different colors. You then use your control board to digitally select the color you want and the scroller moves through the gel string and stops at the right gel.

There is an accessory slot, also known as the *drop-in slot*, in lekos right near the framing shutters that will accept a wide variety of things. The mulitplexer we just talked about uses this. Fixtures used to have an iris installed, but most of the ones made today do not. You can use a drop-in iris to make the projected beam of light smaller while still keeping it round. Special gobo holders fit in the drop-in slot to allow you to use glass gobos instead of metal ones. To have even more fun and create basic moving images, you can use a gobo rotator that spins one or more gobos around at variable speeds. Rotators are, of course, DMX controlled!

A step up from the drop-in slot gobo holder is Rosco's Image Pro®. This accessory allows you to project photographic images that have been printed on acetate. This is awesome for projecting realistic images like an actual forest or a picture of someone or, well, pretty much anything (Fig. 11.45). GAM Products makes a really cool device for the drop-in slot called the Film FX®. With this, you can project moving images like clouds floating through the sky. As you can see, these accessories really open up options for lighting design and effects.

A twist on the accessory slot idea is City Theatrical's EFX Plus 2® (Fig. 11.46). This very cool accessory takes large discs, made like very large gobos, that rotate to project a wide variety of patterns like rain, clouds, snow, and flames. The speed and direction are variable. *Very cool.* Check out Figure 11.47 for a variety of accessories.

■ **Fig. 11.45** Sea Changer's Profile (left) and wash unit (right), both with dichroic color changers!

■ **Fig. 11.46** City Theatrical's VSFX3 effects projector.

For the most part, we talked about hanging lighting fixtures on pipes. While this is the typical situation, you didn't think I'd leave it at that, did you? There are many options for mounting a fixture. You can use extenders that hang a fixture lower or higher than a regular pipe clamp to give you maximum flexibility in making the light go just where you need it. These are also good for those times when the set is high and you need to get above part of it with a fixture. Another option for this is the pipe and base. While the pipes normally found in a theatre are hung horizontally,

sometimes you need to go vertical. The instrument to do this is called a *boom*. Typically, you use a 50-pound base that is threaded to accept a pipe of whatever length you need. You can then hang a fixture anywhere along the height of the pipe. To keep the light consistent with other lights hung on regular pipes, you can use a sidearm. This is a small piece of pipe with a C-clamp. This gets used a lot for dance, where you want a lot of sidelight at several heights. It is also great for putting lights out in the auditorium or somewhere that has no hanging position already. Some bases even have wheels on them, so they can be moved around during a performance. Take it one step further. Use two booms with a horizontal pipe between them. Now you've made a goalpost! The possibilities are endless. You can mount a light anywhere you can safely figure out how to hold it in place!

Occasionally, you come across an accessory made for a particular purpose, and once you get it in your hands, you say to yourself, "Hmmmmmm, I wonder . . . ." The good folks at Meteor Light and Sound Company make a nifty little gadget, the Puppeteer®. This device allows you to create a temporary moving light. It clamps onto a horizontal pipe. You then hang a fixture from the Puppeteer. You can now remotely pan and tilt the light. They are often used with lekos but you can also use Fresnels, PARs, projectors, and as I said, just about anything. There is a weight limit, but after that, just use your imagination.

The light plot, as you know from Chapter 5, shows all the fixtures in their exact locations. This must include the front of house (FOH) hanging positions. (Fig. 11.48). **Front of house** means anything downstage

---

THE LOVE MACHINE
Usher's OMG Tour is a seductive exercise in pop idol worship

Sharon Stancavage

Excerpt 2

At mid-stage, the set features a pair of conveyor belts. "They go in opposite directions; you're either going left or right or right to left," says Lather. "There's a solid surface between the two belts—it's almost like two highways going in opposite directions."

Unlike most conveyor belts on the market, these are part of the actual stage. "The conveyer belt system is a new product for us; it is the first system on the market that I am aware of that actually recesses the belt in the surface of the deck," says Eric Pearce, an SGPS partner and lead mechanical designer.

"It uses a tremendously powerful servo-motor drive and can exceed speeds of 90' per minute, regardless of load. It uses conical drums to keep the belts centered, regardless of what the dancers' moves are. It is completely modular in design, and can be adapted to any length." The production does indeed put up to a half dozen performers on the conveyor belts, and although they can go 90' per minute, Abderrahman adds, "We probably only run it at about 50' on the fast gags."

The 60'-wide-by-48'-deep stage also includes a lift, provided by SGPS, located at upstage center. "The lift can go slow and we have a slow reveal on it, but it can pop up at a rapid speed like a toaster," says Lather. The lift is used for entrances and exits. "If he wants to end a routine, and he hits a pose, he can descend and kind of vanish."

"The toaster is a servo-motor-driven device and is fully programmable for the weight of the artist and the height he wishes to be flown," notes Pearce. "It can be programmed with a shock-reducing slowing ramp at the end of its travel, to reduce the impact on the artist. The unit used on Usher is built into a 4'-by-8'-by-6'-high unit with a traveling deck of 39" by 41"—the traveling deck is fully enclosed in a Plexi tube so the operator can see the artist for visual contact and safety."

OMG has all of the trappings of a huge pop show, including a bevy of gags, the first of which makes its appearance at the very start of the show. It's an "OMG"-worthy moment, starting with a 21st-century magic carpet and ending with a bungee cord. "I really love the bungee; it's crazy stuff he's doing up there," says Allen.

Abderrahman explains the details of the gag: "We have a stage platform that's about 12' long by 8' wide that sits at the very end of the arena behind the mix. Usher gets on that in the blackout, and he comes up and flies over the audience all the way to the stage."

Usher flies from the back of the arena to the stage via 180' of SGPS KB 30 chain hoists to hang this thing, because it has to be picked up in all the right places, says the tour manager. "There's no sag because, when you're moving 4,000 lbs across it, it can't roller-coaster up and down; it's got to be solid."

Once Usher reaches the stage, the second part of the gag begins. "The magic carpet-aerial stage comes to the main stage, it gets on a raked inclined angle, and Usher does a bungee-type performance on that slanted wall," remarks Lather. The gag isn't just for entertainment; it's also an effective way of getting Usher from the magic carpet platform onto the stage proper."

Source: Originally published in *Lighting and Sound America*, February 2011

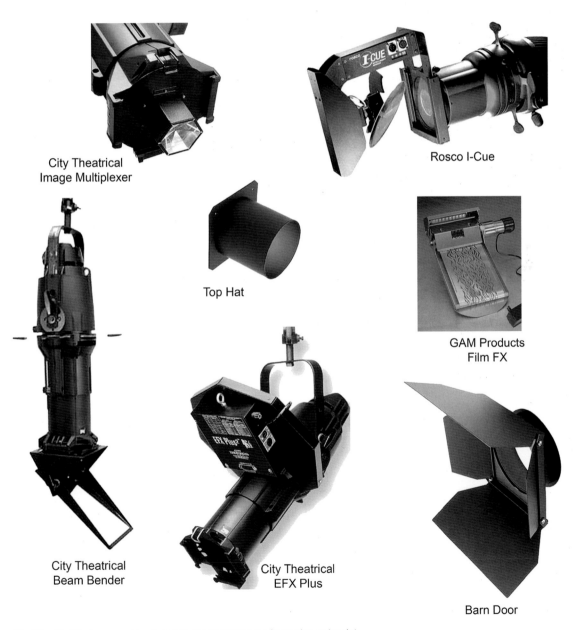

City Theatrical
Image Multiplexer

Rosco I-Cue

Top Hat

GAM Products
Film FX

City Theatrical
Beam Bender

City Theatrical
EFX Plus

Barn Door

■ **Fig. 11.47** Accessories, it is what separates us from the animals!

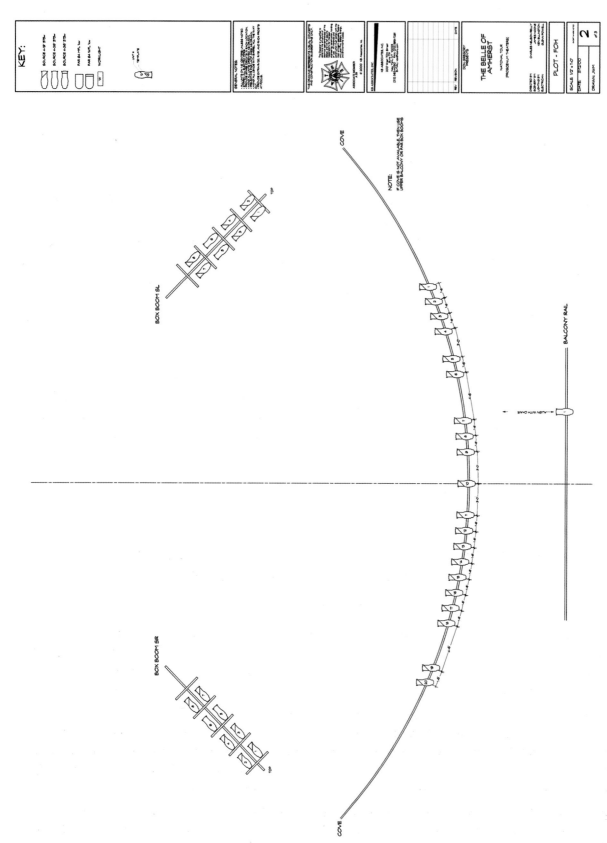

Fig. 11.48 *The Belle of Amherst* FOH light plot. Lighting design by Ken Billington.

of the proscenium or over the audience. Since the FOH is usually quite large, it is common practice to compress the space between the FOH hanging positions, as well as between the pipes and the proscenium. This is done to help all the pipes fit onto one page of drafting! If the FOH is extensive, it can be moved to its own page of drafting.

The light plot shows more than just the lighting fixtures (Fig. 11.49). *It shows the centerline–in case I forgot to mention how important that is!* The lighting equipment, each individual fixture, and any accessories are shown. The symbols used to represent the fixtures are approximately the correct shape and size, in scale, of the real fixtures. This is very important. If you use a symbol that is 6 inches to represent a fixture that is 18 inches, chances are your lights won't fit in the air when they are being hung. The standard default spacing for fixtures is 1–6 inches or 18 inches. This is commonly used and based on fixture sizing and the ability for the electrician to get his or her hands in between everything to focus and tighten the lights. If larger fixtures are used, you obviously need more room.

The light plot needs to have a key to the symbols, so that everyone can understand what each symbol actually means. Without the key, the light plot is almost useless!

Dimensions need to be on the light plot as well. Critical dimensions include spacing between units, as I already mentioned, but also dimensions to locate all the pipes, not only US to DS, but also in terms of height. Take a look at Figures 11.48 and 11.49 for more details.

> If I'm a good designer today it's because I learned so much from Tharon—I always say I went to Musser U.
>
> **—Ken Billington**

Once the lighting designer gets into the theatre, he or she and the assistants make magic sheets (Figs. 11.50 and 11.51). A magic sheet is sometimes called a cheat sheet. It is a quick reference for the design team to be able to find the channel number quickly and easily. A cheat sheet is usually a compressed number list, and a magic sheet is more of a visual reference.

The more complex a design, the more drawings that will be needed to get all the details across. Often several drawings are needed to fully indicate the placement of all the built-in fixtures. Figure 11.52 should give you an idea of this.

INTERESTING AND USELESS FACTOID: DARK SUCKERS
(please note: all Useless Factoids are fictional)

Author Unknown

For years it has been believed that electric bulbs emitted light. However, recent information has proven otherwise. Electric bulbs don't emit light, they suck dark. Thus, they now call these bulbs "dark suckers." The dark sucker theory proves the existence of dark, that dark has mass heavier than that of light, and that dark is faster than light.

The basis of the dark sucker theory is that electric bulbs suck dark. Take, for example, the dark suckers in the room where you are. There is less dark right next to them than there is elsewhere. The larger the dark sucker, the greater is its capacity to suck dark. Dark suckers in a parking lot have a much greater capacity than the ones in this room. As with all things, dark suckers don't last forever. Once they are full of dark, they can no longer suck. This is proven by the black spot on a full dark sucker.

A candle is a primitive dark sucker. A new candle has a white wick. You will notice that, after the first use, the wick turns black, representing all the dark that has been sucked into it. If you hold a pencil next to the wick of an operating candle, the tip will turn black, because it got in the path of the dark flowing into the candle. Unfortunately, these primitive dark suckers have a very limited range.

There are also portable dark suckers. The bulbs in these can't handle all of the dark by themselves and must be aided by a dark storage unit. When the dark storage unit (or battery) is full, it must be either emptied or replaced before the portable dark sucker can operate again.

Dark has mass. When dark goes into a dark sucker, friction from this mass generates heat. Therefore, it is not wise to touch an operating dark sucker. Candles present a special problem, as the dark must travel in the solid wick instead of through glass. This generates a great amount of heat. Therefore, it can be very dangerous to touch an operating candle.

Dark is also heavier than light. If you swim deeper and deeper, you notice it gets slowly darker and darker. When you reach a depth of approximately 50 feet, you are in total darkness. This is because the heavier dark sinks to the bottom of the lake and the lighter light floats to the top.

The immense power of dark can be utilized to man's advantage. We can collect the dark that has settled to the bottom of lakes and push it through turbines, which generate electricity and help push it to the ocean where it may be safely stored. Prior to turbines, it was much more difficult to get dark from the rivers and lakes to the ocean.

The Indians recognized this problem, and tried to solve it. When on a river in a canoe traveling in the same direction as the flow of the dark, they paddled slowly, so as not to stop the flow of dark, but when they traveled against the flow of dark, they paddled quickly, so as to help push the dark along its way.

Finally, we must prove that dark is faster than light. If you were to stand in an illuminated room in front of a closed, dark closet, then slowly open the closet door, you would see the light slowly enter the closet, but since the dark is so fast, you would not be able to see the dark leave the closet.

In conclusion, dark suckers make all our lives much easier. So the next time you look at an electric bulb, remember that it is indeed a dark sucker.

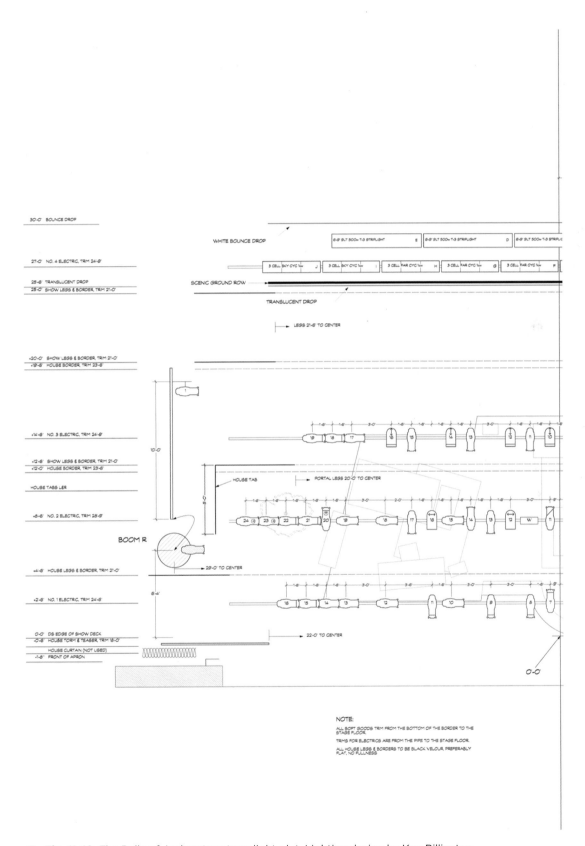

■ **Fig. 11.49** *The Belle of Amherst* onstage light plot. Lighting design by Ken Billington.

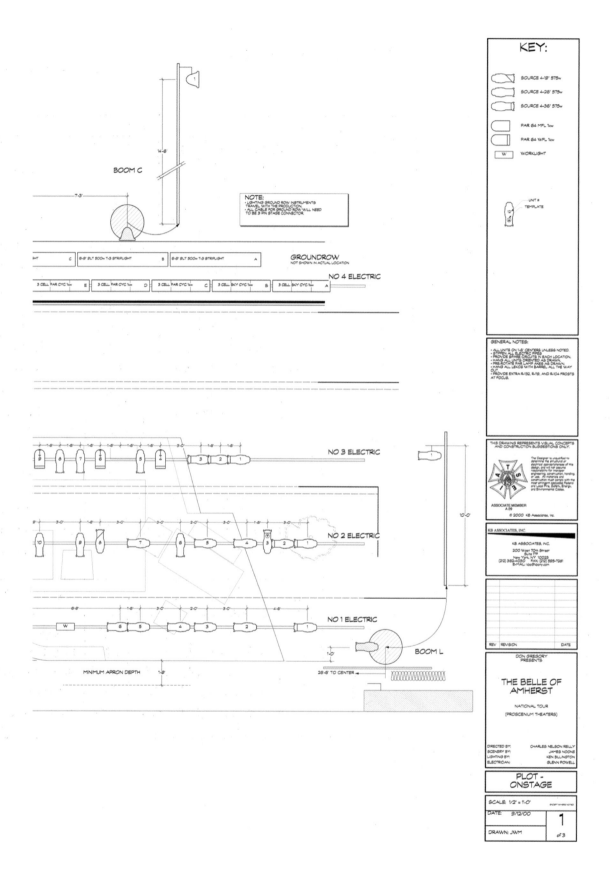

■ **Fig. 11.49** (Continued).

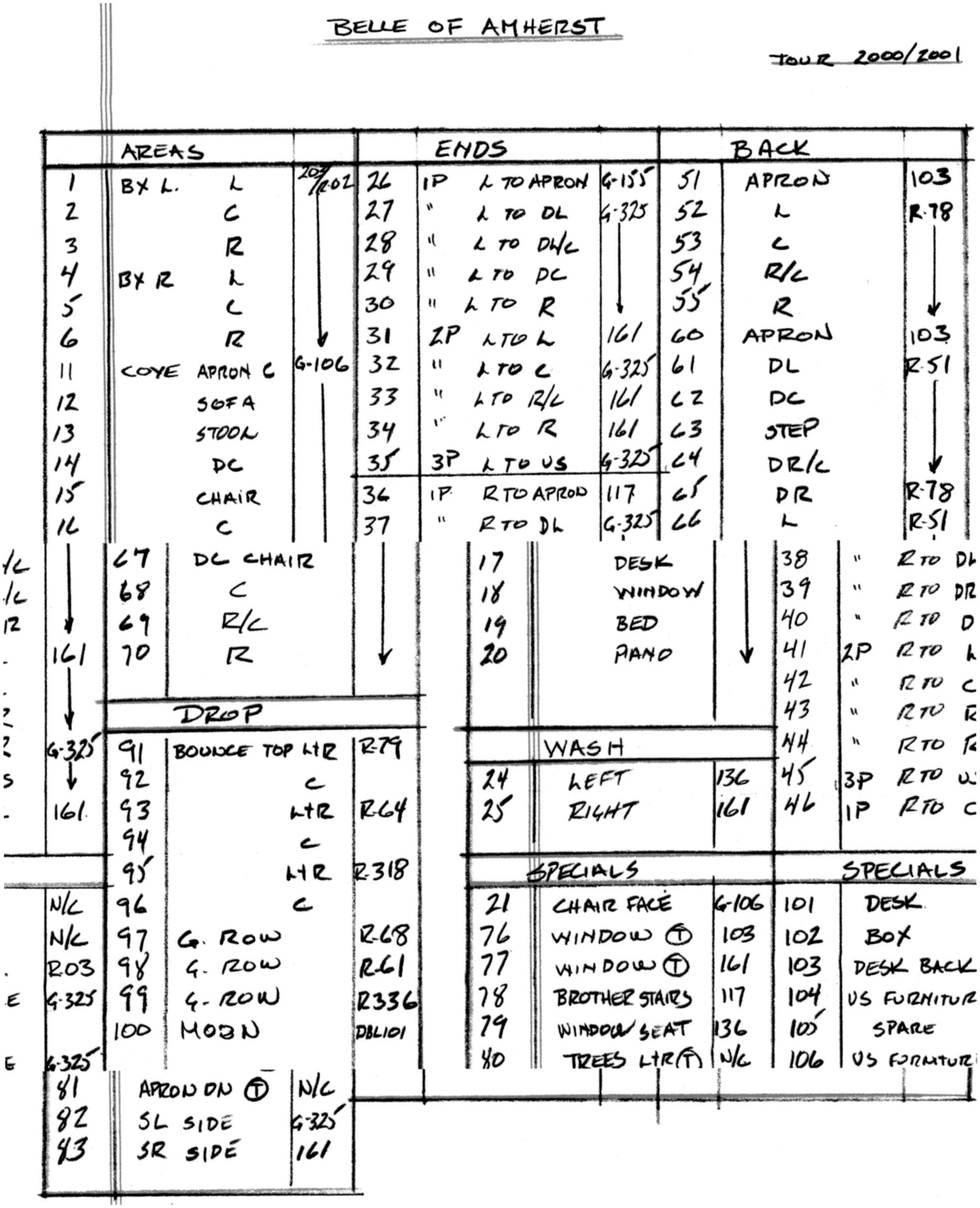

BELLE OF AMHERST

TOUR 2000/2001

AREAS				ENDS			BACK		
1	BX L.	L	20/R02	26	1P L TO APRON	G-155	51	APRON	103
2		C		27	" L TO DL	G-325	52	L	R-78
3		R		28	" L TO DL/C		53	C	
4	BX R	L		29	" L TO DC		54	R/C	
5		C		30	" L TO R		55	R	
6		R		31	2P L TO L	161	60	APRON	103
11	COVE APRON C		G-106	32	" L TO C	G-325	61	DL	R-51
12	SOFA			33	" L TO R/C	161	62	DC	
13	STOOL			34	" L TO R	161	63	STEP	
14	DC			35	3P L TO US	G-325	64	DR/C	
15	CHAIR			36	1P R TO APRON	117	65	DR	R-78
16	C			37	" R TO DL	G-325	66	L	R-51
/C	67	DC CHAIR		17	DESK		38	"	R TO DL
/C	68	C		18	WINDOW		39	"	R TO DR
12	69	R/C		19	BED		40	"	R TO D
.	161	70	R		20	PIANO		41	2P R TO L
							42	"	R TO C
		DROP					43	"	R TO R
2		91	BOUNCE TOP L+R	R-79			44	"	R TO R
2	G-325	92	C		WASH		45	3P R TO US
S		93	L+R	R-64	24	LEFT	136	46	1P R TO C
.	161	94	C		25	RIGHT	161		
		95	L+R	R-318					
		96	C		SPECIALS			SPECIALS	
N/C	97	G. ROW	R-68	21	CHAIR FACE	G-106	101	DESK
N/C	98	G. ROW	R-61	76	WINDOW Ⓣ	103	102	BOX
R03	99	G. ROW	R336	77	WINDOW Ⓣ	161	103	DESK BACK
E G-325	100	MOON	DBL101	78	BROTHER STAIRS	117	104	US FURNITUR
				79	WINDOW SEAT	136	105	SPARE
E G-325				80	TREES L+R Ⓣ	N/C	106	US FURNITUR
	81	APRON ON Ⓣ	N/C					
	82	SL SIDE	G-325					
	83	SR SIDE	161					

Fig. 11.50 *The Belle of Amherst* lighting designer Ken Billington's magic sheet.

BELLE OF AMHERST - Laguna Playhouse Sept. 2000

1	2	3	4	5	6	7	8	9	10	11	12	13	14	15	16	17	18	19	20	21	22	23	24	25
L	C	R	L	C	R					Apr L	Sofa	Stool	DC	Chair	C	Desk	Wind o	Bed	Piano	Chair Face			L136	L161

26	27	28	29	30	31	32	33	34	35	36	37	38	39	40	41	42	43	44	45	46	47	48	49	50
Apr	DL	DLC	DC	R	L	C	RC	R	US	Apr	DL	DLC	DRC	DR	L	C	R	R	US	C				

51	52	53	54	55	56	57	58	59	60	61	62	63	64	65	66	67	68	69	70	71	72	73	74	75
Apr Bk	L161 BACKLIGHTS									R51 BACKLIGHTS														
	L	C	RC	R					Apr	DL	DC	Step	DRC	DR	L	DC	C	RC	R					

76	77	78	79	80	81	82	83	84	85	86	87	88	89	90	91	92	93	94	95	96	97	98	99	100
Window		Broth	Wind Seat	Trees	Apr Temp	Boom L	Boom R								CYC TOP						CYC BOTTOM			Moon
Wm	Cool														R79	R79	R64	R64	R318	R318	R68	R61	R336	

101	102	103	104	105	106	107	108	109	110	111	112	113	114	115	116	117	118	119	120	121	122	123	124	125
Desk Sp.	Box Sp.	Desk Bklt	US Furn	Spare	US Furn																	Run Lts		Hse Lts

■ **Fig. 11.51** *The Belle of Amherst* associate lighting designer John McKernon's magic sheet.

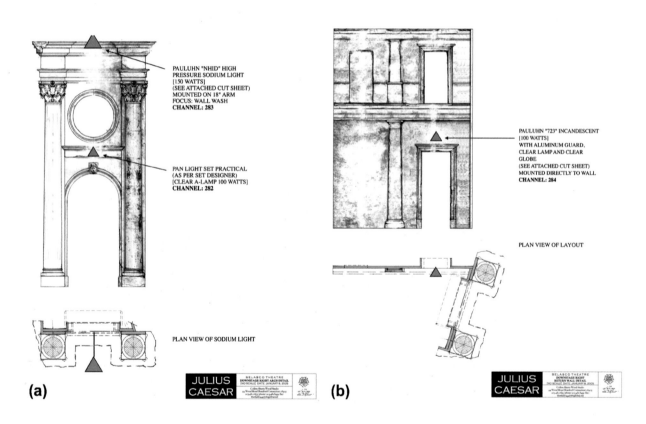

PAULUHN "NHID" HIGH
PRESSURE SODIUM LIGHT
[150 WATTS]
(SEE ATTACHED CUT SHEET)
MOUNTED ON 18" ARM
FOCUS: WALL WASH
CHANNEL: 283

PAN LIGHT SET PRACTICAL
(AS PER SET DESIGNER)
[CLEAR A-LAMP 100 WATTS]
CHANNEL: 282

PLAN VIEW OF SODIUM LIGHT

PAULUHN "723" INCANDESCENT
[100 WATTS]
WITH ALUMINUM GUARD,
CLEAR LAMP AND CLEAR
GLOBE
(SEE ATTACHED CUT SHEET)
MOUNTED DIRECTLY TO WALL
CHANNEL: 284

PLAN VIEW OF LAYOUT

(a)
JULIUS CAESAR

(b)
JULIUS CAESAR

■ **Fig. 11.52** *Julius Caesar* detail drawings.

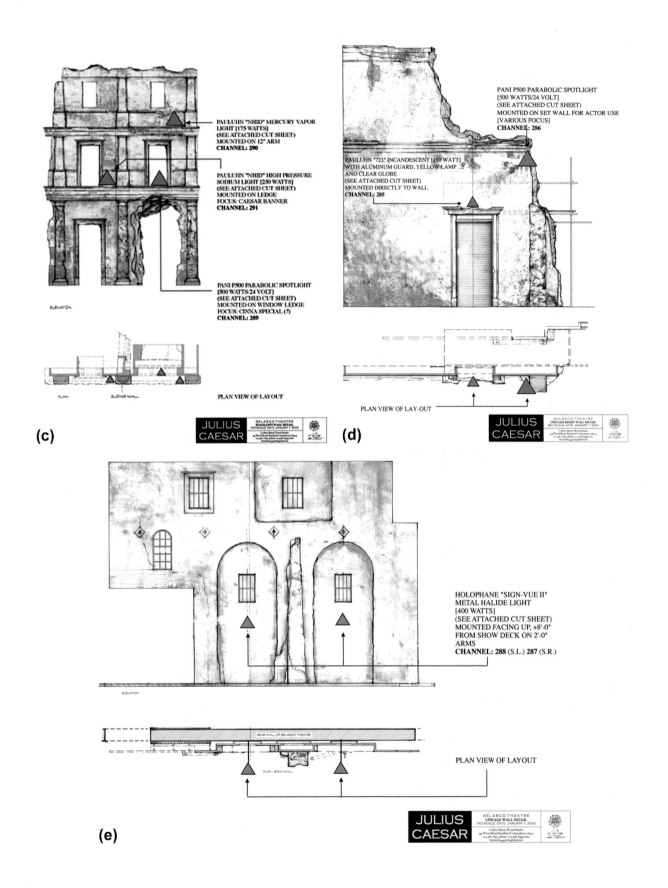

(c)

PAULUHN "NHID" MERCURY VAPOR
LIGHT [175 WATTS]
(SEE ATTACHED CUT SHEET)
MOUNTED ON 12" ARM
CHANNEL: 290

PAULUHN "NHID" HIGH PRESSURE
SODIUM LIGHT [250 WATTS]
(SEE ATTACHED CUT SHEET)
MOUNTED ON LEDGE
FOCUS: CAESAR BANNER
CHANNEL: 291

PANI P500 PARABOLIC SPOTLIGHT
[500 WATTS/24 VOLT]
(SEE ATTACHED CUT SHEET)
MOUNTED ON WINDOW LEDGE
FOCUS: CINNA SPECIAL (?)
CHANNEL: 289

ELEVATION

PLAN   ST. LONG WALL

PLAN VIEW OF LAYOUT

(d)

PANI P500 PARABOLIC SPOTLIGHT
[500 WATTS/24 VOLT]
(SEE ATTACHED CUT SHEET)
MOUNTED ON SET WALL FOR ACTOR USE
[VARIOUS FOCUS]
CHANNEL: 286

PAULUHN "723" INCANDESCENT [150 WATT]
WITH ALUMINUM GUARD, YELLOW LAMP
AND CLEAR GLOBE
(SEE ATTACHED CUT SHEET)
MOUNTED DIRECTLY TO WALL
CHANNEL: 285

PLAN VIEW OF LAY-OUT

(e)

HOLOPHANE "SIGN-VUE II"
METAL HALIDE LIGHT
[400 WATTS]
(SEE ATTACHED CUT SHEET)
MOUNTED FACING UP, +8'-0"
FROM SHOW DECK ON 2'-0"
ARMS
CHANNEL: 288 (S.L.) **287** (S.R.)

ELEVATION

REAR WALL OF BELASCO THEATRE

PLAN - BACK WALL

PLAN VIEW OF LAYOUT

Accessory slot
Alternating current
Ampere
AMX
Autotransformer
Auto Yoke®
AWG
Ballast
Barn door
Beam angle
Beam projector
Beam spread
Cheat sheet
Conventional
   lighting
Dimmer
Direct current
DMX
Ellipsoidal reflector
   spotlight
Filament
Fluorescent
Focus
Footlights
Fresnel
Fresnel lens
Front of house
Gel
Gobo
Ground

Halogen lightbulb
Incandescent
   lightbulb
Intelligent
   lighting
Kelvin
Lamp
Lamp housing
LED
Leko
Lens
Lighting controller
Limelight
Magic sheet
PAR
Pipe clamp
Quartz envelope
Reflector
Scoop
SCR
Shutters
Single phase
Strip light
Three phase
Top hat
Trunnion
Voltage
Wattage
West Virginia
Yoke

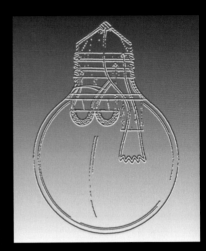

CHAPTER ELEVEN
Study Words

PART
FOUR
Costumes
and Makeup

Chapter XII: All Dressed up with Someplace to Go
Costumes

Chapter XIII: Put on a Happy Face
Makeup

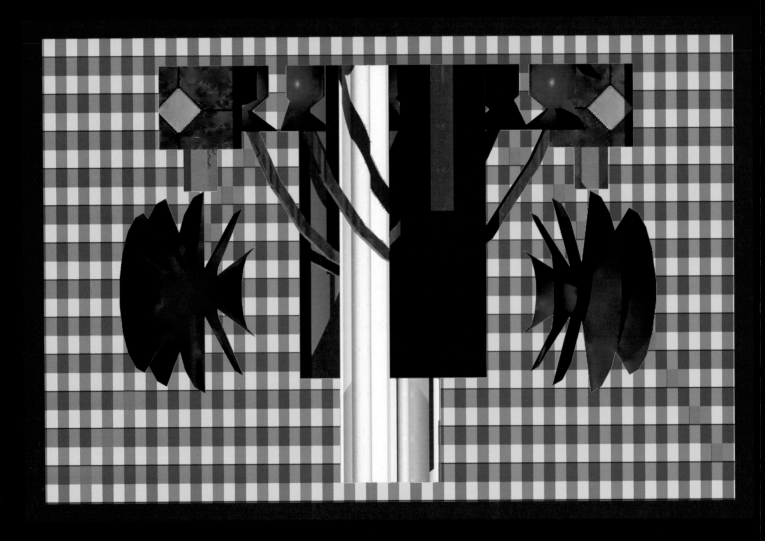

All Dressed up with Someplace to Go

Costumes

This chapter is all about costumes. Now, you may be thinking, "How can costumes use new technology?" Many of the new technologies that costume designers and shops use is not in the actual costumes, but in how they get built. Patterning software has had huge developments recently. Let's get started.

> It's always a group effort . . . . I develop the designs by working with the director and choreographer and, if there is one, a live author. That's how it all begins. And then you get to the actor, and they bring in their elements. It's like cooking! I feel like Julia Child sometimes!
>
> **—William Ivey Long**

The costume designer provides the shop with costume sketches (Figs. 12.1 and 12.2). There is one sketch per costume or character, whichever is required for the show. Each sketch shows the front as

Fig. 12.1 Campbell Baird's costume sketches for a production of *Carousel*, mounted on a wall in the costume shop at Muhlenberg College.

Fig. 12.2 Two of Campbell Baird's costume sketches for a production of *Carousel*.

well as back or side details, accessories, and fabric swatches. This is the first chance the shop has to see what it is about to build. Usually, the entire show's renderings are posted on a shop wall, so that everyone can reference them as needed throughout the entire process.

FABRICS

One of the first choices a costume designer makes is with regard to fabric. So many fabrics are available today. Also, many techniques can add additional design, texture, or color to a fabric. Let's break it down into natural fabrics versus synthetic fabrics.

Natural fabrics can be divided into four basic categories: wool, cotton, silk, and linen. Wool fabric often brings to mind cozy warmth or being scratchy and itchy. The second one gives some people the idea that they are "allergic" to wool. Wool fiber comes from a variety of animal coats and not all wools are scratchy. Wool is also processed in different ways, so you may feel "allergic" to one wool and not another. Some wools are even extremely soft.

The wool fibers have natural crimps or curls that create pocketed areas, making the fabric feel spongy. This also creates a warm insulation for the wearer. Wool can absorb up to 30 percent of its weight in moisture, either from rain, snow, or perspiration, without feeling damp. All these traits combine to make wool the most popular fabric for tailoring fine garments or outdoor wear. Wool is also dirt resistant, flame resistant, and in many weaves, resists wear and tearing.

Cotton is often thought of as cool, soft, and comfortable. The cotton fiber is from the cotton plant's seedpod. The fiber is hollow in the center and, under a microscope, looks like a twisted ribbon. The fiber absorbs and releases perspiration quickly, thus allowing the fabric to "breathe." "Absorbent" cotton retains 24–27 times its own weight in water and is stronger when wet than dry. Cotton can stand high temperatures and takes dyes easily, which is often important in theatrical design. Chlorine bleach can be used to restore white garments to a clear white, but this bleach may yellow chemically finished cottons or remove color in dyed cottons (Figs. 12.3 and 12.4).

Silk is a fabric that has its own reputation. When you hear the word *silk*, what do you visualize? For centuries, silk has had a reputation as a luxurious and sensuous fabric, one associated with wealth and success. No other fabric

Fig. 12.3 *Othello*, as produced by the Shakespeare Theatre Company in 2005. Avery Brooks as Othello; director, Michael Kahn.

generates quite the same reaction. Silk is a natural protein fiber taken from the cocoon of the silkworm. Silk is one of the oldest textile fibers known to humans. Silk absorbs moisture, which makes it cool in the summer and warm in the winter. Because of its high absorbency, it is easily dyed in many deep colors. Silk retains its shape, drapes well, caresses the figure, and shimmers with a luster all its own.

Linen is often confused with cotton or at least with being made of some part of the cotton plant. Linen is actually made from flax, or more specifically, a fiber taken from the stalk of the plant. It has a natural luster from the inherent wax content of the plant. It is an elegant, beautiful, durable, and refined luxury fabric. Linen is the strongest of the vegetable fibers and has two to three times the strength of cotton. Not only is linen strong, it is also very smooth. It is highly absorbent and a good conductor of heat like most natural fibers. Linen is naturally off-white or tan. It can be easily dyed and the color does not fade when washed.

Fig. 12.4 *Othello*, as produced by the Shakespeare Theatre Company in 2005. Avery Brooks as Othello and Colleen Delany as Desdemona; director, Michael Kahn.

MAPPING THE COMPLEX TERRAIN OF JOHN GUARE'S *A FREE MAN OF COLOR*

David Barbour

New Broadway plays don't come more ambitious than *A Free Man of Color,* which opened in November at Lincoln Center Theatre's Vivian Beaumont Theatre. John Guare's sprawling historical comedy/drama practically demands a spectacular production, and that's what it got in George C. Wolfe's staging—complete with a cast of two dozen actors covering three dozen speaking roles and a stunning production design that included, among other things, an elaborate costume parade and more than one coup de théâtre.

Rest assured, nobody involved in *A Free Man of Color* was pursuing spectacle for its own sake. If anything, the play's many critics complained that Guare had overstuffed his script with a superfluity of ideas, characters, and themes. There's no question that the script makes big demands on the audience: It's a pastiche Restoration comedy crossed with a broadly cartooned political satire, climaxing in a starkly dramatic revelation of the horrors of slavery; the author combines these elements to produce a tart history lesson designed to reveal the exact moment when the still-young American republic began its transformation into a bloated, ungovernable superpower.

Source: Originally published in *Lighting and Sound America*, January 2011.

Synthetic fibers are a whole different category. Synthetics are the result of extensive research by scientists to improve on naturally occurring animal and plant fibers. Before synthetic fibers were developed, artificial (manufactured) fibers were made from cellulose, which comes from plants. All these developments happened during times of war. As certain materials were rationed, these developments were necessary to our culture. Rayon, acetate, nylon, and polyester are just a few of the synthetics we discuss.

We start with rayon. Rayon, introduced in 1910, is a very versatile fiber and has many of the same comfort properties as natural fibers. It can imitate the feel and texture of silk, wool, cotton, or linen. The fibers are easily dyed in a wide range of colors. Rayon fabrics are soft, smooth, cool, comfortable, and highly absorbent, but they do not insulate body heat, making them ideal for use in hot and humid climates.

Acetate, introduced in 1934, is low in cost and has good draping qualities. Acetate is used in fabrics such as satins, brocades, and taffetas to accentuate the fabric's luster, body, drape, and beauty. It is soft, smooth, dry, and crisp. It breathes, wicking away moisture and drying quickly, but offers no heat retention. Acetate is an environmentally friendly fabric, as it is made from wood pulp of reforested trees. Deep brilliant color shades are possible through dyeing.

Nylon, introduced in 1935, has the ability to be very lustrous, semi-lustrous, or dull. Nylon was intended to be a synthetic replacement for silk and substituted for it in many products after silk became scarce during World War II. It replaced silk in military applications, such as parachutes and flak vests, and was used in many types of vehicle tires. Nylon fibers are used in a great many applications, including fabrics, bridal veils, carpets, musical strings, and rope.

Last, there is polyester. Polyesters are the most widely used human-made fiber in the world. Polyester fabrics are used in consumer apparel and home furnishings, such as bed sheets, bedspreads, curtains, and draperies. Polyester fiberfill is also used to stuff pillows, comforters, and cushion padding. Polyester fabrics can have a "less natural" feel when compared to similarly woven fabrics made from natural fibers. However, polyester fabrics may exhibit other advantages over natural fabrics, such as improved wrinkle and stain resistance. As a result, polyester fibers are sometimes spun together with natural fibers to produce a cloth with blended properties.

So as you can see, before we even talk about color and pattern of fabric, there are a lot of choices to consider (Fig. 12.5). What type of fabric properties are you looking for?

This is a major question to be answered before you ever go shopping for fabric. And, shopping might not be as much of an option, depending on the costume shop's in-house stock (Fig. 12.6). Most fabrics need to be prewashed before you cut and assemble them into a garment. This allows them to preshrink before fabrication, which basically means your sizing will be, and remain, more accurate.

TOOLS AND ACCESSORIES

Let's talk about basic tools for a little bit. There are many small tools and a few bigger tools. The smaller tools are something that most costume shop workers carry with them from job to job. Once you develop a preference for a specific pair of scissors, you won't leave home without them. So, here goes.

Tape measures are a very important part of the costume shop (Fig. 12.7). These are similar in concept to the scenic tape measures, yet different in fabrication. Huh? Well, basically, they are a soft, flexible tape measure. People are soft and have curves, wood doesn't.

Fig. 12.5 A variety of fabric choices.

Fig. 12.6 Organized swatch books of all in-house fabrics listing amount of yardage available.

Fig. 12.7 Tape measure.

Use your tape measure to take all the appropriate measurements for the actor or actress. More on this later. Once you have the actor's measurements, you work with a pattern. You work with either an existing pattern, create your own, or use some mixture of the two. If you have a pattern, it gives you each piece of the finished garment separately, so that you can lay them out on fabric to begin cutting.

If you are creating a pattern from scratch, you will most likely use a sloper. A sloper is a basic pattern shape in a variety of sizes (Fig. 12.8). Slopers come in many pattern shapes. They help you to get started with a custom pattern by letting you more easily fit the pattern pieces together as you are making adjustments for size and design. As you make these adjustments, a patterning template helps you ease the transitions between pieces (Fig. 12.9).

Next up are pins. This may seem obvious, but there are many kinds of pins—some with different purposes and some that are different just by preference. Differences can vary a pin from a flat metal head to round plastic head, and the length of the pin can change from short to very long for quilting. A pincushion holds the pins all in one place. It is usually a soft, stuffed shape that you stick the pins into. The coolest thing I've seen in a long time is the magnetic pincushion (Fig. 12.10). It's sort of obvious how it works, but wow! What a great idea.

Once the pattern is created and pinned to the fabric, you get to cut it out. Scissors are not new to us, but the scissors you use for fabric are much different (Fig. 12.11). Sewing

Fig. 12.8 Sloper.

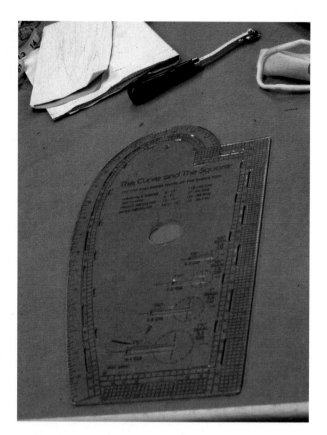

Fig. 12.9 Patterning template.

Fig. 12.10 Magnetic pincushion.

scissors are usually much more expensive than regular scissors because they are made to be adjustable and sharpened as required. Cutting paper dulls a scissors' blades faster than anything else I know of. Never let anyone use your sewing scissors to cut anything other than fabric. And, be aware that there are now great scissors for those of us who are left-handed. Some scissors even have handles that work well for right- or left-handed people.

Continuing in some sort of semilogical order, let's talk about thread (Fig. 12.12). There are almost as many types as there are colors. Thread comes in cotton, rayon, polyester, silk, and so forth. You get the idea. And, the colors are endless. Many manufacturers have their own color list. You can get almost any kind of thread in any color you can think of. The important part of choosing a specific thread is to know what you will be sewing, so that you make sure to match the thread's properties to the fabrics. There are threads for regular sewing, mending, quilting, and embroidering. Just because a thread says it is for a specific purpose doesn't

mean you can't use for it something else. You just have to make a small sample to try it out.

Buttons, zippers, lace, appliqués, beads, and all sorts of other accessories complete the costume and make it truly unique (Figs. 12.13 and 12.14). These are some of the hardest items to find when you are looking for something very specific, and this can become the most time consuming part of making the costumes. Most shops have

Fig. 12.11 Scissors.

Fig. 12.12 Various thread spools.

Fig. 12.13 Buttons.

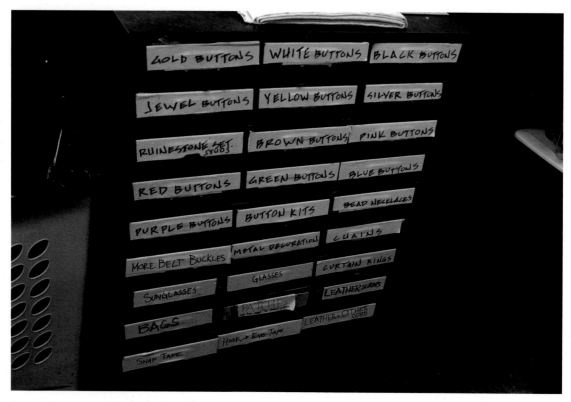

Fig. 12.14 More buttons.

Fig. 12.15 Lots of other accessories neatly stored and ready for use.

Fig. 12.16 Seam ripper.

a stock of accessories, just waiting for the right costume. It is important to store these items in a safe and organized way (Fig. 12.15). If you can't find them when the time comes, they are useless to have.

Seam rippers are almost as important as any other tool (Figs. 12.16 and 12.17). Once you have sewn anywhere from a single seam to a whole garment, there will always be times when you need to open up a seam. Changes happen. The seam ripper is your best tool for this since it is specifically designed for it. If you try to open a seam with a pair

of scissors, you will have a better shot at cutting the fabric than just removing the thread. Similar to scissors, you end up finding a favorite kind of seam ripper and want to have it with you all the time.

Once the garment is made, you need to fit it to the actor or actress. Tailor's chalk is perfect for marking where you need to adjust the fit, either larger or smaller (Fig. 12.18). Of course, you can also use chalk to make markings before you cut and assemble. The reason tailor's chalk is so good for this purpose is that, when you no longer need the markings, the chalk can be brushed away without leaving any residue. During fittings, it is much faster to mark a garment with chalk than to have an actor stand there while you insert pin after pin.

While we're on the subject of chalk, a great use for it is to mark a hem during a fitting. The problem with hems, especially full ones, is that it is very difficult to get them even. This is even more of an issue if a skirt is bustled. There is no way to mark the hem unless it is on the actress. Enter Mr. Puffy! Mr. Puffy is basically the chalk line of costume design (Figs. 12.19 and 12.20). Tailor's chalk, ground to a powder, is put into a small container with a very focused spout. A hose is attached to the container, controlled by a squeeze ball. The whole thing is mounted on a stand that

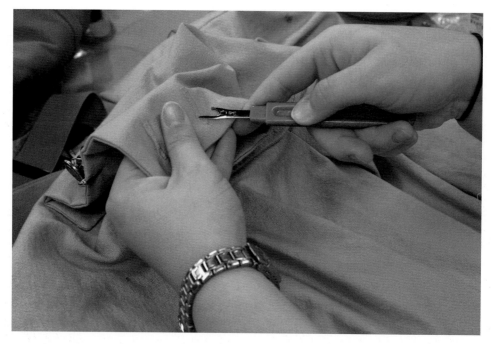

Fig. 12.17 A seam ripper being used to open a buttonhole.

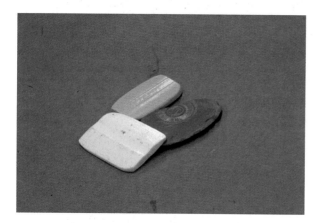

Fig. 12.18 Chalk comes in a variety of colors, so you can easily use the color that shows up best on the fabric.

is measured and marked, so you know how high it is off the ground. Squeeze the ball and *poof*, your hemline is marked. I'm sure Mr. Puffy has another name, but this is the only name I've heard him called.

Useless Factoid: Tripping

If an actress trips on the hem of her dress, she should pick it up and kiss the hem for good luck.

Fig. 12.19 Mr. Puffy.

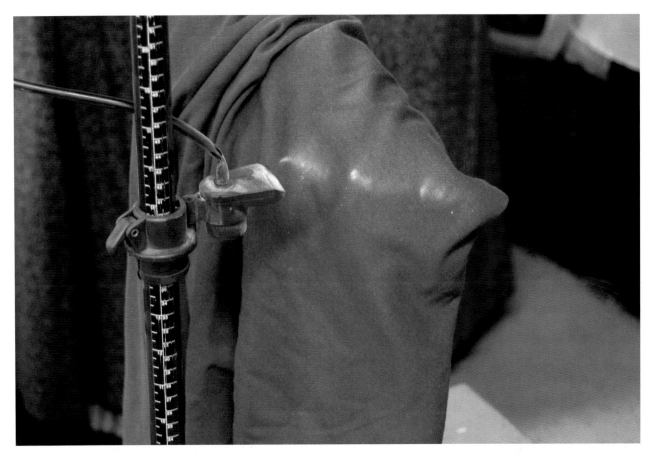

Fig. 12.20 Mr. Puffy in use to mark a hemline.

MEASUREMENTS

Now that we have the basic small tools covered, let's talk for a minute about measurements. All the actors must be measured. *Do not* take their word for it that they are a certain size, dimension, or weight. First off, most people don't know how to properly measure themselves for the purpose of making clothing. Second, we all have our own idea of what our body looks like. Just because you can squeeze into a size 6 pair of jeans without being able to breathe or sit down doesn't mean they fit! Men's and women's measurements are taken slightly differently. Let's go into them one at a time.

WOMEN'S MEASUREMENT INSTRUCTIONS (FIG. 12.21)

Bust: The fullest point of the bust, under the arms and around the widest part of the back.

Chest: Just below the bust measurement, usually corresponds to bra size.

Waistline: The natural waistline is the narrowest part of the body. Firmly measure with your fingers on the outside of the tape.

Outer leg: From the waistline to the anklebone.

High hip: Measure around the high point of the hip bones, usually 3 to 4 inches below the waistline.

Bodice front: From the nape of the neck, down over the bust and to the bottom edge of the waistline. (The nape is where the neck turns toward the shoulder.)

Height: In bare feet, measure from the top of the head to the bottom of the feet.

Weight: Use an accurate scale, and remember all of this information is confidential!

Shoe size: Wide, medium, or narrow plus size.

Head size: Measure around the forehead holding the tape taut.

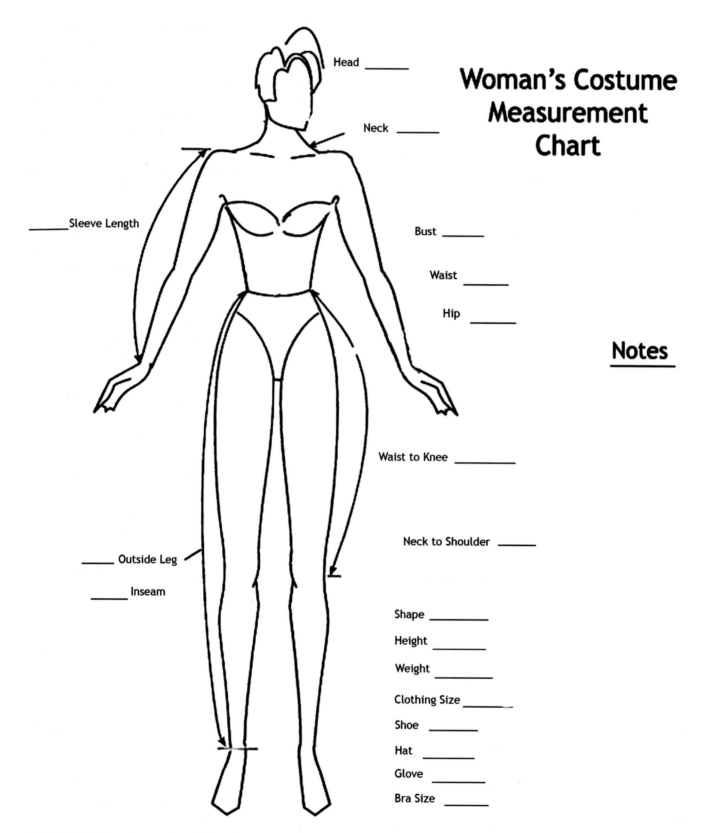

Woman's Costume Measurement Chart

Head _____

Neck _____

Bust _____

Waist _____

Hip _____

Sleeve Length _____

Waist to Knee _____

Neck to Shoulder _____

Outside Leg _____

Inseam _____

Notes

Shape _____

Height _____

Weight _____

Clothing Size _____

Shoe _____

Hat _____

Glove _____

Bra Size _____

Fig. 12.21 Form to use when taking down women's measurements.

MEN'S MEASUREMENT INSTRUCTIONS (FIG. 12.22)

Chest: Measure the widest part of the chest just below the armpits and around the back.

Waistline: Measure the circumference of the waist. If the actor wears his pants at or below the waist, indicate the distance from his navel and in which direction (below or above).

Outer leg: Measure from the waist down to the anklebone.

Inner leg: Measure from the crotch down to the anklebone.

Crotch length: Measure from the waistline at the center back all the way around to the waistline at the center front.

Back width: Measure across the broadest part of the back from armpit to armpit.

Neck: Measure comfortably around the base of the neck. The actor should be able to move his neck and swallow.

Shoulder: Measure from the base of the neck to the outermost point of the shoulder.

Arm: With arms slightly bent, measure from the outermost point of the shoulder down to the wrist bone bump.

Height: In bare feet, measure from the top of the head to the bottom of the feet.

Weight: Use an accurate scale, and remember all of this information is confidential!

Shoe size: Wide, medium, or narrow plus size.

Head size: Measure around the forehead holding the tape taut.

Depending on the costume designs, you may need to add other specific measurements y to those noted. Once the actors have been measured, the next step is to keep track of which actors/characters are wearing which costume pieces and accessories. Yup, this means more paperwork and yet another form (Figs. 12.23 and 12.24). Small accessories can get lost so easily that tracking their use is very important.

Also, every character should have an accessory bag, sometimes known as a **ditty bag** (Fig. 12.25). This is not an item you can easily buy. Costume shops usually make them between shows using leftover muslin. A hanger is sewn into the top of the bag and a series of pockets are created down below. This allows the accessory bag to hang with the actor's costumes. It keeps everything in one place, which means fewer crises before the show and easier maintenance after the show.

At one time, the cutter and draper were two separate positions in the costume shop. More and more these days, the positions have been combined. Originally, the **cutter** was a person who used patterns, or created patterns, and cut the pattern from the fabric. Originally, the **draper** was a person who, instead of using a pattern, created a design by draping the fabric onto the actor or a mannequin. Then, marking and pinning would define where the fabric needed to be stitched. This was all done on the actor or mannequin, with no pattern. Obviously, this was very specific to the actor's body. Mannequins come in different sizes and are adjustable so that you can truly simulate the size and shape of the actor. Certain designs still call for this but not nearly as much as there used to be. So, gradually, the two positions were combined.

> The lighting can make it or break it. You pick a color and you think, "This is going to be great!" And then you get it on stage and you think, "Oh, my, what was I thinking?" Black costumes are a particular problem, due to the many colors and multistep process used to dye the cloth. Certain lights, particularly lavender tints, can pierce through black dye to reveal other colors that had been on the fabric before, ruining the effect. You have to do lots of color testing, but the whole process is "fun."
>
> **—William Ivey Long**

SEWING

It is now time to begin sewing. Finally. Who knew there was all this work to do before you could even stitch your first stitch? OK, so there are many different kinds of sewing machines. There are lots of manufacturers; some are simple and straightforward, while others are more complicated and have specialty things they do, like embroidery. If a costume shop has several sewing machines, it will most likely set each one up for a different task. One might be for straight sewing, while another is set up to only create buttonholes (Figs. 12.26 and 12.27).

There is a stitch called *overlocking* that we should discuss. If you happen to be wearing a T-shirt, turn it inside out and look at the seam … most likely it was seamed with

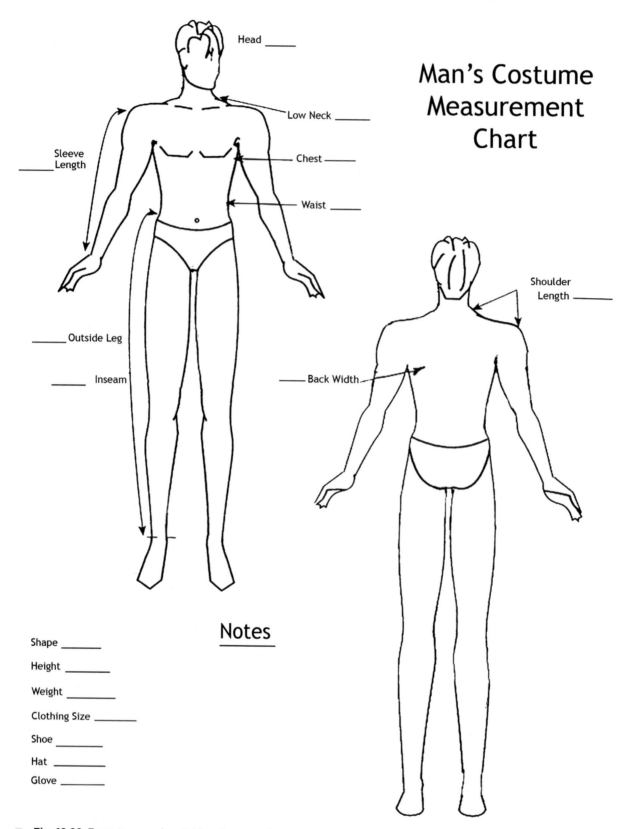

Man's Costume
Measurement
Chart

Head _____

Low Neck _____

Chest _____

Waist _____

Sleeve
Length
_____

Shoulder
Length _____

Outside Leg _____

Inseam _____

Back Width _____

Notes

Shape _____

Height _____

Weight _____

Clothing Size _____

Shoe _____

Hat _____

Glove _____

Fig. 12.22 Form to use when taking down men's measurements.

Actor's Name:		Character:	
Scene			
Undershirt/T-shirt			
Corset			
Bum Roll			
Bustle			
Petticoat			
Tights			
Stockings			
Shoes/Boots/ Footwear			
Bodice			
Skirt			
Bustle Drape			
Apron			
Shawl			
Hair Ribbon			
Hat/Bonnet			
Gloves			
Jewelry			
Parasol/Cane/ Walking Stick			
Pocketbook			
Other (Costume Props)			
Wig/Hair Piece			
Makeup			

Fig. 12.23 Women's tracking form.

Actor's Name: Character:

Scene			
Undershirt/T-shirt			
Dance Belt			
Socks			
Shoes			
Spats			
Shirt			
Overshirt/Dress shirt			
Vest			
Coat/Jacket			
Pants			
Apron			
Suspenders			
Tie			
Hat/Cap			
Gloves			
Jewelry			
Cane/Walking Stick			
Wallet			
Other (Costume Props)			
Wig/Hair Piece			
Makeup			

■ **Fig. 12.24** Men's tracking form.

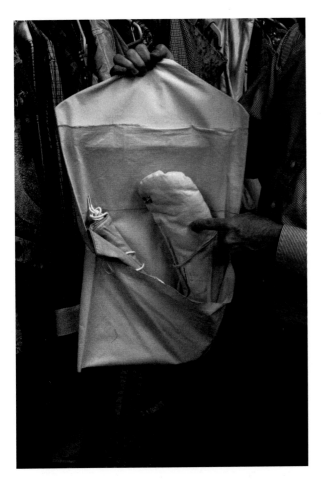

Fig. 12.25 Ditty bag for accessories. These are a great way to keep everything for a character together.

an **overlocking** stitch. This stitch sews over the edge of one or two pieces of cloth for edging, hemming, or seaming. Usually, an overlock sewing machine, or **serger**, will cut the edges of the cloth as it is fed through, though some are made without cutters. The inclusion of automated cutters allows sergers to create finished seams easily and quickly. A serger differs from a regular sewing machine in that it utilizes loopers fed by multiple thread cones rather than a bobbin (Fig. 12.28). **Loopers** create thread loops that pass from the needle thread to the edges of the fabric so that the edges of the fabric are contained within the seam (Fig. 12.29). Overlock stitches are extremely versatile, as they can be used for decoration, reinforcement, or construction.

Let me back up for a second. In extremely complicated costumes, a test garment is made out of muslin. The whole process of patterning, cut, sewing, and fitting is still done. Muslin is a fabric that is relatively inexpensive. Once the garment has been fitted to the actor, the muslin is taken

apart and the pieces used as a pattern to make the real costume out of the real fabric.

OK, so—fittings. Once you've sewn the costume, or at least a part of the costume, you schedule a fitting with the actor. The main purpose at this time is to have the actor try on the pieces that are ready to see how they fit. The costume designer is on hand to oversee all of this, especially for the principal characters. This is also a time when the designer may work out any accessories or decorative items that may be needed (Fig. 12.30). Be ready to help the actor get into the costume, and also take lots of notes!

Take a look at Figures 12.31–12.36 to see how a period costume is tried on in stages. The fit is checked at each step along the way.

Once the costume has been fitted to the actor, much of the trim work can be positioned with the aid of a mannequin and without the actor (Figs. 12.37–12.39). This saves the actor time away from rehearsal and allows the shop to keep working on several projects with mannequins simultaneously.

Accessories come in so many types and styles, never mind specialty items. Simple accessories include jewelry, shoes, wigs, hats, and gloves. If what is needed is basic, or easily attainable, the costume shop can provide it. Most costume shops have a stock of these types of items (Figs.12.40–12.42).

Specialty items are usually shopped or sent out of house to a shop that creates only one thing. Armor and weaponry are two examples of this. Costumes that need to do a "trick" may also be created elsewhere, depending on what the trick entails. The other option is to rent items like this or, for that matter, rent the entire show. If you are going to rent all the costumes, the costume designer must be careful when selecting costumes, to make sure they work together on the stage. Many rental houses allow you to make minor alterations, and this can be the key to unifying a rented design.

Useless Factoid: Knitting

It is unlucky for an actor to knit while on the side of the stage. This is because knitting needles are pointy and can rip expensive costumes, or the needle may fall on the floor and cause someone to fall onstage.

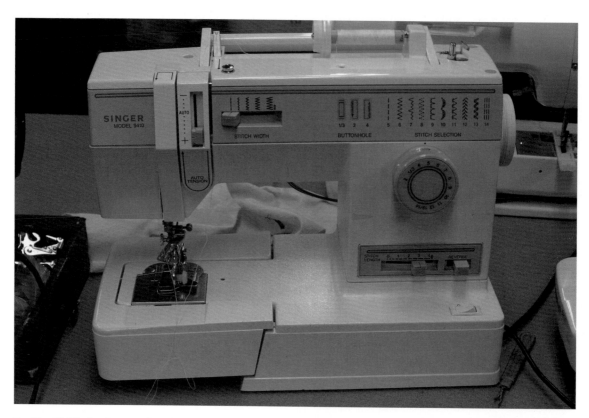

Fig. 12.26 Sewing machine setup for regular stitching.

Fig. 12.27 Sewing machine setup for buttonholes.

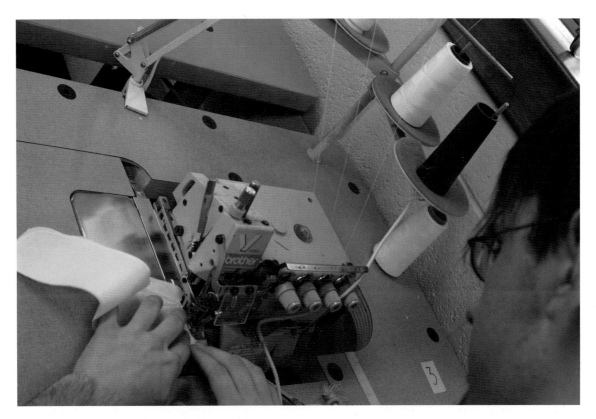

Fig. 12.28 Serger with three loopers.

Fig. 12.29 Serger seam close up.

There are many shortcuts that can be taken to achieve a period feel without building an entire costume from scratch. For example, modern men's shirts with a proper collar design can be altered with the appropriate cuff to work within a costume designer's idea (Fig. 12.43). This saves both time and money. If the look works, do it! These are specialty items that can be created in the costume shop provided enough time and budget are allowed (Fig. 12.44).

One topic I really haven't discussed is the fantasy costume. These can be done for dance, theatre, or opera.

■ **Fig. 12.30** *Hedda Gabler,* as produced by NYU's Tisch School of the Arts, Department of Graduate Acting and Department of Design for Stage and Film. Director, Cigdem Onat; scenic designer, Veronica Ferre; costume designer, Sarah Greene; and lighting designer, Dan Sheehan.

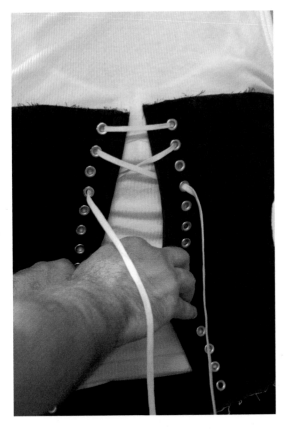

Fig. 12.31 Fitting a corset.

The idea is that you are catering to the specific needs of character creation in a different way than usual. All of your choices, from fabric, to patterns, to cutting, to sewing, to fitting, are slightly different than making a more traditional costume. Each of these situations is slightly different from any other and caters to the needs of that individual production. With that said, take a look at Figures 12.45–12.48, all of which come from a production of the opera: *The Magic Flute* or, as it is also known, *Zauberflote*.

SOFTWARE

We finish up this chapter by talking about software that can make all of this easier. A number of software packages are on the market that help you through the patterning process. The software does not help you design, choose fabric, or sew, but it can be a huge aid in pattern creation. If your shop does not have a set of slopers, or someone who is able to create patterns, then this is the right path for you to consider.

Some of the software patterns available today are Pattern Maker, Dress Shop 7 Pro, Garment Designer, and

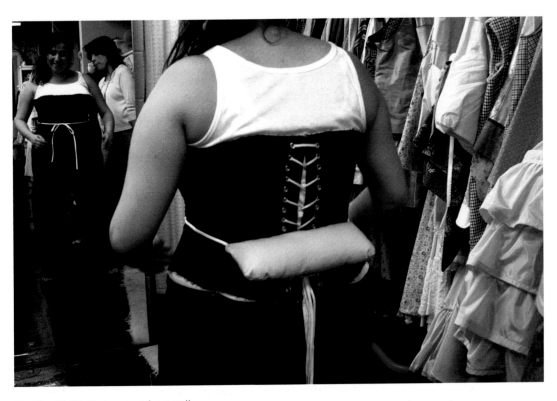

Fig. 12.32 Trying on a bum roll.

Fig. 12.33 Fitting an underskirt and bustle.

Fig. 12.35 Blouse and decoration.

Fig. 12.34 Adding in the skirt and scarf.

My Pattern Designer, to name a few. All have websites, and most have a demo version you can download to try! Most software programs have a series of standard patterns or slopers. You input the actor's measurements, select the different pattern pieces you are interested in using, and *boing*!—pattern pieces can be printed out. Well, it's not quite that easy, but it is close. PatternMaker®, for example, gives you a great deal of flexibility without costing a small fortune. Figures 12.49 and 12.50 show a couple of images from PatternMaker.

I can tell you all about the software, but the only way for you to really get a feel for it is to try it. And, the company now has a 30-day trial for free. This is the case with any tool, not just software. The feel in your hand, or under your control, is completely different than a verbal description. So, go out there, find software to try, and decide for yourself.

■ **Fig. 12.36** Bustle detail.

■ **Fig. 12.37** Pinning trim is the time when the exact placement is determined.

■ **Fig. 12.38** Pinning ruffle.

■ **Fig. 12.39** Costume with all trim pinned in place and ready to be sewn.

Fig. 12.40 Jewelry organized, stored, and ready for its next use.

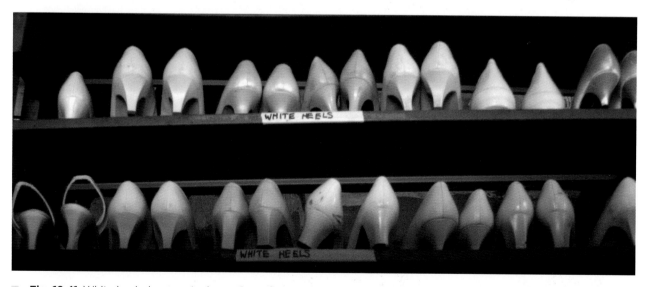

Fig. 12.41 White heeled woman's shoes. One of many categories of shoes a costume shop is liable to have.

■ **Fig. 12.42** A few wigs that have been pulled for a production. When ready, they will be kept on "heads" to help keep their shape.

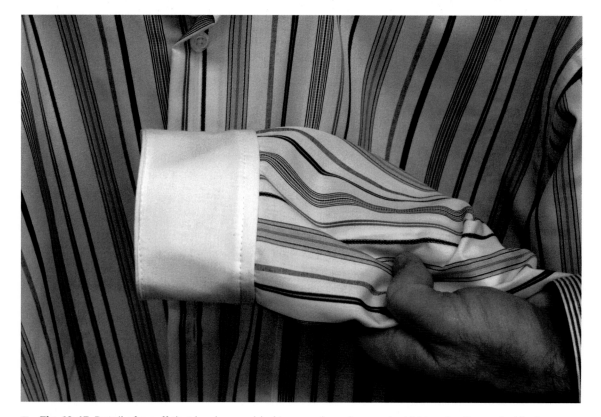

■ **Fig. 12.43** Detail of a cuff that has been added to a modern-day men's shirt to give it a period feel.

■ **Fig. 12.44** A wonderfully done turkey hat, created at Muhlenberg College's costume shop.

■ **Fig. 12.45** Papageno and the three ladies from *Zauberflote*, at the Metropolitan Opera. Director, Julie Taymor; scenic designer, George Tyspin; costume designer, Julie Taymor; and lighting designer, Donald Holder. Puppet designs by Julie Taymor and Michael Curry.

■ **Fig. 12.46** Monastatos, Papageno, and Pamina from *Zauberflote*, at the Metropolitan Opera. Director, Julie Taymor; scenic designer, George Tyspin; costume designer, Julie Taymor; and lighting designer, Donald Holder. Puppet designs by Julie Taymor and Michael Curry.

■ **Fig. 12.47** Papageno from *Zauberflote*, at the Metropolitan Opera. Director, Julie Taymor; scenic designer, George Tyspin; costume designer, Julie Taymor; and lighting designer, Donald Holder. Puppet designs by Julie Taymor and Michael Curry.

■ **Fig. 12.48** Papageno and flamingos from *Zauberflote*, at the Metropolitan Opera. Director, Julie Taymor; scenic designer, George Tyspin; costume designer, Julie Taymor; and lighting designer, Donald Holder. Puppet designs by Julie Taymor and Michael Curry.

Fig. 12.49 PatternMaker screenshot of "costume" options.

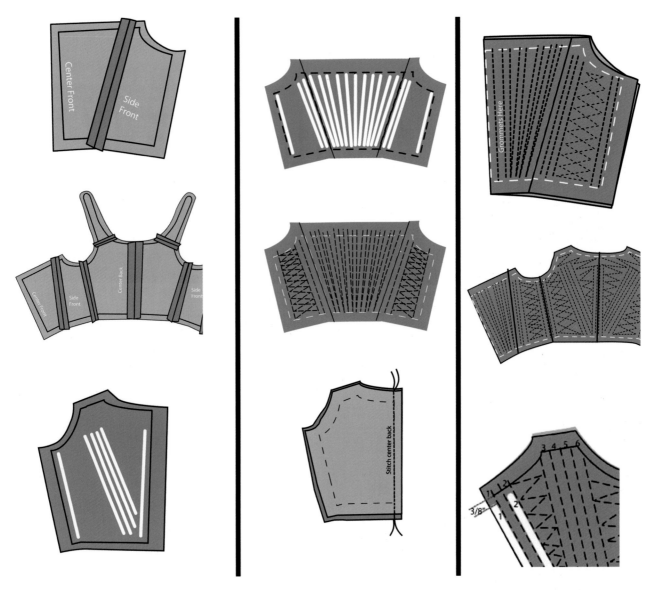

Fig. 12.50 PatternMaker images from a step-by-step instruction for a corset.

Acetate

Cotton

Cutter

Ditty bag

Draper

Linen

Looper

Mr. Puffy

Overlocking

Nylon

Pattern

Patterning template

Preshrink

Polyester

Rayon

Seam ripper

Serger

Silk

Sloper

Tailor's chalk

Tape measure

Wool

CHAPTER TWELVE
Study Words

Put on a Happy Face

Makeup

In our eternal search for the next logical step, we made it to makeup! Makeup, and the concept behind it, has changed greatly over the years. Makeup goes back to Egypt and before. Women of the time would use a product called *kohl* as an ancient eye makeup. Kohl would be made by grinding several natural ingredients together, making a powder. This could be used as an eye shadow, or with water added as a mascara.

Organized makeup as we know it came into fashion during the 1920s and 1930s, when a man by name of Max Factor became intimately associated with the world of Hollywood makeup. Yes, that is right, Max Factor was a real person. And his son, Max Factor, Jr., continued in his father's tradition. Max Factor created the first makeup for the movies in 1914 and coined the term *makeup*, based on the verb *to make up* one's face. Prior to this, all actors and actresses were pretty much on their own for what they used. Max and his company are credited with many cosmetic innovations, such as the first motion picture makeup in 1914, lip gloss in 1930, pancake makeup (the forerunner of all modern cake makeups) in 1937, panstik makeup in 1948, Erace (the original coverup cosmetic) in 1954, and the first "waterproof" makeup in 1971. How is that for one man's history?

Ben Nye is another makeup pioneer, and his company has been very helpful in providing to me information both on tools and techniques. Ben Nye began his career as a Hollywood makeup artist beginning in the 1930s. By the time he retired, his ethnic

CHAPTER THIRTEEN

In this chapter

foundations and unique colors had become standards in most makeup departments. He began formulating his own makeup brand 10 years after his retirement. Today, his son Dana runs the company Ben started in 1967.

FACIAL SHAPES

The first thing to talk about when makeup is the subject are the different face shapes. The face is always balanced. We might not like the balance, but it's always balanced. Analyze the face; take it apart. We always want to be able to see the eyes! They are the window to the soul after all. Double check the wardrobe, check character research, and talk to costumers, lighting designers, and hairstylists. It's an ensemble that all has to work together and all the individual pieces have to add up.

There are six different facial shapes—oval, heart, pear, square, round, and long (Fig. 13.1)—and each has its own specific needs when applying makeup. An oval face is usually considered "perfect," because it is absolutely symmetrical. It has wider cheekbones and is narrow down toward the jaw line and chin and also narrow up toward the forehead. A heart face, which can also be called a *triangle*, is very unique. It is broader at the forehead and then tapers into a small, narrow chin. A pear face is wider at the cheeks and jaw but has a narrow forehead. A square shape is actually the most common facial shape. It is equally wide at the forehead, cheeks, and jaw line. A round shape is fuller and usually makes a person look younger than they are. It has a round forehead and a round chin, with wide, full cheeks. The long shape is similar to an oval face shape but has higher cheekbones and a high forehead.

MAKEUP AND TOOLS

Let's start talking about the tools and makeup of today. There are several manufacturers of stage makeup. Similar to paint from Chapter 9, there are differences between the makeup you buy at the local pharmacy or department store and stage makeup. One of the main differences is that stage makeup is intended to be applied and removed frequently. Stage makeup also lacks perfumes. It is, therefore, easier on your skin and any allergies you may have.

Makeup tools are fairly easy to take about. Makeup brushes, like paintbrushes, come in a number of shapes and sizes. They are also composed of a handle, bristles, and a ferrule, just like the paint brushes we discussed in Chapter 9. There are flat brushes, angle brushes, dome brushes, round brushes, detail brushes, foundation brushes, contour brushes, and rouge brushes. Brushes can be used in whatever way you need to achieve your goal. Here are a few examples, but know that you can use them any way that works for you.

Flat brushes are great for blending (Fig. 13.2). The shape gives you great control when moving the makeup around. You can really control how much makeup you remove versus how much you add. Angle brushes are for very precise work. Applying eye shadow, eyeliner, brow coloring, and lipstick are all good options for the angled brush. Dome brushes, with rounded corners for soft edges, are ideal for under-eye concealer as well as eye shadow (Fig. 13.3). Round brushes are good for lining eyes, etching brows, and applying fine details to effect makeup (Fig. 13.4).

Now wait a minute. Didn't you say the same for dome brushes? Well, yes. But think about it for a second.

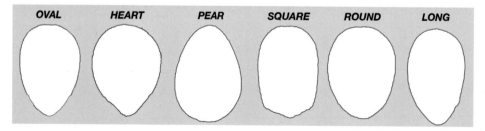

Fig. 13.1 Various facial shapes.

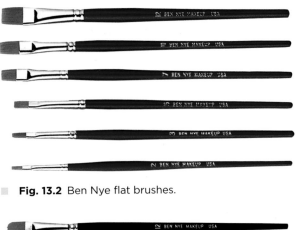

Fig. 13.2 Ben Nye flat brushes.

Fig. 13.3 Ben Nye dome brushes.

Fig. 13.4 Ben Nye round brushes.

Everybody uses brushes in different ways. And the eyebrow, for example, has places where you will need a wider brush and places where you will want a smaller brush. Whoever said you could only use one brush for each purpose? Not me!

Detail brushes come in a variety of shapes. Small powder brushes are soft and rounded, which gives you great control when adding pressed-powder colors to cheeks and eyes. The tapered-point brush is good for contouring eye shadows or applying powders that sparkle or have glitter. The petite shader is a small rounded brush for use when delicate powder detailing is important. The medium blender is a soft, but firm, chiseled-end brush for the precise finishing of powders. Last, the lip brush is a finely tapered brush with a petite shape for applying lip colors and glosses.

Foundation brushes and contour brushes come in a variety of sizes, all with the same shape (Fig. 13.5). They are rounded, with tapered edges that make them perfect for applying crème-style foundations and pressed-powder colors. Rouge brushes come in several different options. The

Fig. 13.5 Ben Nye foundation brushes.

Fig. 13.6 Ben Nye sponge applicators.

professional rouge brush has a full shape for the quick application of powders to the face and body. The touch-up brush is beveled for precise application of powder, especially around the eyes. The angle contour is great for touchups. The contour shader is great for contour powder and shimmer powders, where you want a little extra control. The powder brush is full and luxurious for adding powder or removing excess powder without disturbing makeup. Natural hair smudge brushes are a new design with dense, short bristles that quickly softens or blends eye makeup. Are you starting to see the flexibility available with the wide variety of brushes available?

Brushes are not the only way to apply makeup. There are a few other tools we should discuss. Sponge applicators, for single use, can be very helpful, as they give you a huge amount of control (Fig. 13.6). Spatulas are used for mixing makeup and applying thicker products like nose or scar wax and gel effects. New designs include the tapered blade spatula and the blending spatula. Spatulas are used in conjunction with plastic palettes. Palettes are great for mixing colors to get the perfect color, and they are easy to clean. Powder puffs are usually round and always soft. Some are even washable. They are great for applying powder very specifically and for blotting excess powder away from the face. Foam sponges come in different shapes and sizes (Fig. 13.7). They are ideal for applying crème makeup. To use, dampen them first. They are gentle on the skin and you

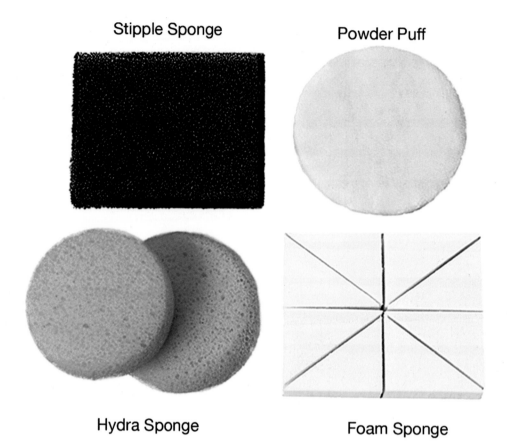

Stipple Sponge

Powder Puff

Hydra Sponge

Foam Sponge

Fig. 13.7 Ben Nye sponges.

will end up using less makeup in the long run. The makeup also blends more easily and wears better. **Stipple sponges** are made of nylon and come in square shapes. New designs include a fine-pore and a medium-pore stipple sponge. These sponges are great for adding texture such as beards, bruising, and road rash to name a few effects.

That should give you a basic idea for the tools (Fig. 13.8). Let's move on to makeup. There are many variations within each category. We discuss foundation, concealers, face powders, cheek colors, eye shadows, eyeliners, eye pencils, mascara, lipsticks, lip pencils, and lip glosses. We also look at hair and character effects, bloods, latex, modeling wax, adhesives, removers, sealers, and cleansers. Wow, that is a lot of stuff. Let's get going!

We are all people of color! Everybody's skin tone is a different color. Color is the key word.

—Linda Mensching

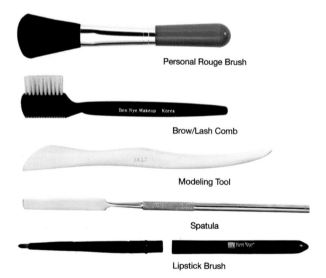

Personal Rouge Brush

Brow/Lash Comb

Modeling Tool

Spatula

Lipstick Brush

Fig. 13.8 Ben Nye other brushes, combs, and tools.

Creamy matte and color-cake **foundations** glide on easily when using a foam sponge (Fig. 13.9). They are long lasting and provide a flawless finish. Foundations come in a wide range of colors to match any skin tone. If, by chance, you can't find the exact color, you can mix them using a

(a)

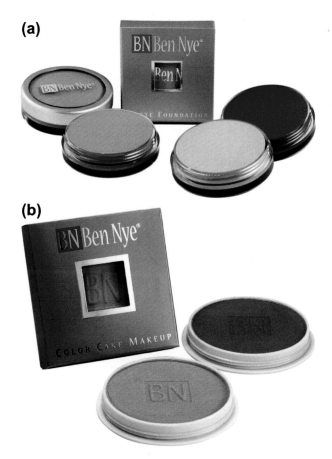

(b)

■ **Fig. 13.9** Ben Nye crème foundations.

■ **Fig. 13.10** Ben Nye neutralizers.

■ **Fig. 13.11** Ben Nye powder cheek colors.

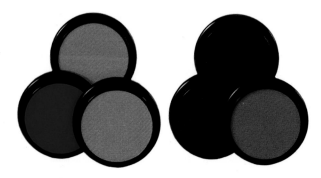

■ **Fig. 13.12** Ben Nye face powder.

spatula and plastic palette to create a new hue. Crème foundations need to be set with powder, but more on that in a minute. **Concealers** blend away temporary and permanent imperfections. These can include birthmarks, blemishes, and tattoos. Concealers are highly pigmented, which helps them to create an even tone to the skin. This is the inherent difference between a foundation and a concealer. Concealers are the perfect way to cover up tattoos. Since tattoos have become much more popular, the need to cover them up for specific characters is frequent. Neutralizers correct specific differences within the natural skin tone, as opposed to just covering something up (Fig. 13.10).

Cheek colors come in a variety of hues from the most pale to the truly strong (Fig. 13.11). Keep in mind that the character may need just a gentle enhancement of the actor's normal look, or you may be creating a fantasy character. Cheek colors can help with all of this including contouring with darker shades for special effect. Powder cheek color is most often applied by gently dusting the color over the cheeks with a rouge brush.

Face powders come in variations from completely translucent to heavily pigmented (Fig. 13.12). Powder sets crème foundations for a durable, soft, and matte finish. A range of colors is available to match any skin tone. In addition, there is white powder for use when you are using a white foundation for effect.

Eye shadows, similar to cheek colors, are pressed powders with pigment (Fig. 13.13). The colors for eye shadow are almost endless: beiges, pinks, browns, purples, blues, greens, grays, and blacks. These colors are overall more intense than the cheek colors. Here is the cool thing. Cheek colors and eye shadows can be used interchangeably. That

Fig. 13.13 Ben Nye eye shadows.

Fig. 13.14 Ben Nye eyeliners.

Fig. 13.15 Ben Nye eyebrow pencils and mascara.

is right—if you want to use navy blue as a cheek color and you happen to have that color as an eye shadow, go ahead and use it.

Eyeliner has three options (Fig. 13.14). Liquid eyeliner packaging looks a lot like mascara. Inside the container is a small fine brush that reloads every time the brush is put in. Liquid eyeliner gives a very precise line. It is smudge resistant, and also comes as water resistant and waterproof. Eyeliner pencils are moist and creamy. They are easy to smudge with a smudge brush or applicator and also easy to blend. Cake eyeliner is applied with a small round brush and a little water. You basically take powdered pigment,

adding water, and making liquid eyeliner that is applied with a separate brush. This is very similar to the how the Egyptian women applied kohl.

Eyebrow pencils are great for enhancing brow contours or for completely changing the shape (Fig. 13.15). They are also great for filling in any minor thin spots in eyebrows. Pencils come in colors from white to black, with a range of browns in between. Mascara is used to coat eyelashes to make them appear thicker, longer, or curlier. The many different formulas enhance eyelashes in different ways and to different degrees. Mascara comes in brown, black, and

Fig. 13.16 Ben Nye lipsticks and lip pencils.

more recently a wide range of colors to match eye shadows. It also comes in white, for aging, and clear for a simpler look. Mascara can be used on all facial hair to enhance and help style it.

Lipsticks are perhaps the most used cosmetic (Fig. 13.16). Everyone knows what lipstick is, right? Moist, creamy color for your lips. Every color from a perfect match to the wildest color you can think of. They come in a standard lipstick package, or you can get them in a

Fig. 13.17 Ben Nye crème colors.

palette. Either way, applying lipstick with a brush is more precise and lasts longer. Lipsticks come in matte, gloss, and iridescent. The combinations are endless. Lip balm is usually used as a protection against the weather, but often men use it to keep their lips more moist without looking like they have makeup on.

Useless Factoid: Lipstick

When applying makeup, an actress regards it as a sign that she will receive a good contract if she accidentally smears some lipstick onto her teeth.

Lip pencils help contour lips. You can also alter the shape of lips with a pencil. Pencils are coordinated with the colors of lipsticks. You have the choice of a natural look, by matching the pencil and lipstick colors, or going for something more dramatic, by using a pencil that is lighter or darker than the lipstick color. Lip glosses come in clear, tinted, and shimmering. They are not meant to be as colorful as lipstick. Glosses are more delicate looking when used alone. When combined with lipstick they create a layered effect that is stunning.

Crème colors began life as crème rouge (Fig. 13.17). They exploded off the chart in terms of color and are now used for rouge and so much more. Crème colors can also be used for such ideas as highlights and shadows for creating contouring and aging details, and rich colors for the more whimsical, dramatic, and magical. This is truly an area where your imagination is the only limit.

Liquid face paints are highly pigmented paints used for face painting and more (Fig. 13.18). They come in a wide variety of colors. Aqua paints are similar to liquid paints in their uses. They come in cakes and need to be used with a brush and

Fig. 13.18 Ben Nye liquid face paints, aqua paints, and sparkles and glitter.

Fig. 13.19 Ben Nye clown colors.

Fig. 13.20 Ben Nye effects wheels.

water. Both of these are created not only for faces but also bodies. Sparkles and glitter come in various colors for multiple uses. These are loose, small pieces of sparkle and glitter that are applied over wet liquid makeup or with a special glue.

Clown white is a foundation that covers your entire skin tone with opaque white (Fig. 13.19). It can be used by, well, clowns, but also if you are creating a geisha look or for certain aging looks. Crème shades in bright colors are packaged together and often called a *clown series*. Keep in mind that the most important thing isn't the product, but how you use it! These are crème shades in bright colors. Use them anyway you can, for whatever purpose. And maybe even to make a clown face!

Crème shades, as we discussed already, come in a wide variety of colors. Now let's take a look at how we can combine them in different configurations for a wide range of effects. Effects wheels often have four shades of crème color that work together to create specific effects, such as bruises, cuts, abrasions, burns, blisters, age, severe exposure, monsters, camouflage, and even death (Fig. 13.20). They are totally cool! As always, remember that your imagination is the only limitation.

Hair color is easy to get at the corner drugstore, right? Well, yes, but it doesn't just wash out. Liquid hair colors can be brushed in for fabulous effects, and they wash right back out when you are done (Fig. 13.21). There is no damage to your hair either. There are a number of colors, and you can combine them for variations. Character powders are pigmented for very specific reasons. Plains dust looks like real dirt. Stipple this powder on to create "dirty" characters. Plains dust is a pale powder that can be used for aging. Charcoal powder can be used to simulate grease stains, powder burns from a gun, and much, much more.

Let's move on to blood and gore. Gee, that is a sentence you don't hear too often! Stage blood has come a long way

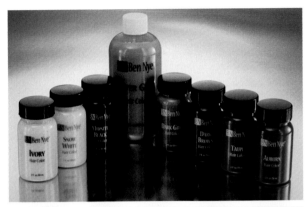

Fig. 13.21 Ben Nye liquid hair color and tooth colors.

Fig. 13.22 Ben Nye stage blood.

(Fig. 13.22). Commercial stage blood has many realistic qualities, including color and viscosity. It can also come in a peppermint flavor so that if the blood must be put in the mouth it is at least palatable. Staining can occur on skin and fabrics, so be careful of this.

The Graftobian Makeup Company makes a powdered blood that is activated by water. It is pretty cool! Here is

Fig. 13.23 Ben Nye nose and scar wax.

how it works. Let's say you put some of the blood powder on your arm. Then someone "attacks" you with a fake knife and the blade is wet. As the knife is dragged across your arm, the blood powder mixes with the water and turns into realistic-looking blood. It looks like you are being cut and the blood is coming out of an unseen wound!

Nose and scar wax are very cool (Fig. 13.23). They are pliable yet firm and can create a number of injuries. They are easy to shape into exactly what you need. They stick to the skin on their own, but applying them with spirit gum allows for longer wear. Wax is always covered with makeup after it is applied, to make it blend in with the other makeup for a seamless effect. For more advanced effects, **liquid latex** is a great product. First off, always check to see if an actor has a known allergy to latex. Even if he or she has never had a reaction, try a small amount of latex on the skin and monitor it carefully for any signs of a reaction, as we discussed in Chapter 6. For certain types of aging or injuries, you can apply the latex with a brush while holding the skin taut. When the skin relaxes, the latex causes wrinkles and puckers. It can be that easy, but again the effect must be covered with makeup to be complete.

Let's talk next about **adhesives**. We talked about glitters needing adhesives and wax needing adhesives. Glitter glue is specifically designed for glitter and sparkles. Spirit gum is sticky when wet but dries to a flat finish. It is used to attach various hairpieces like beards and mustaches, as well as prosthetic pieces made from latex, foams, plastics, and the like. The gum is applied, then allowed to partially dry. When still slightly tacky, place the material on it that you are trying to adhere.

Fig. 13.24 Ben Nye removers and cleansers.

Removers are just as important as adhesives and similarly come in a number of types, depending on what you are trying to remove (Fig. 13.24). Spirit gum remover is specifically made to, well, remove spirit gum and only spirit gum. Other removers are meant to remove a variety of products. Follow up the use of any remover with a cleanser that is delicate on the skin. Massage a cleanser into your skin and then gently it wipe away and, last, follow up with a good-quality

moisturizer. The other cleanser type is for brushes. All of your tools should be cleaned after every use. This is really important to not only the longevity of the brushes but, more important, for the health of the actors you are using the brushes on. Dirty brushes can transfer bacteria and illnesses. It is best to have one set of brushes per actor, if at all possible.

MAKEUP APPLICATION

OK, relax for a minute. We've gotten through all the tools and types of makeup. Exhausted? Excited? Well, next we need to figure out what to do with all that stuff you just read about. We learned about the face shapes. The next thing to do is figure out what the makeup will look like. Makeup designers usually keep a morgue of photos showing different people and character types. They will often then do sketches of the finished makeup design. When applying makeup, it is important to chart what you create, mostly so you, or the actor, can recreate it for the next performance. The chart in Figure 13.25 is used to document the makeup you apply when you need to do the same makeup again. Notice the grid, which makes it easier for others to pick up your notes and create the same design.

The application of makeup happens in a very specific order (Figs. 13.26 and 13.27). But, here is the thing. The order does depend on what type of makeup you are applying. For basic street makeup, whether or not it is "enhanced" for the stage, the steps are as follows:

1. **Foundation:** Blend on a palette if needed. Gently pat the sponge on forehead, nose, and cheeks. Patting doesn't pull skin the way rubbing does. Always work in an upward motion to help fight gravity. You are going for an even look, but be careful not to blend it all away.

2. **Concealer:** If trying to conceal dark circles or marks, the color should be slightly lighter than regular foundation, because it has to counterbalance the darkness. Don't change the hue for the rest of the skin, just use a slightly darker version.

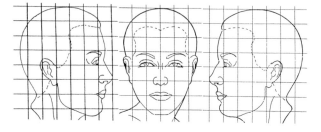

Fig. 13.25 Linda Mensching's makeup chart.

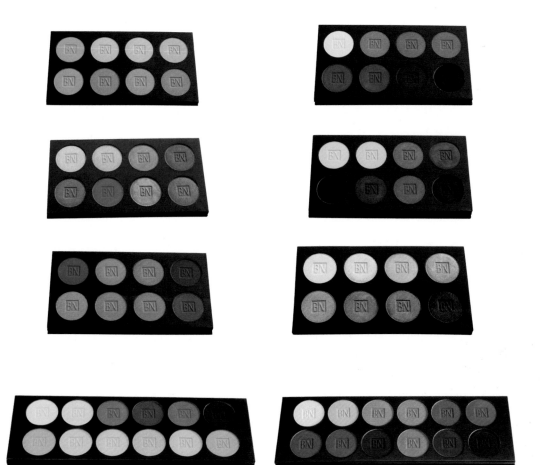

Fig. 13.26 Palettes of combined colors can come in handy for applications as well as touchups.

Fig. 13.27 Kits are also available for a variety of specific needs and effects.

3. **Powder:** This sets the makeup. That means the makeup below the powder stops moving around or blending with the makeup above the powder. Make sure you are happy with the makeup before you powder! You use powder after the foundation and concealer, then again after the cheeks and eyes. And of course at any other point where you need to "lock in" the makeup.

4. **Cheeks:** Both highlights and shadows can be done at the same time. Use two cheek powders for shadowing if the actor's facial structure might have a tendency to get washed out by lighting.

5. **Eyes:** There are so many variations in shadow, highlight, liner, lashes, and brow techniques that it is impossible even to summarize. Look at the makeup you love. Study it and break it down. Figure out how it was done, then you will know how to apply it for yourself. Don't underestimate the power of a well-shaped eyebrow. It frames the eye.

6. **Lips:** Lip liner and lipstick not only color the lips but help define and shape them. Even if color is not desired, a clear gloss or balm makes an actor more comfortable onstage, where the air is sometimes drier.

Ben Nye has been wonderful in sharing information with me, as you can probably tell from most of the images in this chapter. The photos in Figure 13.28 are also courtesy of Ben Nye. They are step-by-step process photos of makeup applications. This is a great opportunity to see the difference makeup can actually make, as well as to study the individual steps. Check it out!

Sometimes makeup is part of what helps an actor get into character. The days are over of makeup being hugely different between street and stage. Heavy shadowing is gone, unless it is for a special effect. Lighting has changed, and makeup has to change with it. Lighting can make or break the makeup design. Everybody has to work together. Linda Mensching did the makeup for a wedding where the bride said, "We all look beautiful, but we still look like ourselves!" Linda then said, "Who do you want to look like?" She also said if she makes up an actor and everyone says, "Wow, that actor is beautiful," then she has succeeded. If they say what great makeup, then she has failed. Last, remember makeup is to enhance, it's not instead of.

(a)

■ **Fig. 13.28** Step-by-step makeup techniques shown over the next several pages. All have different outcomes and different effects.

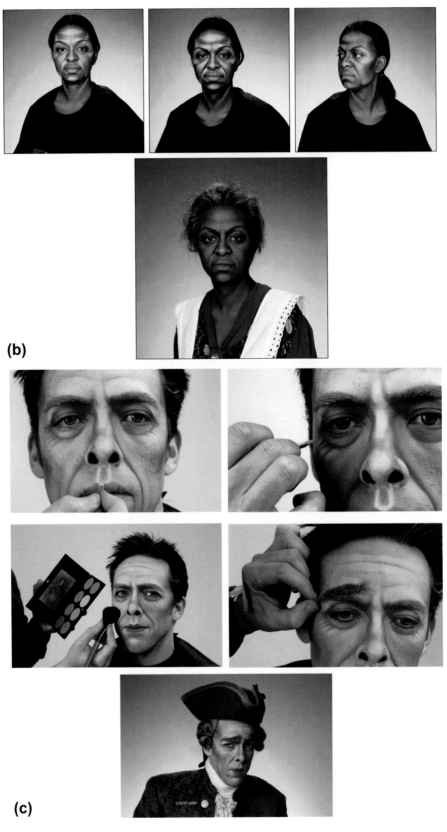

(b)

(c)

Fig. 13.28 (Continued).

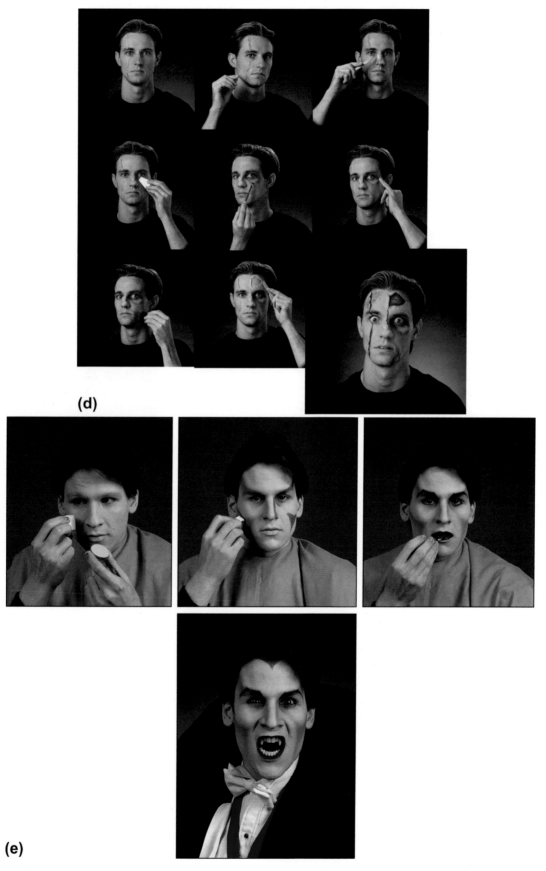

(d)

(e)

Fig. 13.28 (Continued).

Adhesives

Angle brush

Cleansers

Concealer

Detail brush

Dome brush

Facial shapes

Flat brush

Foam sponge

Foundation

Foundation brush

Liquid latex

Palette

Powder brush

Powder puff

Removers

Round brush

Scar wax

Spatula

Stage blood

Stipple sponge

CHAPTER THIRTEEN
Study Words

PART
FIVE
Sound and Special Effects

Chapter XIV: Is This Thing On?
Sound

Chapter XV: The Magic
behind the Curtain
Special Effects

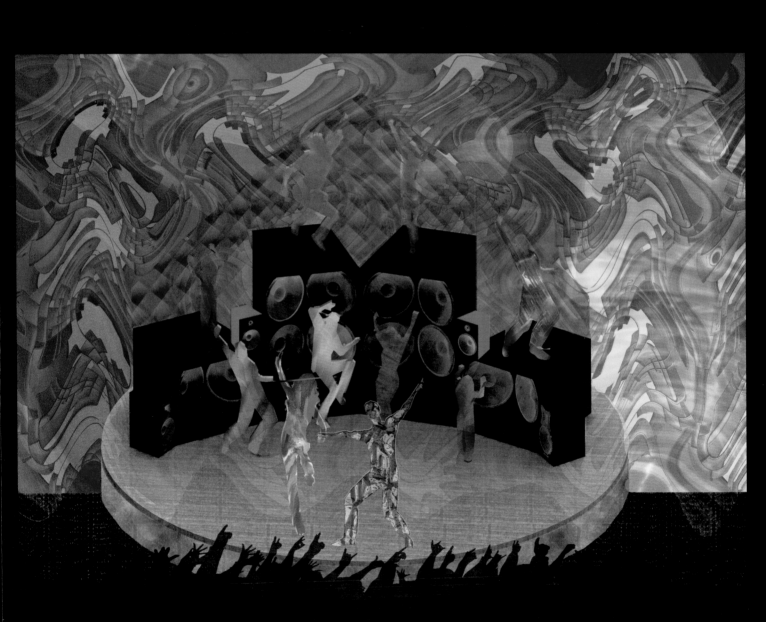

Is This Thing On?

Sound

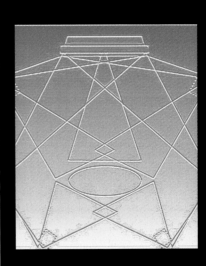

We dealt with the visual, let's move on to the aural! There are many aspects to what sound can do for a theatrical production. At the very least, sound can reinforce the spoken word. Sound can also add direction and effects, just to name a few. With the advent of digital technology, the impact sound can have has drastically improved. Sound can now follow a performer around the stage or around the entire theatre. Digital delays can ensure that audiences of 50–50,000 all hear the same thing at the same time.

Over the past 10–20 years, people's ears have grown more acute or least their hearing has. The general public is accustomed to hearing sound that is very crisp. Now, everyone wants to hear like they are wearing digital headphones. So, basically, the audience's expectations have gone up—way up. This means the sound designer in today's theatre has several parts to their design. Depending on the production, the designer's responsibilities can range from playback of sound effects, to reinforcing the performers, to providing an intercom package.

> For better or for worse, the story is the most important thing. It is up to me to enhance that, but never overshadow it.
>
> **—Kai Harada**

SOUND BASICS

Let's talk for a moment about some basic sound ideas. Acoustics refers to the inherent sound qualities of a room in regard to the overall audio quality when no reinforcement is in use. Ambient noise is the sound in a room when there is no planned audio source. So far, so good? OK. Sound reinforcement happens for a variety of reasons. The auditorium where the show takes place may have bad acoustics, the audience may be too large to hear someone speaking on stage, or maybe an actor never learned to properly project his or her voice. Today's performers are not always being trained to project their voices the way they once were. In the "old days" of actor training, actors were trained to support their voices through breathing to get the words and music all the way to the back of the house.

Gone are the days of most live sound cues performed backstage by stagehands. Gone also are the days when musicals were done without any sound reinforcement. Vocal reinforcement is an everyday occurrence now. Every actor knows about body mics. Orchestral reinforcement works on the basis that every part should be heard and that everything should blend together and be cohesive. The sound operator and the orchestra working together can achieve this goal. Please, please, please, always remember louder *does not* mean better!

UNDER THE TUNGSTEN MOON
Creating the Eccentric, Intimate Style of Neil Young's Latest Tour

David Barbour

Photography by Todd Kaplan

Among the elder statesmen of rock, Neil Young is the great paradox—an icon of integrity who exists in perpetual transition. From his early days as a folk singer in Toronto's coffeehouses, Young's career has followed a singularly winding path, through such groups as Buffalo Springfield; Crosby, Stills, Nash, and Young; and Crazy Horse. Over four decades, he has amassed a catalog of songs numbering in the hundreds and embracing a diversity of styles. According to his citation at the Rock-and-Roll Hall of Fame, Young has "been a cult hero, a chart-topping rock star, and all things in-between, remaining true to his restless muse all the while. At various times, [he] has delved into folk, country, garage rock, and grunge. His biggest album, Harvest (1972), apotheosized the laid-back singer/songwriter genre he helped invent. By contrast, Rust Never Sleeps (1979), Young's second-best seller, was a loud, brawling masterpiece whose title track, an homage to Johnny Rotten of the Sex Pistols, contained the oft-quoted line 'Better to burn out than it is to rust.'" For Young, rusting is simply not an option. In a life marked both by enormous achievement and terrible tragedy, he has emerged as rock's great survivor, always creatively engaged and politically active. (He's known particularly for his defense of the environment and his outspoken opposition to the invasion of Iraq; he was also among the first to respond to the events of 9/11, with the song "Let's Roll.") Indeed, in a here-today-gone-tomorrow pop landscape littered with pretty and pre-processed personalities, Young's flinty insistence on doing things his own way looks positively Lincoln-esque. His latest effort is Chrome Dreams II, a distinctively Young-ian title, as it is a sequel to an album recorded in 1977 and never released. (When asked by a New York Times reporter how the original Chrome Dreams ended up on the shelf, the singer's response is typically oblique: "It just passed me by. I did it, I got to a certain place, and then something would happen and distract me, and I would get into something else and forget what I was doing before. That's happened a lot.") To support Chrome Dreams II—which includes the 18-minute guitar epic, "Ordinary People"—Young hit the road last fall, playing theatres with an intimate, three-part show that showcases songs both old and new. It's a kind of musical triptych: The opening sequence features his wife, Pegi, backed by three musicians; next comes Young performing a

solo acoustic set; finishing the evening, he offers an electric set, backed by three colleagues, featuring plenty of his distinctive guitar jams. The songs are vintage Young—enigmatic, melancholy, and sardonic, a wised-up romantic's elegy to ideals lost and a clear-eyed appraisal of our fallen 21st-century state. Through it all, Young remains indubitably himself. Even as fans cry out, demanding to hear their favorite songs, he deflects their attention with goofy, hilarious musings ("This will probably be disappointing to a lot of you," he says by way of introduction to one number), and a ferocious concentration on his musical mission. The tour features a production design that's perfectly suited to its conceptual, art-rock essence. The musician and his colleagues are placed at stage center, surrounded by an array of elderly looking sound gear and vintage studio lights—not to mention an enormous fan. Located at downstage left is an easel, on which paintings are placed to announce each new song. (Throughout the show, a man in a red suit and white Panama hat—he is, in fact, the tour manager and resident artist, Eric Johnson—paints new works.) On the upstage wall, one sees a jumble of letters, not unlike those found on the refrigerators of young couples with children, only larger. The lighting is defined by warm washes, saturated colors, bold angles, and haunting backlight looks. It's as if you've been invited to wander around in the attic of Young's mind—you wouldn't be surprised if a ghost or two wandered into view.

Source: Originally published in *Lighting and Sound America*, February 2008.

Let's talk for a moment about the difference between amplification and reinforcement. This is a critical part of sound for the theatre, and we better know the difference. *Amplification* means simply making it louder. That equals putting a huge stack of speakers on either side of the stage and cranking the volume. Reinforcement is much more subtle. Reinforcement is all about pushing and pulling the sound to create the right environment. Amplification is obvious, reinforcement should not be. Amplification is easy to notice, reinforcement—when well done—should be a seamless addition to the performance.

Another factor contributing to the differences in theatre sound for today's productions is ambient noise. There is a great deal more street noise. Most theatres are also air conditioned. New technology in other design areas, such as lighting and rigging, brings noise from motors and fans. All this conspires against both the actors and the audience. These factors must be addressed for the reinforcement of the sound to properly do its job. Of course, the director can help through staging, and the conductor can help by controlling the musicians—but the sound department ultimately is responsible for the final way the show sounds.

SOUND SYSTEMS

Let's talk about a basic sound system (Fig. 14.1). This introduces you to each of three main areas of the sound system: input, output, and processing. The inputs in our sample system are microphones. The microphones are connected to inputs on the mixing console. The console provides preamplification, which amplifies the microphone level signals to a consistent level, or line level. The signal then goes through equalization, which provides the means to control each microphone individually. Level control is the last step in the processing. The console takes the processed signal and routes it to the output. The output of the console is sent to the amplifier. The amplifier boosts the output to an adequate level that drives the loudspeaker. The loudspeaker converts the signal into sound waves that people can hear.

Sound equipment has many variations and alternatives. Let me give you some ideas for each of our three categories. Inputs can be microphones, contact pickups, magnetic pickups, laser pickups, and optical pickups. Signal processors can be mixing console, equalizers, reverberation, delay, and amplifiers. Outputs can be loudspeakers (woofers, midrange, and tweeters), headphones, or infrared hearing assist devices. There are variations on all of these options. The last part of choosing equipment is to consider the right speakers, the right microphones, the right mixing system, and most important, the positioning of all of these.

MICROPHONES

Let's start talking about specific equipment. We start with input devices. As I already mentioned, these include microphones and different kinds of pickups. A microphone is a device for converting acoustic sound into electrical energy. The two main types of microphones are dynamic and condenser. Dynamic microphones are good all-around microphones, which are both durable and affordable. Condenser microphones are more versatile, more costly, and less durable. Condenser microphones are the choice for the theatre, given their range in quality for many purposes. Their durability issues though mean backups must be on hand.

There are differences between the various styles of microphones (Fig. 14.2). The handheld microphone was

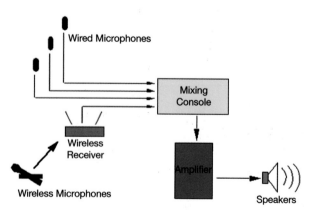

Fig. 14.1 Basic sound design layout.

Fig. 14.2 Different microphone types.

once the most prominent design. It is still used today, although only for effect during obvious "performance" sequences within a play. Almost exclusively, the lavalier microphone has replaced the handheld. Lavaliers are very small and designed to be clipped to clothing or hung around the neck. As the need for sound design in the theatre has grown, lavaliers can now be attached in the hair or wigs, behind the ear, and even sewn into costumes—all to try to hide them while still maintaining adequate usage. The big concern with lavaliers is moisture, as perspiration can cause major issues with these tiny microphones. Hence, the need for backups!

Contact pickups are "like" microphones. They are attached to musical instruments and pick up sound through vibrations instead of from the air. Pressure-response microphones are usually mounted to a flat surface with the attached plate that increases gain.

The impedance of a microphone is the amount of resistance a microphone has to an audio signal. The lower the resistance, the fewer problems the microphone may have using longer cables and dealing with noise interference. Generally, low impedance means a better-quality microphone, which therefore becomes a perfect choice for the theatre.

Gain in a sound system is what we usually think of as volume. However, it is a little different than volume. Gain is the amount of amplification available within the sound system. If set up properly, meaning the system, microphones, and speakers, gain can be maximized, which means you have the most latitude for volume and effects within your microphone. If you think about it, the number of inputs trying to simultaneously use the output divides the potential gain. So, it is important to have open and ready to use only the microphones and contacts that need to be used for a given portion of the show.

So, now that you have all this information, how do you choose a specific microphone?

Handheld microphones have much more latitude in gain than lavaliers. However, most shows want to use the much smaller microphone for aesthetic reasons. The standard is rapidly becoming the lavalier with a wireless transmitter. Sennheiser introduced the MKE-2 lavalier in the early 1980s as a major innovation. It is the smallest, highest-quality lavalier to date.

Most microphones used in theatre are wireless (Fig. 14.3). That means they need a transmitter and a receiver. Wireless microphones operate on radio frequencies. Most transmitters and receivers can be used on a range of frequencies, so that local issues, like television, radio, and taxicabs, can be worked around. If you use a frequency that is already in use or very close to another that is in use, it can cause everything from a hiss, to just plain not working, to interference such as hearing the other frequency.

Lavalier microphones were developed for television news. Originally they were hung around the newscaster's neck on some kind of a loop or clipped on their clothing (Fig. 14.4). Lapel and chest mounts can be used as long as they are taped securely in place. If the microphone needs to be placed between the skin and the costume, the only tape option is to use medical tape. Medical tape has a secure adhesive while being gentle on the microphone and the skin

▥ **Fig. 14.3** Sennheiser wireless microphones.

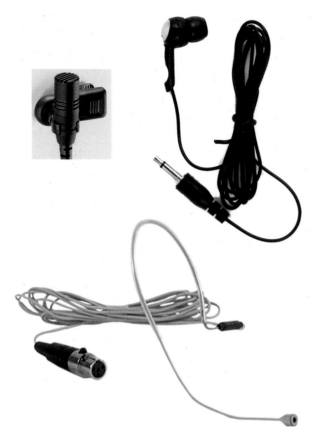

■ **Fig. 14.4** Lavalier mounting options.

MIXING CONSOLES

Next, we talk about the mixing console, which is where the design is implemented. Levels are adjusted both for inputs and outputs. These can vary on a daily basis, as humidity can affect the tonal quality. All consoles work on the same principle. They take inputs, process the signal, and transfer the audio to the outputs. It sounds simple, but there are still many variations that can happen. Consoles allow for only a certain number of inputs and outputs. The individual console also limits the types of adjustments you can make to the audio signal. These combinations of variations are what determine the right console for a show.

Analog consoles are generally used today for smaller-budget shows (Fig. 14.5). As they are the "older" style now, they are generally simpler to operate and less expensive to rent. These boards are large, due to their technology. They are also simpler inside because they don't need all the digital processing and conversions. To operate the analog console, you move the faders up and down, as well as rotate the dials. The drawback is that there is generally no onboard equalizer, delay, or any other effects. This means, if you want them, they cost additional money, and you have to find a place to put them.

Digital consoles are the newest technology, and they are continuing to develop (Fig. 14.6). Overall, digital consoles have more flexibility, are smaller physically, options are limitless, bandwidth is more than double, and all the effects are on board. Other benefits are that the amount of outboard gear is cut down, and there is never a need to repatch cables due to a lack of inputs or outputs. With more control comes a price, in a way. How many faders can you move simultaneously? *Relative mixing* is a term that means individual faders are proportionally controlled by a master fader. That means you move one master fader and all other faders associated with it with move proportionally as well.

of the actor. If the lavalier is to be worn behind the ear, an ear loop holds the microphone in place while a thin boom brings the microphone around and in front of the mouth. This is obvious to the audience, but if the director doesn't mind, it is a good and easy placement.

The forehead lavalier is the best and most popular method in the theatre today. This allows the microphone to land in the middle of the forehead. It uses the natural resonance of the skull. There are a number of ways to secure this in place, depending on the use of hairpieces or hats. The worst thing for the lavalier is if an actor is wearing a hat; the second worst thing is the noise from moving lights. To use microphones on a group of people, like a chorus, a technique known as **area micing** is used. An array of floor or hanging microphones is used and the sound operator raises and lowers the gain as needed. Since so much of theatre can take place on the centerline, it is good to use an odd number of array microphones. This gives you the most options in which microphones to use at what time during any given musical number.

Fig. 14.5 Analog console.

Yamaha 02R96V2

Yamaha 01V96V2

Fig. 14.6 Yamaha 02R96V2 and Yamaha 01V96V2 digital consoles.

The next step is computerized mixing on a digital console. Similar to a lighting controller, this type of digital console can record scenes or cues with all the nuances of input, output, and effects. You can then recall it with the touch of a button! The more the computer can control, the smaller the overall size of the digital console needs to be.

The software has already gone to the next level. It can also control the manual faders via motors. When a scene

SIGNAL PROCESSING

Signal processing is our next topic. Equalizers and effects processors are examples of this. They all change the input signal before it heads to the output signal. Effects processors are something we haven't really talked about yet. They are capable of time delay, echoes, reverberation, and much, much more. We generally tend to use processing, such as equalization and time delay, to get all the speakers to work together and create a unified sound, no matter what seat you are sitting in.

Equalizers are the most common use for a basic signal processor. Think of them as a filter. Equalizers help tune specific sources to a similar base level. If an equalization attempt does too much correction, it can tend to distort the resulting audio. You should try to keep it to the minimum correction needed to do what you want, without overdoing it.

As the system gain is increased, distortion shows up first on any sources where you have overequalized. All this means is that you need to use the tools the way they were intended. You can push it to the extremes, but the equipment lets you know fairly quickly if you've gone too far.

Reverberation is basically reflected sound that has blended with the original sound. This happens normally. Sometimes, you want to try to reduce it. Sometimes you want to enhance it even more. Delay effects are just what the words sound like. They input the audio and hold onto it for a certain amount of time before giving it to the output. This is pretty cool—here is why! If you are in a large auditorium and the speakers are fairly far apart, a delay can make sure the sound comes out of all speakers at the same time.

> People's eyes and ears must go to the same place. Time is the most important thing in a sound system.
>
> **—Tim Mazur**

There are literally hundreds of types to choose from in the mixer console world. If you are renting, you need to find out what is available. Things that may influence you are all the different traits we just discussed. These also include your budget, the space allowed in the auditorium, and the experience of your sound technician.

SPEAKERS

Let's do a little introduction to speakers. There are four types: tweeter, midrange, woofer, and subwoofer (Fig. 14.7). A tweeter is a type of speaker designed specifically to reproduce high frequencies. A midrange is designed specifically for, yes, you guessed it, the midrange frequencies. A woofer is designed to reproduce low frequencies. A subwoofer is designed specifically to reproduce very low-frequency sounds. These types of speakers are used in many combinations, based on your location and the needs of the production.

A line array is multiple speakers hung together, either vertically or horizontally, so that they can act as one huge speaker (Fig. 14.8). Each speaker in an array has a very narrow spread of sound. A cluster is similar to an array, however, it is almost always hung on center right above the edge of the stage. A wedge is a kind of speaker cabinet (Fig. 14.9). It refers to one that is shaped with an angled bottom, placed on the floor; the result is the speaker points up, usually at a 30–45 degree angle. The actors use the wedge to hear themselves isolated from the balanced mix coming out of every other speaker. Last, the sweet spot is the best location in the house. Optimally, it is the place where everyone in the audience is equidistant from each speaker, but that is hard to do in many of today's theatres.

> I did do a show once in which the director ran up to me in a frenzy, and said, "The lighting is dark, the actors can't act, the singers can't sing, the set looks miserable; you are our only hope! We need more thunder cues!" I complied, although that, to me, is putting a band-aid on a gaping wound.
>
> **—Kai Harada**

CONNECTORS AND CABLES

How do we connect all this stuff? Well, there are connectors and there are cables. We take a look at each of the various types. The granddaddy of all audio connectors is

Subwoofer

Woofer   Mid-Range   Tweeter

■ **Fig. 14.7** Tweeter, midrange, woofer, and subwoofer speakers.

■ **Fig. 14.8** Speaker array at the 1869 Bardavon Opera House.

■ **Fig. 14.9** Speaker array on left, and wedges in the center for an outdoor concert.

Fig. 14.10 Various connectors.

the banana plug (Fig. 14.10). Although it can come in various sizes, the 4 mm is the most common. These plugs are single wire. They are often color coded red and black.

The XLR is a connector that can have three pins or more. This connector is one of the most commonly used connectors in the sound world today. Originally called the *X series* when it first came out, the *L* represents the added latch, and the *R* is for the rubber surrounding the internal contacts. The BNC connector is a coaxial connector. It has a miniature bayonet-locking connector. The threaded version of this connector is the TNC connector. The threads replace the bayonet. Both these connectors are locking, which makes them infinitely useful—in addition to the XLR—in theatres where cables may be tripped on or pulled inadvertently.

So much for connectors, let's talk about cable. Coaxial cable, as shown in Figure 14.11, is made up of (D) a single copper core, surrounded by a layer of insulation (B), covered by (C) a copper shield, and then (A) a flexible plastic jacket. Multi-pair cable has a single outer jacket and insulation with many internal balanced, or twisted-pair, lines. Twisted-pair cable has two center conductors twisted together. Many twisted pairs can share one insulation and jacket. All balanced audio cables are twisted-pair cables with a shield, which further protects the signal being transmitted from introduced noise. A shield is a different kind of insulation that is conductive to protect against electromagnetic and electrostatic fields. This helps keep the buzz and hum away from the system. Last, we look at a snake (Fig. 14.12). That is right, an audio snake. Picture several complete audio cables held together in a common jacket. These are awesome for loading in a temporary show.

HEADSETS

Let's talk headsets next. For a show to run smoothly, everyone behind the scenes must be able to communicate easily. This usually requires a combination of wired and

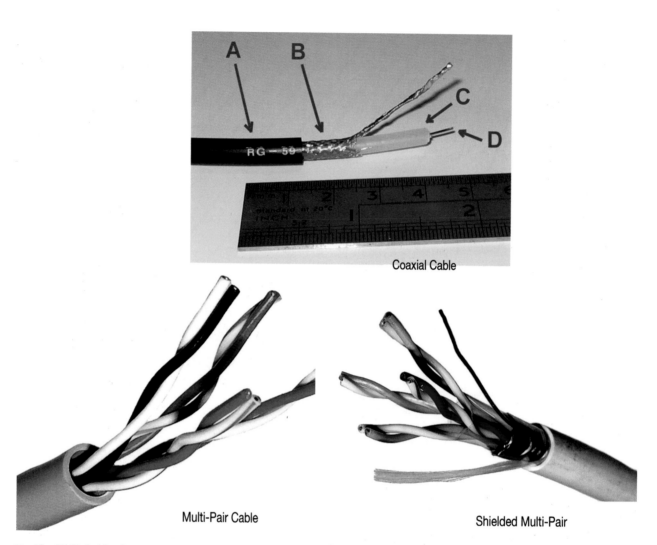

Coaxial Cable

Multi-Pair Cable

Shielded Multi-Pair

Fig. 14.11 Cable diagram—different cable types.

Fig. 14.12 Audio snake.

wireless headset stations on multiple channels (Figs. 14.13 and 14.14). All wired and wireless communication needs to flow through a base station of some kind. The wireless belt pack and wired intercom connection on the rear panel of the base station should have its own full-duplex port. Some manufacturers, like Clear-Com, offer the voice communication from each to be sampled, mixed, and then rerouted throughout the system as desired.

The base station needs to support as many wireless belt packs and intercom connections as the show needs. It also needs to have multiple channels as required for privacy of different departments to talk. LED indicators and a front-panel fluorescent display are nice to show status and battery information. It is important that each belt pack have its own way to be individually addressed by the base—allowing

Fig. 14.13 Clear-Com wireless communication system.

Fig. 14.14 Another model, and style of Clear-Com wireless communication system.

multiple combinations of belt-pack-to-belt-pack and small-group conversations to happen simultaneously.

Some models offer many extra benefits, such as programmable software menus on the base, accessible via the display, and a push-to-enter rotary encoder. All aspects of the belt packs, rear-panel connectors, and creation of communications routes and groups can be addressed. Each belt pack and rear-panel connector can be labeled with a five-character name, which appears on the base station and belt pack displays, uniquely identifying the system users. Relative levels among belt packs and input and output levels for the wired connections are also under software control. This is a long way from a tin can on a string!

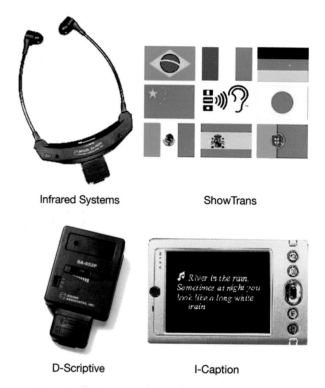

Infrared Systems   ShowTrans

D-Scriptive   I-Caption

Fig. 14.15 Infrared assistive devices by Sound Associates.

ASSISTED-HEARING DEVICES

Our last topic in this chapter is assisted-hearing devices. The first infrared listening system was introduced by Sound Associates on Broadway at the Lunt-Fontanne Theatre to aid hearing-impaired patrons in 1979 (Fig. 14.15). An infrared listening system provides amplification for hearing-impaired patrons through wireless receivers. The sound is transmitted to the receivers using infrared light, which is invisible to the naked eye. ShowTrans by Sound Associates was the next stage in this product's development in 1998, and it added multilingual, scene-by-scene commentary via infrared transmission. This is not a word-for-word translation of the show. Instead the system gives the audience member detailed plot information. The lighting control board can trigger these translations. Each time a lighting cue is executed, the translation software knows to begin the next set of lines.

D-Scriptive by Sound Associates was the next advance. It added a fully automated audio description for the visually impaired audience members, which includes a detailed account of all onstage action including choreography, blocking, lighting, sets, and costume changes. The newest advance is the I-Caption system, also by Sound Associates, which is a state-of-the-art wireless visual aid that provides verbatim real-time closed captions for theatrical performances. By displaying dialogue, lyrics, and sound effects on a handheld device, hearing-impaired patrons can better understand a production or event. The I-Caption System can also be expanded to incorporate subtitles, showing the text in multiple languages and playing audio segments. All of these assistive devices help the theatre take a major step forward to accessibility for the handicapped.

Acoustics

Ambient noise

Amplifier

Area micing

Banana plug

BNC

Cluster

Coaxial cable

Condenser microphone

Contact pickup

Dynamic microphone

Equalization

Gain

Impedance

Input

Lavalier

Line array

Midrange

Mixing console

Multi-pair cable

Output

Pressure-response
microphone

Shield

Signal processer

Snake

Subwoofer

TNC

Tweeter

Twisted-pair cable

Woofer

XLR

CHAPTER FOURTEEN
Study Words

The Magic behind the Curtain

Special Effects

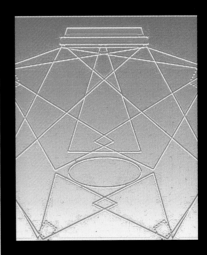

We explore all varieties of effects in this chapter (Fig. 15.1). Effects can fall into any of the departments we already discussed, or the production may add a special effects department if there is a need for many specialized effects. A prop may need to explode into flames, it may need to rain or snow for a certain scene, and a character might need to fly through the air. All of these effects can be handled in a variety of ways, depending on the theatre space and the budget. Bringing in an expert in special effects is sometimes the only way to safely do these effects. Other times, if the effects are done simply enough, someone already on the production team can supervise them.

Effects are a brand-new concept in theatre, right? Wrong! Let's pause for a minute and think back into theatre history. Did the Romans and Greeks use special effects? Well, of course, they did. Effects are *not* a new idea. What is new, however, is the implementation of our ideas into effects (Figs. 15.2 and 15.3). New technologies open up almost limitless possibilities for designing new effects ideas.

■ **Fig. 15.1** At the moment of explosion, a cross explodes during a production of *Laughing Stock*.

COPYRIGHT © BETH BERGMAN 1971, 2006

■ **Fig. 15.2** *Markopoulos Affair* at New York City Opera in 1971. Director, Frank Corsaro; scenic designer, Patton Campbell; slide and projection designers, Gardner Compton and Emile Ardolino; and lighting designer, Hans Sondheimer.

Fig. 15.3 *Tote Stadt* at New York City Opera in 1971. Director, Frank Corsaro; slide and projection designer, Ronald Chase; and costume designer, Theoni Aldredge.

Some effects become more magical and mysterious, while others become overly realistic.

The interesting thing about stage effects is that using the real thing doesn't work. Think about it. Your audience is usually at least 20 feet away from the stage and sometimes hundreds of feet away. The effect has to be seen from many distances and still look realistic from every seat. There are many different ways to create the fake effect in order to make it look realistic.

VINTAGE EFFECTS

NATURE

Let's look at some of the more classic effects in theatre before we move on to the newer generation. The "older" effects were meant to recreate nature. Wind, thunder, rain,

Fig. 15.4 Vintage thunder making machine.

snow, and fire are just a few of the effects that come to mind. The techniques used 100 years ago can still work, especially if you are on a small budget. Wind was easy, and it still is. Any ideas? Yup, use a fan! It can be that easy. Of course, you want to use a quiet fan; otherwise, it will sound like the aliens are landing a spaceship backstage.

Thunder is one of my favorite old-time effects (Fig. 15.4). All you have to do is find a long, thin piece of sheet metal. Drill of couple of holes in the short end and attach a piece of wood that can work like a handle. Drill a couple of holes in the other short end and hang it in the air so that the bottom is right above your head. All you have to do is grab the handle and give it a gentle shake. Once you practice a bit, start it slow, speed up, and slow it down again. It's a cool effect!

Rain was originally a little tougher (Fig. 15.5). A trough would be created with holes drilled in the bottom. The trough was hung in the air at a slight angle to allow gravity to help out. At the high side of the trough, a stagehand would be on a ladder with a bucket of water and would slowly pour the water into the trough. The trough changed to either a garden hose or a piece of small conduit eventually,

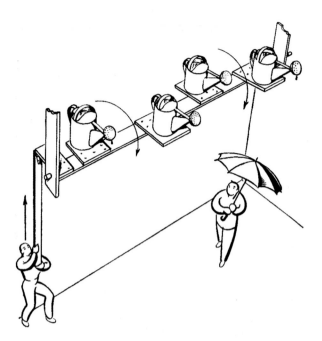

Fig. 15.5 I found this image in a *very* old book. I can't believe anyone actually created a rain effect like this!

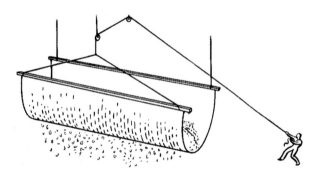

Fig. 15.6 Early snow effect.

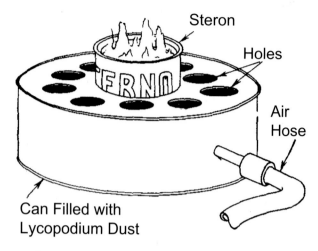

Fig. 15.7 A *very* early fire effect, before we got smarter.

but the idea is the same. The difficulty with this is getting the rain to stop on command!

Snow effects have been around forever (Fig. 15.6). They share the rain problem, in that the snow doesn't stop on command. The original snow bags were long horizontal bags or slings with holes on the bottom. They would be filled with confetti, bleached cornflakes, or any other material that would fall to the floor gracefully. The bag was hung horizontally with strings attached to shake it from the floor to release the "snow."

FIRE

Fire—well, original fire effects actually used real flame (Fig. 15.7). That is why there were so many theatre fires. Once theatre designers figured out this was a *bad* idea,

they started to do it with lighting. Three lights would be hidden in the fireplace, or other appropriate place, with each light gelled to a different color. The colors used were usually amber, orange, and red. Then, a small fan with several flame-shaped pieces of fabric would be placed in the middle of the lights. Turn on the fan and the lights, which would be turned on and off in rapid succession to make it look like the flame was flickering.

PROJECTIONS

As the theatre became a little more modern, a number of inventions took effects to the next level. The following are certainly not modern by anyone's imagination, but they were cutting edge at the time. We call them *vintage*!

A guy named Adolf Linnebach originally developed the Linnebach projector in the late 19th century (Fig. 15.8). This was the first time there was a way to project images as part of the scenic design. Here is how it works. A deep box is made and painted entirely black inside. Then, a high-intensity, concentrated filament is placed inside near the back. One side is open and contains a glass "slide." The slide is hand painted with the image to be projected. That is it. There is no lens; the size of the projection is controlled by the size of the glass in combination with the distance from the surface to be projected on. Due to the lack of a lens, the only way to sharpen or soften the glass image is to move the lamp closer or further away; there is limited room to do this.

The next improvement over the Linnebach was the scene machine (Fig. 15.9). It has a lens! This means you

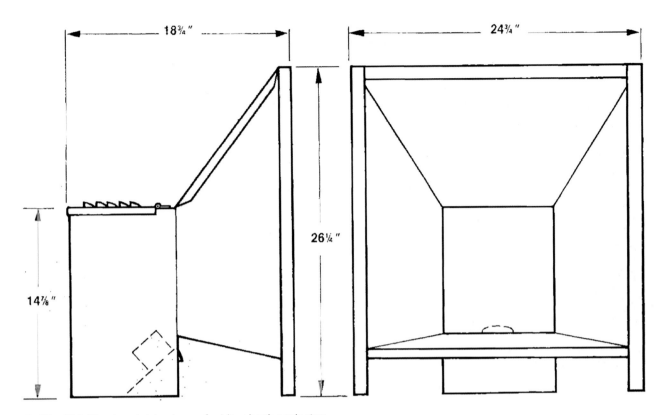

Fig. 15.8 Front and side views of a Linnebach projector.

Fig. 15.9 GAM Products scene machine.

can control the focus and size of the projected image. The wattage of the lamps got higher and became much brighter as well, which means you could project denser designs across longer distances. The images are created out of steel patterns or painted on heat-resistant glass. This is needed, since the focusable lenses and higher-wattage lamps create more heat. The images are still static though; no movement was added as a part of the new invention. Attachments were invented to create spinning effects, and this was somewhat successful.

There was a time when the only way to do a projection was to use a regular slide projector (Fig. 15.10). This was the standard for a long time. Then, we started using two projectors and developed the ability to crossfade between them. Slowly, we added more and more projectors to the design, as the ability to control and align them developed. It seems like such a simple concept now, but it was once the state of the art. One thing to always remember is that today's state of the art is tomorrow's vintage!

The next vintage effect is the lobsterscope (Fig. 15.11). Think of it as the predecessor to today's strobe. The idea is to take a focusable light and mount a motor on the front

Fig. 15.10 *Dr. Faust* at the Metropolitan Opera in 2001. Director, Peter Mussbach; scenic designer, Erich Wonder; costume designer, Andrea Schmidt-Futterer; and lighting designer, Konrad Lindenberg.

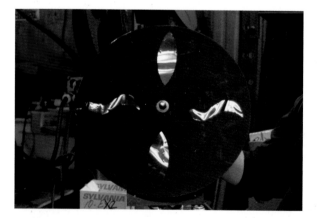

Fig. 15.11 Lobsterscope disk.

of it. Attached to the motor is a metal disk with two slits cut into it. Turn on the motor, and the disk and the light together make a strobing effect. This was *very* popular to

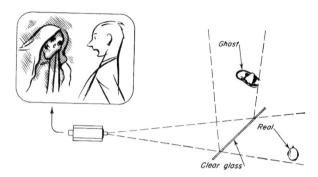

Fig. 15.12 Easy diagram for creating a ghost effect when you have some control over the situation.

create the effect of a moving train or a television's reflected light. The neat thing with this effect is that you can color the light and also dim it. This adds a great deal of variability to its look.

Let's look next at a much more complicated effect that has its roots during the same time frame. How do we make a ghost appear and disappear? How do you turn the reflection of one actor into another? Well, a chemist by the name of John Pepper first saw a technique developed by Henry Dircks in the late 19th century. Dircks's idea was visually successful, but it would never work in the theatre, since it was too complicated and large. Pepper instantly knew how to make it much easier to work with, and it became known as Pepper's ghost. Here is how it works.

For the illusion to work, the viewer must be able to see onto the main stage, but *not* into the secret off-stage area that is hidden by a mirror (Fig. 15.12). The trick is to hide the edge of the glass that separates the areas. Both areas should be identical, yet mirror images, of each other. The off-stage area should be painted completely black and use lighter-colored props and furniture. When the light is turned on the secret area, it reflects in the glass, making the reflections appear as ghostly images on the main stage.

Geoff Dunbar used a similar, yet updated, technique during a production of *Spirit Lodge* (Fig. 15.13). A projector was used to project a film loop onto a rear projection screen that was suspended over the heads of an audience. The audience was constrained to a tight viewing angle. All viewers viewed the virtual image in roughly the same position, and that image was superimposed over an actual theatrical set and actor. With no lights on the set, the audience would see *nothing* except a projected image. With lighting, they would see a magical "How did they do that?" show.

BACK TO THE WALL

A Seminal Concert Production Returns for the First Time in a Touring Format

Sharon Stancavage

Excerpt 1

"So ya

Thought ya

Might like to go to the show."

— "In the Flesh, Part 1"

A unique cross between rock concert, spectacle, and performance art, The Wall has until now only been exhibited in five separate cities. In 1980/81, it was presented in Los Angeles, New York, London, and Dortmund, Germany. In 1990, it was performed in Berlin to celebrate the demise of the Berlin Wall. Now it is on tour for the first time.

Although The Wall was officially a Pink Floyd project, it is in fact the tour de force of Roger Waters. He is the sole author of all but four songs on the album. (According to Wikipedia, the album "was first conceived during the band's 1977 In the Flesh Tour, when bassist and lyricist Roger Waters' frustration with the spectators' perceived boorishness became so acute that he imagined building a wall between the

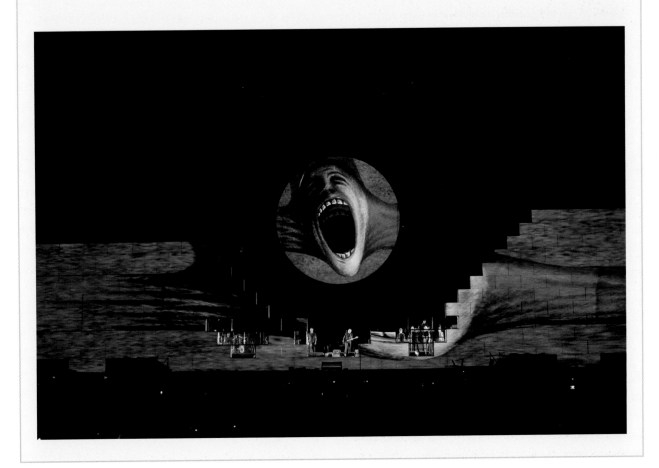

performers and audience.") The result is a rock opera about a young man named Pink, whose lifetime of suffering—a father lost to war, an overprotective mother, abusive schoolmates, and a broken marriage—culminates in his separation from the world, symbolized by the erection of a giant wall.

The production was also an expression of Waters' vision, resulting in an event that was unlike anything previously seen on the concert-touring circuit. As The New York Times noted in 1980, "The Wall show remains a milestone in rock history, though, and there's no point in denying it. Never again will one be able to accept the technical clumsiness, distorted sound, and meager visuals of most arena rock concerts as inevitable." It added, "The Wall show will be the touchstone against which all future rock spectacles must be measured." This was no mere PAR can light show; The Wall set a new standard for concert spectacle. Audiences saw a giant wall built and torn down onstage, along with several inflatables, a plane crash, pyro, and large-scale 35mm projections.

Popular wisdom has long concluded that The Wall could not be toured, but the production designer, Mark Fisher, of London based Stufish, who has worked on all of the live incarnations of the project, disputes that statement. "In 1980, you would have had to load it in the day before the show. So it could have been toured," he says. The issue, according to Fisher, was not the size of the show, but the economics of the era. "Ticket sales today generate proportionally more revenue than they did in 1980—this allows artists to pay for the stage sets of a size that they could not previously afford," he explains. In 1980, the average ticket price was $12.50, which is $35 in 2011 prices. Today, the average ticket price for the tour is $117; the potential gross ticket sales are $257 million; the cost of the production is rumored near $60 million."

Source: Originally published in *Lighting and Sound America*, January 11, 2011.

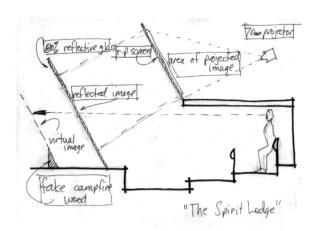

Fig. 15.13 Geoff Dunbar created this section while working on a production.

The lighting works this way. When smoke rises from the campfire, lights inside some fake logs illuminate the actor and the logs for an appropriate amount of time. Then, they dim, and lights at the smoke hole above illuminate the hole as the animated smoke passes through it. And, so on. As the crow "flies" around the room, lights in various positions track it, so that in the end, when the "crow" lands on the actor's hand, the hand is illuminated to reinforce the image.

MODERN EFFECTS

OK, enough of history you say. You want to know about today's effects. OK! So much information is out there. Every day, new ideas create need for technology. Don't let the rest of this chapter limit your imagination. Keep in mind that every piece of machinery or technology was created because someone had an idea. Today, there are many choices, from the most simple to the most extremely advanced. Let's start simply by looking at today's effects that replaced some of the vintage ones.

> Theatre used to be about imagination; now if you're not careful all you look at is the big screen closeup of the star's face. That's TV!
>
> —Anne Johnson

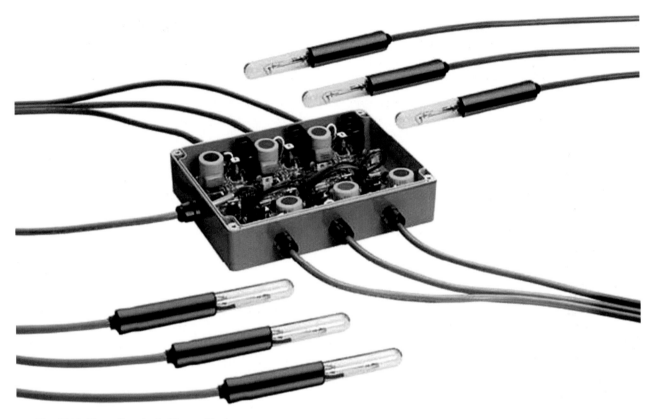

Fig. 15.14 Diversitronics's Finger Strobes.

NATURE

Wind is still created with fans. However, today's fans can vary in speed and direction for a more realistic movement across the stage. The sound designer usually is the one to create thunder today. With the advances in speaker placement and mixing boards, thunder can come from a specific location and move across the stage or throughout the auditorium. Lightning was never dealt with very well during the "vintage" times. Today, it can be done very effectively using a combination of strobes and projections. The advances in lighting control boards have allowed for complicated cueing and triggering of various equipment that can give us quite the lightning storm.

Strobes come in many, many varieties, and all have their uses. Diversitronics makes Finger Strobes® (Fig. 15.14). These are tiny strobes that can be mounted in scenery or even clothing. Diversitronics makes the Superstar Strobe and GAM Products makes the Star*Strobe® (Fig. 15.15). Both strobes are about the size of a standard handheld microphone. They are much more powerful than the finger strobes and are usually hung in varying locations as needed.

Fig. 15.15 GAM Products's Star*Strobe.

Fig. 15.16 Diversitronics's Mark Series high-intensity strobe.

Fig. 15.17 Little Blizzard snow machine.

Moving to bigger units, Diversitronics makes the Mark Series® (Fig. 15.16) and Luminys makes LightningStrikes®. These are some of the brightest on the market. They have so much flexibility that you can create almost any effect you can imagine: one channel, two channels, or stand-alone mode; analog or digital control; varying brightnesses; and wide versus narrow beam field modes.

Remember when I said ideas could generate the technology. Well, remember the musical *Singin' in the Rain*? That show forced the issue of how best and most safely to do rain onstage. A full stage deck was built with a drain in it for the rain to pass into. Overhead there was a complicated plumbing setup with multiple pipes to produce the rain. Off stage there was a pressurized water tank that fed the overhead pipes, and recycled the water from the deck. The water was also temperature controlled for actor safety—not too hot and not too cold.

Snow has come a long way! Although we can still use the snow bag idea, there are many other options. You can rent or buy a snow machine (Fig. 15.17). The machine takes a liquid formula and turns it into snow at the same time it blows the snow out of the machine with a fan. Most machines work only when the temperature is over 40 degrees. The nice thing is that, once the snow melts, it leaves almost no residue. That means no cleanup either! The newest of the machines can vary the size of the snowflakes, the speed at which they are generating, and the distance that they blow. All of this can be very realistic, if that is what you are going for.

FIRE

Real fire is always a danger on stage, which is why many cities and towns have regulations governing its use and the training you need to become certified. This is truly a specialized area. You can buy products to create flames and smoke, but most of them require you to have a special effects license before you purchase or operate them (Fig. 15.18). With all that said, there are still ways to create a simulated fire on stage. Most of the best ones are packaged units that you simply plug in and control via a remote or the lighting control board.

FOG AND HAZE

The developments lately in fog and specifically fog fluids are amazing. Early fog fluids were mineral-oil based. Water-soluble foggers replaced them. A number of factors went into this transition. First, the oil would often coat the stage when the fog dissipated, leaving it slippery. The oil also didn't agree with a singer's voice. Last, the oil was combustible. The water-soluble fluids solved all these problems. The basics of any fog machine are relatively simple (Fig. 15.19). Fog fluid is moved into a heater by a pump. The heater maintains a high temperature at which the fluid vaporizes. As the fluid vaporizes, it rapidly expands, and that expansion forces the vapor through the nozzle of the machine. When the vapor mixes with cooler air outside the machine, it instantly forms an opaque aerosol—the effect we call *fog* or *smoke*.

There are many manufacturers today for fog machines. Every machine is a little different and has different features. These features can control the start and end of the fog, overall quantity of flow, and the speed at which the fog dissipates. Some machines even have a timer that you can set for turning them on and off. The other factor is whether

Fig. 15.18 *Ghosts of Versailles* at the Metropolitan Opera in 1991. Director, Colin Graham; scenic and costume designer, John Conklin; and lighting designer, Gil Wechsler.

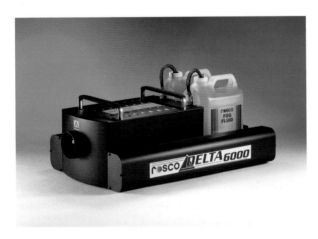

Fig. 15.19 Rosco Delta 6000® fogger.

the fog hangs in the air or on the ground. What we've been discussing is fog that hangs in the air.

If you want fog to hang on the ground, you need dry ice. First, let me say a word of caution. Dry ice can be tricky to deal with. You can't just pick it up with your hands; you have to use gloves. It burns your skin with only momentary contact! Dry ice is basically solid carbon dioxide at a temperature of −109.3 degrees Fahrenheit or −78.5 degrees Celsius. That is *negative*! So be careful. You put the dry ice in a large container and pour water over it; it instantly starts to melt, giving off a dense fog. Dry ice machines are typically made from a 55-gallon drum (Fig. 15.20). You put water in the bottom, where there is a heater element. You put the dry ice in a basket at the top. When you are ready for fog, you lower the basket into the water, and a hole in the side of the drum connects to a hose that points the fog in a specific direction. When dry ice fog dissipates, no residue is left.

Haze is yet another kind of fog that can be created with today's machines. Haze is about revealing light beams more than it is about being seen on its own. Haze is a water-soluble liquid that, when heated, turns to haze. Sound familiar? It works just like the foggers; the difference is in the fluid.

Fig. 15.21 Rosco X24 X-Effects 3D projector.

Fig. 15.20 A 55-gallon dry ice fogger.

PROJECTIONS

The Rosco X24® projector provides large-scale rippling light effects (Fig. 15.21). The X24 uses an incredibly bright lamp, with a long life and a high Kelvin temperature.

Rotating two X-size glass gobos off center of the optical path creates the effect. This results in a projection that does not appear to have a visible direction or pattern. The lens is available in 30-, 50-, and 70-degree configurations.

Let's move on and take projections to the next level. This is where a great deal of the new technology is happening today. What is so amazing is that projections can be both scenery and lighting, so a new department dedicated to projections has been formed. This makes room for another designer on the team, one who is focused on the projections and only the projections. Originally, theatre productions could not afford the new technology. Musical concerts were the first to use this kind of projection on a regular basis.

The best way to introduce you to this idea is to profile one person's journey in the part of the business. Anne Johnston is currently the vice president of marketing for the Production Resource Group in New Jersey. She started working for Production Arts (PA) in 1985 and worked in the office. It was supposed to be her "day job" while she stage managed at night. Anne took an instant liking to projections, as it was so different from lighting and 3D scenery. PA was the only shop to have access to Pani projectors, which at the time were the state-of-the-art projectors (Figs. 15.22 and 15.23).

A typical equipment list for a Pani projector includes much more than just the projector. Take a look at the next box and see how many other items have to be specified. As the technology advances, the equipment lists get longer. That is not a problem, just something to be aware of. If you are the one writing the equipment list, make sure you

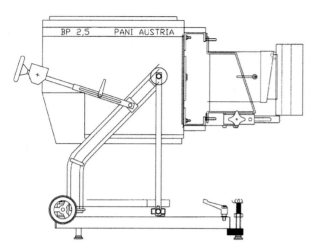

Fig. 15.22 Line drawing of a Pani projector, side view.

understand the technology and all that it entails. Figure 15.24 shows a flowchart for connecting all the parts.

1 Pani BP 2.5 compact HMI projector

1 Pani 2500-watt HMI power supply

1 Pani AMD 32 random-access slide changer

1 Pani G405/PCS gray scale dimming shutter

1 Lighting control console with DMX 512 outputs

1 100-foot power supply extension

1 5-foot three-pin XLR analog control cable

1 50-foot DMX 512 control cable

The "Who's That Girl" tour wanted to use projectors, so the group came to PA. Anne had to figure out road boxes for shipping, coordinating spare lamps and fixtures, as well as onsite technical support. The new projection department of PA was learning quickly and Anne was now working full time. The next call was from the "Steel Wheels" tour, and the rest, as they say, is history.

Remember when I said, if you have an idea, the technology would be developed to help you create that idea. Well, Pani didn't make an automatic slide changer for its projectors at this point, so PA started developing and building its own accessories for the projectors. The first was the automatic slide changer. It also developed the ability to

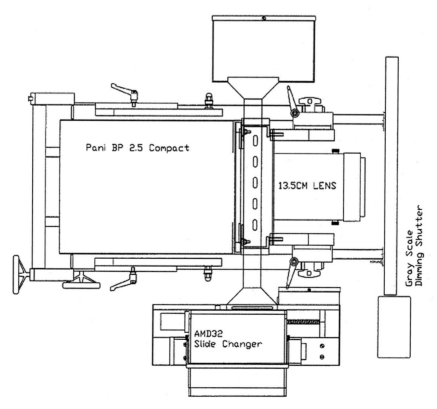

Fig. 15.23 Line drawing of a Pani projector, top view.

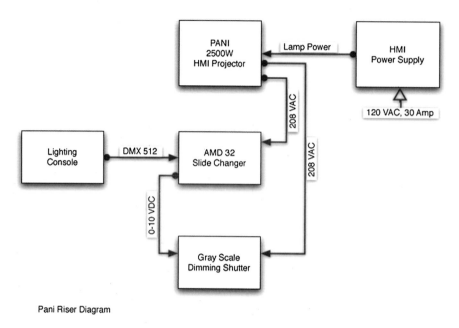

Pani Riser Diagram

Fig. 15.24 Riser diagram shows how to hook up a Pani projector.

control the projectors via DMX, so the lighting board could control everything together.

The next major development in projectors came from a different manufacturer, PIGI. PIGI projectors added a new feature, film. This had never been seen before, and it was amazing to witness for the first time. The rotating double scroller added the ability to change the orientation of the projection at will. The PIGI system could also be controlled through computer software. This became a major step in the process toward today's projections.

Enter the world of video projection! Most dedicated projectors have slowly been phased out. They are still in use, but the larger shows are going all digital with their projections (Fig. 15.25). Digital projection gives way more control and, in combination with moving lights, gets the best of both worlds. Most technicians from the projector departments are being cross-trained onto digital equipment. It is the inevitable next step.

The toughest part of new technology for the rental shops is to know which equipment to invest in. Think about it. If your laptop computer becomes obsolete in 18 months, doesn't the same happen with higher-end equipment? Of course, it does! European theatres are different, in that they tend to own the equipment, as opposed to American theatres, which tend to rent it. If you own, you keep using it

until it stops working. European theatres also have stage-hands on staff, so it is easier to get familiar with the equipment.

So, now, we have moved almost completely to video. Let's talk about that. It is simple and yet not. Huh? Well, it can be simple. You can use a PowerPoint slide show connected to a projector and be done, if that is all you need. I designed a production of *Personals* that used this method (Figs. 15.26 and 15.27). We built a large back wall that was framed to look like the columns from a newspaper. I imported the design drawing into Photoshop to create the template or matte. Then, all the graphics were inserted into it.

Using this simple method you can project still images or video or video with audio. You need someone to run the computer and advance the slides on a cue from the stage manager (Fig. 15.28). You can also use a Rosco Keystroke® (Fig. 15.29). The Keystroke hooks up your computer to your lighting board and gives the light board control of the slide show. Regular cues in the light board can advance the slides. Pretty cool, huh?

I got a little ahead of myself. Let's talk about creating the images for this new video technology. There are a variety of ways to come up with content. First, stock images and video clips can be purchased from a variety of places. These images are very high quality, but they are stock. That means they are not specific to your show. And, stock images usually can't be altered even after you've purchased them. But, they are a good way to create content quickly.

Fig. 15.25 Production Resource Group's video projections for an industrial show.

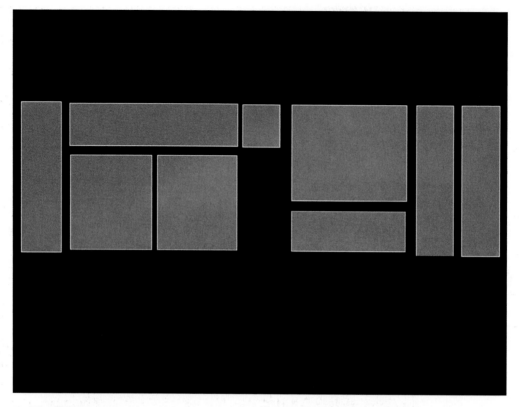

Fig. 15.26 Template created of the projections for a production of *Personals*.

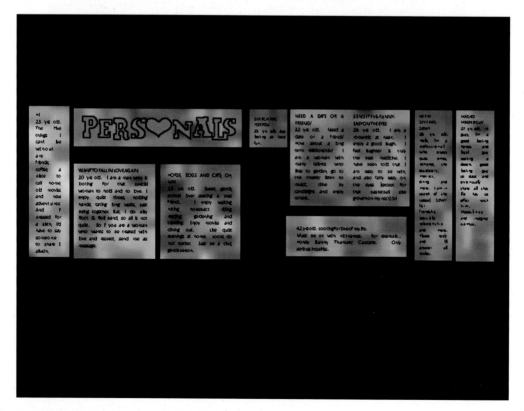

Fig. 15.27 Graphics inserted into the template of the projections for a production of *Personals*.

■ **Fig. 15.28** A production at the 1869 Bardavon Opera House using super title projections.

BACK TO THE WALL

A Seminal Concert Production Returns for the First Time in a Touring Format

Sharon Stancavage

Excerpt 2

Although he is credited in the program as production designer, Fisher freely admits that his role in this project is somewhat different. "Roger is the author of the show. My role has been much more that of being a realizer of Roger's vision and a creator of new ideas that Roger then approves of," he says, "It's at the very least collaborating, at the very most following strict instructions," he concludes with a chuckle.

From a design standpoint, the past is indeed analogous to the present, Fisher notes: "The 2010 show is mechanically a facsimile of the original 1980 show—everything has been rebuilt, but there is nothing significantly different in the way that the thing is done, right down in the small print of the engineering to the fact that some of the components are sourced from the same company that we sourced them from back in 1979 when we were building it for the first time." In 1980, the primary vendor was Britannia Row [at that time, Pink Floyd's wholly owned staging, lighting, and sound company]; this time out, scenic fabrication was handled by Tait Towers of Lititz, Pennsylvania. Waters, who is also the production's director, says he had confidence in his team from the very start. "My experience has been that when

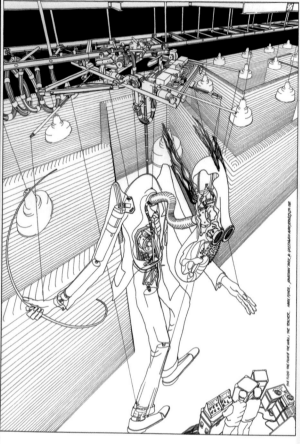

you have a good team of people around you, and you start to work as a team, most of the problems can be solved."

Working with Fisher to complete the vision was technical director Jeremy Lloyd, who typically handles all stadium and larger arena shows at Stufish. "Basically, we had to take paper drawings, things on transparencies and tracing paper that had been drawn by hand, and go over every single piece," he explains. It was, he adds, "a very boring, slow process." However, it did guarantee that the integrity of the original design would indeed survive.

"Mother, should I

build the wall?"

— "Mother"

Source: Originally published in *Lighting and Sound America,* January 11, 2011.

Fig. 15.29 Rosco Keystroke.

If you want something more specific or original to your show then you need to create it from your own material. This means you need a good working knowledge of a variety of software. Four programs are really useful for this: Photoshop®, Illustrator®, Painter®, After Effects®, and Final Cut Pro®. The first three programs allow you to create and manipulate images. The last two add motion. Other programs out there will work. Two others worth mentioning are Avid® and Premiere®. They do very similar things to Final Cut Pro. It's a matter of preference, your budget, what computer platform you are working on, and what you are familiar with. The ultimate goal in creating content is to create the highest resolution images and video possible. The better the resolution, the better the projection looks in the end.

If you are renting equipment from a rental shop, you may end up renting a media server. Media server is a fancy name for a computer with a massive hard drive and a great graphics card. If you rent a media server from a rental shop, it may come with some of the software I just mentioned. The media server is easy to integrate into the projection equipment you will most likely be renting as well. If you rent everything you need, you know it will work together. This is great for bigger shows and more complicated designs. Keep in mind the design is the key to how everything is done.

If the design is figured out before you get to the space, you need less equipment. Sometimes, things can't be figured out in advance. This means you need to have lots of extra "cover your butt" stuff. If you bring the right stuff to begin with, it makes the whole process easier. A lot of people say they'll figure it out when they get there. That is the equivalent of "we'll fix it in post," which usually means more money is needed and potentially wasted. Once you are in the theatre, never ignore the "Hey, what if..." comments, as they are a very creative part of the process. You don't want to do everything that way, but some amount of experimentation and "happy accidents" can really add to the production.

Now, here is a bit of a twist on everything we discussed so far. As the audiences' expectations go up, so must the shows' expectations. In today's culture, you really can't ignore all the influences from other art forms. The audience is savvier today. People want a show to look high tech and modern. All the energy in what we look at everyday has affected us. It has to have a slickness and modernism to the design. It can't look dated. Current movies are the pulse of today. The technological advances of other areas—film, television, and even video games—influence our audience. We have to adapt to those expectations or, at the very least, acknowledge them. However, we should not, I repeat, should not try to compete with those medias.

OK, so we talked about video projection. And, you assume that means you need a video projector. Right? Wrong! The latest technology is the advancement of LED lights (Fig. 15.30). LEDs are still in their infancy, but the options are amazing. Picture a whole wall of LEDs controlled by the media server! The possibilities are endless. And, I mean that! With any new technology, you have to be willing to make a leap of faith. That doesn't mean you jump with your eyes closed. You have to do your research and be informed about the technology. It is only a tool. And, any tool, as we know, is only as good as the person who uses it!

Let's talk about high definition for a moment. HD is all the rage now. Television sets and video monitors are available in HD. The 16 × 9 format is perfect for theatre, as it is a similar proportion to most proscenium arches. The projectors for HD are larger than standard-definition ones, so that is a consideration that should be dealt with. Space in the theatre is always at a premium; if a projector is going to be used, it has to be accounted for early on in the process. If you are going to use LEDs in some configuration instead of a projector, then that too has to be incorporated into the design and budget.

■ **Fig. 15.30** Main Light Industries' Hard-LED Series® panels.

> Just because you can, doesn't mean you should!
>
> —Curt Ostermann

The projection world has gone in two directions. We discussed a little of this, but let's go into more depth. There is still the concept of traditional projection; then, there is fully digital scenery. Still projections to an RP screen or TV set are still possible and used frequently. These can include a static backdrop, a skyline, a grotto, and so forth. The computer technology available today can create all sorts of projection effects. At a very high level, this replaces the lobsterscope effect. Digital projections have come so far that they are now amazing and beautiful and can be used in abstract ways as well as realistic ones. The projections have become more of a lighting effect when used this way.

The first try with almost any new technology is not a good experience. The key to much of the success is working with the manufacturer. If the manufacturer's responsiveness to our needs is good, then the technology can continue to develop and become a great tool for us in the theatre. One of the first huge successes on Broadway with LEDs was on a musical called *Ring of Fire*. The scenery was made of LED panels controlled by a media server. This allowed the scenic images to change on a moment's notice. It was very impressive from a technology standpoint, and even more important from a design standpoint.

The new title in the theatre is projection designer. It is becoming more of a standard and is recognized by other designers, who understand what the projection designer does. It is not just about making pretty pictures. You have to do all the math to figure out the types of equipment needed, specify equipment, then oversee the installation of both computers and projection equipment. Working closely with the director as well as both the scenic and lighting designers means often creating a storyboard of the images, so that everyone understands what the images will eventually look like. During technical rehearsals, the projection designer is in the theatre, continuing to revise and create images, alter the cueing with the computer, and troubleshoot any technical issues with the projection system.

There are many ways to work with directors. It is mostly about the director and what he or she brings to the production as well as his or her background. Some directors have a visual concept for exactly what they want. Others are unsure and may just want a traditional background. Some directors may even shoot a short film themselves and want it projected. In terms of the kind of productions that use projections, they are mostly new plays (Fig. 15.31). Classic plays that are completely reinterpreted may also use projections as opposed to being done more traditionally (Fig. 15.32).

I interviewed Michael Clarke, who is a Broadway projection designer, about his process and he had the following to say. "A truly successful production is when collaboration happens and no one makes assumptions. . . . Then work can be more unified—or not depending on what the team is going for. If everyone does their homework, and shares their ideas . . . the work is done and you go to the theatre and 'plug it all in' . . . until script changes—the work is done."

Michael uses email, FTP, and his web site to the fullest. He gives the director a Web link for him or her to see his process. It is a more environmentally friendly and less costly way to work. Directors can comment right on the web site, or call, email, fax, or whatever. He said he doesn't find the potential color shift of the web site a hindrance. "You don't really know what you're going to get into until you're in the theatre, due to ambient lighting, reflections of scenery and props."

Arizona State University now has a projection designer program. The New School is trying to start one. As more colleges recognize the need to have a specialized program for projections, it will help everyone to get the job they love to do. Keep in mind that you need to understand art and theatre history, just like all the other designers. Computer skills are important, but they are secondary to the design. Software is a tool!

SOFTWARE

I haven't talked yet about 3D software and image creation. This could obviously be a whole book on its own, and it is. Let me address some of the basics here. There are a number of software programs for creating 3D images. They all have their specialties. Maya, 3D Studio Max, Cinema 4D, LightWave, and Softimage are just a few. All these programs work amazingly well for creating content. They have a much higher learning curve than other software,

Fig. 15.31 The Theatre de la Jeune Lune production of *Amerika* in 2006.

mostly because of their capabilities. There are demo versions of most of these and student versions as well. My recommendation is to try a couple of them, if you have an interest, and see which one "fits" you and your needs.

Now that you have all this information, how do you use it? Well, I spoke with Curt Ostermann who designs a lot of industrials (Figs. 15.33 and 15.34). He had some interesting things to say about his process:

The work I do has no script. The show must be designed before there is a rundown or even a show flow. The hardest thing about those shows is to understand how it looks for the audience. Corporate clients have their own very distinct look. The tone and color palette are already set by the company's logos.

The client will buy a set and use it for up to five years. You have to critique your own work, and then make notes to try and fix things for next year. Always keep in mind the client has "bought" the set designer's rendering, it is the key. The client wants it to look like that and they will refer to the rendering during rehearsals.

When I asked Curt about his career and whether he misses doing theatre he said:

I started out my career in Europe, opera, and ballet. I have also designed television and amusement parks. It's all about art when you start out. I don't miss theatre; I don't feel I've missed anything. I've been very lucky.

I love working in television, you get to work in the closeup. You never get to do that in theatre. That's what Rembrandt did his whole life. With industrials, you have the theatrical wide shot, and the television extreme closeup. Designing for television is not selling out! It's the art that you know and making it work is the key. Your attitude is everything, if you think it's selling out, then you are. I haven't sold out, I've cashed in!

■ **Fig. 15.32** The Minnesota Opera's production of *Lucrezia Borgia*. Designers, Tom Mays and Gail Bakkom.

■ **Fig. 15.33** Tom Cariello's Photoshop® rendering for an industrial.

Fig. 15.34 Photo from the same industrial. Scenic designer, Tom Cariello; lighting designer, Curt Ostermann.

Dry ice

Fog

Haze

Linnebach projector

Lobsterscope

Media server

Pepper's ghost

Scene machine

Strobe

CHAPTER FIFTEEN

Study Words

PART
SIX
Stage
Management
and Careers

Chapter XVI: Warning,
Standby, Go!
Stage Management

Chapter XVII: What's Next?
Career Choices

S	M	T	W	Th	F	Sa
1 Update Call Sheet	**2** Prod Meet 10AM Rehearsal 2 - 5 Turn In Petty Cash R	**3** Rehearsal 2 - 5 Dinner 5 - 6 Rehearsal 6 - 8	**4** Rehearsal 2 - 5 Dinner 5 - 6 Rehearsal 6 - 8	**5** Prod Meet 10AM Rehearsal 2 - 5 Dinner 5 - 6 Rehearsal 6 - 8 Update Blocking Book	**6** Prod Meet 10AM Rehearsal 2 - 5 Dinner 5 - 6	**7** Script change review Dir apartment
8 Del Notes to WR/Prod	**9** Actors off book Turn In Petty Cash R	**10** Rehearsal 2 - 5 Dinner 5 - 6 Make copies changes & issue	**11** Rehearsal 2 - 5 Dinner 5 - 6 Rehearsal 6 - 8	**12** Rehearsal 2 - 5 Dinner 5 - 6 Rehearsal 6 - 8	**13** Prod Meet 10AM Rehearsal 2 - 5	**14** Meet 10AM w/ TD & ME
15 Sleep Late Pay my bills & send	**16** Rehearsal 2 - 5 Turn In Petty Cash R	**17** Rehearsal 2 - 5 Dinner 5 - 6 Rehearsal 6 - 7	**18** Rehearsal 2 - 5 Dinner 5 - 6 Rehearsal 6 - 7	**19** Rehearsal 2 - 5 Dinner 5 - 6 Rehearsal 6 - 7	**20** Prod Meet 10AM Rehearsal 2 - 5	**21** Rehearsal 1 - 6 Load In 10AM At Theater Cue Meet 11AM w/LD
22 Rehearsal 1 - 6 Load In 10AM At Theater	**23** Rehearsal 2 - 5 Dinner 5 - 6 Rehearsal 6 - 8 Turn In Petty Cash R	**24** IN THEATER Run Crew Rehearsal 10 - 1 Rehearsal 2 - 5 Dinner 5 - 6 Rehearsal 6 - 8	**25** Run Crew Rehearsal 10 - 1 Rehearsal 1 - 5 Dinner 5 - 6 Rehearsal 6 - 9 T-Rehearsal 6-10-Rehearsal 6-10 Update Cue Log	**26** Run Crew Rehearsal 10 - 1 Rehearsal 1 - 5 Dinner 5 - 6 Rehearsal 6 - 10 Full Run Thru 6 - 10......	**27** Run Crew Rehearsal 10 - 1 Rehearsal 2 - 5 Dinner 5 - 6 Full Run Thru 6 - 10......	**28** OPEN 7PM CALL 8PM Curtain Cast Party at Freddy's Bar
29 OPEN 7PM CALL 8PM Curtain	**30** OPEN 7PM CALL 8PM Curtain Turn In Petty Cash R					

NOTES:

Call Theater about repair fan in actors dressing rm #1

Buy new first aid kit check Fire ext at theater

Find copy shop near theater

22 Margret's Birthday (arrange cake)

Call producers and check bond

Call Equity check bond in place

Set up account w/ cleaner & laundry service for costume crew

Warning, Standby, Go!

Stage Management

Now that we have all the technical stuff done, what next? Well, as Mickey once said to Judy, "Let's do a show." The culmination of working in the theatre is the actual performance. I don't think we'd ever get much of an audience if all we did was put the fabulous set on stage and do some really cool lighting cues. The audiences have come to expect actors as well!

This chapter goes into the details of stage management. The stage manager is responsible for organizing the auditions, rehearsals, running the technical rehearsals, and taking charge of the performances. Without the stage manager, we would never get as far as *house to half*. Stage managers have to be organized, they have to love paperwork, and they need to work well with a variety of people with artistic temperaments—from directors, to designers, to actors, to technicians. Quite frequently, the stage manager comes from the acting side, but that is not to say a good bit of technical knowledge isn't helpful and useful!

Stage management is a unique job within the industry. No other job goes through so many different phases within the production timeline, and with so many varying responsibilities. I think the hardest part of the job is to handle many of the human resource issues that arise. The cast and crew look to the stage manager as the guiding beacon. They come to you with their personal problems, relationship problems, car problems, and of course, their stage problems.

STAGE MANAGER KIT

You need to develop a stage manager kit. Often, it is in a fishing tackle box or a rolling bag or box of some kind. This kit should contain a range of items such as pencils, erasers, highlighters, pads of paper, post-it notes, paper clips, stapler, and so forth. These are all typical office supply items. You also need access to a standard first aid kit. Each show may require specific additions and your personal preferences or actor's needs may be different as well.

Stage Manager Kit Supplies

Briefcase or backpack.
Supply of pencils.
Supply of erasers.
Small supply of pens.
Pads of note paper.
Three-ring binder.
Three-ring dividers (with pocket is better).
Stapler and staple remover.
Three-hole punch.
Ruler, scale rule.
Highlighters, several colors.
Post-it notes, several colors to match
   highlighters.
Personal reading lamp.
Flashlight.
Tape (masking, clear, spike).
Watch, stop watch.
First aid items (band-aids, alcohol swabs,
   tweezers, facial tissues).
Personal tools (jeweler's screwdrivers, needle-
   nose pliers, adjustable wrench, utility knife,
   head phones or ear buds).

The stage manager's professional life is somewhat ruled by paperwork and forms. Every stage manager has his or her favorite forms, designs he or she has developed through years of experience. We address each phase of a show by seeing the various forms that might be needed. Keep in mind that every production is unique. Not all forms are needed for all shows. And, some shows need newly customized forms. At least, the following will get you started. Don't be afraid to alter or create forms as needed for your specific needs or tastes.

AUDITIONS

The stage manager should always arrive early, but especially for auditions. You need to organize the space: setting up a table and chairs for the director and producer, a holding area for the actors, a space for the actual auditions, and a table to greet actors and hand out the audition forms (Fig. 16.1). When the forms are completed, they should be returned to you. If the actor has a resume, it should be attached to the form. Then, the actor should also be photographed for reference. Traditionally, a Polaroid camera was used and the photo was attached to the audition form. Today, a digital camera and printer are more the norm. You can use any method that works for you. The goal is to remember the actor's face after he or she has left the auditions.

Take a look at the sample audition form in Figure 16.1. Contact information and schedule conflicts are critical to casting for obvious reasons. Also notice the paragraph and signature line at the bottom of the page. Think of the audition form as a contract. If the actor is willing to sign on the line, it means he or she agrees to the ground rules that have been established for this particular production.

Once auditions are over, the forms and any other documentation should be handed over to the director or producer. Depending on the stage manager's relationship with the director, you may or may not be a part of the casting process. If you are a part of the casting process, you will be asked for your opinion about various actors. Some of your input can be observations you made while running the audition. Details of import may be did the actor arrive on time, did the actor seem prepared, was he or she courteous. If you are not included in casting, you get to go home and wait for the decisions to be made, so that you can start your next round of paperwork.

REHEARSALS

The stage manager's first step once the show is cast is to create a contact sheet. The contact sheet needs to show everyone involved with the production. Depending on the

Laughing Stock
AUDITION FORM

Performances:
Thursday, March 1 through Saturday March 3 at 8pm
Sunday, March 4 at 2pm

NAME: _____

PHONE: _____

EMAIL: _____

Please list below your class/work schedule...and any other weekly commitments:

	Sun	Mon	Tues	Wed	Thur	Fri	Sat
9a-12p							
12p-3p							
3p-6p							
6p-9p							
9p-12a							

Please Note:

Rehearsals will most likely be during 2 weekday evenings, and 1 weekend afternoon. Load-in will be on Saturday, February 24. Cue-to-Cue will be on Sunday, February 25. Technical rehearsals will be Monday, February 26 through Wednesday, February 28th.

Role you would like to audition for: _____

If auditioning for a specific role, will you accept a different role: _____

I agree to the above schedule of rehearsals and performances for Laughing Stock. I understand that this production is striving to achieve the highest standards of performance and I agree to make all arrangements with other classes and/or my work schedule to participate in the all listed rehearsals and performances. I also understand that should I miss rehearsals or not maintain a professional work ethic, I may be released from my role.

Signature: _____ Date: _____

■ **Fig. 16.1** Sample audition form.

production, and more important the venue, there are two different styles of contact sheets. A production contact sheet is used primarily by schools and community theatres (Fig. 16.2). A company contact sheet is used by professional theatre companies that have many more people involved (Figs. 16.3–16.5). The production contact sheet sample (Fig. 16.2) does not include addresses, but that is easy to add if you need them. The company contact sheet allows for the possible involvement of a separate producer or technical shops, so they are therefore included. Think of the contact sheet as your phone book for the show. Any information you might need should be there. You can even include rehearsal and performance spaces as on the company contact sheet. Feel free, as always, to alter

Show Name
Production Contact Sheet

TITLE	NAME	EMAIL	CELL PHONE	HOME PHONE
Director				
Asst. Director				
Musical Director				
Choreographer				
Scenic Designer				
Lighting Designer				
Costume Designer				
Sound Designer				
Effects Designer				
Production Stage Manager				
Stage Manager				
Wardrobe				
Property Manager				
Hair/Makeup				

CHARACTER	NAME	EMAIL	CELL PHONE	HOME PHONE

Fig. 16.2 Sample production contact sheet.

Show Name
Company Contact Sheet

SEND PACKAGES/ MAIL TO:

<NAME> (212) 555-1234 Box Office
Theatre Name/Production Name (212) 555-2000 Stage Mgmt Office
Mailing Address (212) 555-2100 Backstage Security
City, State, Zip (212) 555-1235 Opening Night Tickets

Role/ Position	First	Last	phone	email	Personal/ Company Address	Representative Contact
Company Staff						
Artistic Director						
Managing Director						
General Manager						
Associate Producer						
Assoc. General Manager						
Company Manager						
Asst. to General Manager						
Casting Director						
Director of Marketing & Communication						
Creative						
Playwright						
Director						

Fig. 16.3 Sample company contact sheet.

Creative					
Asst. Director					
Musical Director					
Choreographer					
Scenic					
Scenic Designer					
Associate Scenic Designer					
Asst. Scenic Designer					
Lighting					
Lighting Designer					
Assoc. Lighting Designer					
Asst. Lighting Designer					
Costume					
Costume Designer					
Assoc. Costume Designer					
Asst. Costume Designer					
Hair Designer					
Makeup Designer					
Sound					

Fig. 16.4 Another company contact sheet.

Sound Designer					
Associate Sound Designer					
Asst. Sound Designer					
Stage Management					
Production Stage Manager					
Stage Manager					
Cast					

Fig. 16.5 Yet another company contact sheet.

these samples and make a hybrid version as needed for your own use.

The rehearsal schedule is the next thing that needs to be published (Figs. 16.6 and 16.7) to the company. You will work closely with the director to create this. The rehearsal schedule becomes your master calendar. It should show dates, times, places, and which members of the cast are required to attend. Be prepared to revise the schedule throughout the rehearsal process as frequently as needed. Make sure to number or include a date on the revisions so that everyone knows which schedule is the most current. This is one of those times that can become frustrating, given the amount of revisions possible. Changes can be due to a number of things, people's schedule can have unforeseen conflicts or

Laughing Stock Rehearsal Schedule

Day	Date	Time	Place	Scene(s)	Notes
Sunday	01/28/07	12pm - 4pm	DHT	*2-4, 2-5*	
Sunday	01/28/07	5pm - 9pm	DHT	*1-3, 1-6*	
Wednesday	01/31/07	6pm - 10pm	DHT	*1-9, 2-2*	
Friday	02/02/07	5pm - 9pm	DEL	*1-1, 1-7,* Shakespeare	
Sunday	02/04/07	12pm - 4pm	DHT	*1-2,* Shakespeare	
Sunday	02/04/07	5pm - 9pm	DHT	*1-4, 1-9*	
Wednesday	02/07/07	6pm - 10pm	D205	1-3,2-3, 1-5	
Friday	02/09/07	5pm - 9pm	DEL	*2-1, 1-8*	
Sunday	02/11/07	12pm - 4pm	D209	1-6, 2-4	OFF BOOK
Sunday	02/11/07	5pm - 9pm	D209	2-2	
Wednesday	02/14/07	6pm - 10pm	D205	Snow Day	
Friday	02/16/07	5pm - 9pm	DEL	*2-1, 2-3,1-2, 1-1*	
Sunday	02/18/07	12pm ·4pm	D209	1-4,2-5	
Sunday	02/18/07	5pm - 9pm	D209	1-5,2·2	
Monday	02/19/07	12pm - 4pm	DHT	Runthrough Act 1	*President's Day*
Monday	02/19/07	5pm - 9pm	DHT	Runthrough Act 2	*President's Day*
Wednesday	02/21/07	6pm - 10pm	D205	Runthrough Acts 1&2	
Friday	02/23/07	5pm - 9pm	DEL	*As Needed*	
Saturday	02/24/07	10a-8pm	DHT	Load-in	
Sunday	02/25/07	12pm -6pm	DHT	Cue-to-Cue	
Sunday	02/25/07	7pm - 10pm	DHT	Tech Rehearsal-Costume Parade	
Monday	02/26/07	6pm -10pm	DHT	Dress Rehearsal	
Tuesday	02/27/07	6pm -10pm	DHT	Dress Rehearsal	
Wednesday	02/28/07	6pm -10pm	DHT	Invited Dress	
Thursday	03/01/07	6pm	DHT	Opening Night	
Friday	03/02/07	6:30pm	DHT	Performance #2	
Saturday	03/03/07	6:30pm	DHT	Performance #3	
Sunday	03/04/07	12:30pm	DHT	Performance #4	
Sunday	03/04/07	5pm - 8pm	DHT	Strike	

■ **Fig. 16.6** Sample rehearsal schedules. Everyone has a preference for what the schedule should look like.

March 30 to April 5, 2008

	Sunday 30	Monday 31	Tuesday 1	Wednesday 2	Thursday 3	Friday 4	Saturday 5
9:00 AM							
10:00 AM		Character work-Leads only	Block Act 2, scenes 3-5		Work Through Act 1		
11:00 AM	Musical Rehearsal-Full Cast					Run Through w/Designers	
12:00 PM				Dance Rehearsal-Full Cast			
1:00 PM		Lunch	Lunch		Lunch		
2:00 PM		Ensemble choreography	Fight rehearsal		Work Through Act 2		
3:00 PM							
4:00 PM							
5:00 PM							

■ **Fig. 16.7** Here is another version.

SP4 CAST CREW CONTACT LISTING

Live and Unrehearsed

Sign In Sheet
Thursday, September 11th 7:00 pm – 10:00 pm

ACTOR NAME	CHARACTER	SIGNATURE

Fig. 16.8 Sample sign-in sheet.

more rehearsal time may be needed for a particular scene. I always believe that every schedule I publish is "tentative" until the show is open. Then, we have a final schedule.

Once rehearsals begin, you need to keep track of many things simultaneously. The first thing each day is to determine who is at rehearsals. If actors are late, you need to phone them to find out where they are and when they expect to arrive. You need to establish a sign-in sheet (Fig. 16.8). It should be posted in the same place at every rehearsal. This is your only way to keep track of missing actors and crew. A policy should be in place regarding lateness and the ramifications to the actor or crew member. This should be decided by the director in escalating steps of consequences for repeat offenders. Remember this is show business—not show fun.

During each day's rehearsal, the stage manager keeps notes for each department (scenery, costumes, lighting, props, etc.) as a daily rehearsal report (Fig. 16.9). These notes include any changes or additions to the lists based on the script that may come up during the rehearsal. A script change, the addition of a prop, rescheduling rehearsals, specific requirements for lighting or costumes, a sound cue that will be needed, anything like that is noted. This information then needs to get to all the right people. The stage manager is responsible for disseminating all this information to the departments heads. Printed copies or emails are sent at the end of each rehearsal day. Any questions that arise are directed at you, so be ready to explain your notes. You become a librarian in a way. Your files for the show are the master copy of everything that people will reference. Keep

A Midsummer Night's Dream
Rehearsal Report

Day: Sunday **Date:** April 18 **Rehearsal:** #1	**Start time:** 7:00 pm **Break:** 8:20-8:30 **End Time:** 9:57
Attendance: TC, SB, MMS until 9:05, DS, BLO	**Prod. Attendance:** KLT, EAK, SW, EW, JA
Today's Schedule: block and work Ii	**Tomorrow's Schedule:** block and work Iii
Set:	**Props:** guitar (EAK has one we can restring and teach SB to play), blanket, poetry book, picnic basket, picnic food (tbd—grapes?)
Lighting:	**Sound:** song for introduction to characters for opening sequence, SB song?
Costumes:	**Box Office:**
Rehearsal Notes:	**Misc:** tomorrow start at 8pm; Wednesday don't start until 9pm; fill open roles at 7pm

Fig. 16.9 Sample daily rehearsal report.

every piece of paper, even little notes on napkins. You never know what you may need in the future.

Your next job is to begin the process of breaking down the script into manageable bits of information. You need to make a spreadsheet of all the acts and scenes in the play. Then, add a list of all the characters. This is the beginning of a matrix that shows which characters are in which scenes. This is called a French scene breakdown (Fig. 16.10). A French scene breakdown is invaluable in mapping the progression of a play. The chart is based on character entrances and exits, the names of the characters in the scenes, and a scene title that summarizes the action. By looking at a French scene breakdown without knowing the play, it's possible to understand major scenes and central characters, as well as analyze the sequence and duration of

scenes that constitute the overall rhythm of the play. This is a critical piece of paperwork, since all rehearsal call sheets are based on it. Take your time to double and triple check that it is accurate. The director will use this as a part of his or her process, potentially changing or adapting it as the need arises. Keep in mind that, if the script is changed in any way, this breakdown needs to be updated. There is no reason to hand out this form. It is for you and the director to use.

Although we don't really like to talk about accidents in the theatre, they do occasionally happen. Every mishap, small or large, requires an accident report to be filled out and filed with your producer as well as with your show's paperwork (Fig. 16.11). Ideally, you will never deal with anything major, but even small accidents must be documented. Should a mishap occur, the first thing to do is

Laughing Stock Characters by Scene

	Dracula	Charley's Aunt	Hamlet	Act 1-1	ACT 1-2	ACT 1-3	ACT 1-4	ACT 1-5	ACT 1-6	ACT 1-7	ACT 1-8	ACT 1-9	ACT 2-1	ACT 2-2
Gordon Page			Hamlet	x	x	x	x	x	x	x		x	x	
Jack Morris	Harker	Fancourt	Horatio	x		x	x		x					x
Susannah Huntsmen	Peasants		Player King		x	x	x		x					x
Mary Pierce	Mina	Kitty	Ophelia		x	x			x		x			x
Tyler Taylor	Dracula	Jack	Laertes		x	x	x		x		x		x	x
Vernon Volker	Dr. Seward		Claudius		x	x			x		x		x	x
Richfield Hawksley	Van Helsing	Spettigue	Polonius/Gravedigger		x	x			x		x		x	x
Daisy Coates	Peasants	Donna Lucia			x	x	x		x					x
Craig Conlin						x		x	x	x			x	
Sarah McKay						x	x	x	x			x	x	x
Henry Mills						x		x	x				x	
Brooke Oakes	Workman	Brasset				x			x				x	x
Karma Schneider	Peasants	Amy	Player Queen			x	x		x					x
Ian Milliken		Charley	Lucianus			x			x					

▓ **Fig. 16.10** French scene breakdown, characters by scene.

Accident Report

Employee(s) name(s): _____

_____

Time & date of accident/incident: _____

Job title(s) and department(s): _____

_____

Supervisor/lead person: _____

Witnesses: _____

_____

Brief description of the accident or incident: _____

_____

_____

Indicate body part affected:

Did the injured employee(s) see a doctor?   ( ) Yes ( ) No

If yes, did you file an employer's portion of a worker's compensation form?   ( ) Yes ( ) No

Did the injured employee(s) go home during their work shift?   ( ) Yes ( ) No

If yes, list the date and time injured employee(s) left job(s): _____

_____

Supervisor's Comments: _____

_____

What could have been done to prevent this accident/incident? _____

_____

Have the unsafe conditions been corrected?   ( ) Yes ( ) No

If yes, what has been done? _____

_____

If no, what needs to be done? _____

_____

_____

Employer or Supervisor's signature: _____

Date: _____

Additional comments/notes: _____

_____

_____

▓ **Fig. 16.11** Sample accident report from OSHA.

evaluate the situation to see if a doctor or ambulance is required. If the accident is minor and does not require professional medical intervention, potentially able to be remedied with an ice pack or bandage, you still need to fill out an accident report. Obviously, the most important thing is to get the injured person the help he or she needs, then—and only then—fill out the necessary paperwork.

For small incidents such as scratches or bruises you should be prepared to offer any items from your first aid kit, or the theatre's, to the injured person. You should not, however, directly give them any medications or apply any first aid directly to the injury. Unless—and there always is an *unless*—the person specifically asks you to. There are many medical and legal ramifications on this subject should something go wrong. Have plans in place for all contingencies—that is the best advice. Sometimes, after an accident, it is rather hectic. It is your job to keep everyone calm, deal with the situation, and get everyone focused again on rehearsal as soon as possible. And, don't forget to fill out the accident report.

Now is the time to begin putting together your script. Get a three-ring binder with dividers. You will get a copy of the script in one of two forms. The first way is to get a copy of the published script. You need to cut this script apart in order to have single pages. Now, get some paper that is the right size for your binder. Cut a square hole in the paper that slightly smaller than your script pages. Line the script pages up with the "frame" you created and glue or tape the script in place. The frame allows you to see both sides of each page. The other way to get a script, especially if it is an unpublished script, is on regular paper. So you have your script. Punch holes in it and put it in your binder. Use the other dividers for all the forms and spreadsheets you've been creating.

A big part of the stage manager's job during rehearsals is to take down the blocking in your script. Blocking, simply, is the actor's movement around the stage. It is important to notate this for several reasons. The first is that the actors are trying to remember their lines, develop their characters, and many other things. Remembering blocking is often difficult, so they may need a friendly reminder of when they move and to where. Throughout rehearsals, blocking may change several times so always work in pencil and always carry a *big* eraser. Blocking changes can be confusing for everyone, actors and directors alike. The stage manager should *always* have the most up-to-date version. Another

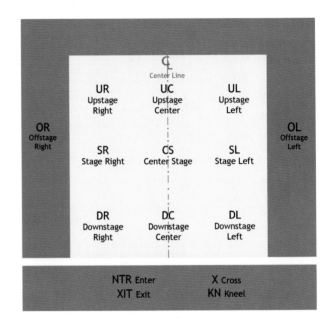

Fig. 16.12 Symbol key for taking blocking notes.

reason for taking down the blocking is for actor understudies, replacements or touchup rehearsals, especially during longer running shows. The stage manager is the person who works with the new actors to help provide a seamless transition between old and new cast members.

Blocking notation can be written in a wide variety of ways. A standard notation is taught in stage management classes (Figs. 16.12 and 16.13). The symbols are used in conjunction with arrows and the initials of the characters as needed for clarity. The standard symbols are important to use, so that anyone else can pick up your book and understand it. If you decide to create your own conventions, then only you can read it. Should you get sick or have to miss a rehearsal, then your assistant or the director will be at a major loss. Since the goal of the stage manager is to organize the production and keep it moving forward in an orderly way, using your own notation is not a good idea.

Throughout the course of rehearsals, you need to make notes about props. Some props are needed for rehearsal, others for the actual production. Certain props can function for both. Your notes should include not only hand props, which the actors handle, but also scenic props, such as furniture or specific pieces of scenic dressing mentioned by the script or through the actors' actions. Keep good notes about the props. They can change almost as frequently as the blocking. Make a spreadsheet of which actor(s) uses a prop, where he or she enters from when the prop is needed,

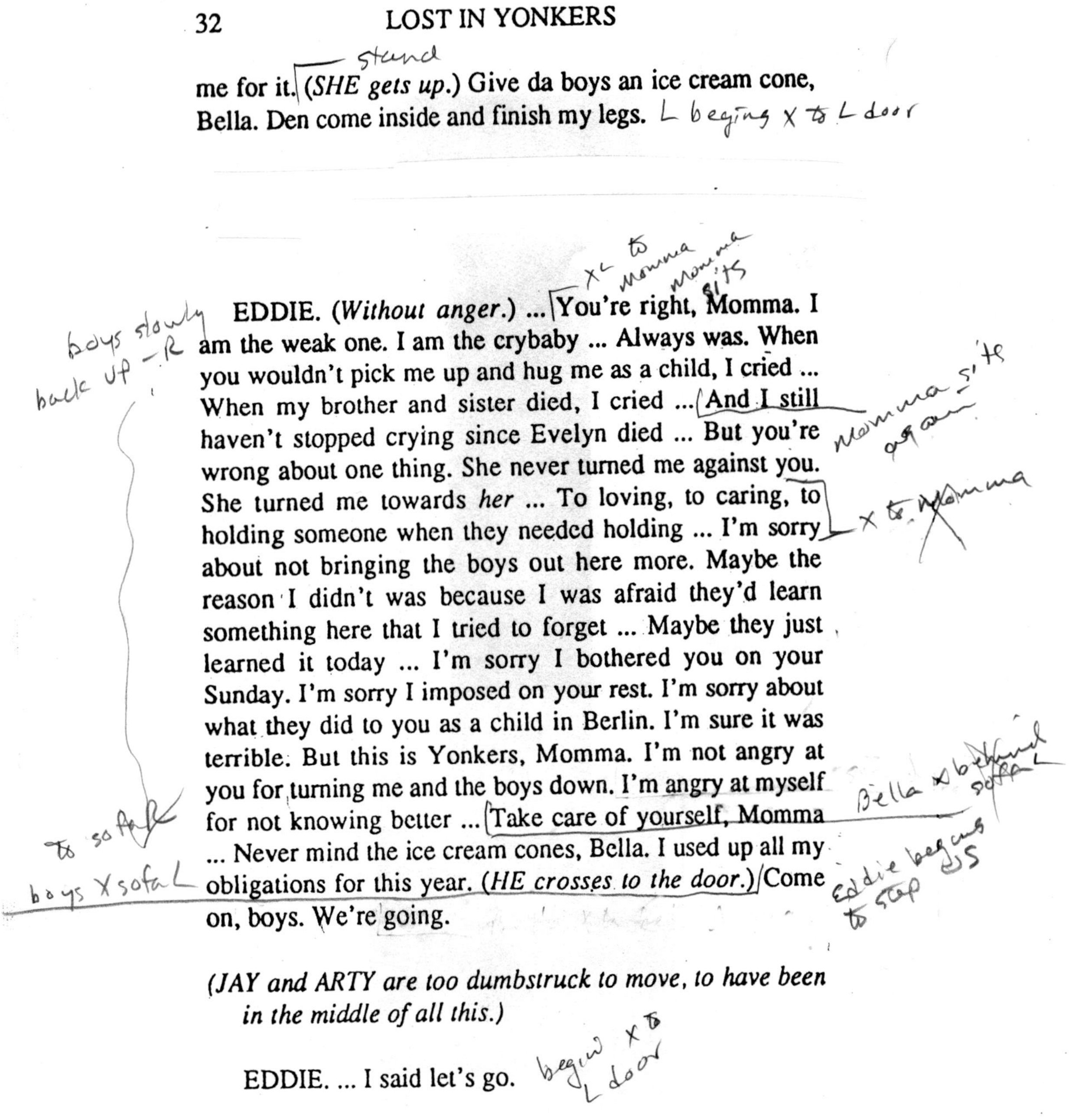

me for it. *(SHE gets up.)* Give da boys an ice cream cone,
Bella. Den come inside and finish my legs.

(handwritten: stand)
(handwritten: L begins X to L door)

EDDIE. *(Without anger.)* ... You're right, Momma. I
am the weak one. I am the crybaby ... Always was. When
you wouldn't pick me up and hug me as a child, I cried ...
When my brother and sister died, I cried ... And I still
haven't stopped crying since Evelyn died ... But you're
wrong about one thing. She never turned me against you.
She turned me towards *her* ... To loving, to caring, to
holding someone when they needed holding ... I'm sorry
about not bringing the boys out here more. Maybe the
reason I didn't was because I was afraid they'd learn
something here that I tried to forget ... Maybe they just
learned it today ... I'm sorry I bothered you on your
Sunday. I'm sorry I imposed on your rest. I'm sorry about
what they did to you as a child in Berlin. I'm sure it was
terrible. But this is Yonkers, Momma. I'm not angry at
you for turning me and the boys down. I'm angry at myself
for not knowing better ... Take care of yourself, Momma
... Never mind the ice cream cones, Bella. I used up all my
obligations for this year. *(HE crosses to the door.)* Come
on, boys. We're going.

(handwritten: boys slowly back up - R)
(handwritten: X L to Momma)
(handwritten: Momma sits)
(handwritten: Momma sits again)
(handwritten: X to Momma)
(handwritten: to sofa R)
(handwritten: boys X sofa L)
(handwritten: Bella X behind sofa L)
(handwritten: Eddie begins to step DS)

*(JAY and ARTY are too dumbstruck to move, to have been
    in the middle of all this.)*

EDDIE. ... I said let's go.

(handwritten: begin X to L door)

■ **Fig. 16.13** Sample blocking notes from a script.

which scene the prop is in, and when and where the prop
comes back offstage. Also, and very important, how does
the prop get offstage if the original actor doesn't carry it?
Often this crucial detail is forgotten until the technical
rehearsals, if you are not careful. This coordination is very
important and your spreadsheet will be the basis for a **prop**

breakdown (Fig. 16.14). Again, remember that the designers and technicians don't know what is going on in rehearsal
unless you tell them. The daily reports are critical, but so
is a comprehensive, coordinated list. A specific prop might
require "fitting" to an actor. Depending on the prop, you
need to coordinate with the scenic or costume designer and

<u>**Laughing Stock Prop Breakdown**</u>

Act 1-1

Gordon   flashlight

Act 1-2

Gordon	pictures/resumes
Gordon	scripts
Mary	flyer for "Epic of Gilgamesh"
Mary	bag
Tyler	script
Vernon	briefcase
Gordon	cell phone

Act 1-3

Craig	handouts - thick and impressive
Henry	script
Sarah	gin and tonic

Act 1-4

Act 1-5

Henry	Ethel's will
Henry	hat box with skull

Act 1-6

Jack	rehearsal skirt and wig
Gordon	hat box with skull
Braun	tea service w/4 cups, sugarer, creamer
Richfield	hat that can hold liquid
Sarah	stop watch

Act 1-7

Craig   several trays of coca-cola products

Act 1-8

Tyler	cape
Tyler	vampire teeth
Richfield	script

Act 1-9

Gordon   ghostlight

Act 2-1

Gordon	cell phone
Craig	several garbage bags of empty coca-cola products
Henry	roll of fabric
Henry	tiny pencil
Apprentices	straight ladder
Richfield	script

Act 2-2

Peasant woman	crucifix
Dracula	teeth
Dracula	door
Dracula	claw-like hand
Harker	change
Harker	eye drops
Harker	journal
Seward	newspaper "The Whitby Daily Telegraph, 8 August 1892"
Mina	diary, pen
Mina	letter from Professor Szgany
Harker	gun that doesn't fire
Braun	tea service
Mina	broken lighting instrument
Dracula	door
Van Helsing	exploding cross
Seward	pry bar
Karma	mallet and stake

Act 2-3

Gordon	Hamlet costume
Company	Chairs
Company	Costume Rack
Company	Props Table

Act 2-4

Brooke	cardboard box w/cantaloupe and magic marker
Sarah	tea
Henry	skull
Craig	pencils
Sarah	ghostlight

Act 2-5

Henry	hatbox
Sarah	2 drinks
Henry	skull
Susannah	dip on her head

Fig. 16.14 Sample prop breakdown.

Laughing Stock Costume Breakdown

		description	costume provided	personal clothes	accessories
Gordon Page	1-1	black pants, turtleneck, leather jacket		black pants, turtleneck, leather jacket	
	1-2	black pants, plain black T-shirt, leather jacket		black pants, plain black T-shirt, leather jacket	
	1-3	khaki pants, polo shirt	blue ss shirt	khaki pants	
	1-4	khaki pants, polo shirt		khaki pants, green polo shirt	
	1-5	khaki pants, polo shirt	maroon ss shirt	khaki pants	
	1-6	khaki pants, polo shirt		khaki pants, green polo shirt	
	1-7	khaki pants, polo shirt		khaki pants, polo shirt	
	1-9	khaki, polo, blazer		khaki, green polo, blazer	
	2-1	khaki pants, polo shirt		khaki pants, green polo shirt	
	2-3	tux pants, white shirt, black jacket		tux pants, white shirt, black jacket	
	2-4	Hamlet in Hamlet performance	beige/aqua tunic	black pants, white T-shirt	
	2-5	tux pants, white shirt, black jacket		tux pants, white shirt, black jacket	
Jack Morris	1-1	jeans, coat, hat, gloves		jeans, turtleneck, coat, hat, gloves	
	1-3	shorts, T-shirts		shorts, T-shirts	
	1-4	Harker of Dracula rehearsal	maroon pineapple shirt	shorts	
	1-6	Fancourt in Charley's Aunt rehearsal	dress, wig, hat, shoes, fan	jeans	
	2-2	Harker of Dracula performance	plaid vest	brown pants, green turtleneck	
	2-3	shorts, T-shirts		shorts, T-shirts	
	2-4	black jeans	navy tunic	black jeans	
	2-5	suit, dress shirt	blue sailboat shirt	blue or khaki pants	
Susannah Huntsmen	1-2	flowy dress	dress from costume stock	spaghetti strap top	
	1-3	spaghetti strap top, skirt	katia's dress		
	1-4	Bride of Dracula rehearsal	brown velvet hippie	khaki pants/skirt	
	1-6	flowy sleeves, pants	crocheted dress		
	2-2	Bride of Dracula performance	black skirt, cravat	white blosue	
	2-4	black pants, gravedigger	pink tunic	black pants	
	2-5	beaded dress	blue beaded dress		
Mary Pierce	1-2	very NYC - all in black, sexy and suggestive without her being aware of it.			black character shoes
	1-3	summer, first day of rehearsal	striped dress		shorts, T-shirts
	1-6	Kitty in Charley's Aunt rehearsal			shorts, T-shirts
	1-8	Mina in Dracula rehearsal	vintage gown/shawl		
	2-2	Mina in Dracula performance	vintage gown/shawl		
	2-4	Ophelia in Hamlet performance	yellow tunic	black pants	
	2-5	closing night attire	taupe sparkle gown		
Tyler Taylor	1-2	Typical "NYC actor" wanna be, jeans, loafers, no socks, jacket with scarf			jeans, shirt, jacket, scarf
	1-3	summer, first day of rehearsal			jean shorts, gray T-shirt
	1-4	Dracula in Dracula rehearsal			jean shorts, gray T-shirt
	1-6	Jack in Charley's Aunt rehearsal			khaki shorts, blue T-shirt
	1-8	black pants, white shirt	cape		khaki shorts, blue T-shirt
	2-1	summer casual			khaki shorts, colored T-shirt
	2-2	black pants, white shirt	cape		black pants, white shirt
	2-4	Laertes in Hamlet performance	yellow tabard		black pants, black shirt
	2-5	closing night attire			dark suit, white shirt, tie
Vernon Volker	1-2	pants, blazer, Steve Press's T-shirt	Steve's T-Shirt	jeans, blazer	
	1-3	jeans, button shirt	green ss shirt	khaki pants	
	1-6	jeans, button shirt		khaki pants, button shirt	
	1-8	Dr. Seward in Dracula rehearsal		khaki pants, button shirt	
	2-2	Dr. Seward in Dracula performance		sweater, black pants	
	2-3	jeans, button shirt		khaki pants, button shirt	
	2-4	black pants, Claudius	black/red costume	black pants	
	2-5	tuxedo		tuxedo	

Fig. 16.15 Sample costume breakdown.

schedule a time between the designer and the actor for the customization of the prop.

The costume breakdown is similar, in theory, to the prop breakdown (Fig. 16.15). Costume notes should include a description of the costume, the character name, accessories, what scene(s) it is worn in, and any special notations if a fast change is needed or if it needs a special effect to be rigged. Accessories can include jewelry, hats, undergarments, handbags, briefcases, canes, and the like. Special effects can include distressing, blood packs, tearaways, and so on. The individual notes are somewhat different from the props, although they can include related props as listed in Figure 16.15. The breakdown should be sent to the costume designer for verification. Keep in mind that part of creating the breakdown includes making actors available for all costume fittings as required by the costume designer.

CALLING SCRIPT

As rehearsals progress, the stage manager starts to accumulate even more information. Designers often begin coming to run-throughs to see how the show is shaping up. They make notes on what is needed within their designs to complete the director's vision and needs for the movement of the actors. It is your job to keep the designers informed of any changes that happen during rehearsals, so the designers are working with the most up-to-date information. The designers then go away to do their work and eventually begin to provide you with paperwork that will be needed once you get into the theatre for technical rehearsals. All of this compiled information turns your binder into the beginnings of your calling script. This then becomes *the* definitive authority for information about the show. The calling script is

Lost in Yonkers
Lighting Cue Synopsis

Cue	Time	Purpose	Placement	Page
97	5	Preset	1/2 Hour	5
98	5	Rita's Speech	Places	5
99	8	End Rita's Speech	FTB	5
		ACT 1 SCENE 1		
100	3	Sunlight	Actors in Place	5
100.1	6	Hot August Early Evening	AUTO FOLLOW	
101	6	Front Door	Knock on Door	10
102	12	Front Door out	Bella hugs boys	10
103	6	Momma Chair	"*Her back is killing her"	26
103.5	30	Momma Sits	Walls toward red	27
104	3	Fade to Momma Chair	"Won't that be fun Momma*"	34
104.1	2	FTB	AUTO FOLLOW	
		ACT 1 SCENE 2		
105	4	Moonlight	End of Voice Over	35
105.1	8	Late at Night	AUTO FOLLOW	
106	0	Light Switch	Jay turns off Table Lamp	37
107	3	Fade to Couch	"fingers chopped off*"	37
107.1	2	FTB	AUTO FOLLOW	
		ACT 1 SCENE 3		
108	3	Sunlight	End of Voice Over	38
108.1	6	Sunday Afternoon	AUTO FOLLOW	
109	2	Fade to Couch	"Jew in Alabama*"	43
109.1	1	FTB	AUTO FOLLOW	
		ACT 1 SCENE 4		
110	3	Moonlight	End of Voice Over	44
110.1	6	Midnight	AUTO FOLLOW	
111	0	Table Lamp On	Louie turns on lamp	45
111.1	15	Walls up	AUTO FOLLOW	
112	0	Table Lamp Off	Jay turns off Table Lamp	53
113	3	Fade to Couch	"Save it*"	53
113.1	2	FTB	AUTO FOLLOW	53
		INTERMISSION		
197	5	Preset	Actors Clear	53
198	5	House to Half	Places	53
199	8	House Out	When Ready	53
		ACT 2 SCENE 1		
200	3	Sunlight	End of Voice Over	55
200.1	6	Weekday Daytime	AUTO FOLLOW	55
200.5	30		Bella Enter	63
201	8	Reinforce Jay's speech	"*Don't do it"	71
202	12	Restore	"What's moxie*"	72

Fig. 16.16 Sample light cue synopsis.

sometimes a completely different copy of the script than what you have been using so far for rehearsals, but often it is the same.

As technical rehearsals approach, the lighting designer needs to give you information regarding when the light cues are to happen. He or she should also give you an idea of how long the lighting change takes to happen and a brief idea of what the change does (Fig. 16.16). This is the only way you know what to expect and how to anticipate other cues that you need to call. The sound designer does the same. If there are a lot of scenery movements, motorized or not, the technical director may give you a similar list. These cues need to be noted in the calling script along with warnings and standbys for the cues.

The last thing you might do in the rehearsal space is block out the curtain calls. This may not happen until you are in the theatre. Either way, it is good to have it written down. You want to know the order in which the actors appear, where they come from, and whether they appear by themselves or in groups. A great deal of political craziness goes on with the curtain call order. Stay out of that part of it and let the director work it out. Simply document what is supposed to happen.

TECHNICAL REHEARSALS

Oh goody! You finally made it into the theatre. Now, what? Well, frankly, the only guarantee is that craziness will ensue. The actors have finally begun to feel at home in the rehearsal studio, and now they have to get used to the stage. The long-awaited crew has finally shown up and has to get to know each other. The director, and everyone else, has suddenly realized that the show is *actually* going to happen. Holy crap! OK, keep calm. You are probably the only one who can and needs to. Here is the deal.

As stage manager, you have now become the captain of the ship. You set the call times for crew and cast. You also establish the schedule for what should happen in the rehearsal. Of course, you don't do all this by yourself. You consult with the director, designers, and union representatives, if they exist. There are many details to deal with in the theatre. Your assistants and crew should help with all of this.

The actors need to be assigned dressing rooms. You can make a chart for this that shows the location of the dressing room and the names of the actors who are assigned to it. Each dressing room should also be labeled so there is no

confusion. The green room needs to be established, where everyone can relax between rehearsal scenes and before shows. Even small details like which restaurants in the area deliver and where the closest Starbucks is are pieces of information that make life easier.

The sound department is responsible for getting and setting up the headset you need to talk to the technical crew. However, you must let them know where you want headset stations, as well as if the stations can be wired or must be wireless. Headset systems can also have multiple channels. This is critical for communication in two ways. People must be able to talk to those with whom they need to communicate and, more important, not to talk to those they don't need access to. If everyone is on one channel, the chatter can become overwhelming. If one channel is all you can get, then you have to be very strict about who talks and when.

The sound department can also provide a paging "God" microphone. The paging mic is set up so that you can make theatrewide announcements. There should be speakers in the dressing rooms, green room, backstage, control booth, and so forth. You won't use this when there is an audience in the house, but it is very handy during rehearsals. The God microphone is used during technical rehearsals, so that those not on headset can hear any special information or announcement that must be made to the whole company. We used to just yell, but the microphone saves us a sore throat or even worse, laryngitis!

The lighting department can provide cue lights if needed. Visual cues work great but only if you can actually see each other. Headset cues work great, but only if you have enough headsets for everyone. Cue lights can be placed in locations around the set and the theatre where visual or headset cues are not an option. Cue lights are small lights that can be different colors. You establish with your cast and crew what the cue light colors mean as well as whether the light is on, off, or blinking—and then all should go smoothly. Cue light products now are available that make this idea much easier to set up. GAM Products recently came out with with the Go-Lite™ system (Fig. 16.17). All connections are with RJ-25 cable, regular phone wire. You can link up to 20 boxes in a series. Use standard six-wire phone cable to link 20 or more in series. Control the four LED cue lights, white, red, blue, and green, with the GAM four-way controller and power

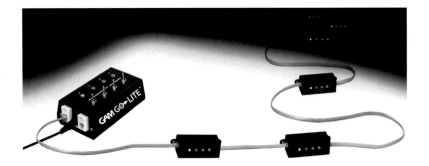

■ **Fig. 16.17** GAM Products Go-Lite, the cue light solution.

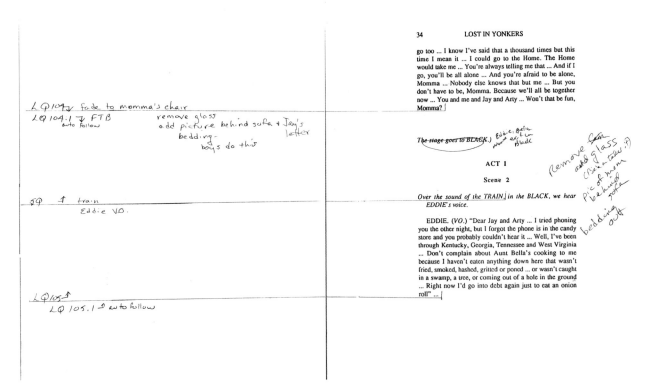

LQ 104 ↓ fade to momma's chair
LQ 104.1 ↓ FTB
auto follow
remove glass
add picture behind sofa & Jay's letter
bedding-
boys do this

SQ ↑ train
Eddie V.O.

LQ 105 ↑
LQ 105.1 ↑ auto follow

34   LOST IN YONKERS

go too ... I know I've said that a thousand times but this
time I mean it ... I could go to the Home. The Home
would take me ... You're always telling me that ... And if I
go, you'll be all alone ... And you're afraid to be alone,
Momma ... Nobody else knows that but me ... But you
don't have to be, Momma. Because we'll all be together
now ... You and me and Jay and Arty ... Won't that be fun,
Momma?

~~The stage goes to BLACK.~~ Eddie, Bella must exit in Black

ACT I

Scene 2

*Over the sound of the TRAIN, in the BLACK, we hear
EDDIE's voice.*

EDDIE. (*VO.*) "Dear Jay and Arty ... I tried phoning
you the other night, but I forgot the phone is in the candy
store and you probably couldn't hear it ... Well, I've been
through Kentucky, Georgia, Tennessee and West Virginia
... Don't complain about Aunt Bella's cooking to me
because I haven't eaten anything down here that wasn't
fried, smoked, hashed, gritted or poned ... or wasn't caught
in a swamp, a tree, or coming out of a hole in the ground
... Right now I'd go into debt again just to eat an onion
roll" ...

Remove glass add glass (Bella takes?) pic of mom behind sofa bedding out

■ **Fig. 16.18** Sample calling script.

supply. Place the control box anywhere convenient for you.
Go-Lite can also be controlled from a DMX Go-Lite
power supply to operate from your show's light board.
Rack mount controls are also available.

The calling script that we already talked about
becomes the most important binder of paperwork at this
point in the process (Fig. 16.18). A copy should always
be left at the theatre and a copy taken home, just in

case. The calling script should be viewed as the show's
blueprint. All cues, warnings, standbys, and gos should
be clearly labeled for all departments. This can include
color coding the different departments' cues. Remember
those highlights and post-it notes? Well, now is the time
they really come in handy. Let me explain.

For the technicians to be able to execute their technical movements, the stage manager has to let them know

Fig. 16.19 Global Design Systems SM Console.

that the cue is coming up soon. This is called a warning. A standby means the cue is imminent. The go should be obvious, but just in case it's not, *go* means do the cue! *Never* joke around or say "go" when you don't mean it, or things will happen that you didn't intend. Most stage managers go so far as to spell it, g-o, if they have to use the word for another meaning. Your calls should always be acknowledged: warned, standing by, going. Otherwise, you won't know if they have been heard and are being done.

If the placement for the stage manager to call the show does not provide adequate visibility of the stage, you can request a video monitor. This works well if a camera is out in the house on a balcony, if it exists. The camera is set to give a full view of the stage. A monitor is then placed at your station so you can see everything. This becomes critical if you have lots of moving scenery, as the video camera can be set up to get the image even in very low-light situations. Other possible camera locations that can be useful are in the orchestra pit, pointing toward the conductor, and possibly in the green room. These cameras can be particularly useful if there are large scenic elements moving during the show that prevent areas of the stage from being seen.

It is important for the stage manager to have visual as well as physical access to all areas of backstage in case of emergencies. Therefore the positioning of the stage manager is usually downstage left or right, depending on the layout of the theatre. It is a complicated position to set up, as the stage manager needs plenty of room for the calling script, headset station, video monitors, and so forth. A few companies now make customized desks with everything built in. And by everything, I mean communications, video monitors, God microphones, and so on.

GDS Design Systems is one of those companies. The enclosures can be either fiberglass or wood. SM Console is ideally suited for a range of venues that require 12–24 cue light channels (Fig. 16.19). Additional touch panels for working light controls and a further 19" panel section on the right for extra facilities. The larger console case can be made any width, depending on the facilities required. In general, the left section is reserved for clocks, timers, and intercom; the middle section is cue lights; with functions such as paging and intercom on the right panel. The cue light section normally comes with a padded wrist rest for the operator when using cue lights. LED Littlelites and a digital step dimmers are supplied as standard.

PERFORMANCES

So, by now I hope you've gotten through the technical rehearsals. You're now ready for previews and performances. The next thing to formulate is the preshow checklist. This list should include *everything* that must be set up before you start the show. It should include checking props, placing furniture, setting any scenery that moves to the starting position, making food or drinks, setting any effects to be ready. You get the idea. Keep in mind that you don't personally do all these things. But you have to check to make sure they've been done, including lighting and sound checks.

The call time for the actors is set based on how much time they need to get ready. This is usually an hour to an hour and a half prior to curtain time. This is the prep time for actors to get into hair, makeup, and costume. They also warm up during this time and do whatever preparatory work they need to get into character. Half hour is then called using the paging mic. This lets everyone know that you are opening the house to the audience and that they can no longer walk into the house. Places is called a few minutes before the show begins. This means that all actors and technicians should go immediately to the positions where they will be needed to start the show.

During each performance, the stage manager continues to keep notes for each department. These performance notes include any problems that may have arisen during the performance, such as a broken prop or ripped costume. The stage manager continues to be responsible for disseminating all of this information. These reports are added to your files and follow-up must be done to make sure problems have been dealt with in a timely fashion, usually before the next performance.

Accident report

Audition form

Blocking

Calling script

Call time

Contact sheet

Costume breakdown

Cue lights

Curtain calls

Daily rehearsal report

French scene breakdown

Go

Half hour

Places

Preshow checklist

Prop breakdown

Rehearsal schedule

Sign-in sheet

Standby

Stage manager kit

Warning

CHAPTER SIXTEEN

Study Words

What's Next?

Career Choices

OK. Great! You learned all this stuff. We're almost at the end of the book. Ideally you had fun learning and are now wondering, "What is next?" Everybody always tells you that you can't make a living in the theatre, right? Wrong! The first thing you need to think about before you look for a job is this: Do I really want to work in the theatre? Huh? What am I talking about? OK, now pay attention, this is important.

Being successful isn't about getting a prestigious job, having your name in lights, or making a boatload of money. If it isn't about those things you might ask, then what is it about? Well, it's about *passion*. Your passion. What do you love to do? What would you miss the most if you could no longer do it? For some people, the answer is theatre. The job itself doesn't matter; just being a part of the theatre is enough. For others, it is very specific, say, makeup. They can do makeup in any situation and be happy; it isn't limited to theatre makeup. Only once you identify your passion will you be able to truly find a position, a job, and a vocation!

> There's a lot of different kinds of jobs out there, and not everyone ends up being a designer or stagehand.
>
> **— Anne Johnson**

This chapter works through how to take this new knowledge and excitement to find all the places you might find employment.

Many job opportunities are out there, some of which are actually related to the theatre. Many of the possibilities are in related fields, and some are in what seems at first to be totally unrelated fields. We explore all these options to make sure your training gets put to good use and in an area where you will be happy.

> ### Useless Factoid: Bad Dress Rehearsal—Good Opening
>
> There is a saying that "a bad dress rehearsal will equal a good opening night." It might have started with a producer who had a show underway that had an absolute disastrous dress rehearsal. Not knowing how else to build morale, the producer glibly invented a quick excuse: "Well, you know the old saying that a bad dress rehearsal guarantees a great show!" And that propaganda is hauled out by its hind legs every time a dress rehearsal goes down the tubes. Plah! Most times, a cruddy dress rehearsal means a cruddy opening; a potent dress rehearsal, on the other hand, builds confidence and morale and it is a marvelous high leaping off place for the growth that will follow.

THEATRE CAREERS

Theatre jobs. OK, we discussed these and most of you have now had experience with some of them, or at the very least working with people who do these jobs. Let's make a list.

Box office manager

Carpenter

Company manager

Costume designer

Director

Electrician

Engineer

Flyman

Follow spot operator

General manager

House manager

Lightboard operator

Lighting designer

Makeup artist

Master carpenter

Master electrician

Playwright

Producer

Production manager

Project manager

Projection designer

Prop master

Publicist

Rentals supervisor

Rigger

Scenic artist

Scenic designer

Sound designer

Sound operator

Special effects designer

Special effects technician

Stagehand

Stage manager

Technical director

Technical supervisor

Wardrobe

Welder

Keep in mind that every one of these jobs has the potential for associates, assistants, and entire staffs within the department. There are also specialties within each department that aren't listed, as these specialties are endless. Every time a new technology is introduced to the theatre, it causes new jobs to be created to keep up with the demand.

A quick word about unions. Various unions, in certain situations, can represent many of the jobs just listed. Some of the same jobs are nonunion positions in other situations.

If union jurisdiction applies to a job you want to do, contact the union. Many have apprenticeship programs that help you to gain admission to the appropriate union. There are different unions for each job, depending on whether you want to work in theatre, television, or film. All of this can seem overwhelming at first. Don't panic. Just take it one step at a time.

Let's take a look at a few job descriptions. You might be surprised at what each position does. I won't go into each job from the list, but the following should give you a pretty good idea of what the business of show business is really like.

BOX OFFICE MANAGER

The box office manager's responsibilities include overseeing all ticketing and accounting, including daily receipts, deposits, and cash handling; supervising, instructing, and training all box office personnel; and maintaining and monitoring the electronic ticketing system. Other possible duties include partnering with event promoters and appropriate facility personnel to establish ticket pricing and seating configurations, updating management and promoters with ticket sales information, preparing final box office reports, completing event settlements, and establishing files on each event that consist of seats on hold for the building and promoter, complimentary ticket vouchers, event audits, and ticket inventory schedules.

COMPANY MANAGER

The company manager's responsibilities include traveling, accommodations, and day-to-day needs of the acting, design, and technical company members. Often included are renting apartments and hotel rooms, booking plane tickets, dealing with furnishing and cleaning for rented apartments, and dealing with special needs and requests.

COSTUME DESIGNER

Costume designers seek to enhance a character's persona, within the framework of the director's vision, through the way that character is dressed. At the same time, the designer must ensure that the designs allow the actor to move in a manner consistent with the historical period and enables the actor to execute the director's blocking of the production without damage to the garments. Additional considerations include the durability and washability of garments, particularly in extended runs. The designer must work in consultation with not only the director, but also the set and lighting designers to ensure that the overall design of the production works together. The costume designer needs to possess strong artistic capabilities as well as a thorough knowledge of pattern development, draping, drafting, textiles, and costume and fashion history.

DIRECTOR

Directors oversee and orchestrate the mounting of a theatre production (a play, an opera, a musical, or a devised piece of work) by unifying various endeavors and aspects of production. The director's function is to ensure the quality and completeness of theatre production and lead the members of the creative team into realizing their artistic vision for it. The director, therefore, collaborates with a team of creative individuals and other staff, coordinating research, stagecraft, costume design, props, lighting design, acting, set design, and sound design for the production. If the production he or she is mounting is a new piece of writing or a (new) translation of a play, the director may also work with the playwright or translator. Directors also preside over the auditioning process as well as all rehearsals, guiding actors, designers, and all other staff toward their vision.

> The reason I became a dancer is because I asked myself at a certain point, "What do you do best?" And I said, "Dance." And then I said, "Well, that's a stupid choice to make, there's no career to be made in dance, this is really foolish." And I said, "Too bad, this is what I do best, and this is what I'm going to do." Because in a way I owe it, to whatever, whomever, wherever I come from, to do that. The commitment is ever absolute. And that is what faith is about.
>
> —Twyla Tharp

HOUSE MANAGER

The house manager's responsibilities include the selling of tickets, the ushering of patrons in front-of-house areas, and the maintenance and management of the theatre building itself. House management staff usually work for the theatre, under the supervision of the house manager, and not for the theatrical company that is currently occupying it. Often, in regional or smaller theatres, the responsibility falls under the aegis of the production manager. In any case, house management works closely with the production management team for the presentation of the theatrical production.

LIGHTING DESIGNER

Lighting designers are responsible for creating the overall mood or feeling of the show utilizing the ethereal concept of lighting and shadow. They read the script carefully and make notes on changes in place and time and have meetings with the director, designers, stage manager, and production manager during the preproduction period to discuss ideas for the show and establish budget and scheduling details. They also attend several later rehearsals to observe the way the actors are being directed to use the stage area (blocking) during different scenes and receive updates from the stage manager on any changes that occur. It is also important for them to make sure they have an accurate plan of the theatre's lighting positions and a list of their equipment, as well as an accurate copy of the set design, especially the ground plan and section.

PRODUCER

The producer is the person ultimately responsible for overseeing all aspects of mounting a theatre production. The producer finds the script and the director, then begins the primary goal, which is to balance and coordinate the business and financial aspects of mounting the show in the service of the creative realization of the production's vision. This may or may not include casting, but often includes casting approval. The producer is responsible for securing funds for the production, either through his or her own company or by taking on investors. The producer will have optioned the play from the playwright, which would include all rights including film and television rights, if the production will enhance their value, and may include the royalty agreement. Then comes the time to work with theatrical agents, negotiate with the unions, find other staff, secure the theatre and rehearsal hall, obtain liability and workers' compensation insurance, and post bonds with the unions.

> Why didn't I listen to my mother and become a lawyer so I could be producing this and taking home real money.
> —Michael A. Fink

The producer also hires the production team including the general manager, production manager, house manager, stage manager, and the like at his or her own discretion. In many cases, the producer is required to use front-of-house people (such as the house manager, box office manager, and ushers) and backstage personnel (stagehands, electricians, carpenters, etc.) supplied by the theatre owner. The owner sets ticket prices, performance dates and times, and develops a marketing and advertising strategy for the production. The hiring of a publicist and marketing team is one of the most important responsibilities of the producer. Last, the producer hires accountants and perhaps already has legal representation.

PRODUCTION MANAGER

The production manager's responsibilities include coordinating the operations of various production departments including scenic, wardrobe, lighting, sound, projection, automation, video, pyrotechnics, and stage management. In addition to management and financial skills, a production manager must have detailed knowledge of all production disciplines including a thorough understanding of the interaction of these disciplines during the production process. This may involve dealing with matters ranging from the procurement of staff, materials, and services, to freight, customs coordination, telecommunications, labor relations, logistics, information technology, government liaison, venue booking, scheduling, operations management, and workplace safety.

PROJECT MANAGER

The project manager's responsibilities include the planning, execution, and closing of any project. A project manager is the person accountable for accomplishing the project's objectives. Project management responsibilities include creating clear and attainable objectives, building the project requirements, setting deadlines, overseeing budgets, and managing the triple constraint for projects, which is cost, time, and scope. The project manager is with the production from its inception through striking the production after closing.

RIGGER

Riggers specialize in the lifting and moving extremely large or heavy objects. Riggers tend to be highly specialized in moving elements that cannot be accomplished by ordinary means, and use equipment expressly designed for moving and lifting objects weighing hundreds of thousands or even millions of pounds in places where ordinary material-handling equipment cannot go. There are two main divisions of riggers in entertainment, theatrical and arena. The main difference is that arena riggers need to be trained in high steel work. Because of the highly specialized nature of the work riggers do, it is one of the few remaining occupations that can be learned only by apprenticeship. Riggers must work together as a cohesive team, and there must be an environment of trust among riggers because of the potentially dangerous nature of rigging.

SCENIC ARTIST

The scenic artist's responsibilities include reproducing color, texture, and aging of all building surfaces, whether they be two dimensional or three dimensional. They also interpret the scenic designer's sketches, models, and paint elevations to establish the best supplies and techniques to achieve the design. Similar to rigging, due to the highly specialized nature of the work, it is one of the few remaining occupations that has an extensive apprenticeship program.

SCENIC DESIGNER

Scenic designers are responsible for collaborating with the director and other members of the production design team to create an environment for the production and communication of the details of this environment to the technical director, production manager, charge scenic artist, and prop master. The designer is also responsible for creating scale models of the scenery, renderings, paint elevations, and scaled drawings as part of the communication with other production staff.

The scenic designer must possess strong artistic capabilities as well as a thorough knowledge of architectural history, color and symbol meanings, and building. In Europe and Australia, scenic designers take a more holistic approach to theatrical design and often are responsible not only for scenic design but costume, lighting, and sound, and are referred to as *theatre designers*, *scenographers*, or *production designers*.

SOUND DESIGNER

Currently, it can be said that there are two variants of theatrical sound design. Both are equally important but very different, though their functions usually overlap. Often a single sound designer fills both these roles, and although on a large-budget production, two sound designers may work together, for the most part there is only one sound designer for a given production. Where such distinctions are made, the first variant is technical sound design (which has also been termed *theatre sound system design* by the United States Institute for Theatre Technology's [USITT] Sound Design Commission), and the second is *conceptual sound design* (which has also been termed *theatre sound score design* by the USITT). These terms are really examples only and not generally used in practice, since most sound designers simply call themselves *sound designers*, no matter which role they are filling primarily.

Technical sound design requires the sound designer to design the sound system that fulfills the needs of the production. If a sound system is already installed in the venue, it is the sound designer's job to tune the system for the best use for the given production using various methods including equalization, delay, volume, and speaker and microphone placement; and this may include the addition of equipment not already provided. In conjunction with the director and musical director, if any, they also determine the use and placement of microphones for actors and musicians. They make sure that the performance can be heard and understood by everyone in the audience, no matter how large the room, and that the performers can hear everything they need to in order to do their job.

Conceptual sound design is very different from technical sound design but equally important. The designer must first read the play and talk to the production's director about what themes and messages they want to explore. It is here that, in conjunction with the director and possibly the composer, the designer decides what sounds he or she will use to create the mood and setting of the play. He or she may also choose or compose specific music for the play, although the final choice typically lies with the director, who may want nothing but scene change music or, at the other extreme, ambient beds under every scene. Many sound designers are indeed accomplished composers, writing and producing music for productions as well as designing sound. With these designers, it is often difficult to discern the line between sound design and music.

STAGE MANAGEMENT

The stage manager acts as an adjunct to the director in rehearsal, recording the blocking and seeing that cast members stay on script, have necessary props, and follow the blocking. As the lighting, sound, and set change cues are developed, the stage manager meticulously records each as it relates to the script and other aspects of the performance. Once the house opens, the stage manager essentially takes control, calling the cues for all transitions (this is known as *calling the show*) as well as acting as the communications hub for the cast and crew. After a show opens, the stage manager is also responsible for calling brush-up, put-in, and understudy rehearsals to make sure that the show's quality is maintained.

TECHNICAL DIRECTOR

It is a technical director's job to make sure the technical equipment in the theatre is cleaned and safe, although these duties may be delegated to a shop or house manager. For a specific production, the technical director is responsible for working closely with the scenic designer and director. It is his or her responsibility to determine how the scenery will be built, out of what materials, and to oversee the implementation of all elements.

INTERVIEWS

OK, so that should give you an idea of the theatre jobs and what they entail. There are many other theatre jobs, but here is the key: What common traits do you need to land a job? Well, you need to be a responsible person, follow through on tasks, take initiative, and have a love of the *theatre* that inspires you to learn what you need so that you can stay in the business.

> Keep up the good work . . . whoever you are!
>
> —Noel Coward

OK, great you say. So what can I do other than theatre work with all these fabulous skills? Well, have I got answers for you: television, film, architecture, advertising, Internet design, gaming, military, to name just a few. Or maybe you'll find some combination that works for you. Perhaps, you'll get a job in a related field working full-time with benefits and vacations, and you'll use your vacation time to do shows. Oh, yeah, and how do you get that all-important job so you can show yourself off? I interviewed many people who all have one thing in common—theatre training. Here are a few stories from their travels.

FERNANDO BERMUDEZ INTERVIEW

Theatrical design training gives you the basic knowledge you need to design for all of the performing arts. The method you use in theatre design can be applied to all the different forms of design for the performing arts. You need a concept, research, a design and production process, as well as evaluation of the product with directors and producers. I see this going on, not only in my professional career as a television costume designer but as a teacher as well. I teach students how to design for the theatre, and at the end, they choose a variety of professions. Some of them do theatre, others movies or television, or even advertising. They choose what interests them the most. At the end, the method fits every shoe! By understanding the way a theatre designer works, you are able to be in touch with literary analysis; understanding characters through light, sets, or costumes; learn how to communicate atmospheres or personalities; manage budgets; and understand production. All of these are essential parts in the craft of designing for the performing arts. My job as a costume designer for television is not much different than that of a theatre designer. Only the timing changes. . . . Television is an ongoing process, it never ends, or at least it feels that way, as some projects can last for a year or more. You work on a show or series for maybe 10 to 12 months and then you might move to another one. Theatre and film don't usually take this long. Television is more immediate. You need to change design choices according to ratings *or* because no story is ever fully developed. Things change and you must be ready for this.

GRACE BRANDT INTERVIEW

In high school, I painted backdrops for the school plays. I have a very heavy art background. Both my mother and grandmother were artists. In college, I became an art major, then found the theatre department, which led me to set design. I loved scenic painting immediately and moved to NYC as soon as I could. I knocked on Joe Papp's door and he answered. I was very naïve. I was new and nonunion.... I ended up meeting a scenic artist and took the apprentice exam at USA—and passed! I made it my mission to know all the scenic artists and know their stories. I spent a lot of time cutting paper for all painters just to learn from them. You have to want it really, really bad!

HEATHER CARSON INTERVIEW

After 32 years of lighting shows, I find myself focused solely on being a visual artist these days. Without realizing it at the time, my theatre work functioned as an artistic practice—meaning that each piece built on the last. When I was 28, my dad gave me the book *Seeing Is Forgetting the Name of the Thing One Sees*, the seminal book by Lawrence Wechsler. It's a meditation on the work of artist Robert Irwin, one of the key members of the Light and Space art movement birthed in Los Angeles, California. Up to that point, it had never occurred to me that you could make "art" with light.

In 1995, I did my first lighting installation as part of Elizabeth Streb's *Action Occupation* performance that reopened the Temporary Contemporary Museum (MOCA) in Los Angeles. My work for Streb was static—for each piece she created, I did a response to the structure she was interacting with and a response to the architecture of the movement. The structure was lit, when the movement started the lights changed and when it finished the lights went out. Or, as it evolved, the piece would end in a white-out instead of a blackout—with a quick flash of light flooding the audience as the lights simultaneously went out on the performers before going to total black.

Somehow, it came about that I proposed making a piece that was just about light. I wanted it to be "before" the performance—both spatially and temporally. It was called *up/Down*. A grid of fluorescents facing up mirrored the lines in the wooden beamed ceiling; and a grid of sodiums facing down echoed the number of panels in the skylights above. The lights facing up went on, the lights facing down were added, then just the lights facing down were left on. That was the sequence—up/down—and it kept repeating from the time the audience entered until the performance began.

Little did I know that I would continue exploring the grid for the next 15 years, using the language of sodium vapor and fluorescent light to explore interior and exterior volumes of light. At that time, my lighting career had just taken off and I was primarily lighting opera in Europe. Shortly after that, I read about a place called the Skowhegan School of Painting and Sculpture, a 9 week summer residency. You are given room and board and your own studio. You can do whatever you like and are heavily mentored by visiting and in residence guest artists as well as weekly lectures. It was transformative for me to spend that kind of time with young artists – most were in their 20s and I was in my late 30s. While there, I made three pieces.

I began to realize that what I was doing was installation, sculpture, emerging art, etc. and realized there were many opportunities for this. I received a NY Foundation for the Arts Artists Grant in Architecture/Experimental forms. A few years after that I received The Rome Prize in Design Arts. I was the first lighting designer to receive it and now it is listed as one of the categories. During my 6 months in Rome I made two pieces. A few years after that, I got another NYFA grant to make another piece. And so I continued, lighting shows and doing my own work when I had the time or the funds, or the opportunity arose.

In 2004, I moved back to LA to head the lighting program at Cal Arts. I took advantage of that shift to get an artist's studio for the first time and commit to a studio practice. In 2006, I was invited by the same curator who had curated the Streb piece all those years ago, Julie Lazar, to be in my first "real" gallery exhibition. Shortly after that, I was asked to do an exhibition by Liza Simone of Phantom Galleries LA, which presents work in empty storefronts. That piece was seen by Doug Chrismas of Ace Gallery and he signed me immediately on seeing it.

And so all these years later, I find myself back where I started out, but having come full circle to creating my own work. The theatre was the place where I developed all my ideas. It's where I sat in the dark, hour after hour, looking and thinking, making small adjustments, looking again. There is absolutely no way I would be making the work I'm making now without having spent all those years in the theatre and specifically in New York.

ANNE JOHNSON INTERVIEW

I have a BFA in dance.... I started at Production Arts in 1985, working in the office. It was supposed to be my day job while I stage managed at night. Madonna's Who's That

Girl tour wanted to use the projectors but no one knew how to pack projections for touring. They needed good road boxes, needed spares, needed tech, etc. I learned a lot quickly. We got the call about the Steel Wheels tour right after the Madonna tour. By 1988, I was working full-time doing projection stuff. It was so different from lighting and 3D scenery; I really liked it. A couple of years ago, video started to approach the brightness and contrast to be usable in the theatre. When new technology starts in theatre, there is a big growth curve. Now, with media servers, you can make instant changes to the projections. Video has decreased the desire for still projections. The technology creates lots of new positions for the creative and technical team. You have to be willing to make the leap.

MICHAEL RIZZO INTERVIEW

I left NYC in 1987 because the theatre industry was a dead end for me. How could I've decided this having just graduated from NYU Tisch School of the Arts just two years earlier? Once graduated and out in the world, it was obvious that New York theatre supported a finite and highly coveted population of professionals. Although passion and longevity would have been essential to maintain even a basic foothold, the payoff was not assured and unlikely at best. At the same time, a friend was headed toward Los Angeles with extra room for some basic essentials, so I closed up my life and copiloted the self-drive van to the West Coast. Granted this was a cavalier thing for someone with no connections or hope for ready-made work, but I saw the same opportunity available to me, an eager newcomer, on both coasts. The only difference was LA, city of reinvention, held the promise of Hollywood and a more tangible kind of immortality. My hunch turned out to be dead-on for two reasons: a larger industry base and my theatre training. Broadway is a tiny creative community tucked securely into the bustling northeast corner of the country. It is insular and self-driven—a complete ecosystem. Hollywood was and still is no longer in a centralized, studio-driven location; its expansion into Canada, Europe, and right-to-work states in America allowed me to work in locations I would've only imagined had I stayed put and carved a niche onstage. On top of that, my new employers on independent film projects were welcoming and the work was dependably steady. I had little difficulty adjusting myself to the fast and furious pace. The social nature of the business was familiar enough, as were the large egos I had previously encountered. My transition was relatively easy. Mind you, none of this would've been possible without my comprehensive and practical theatre training borne from firsthand experience in regional theatre and Off-Broadway. I unwittingly drove away from the richness of my creative development fully prepared to perform as a "can-do" lighting tech, costumer, scenic painter, or draftsman/designer in any situation I encountered. Without the depth of such a technical/creative foundation, my emergence as a successful art director would've had little chance of happening. Although there are noticeable differences in each of these media, the basis of design for a play manuscript or TV/film screenplay is the same: the translation of the literature into an appropriate visual concept. I simply transferred my knowledge of theatre craft directly into the other media.

> I can't make you a great dancer . .. or even a good dancer. But, if you keep trying and don't quit, I know I can make you a better dancer.
>
> —Joe Gideon, *All that Jazz*

APPENDICES
Still Confused?

A

Accessory slot

Also known as the drop-in slot, this is a slot in a leko near the shutters made to hold specialized accessories.

Accident report

This form is to be filled out *every* time there is some sort of accident, so that everything is documented.

Acetate

Acetate is low in cost and has good draping qualities.

Acoustics

Acoustics refers to the inherent sound qualities of a room in regard to the overall audio quality when no reinforcement is in use.

Additive

Additive color mixing means, when all three primary colors of light are mixed together in equal parts, they make white light.

Adhesives

These are products that will make things stick to the actor. They are used for things such as glitter, sparkles, and hair pieces.

Adjustable wrench

Often called a *crescent wrench*, it is an open-ended wrench with one fixed jaw and one adjustable jaw. The adjustment works by a screw positioned within the handle.

Allen keys

This is a tool with a hexagonal head for adjusting screws or bolts with a recessed six-sided opening.

Alternating current

AC is electric current whose direction reverses cyclically.

Ambient noise

This is the sound in a room when there is no planned audio source.

Ampere

Amp (A) is a unit of electric current, or amount of electric charge per second.

Amplifier

An amplifier boosts the output to a level that drives the loudspeaker.

AMX

Analog multiplex is a control signal used to control SCR dimmers.

Analogous

This describes a number of different hues, instead of just one, that come from within the same area of the color wheel.

Apron

This is the area of the stage that extends downstage of the proscenium arch.

Arbor

An arbor is a carriage or rack that contains weights, usually of cast iron, called *pig iron*.

Arc dimensions

Arc dimensions are used when measuring some kind of angle or radius.

Arc weld

Arc welding involves two large metal alligator clips that carry a strong electrical current. One clip is attached to any conductive part of the project being welded. The second clip is connected to a thin welding rod. When the rod touches the project, a powerful electrical circuit is created. The massive heat created by the electrical current causes both the project and the steel core of the rod to melt together, cooling quickly to form a solid bond.

Arch

Simply put, it is a large hole in a wall. There are many different styles of arches: Roman, Tudor, and Gothic just to name a few. Make sure to follow the designer's drawings to create the correct shape for the arch.

Area micing

An array of floor microphones is used, and the sound operator rises and lowers the gain as needed.

Arena

Arena stages are truly theatre in the round. The stage is in the center of the space and the audience is seated on all sides.

Audition form

Actors fill out this form on arriving for an audition; it contains all pertinent information about the actor.

Auditorium

The audience sits in seating called the *auditorium*.

Autotransformer

This is a mechanical device used to dim lights. It works by moving a handle that physically moves a brush against a coil to change the voltage going to a lamp.

Auto yoke

This motorized device allows the user to pan and tilt a number of lighting fixtures from the control console. Newer models can also control color scrollers and irises.

AWG

American wire gauge.

B

Backdrop

This is the painted back wall used to help create the environment for the play. This backdrop serves two purposes. It helps the audience to better understand where the play is taking place, and it provides a space for the actors to change their costumes and masks outside the sight of the audience.

Balance

This is the contrast between all the different visual characteristics of a scene.

Ball peen hammer

A hammer used to bend, flatten, or shape metal.

Ballast

Ballast is used to start and properly control the flow of power going to a lamp.

Bamboo

This is a hollow stick used on the end of a paintbrush or stick of charcoal to extend an artist's reach.

Banana plug

Although it can come in various sizes, the 4 mm is the most common. These plugs are single wire. They are often color coded red and black.

Band saw

This is a stationary motorized saw used for cutting wood or metal into nonlinear shapes. The blade is one continuous loop, or band, stretched over two pulleys.

Bar clamp

Bar clamps have a fixed jaw and a sliding jaw, which makes them easily adjustable to different lengths. The determining factor of their usage is the bar to which they are attached. The longer the bar, the bigger an object they can clamp.

Barn door

This accessory fits on the front of a lighting fixture with movable blades used to cut light off of curtains or scenery projected from a soft-edge fixture.

Base paint

This is the color that is put on first. Other colors are applied over this to create textures.

Beam angle

This is the part of the light beam where you get the best light. It is measured to be at a level of 50 percent of the maximum intensity of the beam.

Beam projector

A beam projector is an open-face fixture that produces a narrow beam of light. The result is an intense shaft of light.

Beam spread

This is the part of the light beam measured to where you get down to 10 percent of the maximum intensity of the beam.

Belaying

This means to secure a rope by winding it in a figure-eight pattern around the cleat. To secure the belay, the final figure eight wrap gets a 180-degree twist, turning the end of the rope to the inside, before being put on the cleat.

Bevel gauge

This is used to check or copy the angle of an existing unit or drawing. It consists of a handle or stock and a blade or tongue, connected by a wing nut. This tool *does not* measure an angle. It simply copies the angle from something that already exists.

Black box

The black box is the most flexible of all the theatre types. Basically, black box is just what it says. It's a big black room with absolutely nothing in it. Very simple, very plain. It's a space in need of a production! The production brings in chairs and maybe risers for the audience. They also bring in a stage, raised or not. This allows for infinite possibilities within one space.

Block and fall

This is a piece of equipment that simulates standard blocks, allowing multiple ropes to come in through the top. The difference is in the "fall" side, as it reduces the number of ropes coming back out to one.

Blocking

This is the actor's movement around the stage.

BNC

A coaxial connector, BNC has a miniature bayonet-locking connector.

Borders

Hung overhead, originally painted to simulate the heavens, borders were added to complete the visual effect complementing the backdrop. They also became known as *masking*, which had the added benefit that they blocked the audience's view of rigging and lights hung over the stage.

Bowline

This is one of the most important knots to know. If properly tied, it does not slip and can be used to secure things or lift people.

Box set

This is a set usually containing three walls and perhaps a ceiling. It was, and still is, used to represent interiors.

Box wrench

This closed-end wrench fits only one size of hardware. Typically, it has between 6 and 12 points of contact to the hardware.

Brazing

This uses molten metal to join two pieces of metal. The metal added during the process has a melting point lower than that of the material, so only the added metal is melted, not the material. Brazing uses metals with a higher melting point. Brazing produces a stronger joint than does soldering and often is used to join metals other than steel, such as brass.

C

CAD

CAD is computer-aided drawing and drafting software.

Call script

This is *the* authority for information about the show. This script contains all of the information needed to call the show once you are in the theatre.

Call time

This is the time when people are to arrive and be ready to work. On any given call, there may be several call times for different groups of people.

Carpenter clamps

These are the basic clamps found in a scene shop. They are shaped like a C with a screw that tightens and loosens. They can leave marks on wood, so they are usually used when that is not a factor.

Carpenter pencil

This pencil is made in a flattened octagon shape that prevents it from rolling. The "lead" is thicker and stronger than in a regular pencil, which comes in handy when writing on wood instead of paper. You cannot sharpen this in a standard pencil sharpener; most people just use their pocketknife or a utility knife.

Cartoon

Cartoon refers to drawing the basic design at full scale using vine charcoal.

Center Line

Our only reference for left and right measurements in the theatre is the center line.

Center punch

This is used primarily on metal to mark a starting point for drilling into the material. Once you have used the center punch, it is much easier to begin drilling into metal without the drill slipping.

Chalk line

An almost diamond-shaped container containing a very long string and powdered chalk, a chalk line is used to mark a straight line between two points.

Cheat sheet

Sometimes called a *magic sheet*, it is a quick reference for the design team to be able to find the channel number quickly and easily. A cheat sheet is usually a compressed number list.

Chip

A very inexpensive alternative to the standard paintbrush, a chip is less durable and considered to be disposable.

Chisel

A tool with a cutting edge on its end, it is used primarily for carving and cutting hard materials like wood, stone, or metal and is specifically designed for each type of use. The sharp edge of the chisel is forced into the material, usually with a hammer or mallet.

Chop saw

Chop saws have a circular saw blade similar to a circular saw but usually larger in diameter. Chop saws work by having a pivoting arm containing the blade, which is brought down to cut the material.

Chroma

Chroma is a hue in its purest form.

Circular saw

One of the more popular portable tools in the shop, it gets its name from the circular saw blade it uses. It is designed to make long, straight cuts. This saw can crosscut or rip wood. The bottom foot can be angled to allow for a consistent angled cut.

Classicism

Based on idealistic models or established conservative standards, this style embraces a high level of taste, sobriety, and proportion. Conventional formality is another way to think of classicism.

Claw hammer

This is the hammer you see the most in the scene shop. It has a metal head for striking a nail, or whatever else you need to hit, and a curved claw for ripping nails back out of the wood.

Cleansers

These products are made to clean a variety of things, such as skin or brushes.

Clove hitch

This knot is important to almost every rigging job in the theatre. Used as a traditional hitch, securing only one end, the clove hitch is liable to slip. It requires a load attached in each direction to be effective. The clove hitch is almost always a load-bearing knot.

Cluster

This is similar to an array; however, it is almost always hung on center right above the edge of the stage.

Coaxial cable

This cable is made up of a single copper core, surrounded by a layer of insulation, covered by a copper shield, then a flexible plastic jacket.

Coiling

This is one of the few ways you can safely store rope without putting any bends, kinks, or knots in it.

Collaboration

Collaboration means to work as a team. Collectively, you create a production where there once was none.

Combination square

A combination square can handle 90-degree angles, and it can also help you draw 45-degree angles. You can loosen a knob and slide square's head along the ruler, then tighten it down at a different location on the ruler. This allows you to transfer measurements from one place to another. The sliding head of the square contains a level. This can be very useful for certain types of measuring.

Complementary

Complementary colors are opposite each other on the full color wheel.

Composite

An order of architecture devised by the Romans, the composite first appeared on the arch of Titus in Rome in 82 CE.

Concealer

Used to blend away temporary and permanent imperfections, which can include birthmarks, blemishes, and tattoos, concealers are highly pigmented makeup. This is what helps them to cover up and is the inherent difference between a foundation and a concealer.

Concept

A concept is your unique way of looking at the show.

Condenser microphone

More versatile, more costly, and less durable than dynamic microphones, the condenser microphone is the choice for the theatre, given its range in quality for many purposes.

Construction drawings

These are technically detailed drawings created by the shop to build from.

Contact pickup

Like microphones, they are attached to musical instruments and pick up sound through vibrations instead of from the air.

Contact sheet

This form shows everyone involved with the production, including directors, actors, producers, technicians, shops, and so on. The contact sheet is the phone book for the show. Any contact information you might need should be there. It should also include rehearsal and performance spaces.

Contrast

Variations in line weight, direction, shape, texture, balance, proportion, pattern, and scale add interest to a composition. Contrast can help focus the viewer's eye. The better and more varied your contrast, the less you need other factors to define your shape.

Conventional lighting

Conventional lighting comprises nonmoving fixtures.

Coping saw

A coping saw has a handle with a U-shaped steel frame. The very thin blade is held between the arms of the U. Turning the handle tightens or loosens the tension on the blade. Holders at either end of the blade can also be pivoted so that you can adjust the angle of the cut.

Corinthian

An order of architecture, the Corinthian was little used until the Romans adapted it. This order included leaves on the capitals in a more natural replica and dates from the end of the 5th century BCE.

Corner block

This is triangular pieces of ¼-inch plywood used to hold together corners of a soft flat frame.

Costume breakdown

A costume breakdown contains all information about each of the costumes used in the production. It should include a description of the costume, complete with any accessories, what scene(s) it is worn in, how it gets on and off stage, the character name, and any special notations if a fast change is needed or if it is used with a special effect like blood.

Cotton

Often thought of as cool, soft, and comfortable, the cotton fiber is from the cotton plant's seedpod. The fiber is hollow in the center and under a microscope looks like a twisted ribbon. This fiber absorbs and releases perspiration quickly, thus allowing the fabric to "breathe."

Counterweight

This is a weight used to offset the weight of what you are trying to lift.

Crosscut blade

A saw blade for cutting wood, the teeth are designed to cut across the grain.

Cue lights

These can be placed in locations around the set and the theatre where direct visual or headset cues are not an option. Establish with your cast and crew what the cue lights mean.

Curtain calls

Documentation is needed of the curtain call blocking, including the order in which the actors appear, where they come from, and whether they appear by themselves or in groups and any other information about the curtain call.

Cutter

Originally, the cutter was a person who used patterns, or created patterns, and cut the pattern from the fabric.

Cyc

Cyc is shorthand for cyclorama, now used almost interchangeably with *backdrop*.

Cyclorama

Traditionally, this was a backdrop placed upstage, wide enough that the sides wrapped around and came downstage toward the audience.

D

Daily rehearsal report

This report is given to all departments concerning any changes, cuts, or additions that affect them as a result of the daily rehearsal.

Dead lift

This is used to lift the full weight of something with no help from counterweights.

Deck

This is a complete replacement for the existing stage floor.

Deck plan

This is a drawing of the floor.

Deluge

Deluge is similar to a sprinkler system, except the sprinkler heads are open and the pipe is not pressurized with air.

Designer drawings

Drawn by the designer, they are meant to convey the artistic vision of the designer. They are critical to informing the shop what the designer's ideas and goals are.

Detail brush

Detail brushes come in a variety of shapes to help add or remove just the right amount of makeup.

Detail drawing

Used when parts of the set require a much closer look, these are drawn in full or close to full scale. They make dimensioning easier. Detail drawings also include practicals, scenic elements, or props that plug in to some form of electricity or require finer work that cannot be drawn in a smaller scale. These items must be planned out in great detail to make sure that they work properly and are safe.

Deux ex machina

Literally, "God from machine," this usually involves moving scenery.

Dimmer

Simply put, its job is to make lights go up and down. A variety of technologies have been utilized over the history of dimming, from mechanical, manual devices to electronic, digitally controlled dimmers.

Direct current

DC is an electric charge that flows in one direction.

Direction

Direction creates visual movement.

Distressing

This is a way to make something new look like something old.

Ditty bag

A ditty bag is an accessory bag.

DMX

Digital multiplex has become a standard control signal for dimming and many other devices.

Dome brush

Made with rounded corners for soft edges, these are ideal for undereye concealer as well as eye shadow.

Doric

An order of architecture, it was the earliest order to develop and was used for the Parthenon and most early Greek temples. Its columns have no base; it was developed around the 5th-century BCE.

Double purchase

A double-purchase system puts the loading floor halfway between the stage floor and the loft blocks. Extra pulleys are both above and below the arbor to double the wire rope length. This is necessary to make this system work properly. The pipe travels 1 foot for every 2 feet the rope has to travel. You need to use twice the amount of weight of what is hung on the pipe. The advantage is that you lose no floor space. This is often the major deciding factor in which type of system to use.

Downstage

This is the stage area closest to the audience.

Drafting

Usually done shortly after the drawing and rendering are completed, drafting is meant to convey information not an emotion.

Drafting stool

This is a stool (or chair) that goes up and down to adjust to the height of your drafting table. It should be comfortable and support your back.

Drafting table

Often used for sketching and layout as well as for drafting, the table height and angle can be adjusted to whatever is the most comfortable.

Drafting tape

Looks like regular masking tape, but it is less sticky. That means you can pull it up without leaving residue or tearing your paper.

Draper

Originally, the draper was a person who, instead of using a pattern, created a design by draping the fabric onto the actor.

Drawing

Often used interchangeably with *sketching*. drawing pulls our ideas together and allows them to form on the outside of our head and puts them on paper.

Drill

This is a tool for making holes.

Drill press

This is a stationary tool that does the same job as a regular drill. It has the added advantage of being mounted over a tabletop.

Dry brush

Dry brushing means you keep your brush as dry as possible, using only a minor amount of paint. Or, you use a brush with no paint to move around or remove paint that has already been applied to the surface.

Dry ice

Dry ice is solid carbon dioxide that exists at a temperature of −109.3 degrees Fahrenheit or −78.5 degrees Celsius. Those are *negative* temperatures! It must be handled with extreme care.

Dust mask

A dust mask helps protect you from inhaling many types of small particles.

Dynamic microphone

This is a good all-around microphone that is both durable and affordable.

E

Earmuffs

Earmuffs are full ear covering used to protect the ears from loud noise.

Earplugs

Earplugs go into the ear to provide some protection from loud noise.

Elevation

An elevation takes the ground plan and stands it up in three dimensions, one element at a time. This allows the scene shop and carpenters to see an individual piece as it is intended to be built.

Ellipsoidal reflector spotlight

Also known as ERS, this is a focusable fixture with one or more lenses. The defining part is the ellipsoidal-shaped reflector.

Emphasis

Emphasis means to place particular importance on a particular area or item in the scene.

Environmental

This type of theatre came about during the 1960s with the help of many avant-garde groups. The basic idea is to provide integration between the audience and the actors. The audience was expected to participate in the performance at some greater level than usual. There are multiple areas of focus in the performance simultaneously. The chaos created by dividing the audience's focus is the whole point of the style. The actual spaces for these performances range from converted garages, to parks, to castles, to monuments. Scenery is used at a minimum, as the whole point is to go to a "realistic" setting. As the name suggests, environmental theatre brought the audience to the environment instead of creating a manufactured environment through traditional theatrical conventions.

Equalization

Equalizers are the most common use for a basic signal processor. Think of them as a filter. Equalizers help to tune specific sources to a similar base level.

Erasing shield

This is one of the coolest things ever invented. A small, thin piece of polished steel has different shapes cut out of it. You lay the shield over your drawing, specifically the part you want to erase. Then, while holding it in place, you erase the offending line without the possibility of your eraser touching anything else on the paper. It's like magic, only better!

Expressionism

Expressionism is a style in which the artist seeks to express an emotional experience placed onto the subject matter. This style allows the artist and the art to combine and form an altered reality.

Eyecup

This is ergonomically designed to be used for single eyewash.

Eyewash station

An eyewash station provides an effective means of washing your eyes quickly to minimize the time an irritant comes in contact with them.

F

Face shield

A face shield is worn over the entire face to prevent flying items from hitting the face.

Facial shape

There are six facial shapes—oval, heart, pear, square, round, and long—and each has its own needs when applying makeup.

Fence

A fence is a guide for cutting straight lines.

Filament

This is the element of glowing wire carrying the current within a lightbulb.

Files

A file is similar to a rasp but with much finer teeth. It is used for fine shaping in wood or metal.

Fire curtain

A fireproof curtain is hung between the audience and the stage, usually just upstage of the proscenium arch. Its main purpose is to keep the audience safe from a fire on stage.

Fireproof

Fireproof means an item will not burn, smoke, or flame.

Fire retardant

Fire retardant means an item will burn, smoke, and flame although it will do all of these slower than anticipated.

Fitch

A fitch is a type of lining brush with a defined shape, seamless ferrule, and natural bristles. It comes in a wide variety of sizes.

Flat brush

This is great for blending. The shape gives you great control when moving makeup around.

Flogger

A paintbrush with really, really long bristles, the flogger can be used for creating textures in wet paint or removing cartooned chalk and charcoal from the material's surface.

Floretta

This is a small, handheld version of the compression sprayer.

Fluorescent

This is a gas-discharge lamp that uses electricity to excite mercury vapor.

Flush cut saw

This saw has a handle with the blade coming straight out of one end. The blade is very flexible. It cuts flush with the bottom surface and has a very fine set of teeth that cut in one direction.

Foam

Foam brushes and pads come in a variety of sizes and are mostly rectangular or round. Instead of bristles, these brushes have a foam block that comes to a wedge at the tip. These are great for cutting in and keeping a straight line.

Foam sponge

These come in different shapes and sizes. They are ideal for applying crème makeup.

Focus

Focus is the process aiming the lights to the place the designer wants the light to be.

Fog

When heated vapor mixes with cooler air outside a fog machine, it instantly forms an opaque aerosol—the effect we call *fog* or *smoke*.

FOH

FOH stasnds for front of house.

Folding rule

This is a combination of a regular ruler and a yardstick. It is made up of small sections in 6-inch increments connected by pivot points.

Footlights

Traditionally located on the downstage edge of the stage and/or apron, they focus upstage toward the back wall, pointing up into the actors' faces from below.

Foreshortening

This is an optical illusion created by changing one's view of the vanishing point to one side rather than directly in front of the viewer.

Foundation

Usually the first layer of makeup to be applied, foundations glide on easily when using a foam sponge. They are long lasting and provide a flawless finish. They come in a wide range of colors to match any skin tone. If, by chance, you can't find the exact color, you can mix them to create a new hue. Crème foundations need to be set with powder.

Foundation brush

These brushes are made for applying foundation.

Fourth wall

The proscenium acts as a frame through which the audience views the play. This frame is often referred to as the *fourth wall*. The actors treat the "fourth wall" as if it is a real wall and ignore the audience. Some plays call for the actors to look right at the audience and deliver their lines. This is called "breaking the fourth wall."

Framing hammer

A framing hammer is heavier and meant for larger nails and harder woods than the standard claw hammer. The claw is not as curved as on a standard claw hammer.

Framing square

A framing square looks like a big L with the long side 24 inches long and the shorter side 16 inches long. It is made out of metal. It is the most accurate of the squares because it has a fixed angle; there are no adjustments you can make.

French curve

A french curve is a template for drawing curves. It has curved edges and several scroll-shaped cutouts in the middle. The French curve is used by tracing along its edges.

French scene breakdown

This is a spreadsheet of all the acts and scenes in the play with a list of all the characters laid out in a matrix to show which characters are in which scenes.

Fresnel

A Fresnel is a soft-edge light that can focus as a spot or flood. The defining part is the shaped lens.

Fresnel lens

A Fresnel lens is divided into a series of concentric circles that step in toward each other in such a design that light output is not sacrificed.

Frisket

This is a plastic sheet with an adhesive back. It is used when you need to mask a specific part of a design. You lay it down and cut a design out to reveal the portion you need to work on, leaving everything else masked.

G

Gain

Gain is what we usually think of as volume. However, it is a little different than volume. Gain is the amount of amplification available within the sound system.

Gel

Originally made of gelatin, which could melt or catch fire, gel is now made of a polyester film. The process to make gel involves adding color to the actual production process of the polyester sheeting. In this way, color is actually incorporated into the polyester.

Genre

This is a category of artistic composition characterized by similarities in form, style, or subject matter.

Glazes

Glazes are thinner than paint and transparent instead of opaque. Glazes are used for a variety of effects.

Go

Go means do the cue!

Gobo

Also known as a *template* or sometimes a *cookie*, a gobo is placed within a leko or other focusable fixture to project patterns.

Goggles

Goggles are the first line of defense for your eyes. Many styles can be worn over eyeglasses.

Graining

Graining involves using specially textured brushes and tools to create wood grain pattern and texture.

Grand border

Downstage of the house curtain usually hangs the grand border. A border is a short curtain that hangs in the air and goes all the way across the stage. It helps mask the workings of the theatre from the audience's view. In this case, the grand border is the one closest to the audience. It is often made of fabric to match the house curtain, rather than the plainer fabric traditional for other borders.

Grayscale

This is the chart of tones and tints from black to white with no actual hue.

Grid

A grid comprises horizontal and vertical lines, creating equal-size squares, drawn on a drop to help enlarge an image to full size.

Grinder

This is a tool that drives an abrasive disc mounted to a geared head.

Ground

The ground wire is there as a safety measure in case there is some sort of short circuit.

Ground plan

This is a drawing of the stage or set as seen from above.

H

Half hitch

This is a knot that forms the basis for a multitude of other knots.

Half hour

A call is given to everyone backstage 30 minutes prior to the curtain going up that lets everyone know that the house is being opened up to the audience and they can no longer walk into the house.

Halogen lightbulb

It is an incandescent lamp with a tungsten filament.

Hammer drill

This looks similar to an electric drill. It works in a similar way, with a drill bit that does the cutting. The added feature in a hammer drill is that the chuck creates a short, rapid hammer-type action to break through hard or brittle material. Hammer drills are used mostly when working with masonry or stone.

Hand pull

This is a big, thick, synthetic rope that attaches to the bottom of the arbor and goes around to the head block.

Hand screw clamp

An older style of clamp that is still used today, they are great when you need to be careful not to destroy your surface. This clamp is easy to recognize by its two heavy, broad wooden jaws. Passing through the jaws are screws with reverse threads at the ends, so the jaws come together rapidly and can clamp at many different angles.

Hard flat

This is a flat covered with ¼-inch plywood forming a hard surface.

Haze

Haze is about revealing light beams more than it is about being seen on its own. The machines use a water-soluble liquid that, when heated, turns to haze.

Head block

This is a pulley mounted to overhead steel above the fly loft that changes the direction of multiple ropes.

Hemp house

This is a theatre where the lift lines from the battens are rope, either organic or synthetic.

Hole saw

Used to cut larger holes, it is a piece of thin metal wrapped in a circle with teeth added on one side. Usually, a small twist bit in the center allows you to get the hole started in the exact place you want it.

Horizon line

This is the line that separates the earth from the sky. In the theatre, it is the horizontal line that comes closest to the height of your eye.

Hot-glue gun

This is used for heating and dispensing hot melted glue.

House curtain

Often a curtain is placed directly upstage of the proscenium and acts as a house curtain. The house curtain is used to mask the stage from the audience's view prior to the performance. The house curtain is not always used in this manner today, as some less-traditional productions choose to expose the stage and the scenery rather than hide it.

Hudson sprayer

The brand name Hudson has become synonymous with the canister type of compression sprayer.

Hue

Hue is another word for color.

I

Impedance

Impedance is the amount of resistance a microphone has to an audio signal. The lower the resistance, the fewer problems the microphone may have using longer cables and dealing with noise interference. Generally, low impedance means a better-quality microphone and therefore becomes a perfect choice for the theatre.

Impressionism

Impressionism, is a combination of realism and romanticism that seeks to allow the artist to define the personality of the subject matter. Through the use of color and light, the subject matter's personality is revealed.

Incandescent lightbulb

This is a carbon filament electrified within a vacuum in a glass envelope.

Input

Input can be microphones, contact pickups, magnetic pickups, laser pickups, and optical pickups.

Insight

Insight is observing the world around you and forming opinions.

Intelligent lighting

This is lighting fixtures that move via remote control.

Intensity

Intensity is the brightness or dullness of a color. This helps describe our perception of a color.

Ionic

An order of architecture. Ionic columns with scroll-like capitals followed soon after Doric.

J

Jig

This is a guide used with cutting or joining tools to produce multiple cuts of the same size or assemble many identical items.

Jigsaw

Also known as a *saber saw*, it has a small straight blade that cuts with an up and down motion. Because of its small blade, it is great for cutting curves but not as good for cutting straight lines.

K

Kelvin

This is color temperature scale for lighting sources; lower numbers are warm, higher numbers are cool.

Key to symbols

This is a box with different symbols to represent various items, such as different lighting units.

Keyhole saw

Also known as a *drywall saw*, it is a long, narrow saw used for cutting small, awkward holes into a variety of building materials.

Keystone

Originally shaped like a keystone, these rectangular pieces of ¼-inch plywood are used to hold the rails to the stiles in a soft, flat frame.

Kick-off meeting

This is the first major meeting once a job is awarded to a shop. It involves all of the pertinent people. Schedules and many other details are laid out.

Kraft paper

Kraft paper is paper produced by the kraft process from wood pulp. It is strong and relatively coarse. Kraft paper is usually a brown color but can be bleached to produce white paper. It is used for paper grocery bags, multiwall sacks, envelopes, and other packaging.

L

Lamp

A lamp is a lightbulb.

Lamp housing

This is the part of the fixture into which the lamp is installed.

Laser measure

A laser measure is typically more accurate than a traditional tape measure. Human error is all but eliminated. In most cases, you just press a button, the laser emits its beam until it hits a solid surface, then a digital display shows the distance measured.

Lavalier

This is a very small microphone designed to be clipped to clothing or hung around the neck. As the need for sound design in the theatre has grown, lavaliers can now be attached in the hair or wigs, behind the ear, and even sewn into costumes, all to try and hide them.

Lay-in

This is a specialty brush used specifically for painting large areas, such as a drop or a large expanse of scenery. It is larger than most other brush types, with typical sizes of 5 and 6 inches.

LED

Light-emitting diode technology has been around for a long time. This high-output, low-wattage light source has only recently been integrated into theatrical lighting fixtures. When using color mixing of red, green, and blue, you can create virtually any color.

Leg

A leg is a visual extension of the backdrop, also used for masking the wings.

Leko

Named after Mr. Levy and Mr. Kook, this is one of the original ellipsoidal spotlights. Leko has become the common name for virtually all ellipsoidals.

Lens

On a fixture, the lens helps to focus the light beam.

Lettering guide

This is a template designed to make you letter perfectly.

Light plot

The light plot is a drawing to show the lighting equipment for the show, in relation to the scenery and masking.

Lighting controller

This is a piece of electronics that sends a low-voltage or digital signal to the dimmers and other devices to control them.

Limelight

An intensely bright light created when a gas flame is directed at a cylinder of calcium oxide.

Line

The mathematical definition of a *line* is the shortest distance between two points. A line has direction. The designer or artist often uses this to infer what that direction is as part of the composition.

Line array

This comprises multiple speakers hung together, either vertically or horizontally, so that they can act as one huge speaker.

Line weight

Line weight is the thickness of a line. Varying the line weight within a composition creates contrast.

Linear dimensions

These are used when measuring in a straight line.

Linen

Linen is made from flax, or more specifically, a fiber taken from the stalk of the plant. It has a natural luster from the inherent wax content.

Lineset

These are the individual rigging points for hanging pipes and scenery in the air.

Lineset inventory

This tells everyone where the pipes are in relation to the plaster line.

Linesman pliers

An all-around great pair of very strong pliers, they are great for holding, bending, and forming. The jaw surfaces are slightly toothed for better gripping. The jaws also have a built-in side-cutter tool.

Lining

This is also known as a *fitch brush*.

Lining stick

This is a beveled straight edge that allows you to run a brush along the side, using it as a guide for creating precise lines. It usually has a handle to make holding it easier when working from a distance.

Linnebach projector

This is an early large-format image projector. The size and focus of the projected image was determined by the size of the glass slide installed and by moving the projector.

Liquid latex

This is made for a variety of effects from wrinkles, to filling in pock marks, to building up wounds. *Always* check for allergy possibilities.

Loading floor

The loading floor is where the technicians add and remove counterweights from the arbors.

Lobsterscope

This is a motorized disk with slits in it placed in front of a focusable light fixture used to project a strobe-like light.

Loft block

A loft block is a pulley mounted to the gridiron or support steel that supports and changes the direction of a lift-line rope between the load and the head block.

Looper

Loopers create thread loops that pass from the needle thread to the edges of the fabric so that the edges of the fabric are contained within the seam.

M

Magic sheet

Sometimes called a *cheat sheet*, it is a quick reference for the design team to be able to find the channel number quickly and easily. A magic sheet is a visual reference.

Mallet

This is a type of hammer with a soft head that helps avoid damaging delicate surfaces. The head is also substantially larger than a regular hammer, which helps to spread out the force of the hit.

Masking

Masking includes legs, borders, or flats used to block the audience's view of backstage or anything you don't want the audience to see.

Material safety data sheets

Also known as MSDS, manufacturer-supplied data sheets provide detailed hazard and precautionary information for hazardous materials.

Media server

This is a fancy name for a computer with a massive hard drive and a great graphics card.

Midrange

This is a speaker designed specifically for the midrange frequencies.

MIG

MIG (metal inert gas) uses a spool of continuously fed wire that allows the welder to join longer stretches of metal without stopping to replace rods.

Miter box

A miter box has precut slots or a movable guide in it to fix a saw into a certain angle.

Miter saw

Having fine crosscut teeth, miter saws are often used in conjunction with a miter box.

Mixing console

This provides preamplification, which amplifies the microphone level signals to line level.

Monkey's fist

This knot adds a substantial amount of weight to the end of the rope.

Monochromatic

This refers to an entire composition made up of tints, tones, and shades of the same hue.

Mr. Puffy

Mr. Puffy is basically the chalk line of costume design. Tailor's chalk, ground to a powder, is put into a small container with a very focused spout. A hose is attached to the container, controlled by a squeeze ball. The whole thing is mounted on a stand that is measured and marked so you know how high it is off the ground. Squeeze the ball and *poof*, your hemline is marked.

Multipair cable

This is a single outer jacket and insulation with many internal balanced, or twisted-pair, lines.

Multiple dimensions

These are used when measuring several things in a row from the same starting point.

N

Nail set

This is used for driving the head of a nail either flush or just below the finished surface.

Naturalism

Naturalism is quite specific. There are no stereotypes per se, but specific characters in specific environments. The purpose of this very detailed world is to show how a person's character and life choices are determined in part by the environmental or social forces.

Needle-nose pliers

Needle-nose pliers are good for smaller jobs. They are similar to basic pliers, but the gripping end is not flat but comes to a small narrow point. This makes them great for holding much smaller items with more precision.

Nut driver

This is sized to fit specific nut or bolt head dimensions. Made up of a handle and driver as a single tool, it does not ratchet.

Nylon

Nylon has the ability to be very lustrous, semilustrous, or dull.

O

Open-ended wrench

This nonadjustable type of wrench fits a specific size of hardware and has an open end.

Orchestra pit

This is the area between the stage and the auditorium. The orchestra occupies this space if there is an orchestra for the show. If there is no orchestra in the show, the pit may be covered to provide extra acting area. The name *pit* comes from the fact that most often this area is lower than the auditorium floor, creating a "pit," similar to the standing-room area in Shakespeare's time.

Orthographic projection

An orthographic projection is a way of representing a 3D object in two dimensions using multiple views.

OSHA

The Occupational Safety and Health Administration is an agency of the U.S. Government's Department of Labor. OSHA's mission is to "assure the safety and health of America's workers by setting and enforcing standards; providing training, outreach, and education; establishing partnerships; and encouraging continual improvement in workplace safety and health."

Output

Output can be loudspeakers (woofers, midrange, and tweeters) and headphones.

Outrigger

These are stabilizing legs that attach to the base of a lift or other potentially unstable item.

Overhand knot

This is the simplest knot of them all.

Overlocking

An overlocking stitch sews over the edge of one or two pieces of cloth for edging, hemming, or seaming.

Oxyacetylene

Commonly referred to as gas welding, it is a process that relies on the proper combination of oxygen and acetylene.

P

Paint elevation

This is a 2D, full-color, to-scale representation of exact paint details.

Palette

Typically made from plastic to hold a variety of colors or types of makeup, it is also used for custom mixing.

Panel saw

A panel saw is a circular saw with a big bracket on it to allow for movement across a large-scale predetermined grid. The saw can be either horizontal or vertical, although most scene shops prefer the vertical type to save space. Cutting sheets of plywood into smaller pieces is this tool's specialty.

PAR

This is the light fixture that holds a PAR (parabolic aluminum reflector) lamp.

Parallel rule

This is a straight edge that travels up and down the drafting table on two cables. It allows you to draw horizontal lines that are consistently parallel to each other.

Pattern

This is a repeated element within a composition. Any shape, repeated, becomes a pattern.

Patterning template

This is a tool to help ease the transitions between pieces in a custom pattern.

Patterns

These are the diagrams of the pieces and parts of a garment that act as a guide for its construction.

Pepper's ghost

This is a stage illusion developed by chemist John Pepper to make a ghost appear and disappear or turn the reflection of one actor into another.

Periaktoi

These triangular columns revolve to reveal other sides, and other sets.

Perspective

This type of drawing uses a 2D technique to approximate a 3D object.

Phillips screws

This is a screw with an X slot indented into the top.

Pin rail

A locking device to hold ropes attached to things to be lifted, the ropes get belayed onto the pins.

Pipe clamp

This is hardware to attach a fixture to a pipe.

Pipe cutter

Shaped like a C with a handle coming out the bottom, the handle is tightened, which tightens the pressure onto the pipe. This forces the sharp blade into the pipe while wheels around the clamp continuously rotate the pipe.

Pipe reamer

A reamer is used whenever pipe or tube is cut to remove burrs.

Pipe threader

This is used to cut threads into pipe.

Pipe wrench

Meant for gripping round objects, primarily it is used for metal pipes, hence its name. It has an adjustable jaw similar to the adjustable wrench. It closes and opens by screwing itself tighter as the wrench clamps down on the pipe.

Places

Called a few minutes before the show begins, this means that all actors and technicians should go immediately to the places where they are needed to start the show.

Plan view

This is an overhead view of the architecture of the theatre or scenic or lighting elements.

Plane

Used to flatten, reduce the thickness of, and smooth a surface of a generally rough piece of lumber, planes usually have a cutting edge on the bottom attached to the solid body of the plane. They can also be used to cut specific shapes depending on what cutting edge is installed.

Plaster line

Where the apron meets the stage deck, this is our reference for all upstage and downstage measurements.

Platform

This is a small section of flooring that adds height to the existing stage.

Plumb bob

A plumb bob is used when trying to determine a level line from one point only. That means you can attach a string to the top of a wall. Let the string drop down with a plumb bob attached the bottom. The plumb bob is a weight and stops swinging at the point of making the string level, also useful for determining a point directly below something hung over the stage.

Pneumatic

This refers to any tool that requires a compressor to generate air pressure.

Polyester

This is the most widely used human-made fiber in the world.

Postmodernism

This style rejects the preoccupation with purity of form and technique. Mixtures of style elements from the past are applied to spare modern forms. The observer is asked to bring his or her opinions of this combined form, as there is no real standard or unity.

Pounce

A pounce wheel, a small tool with sharp teeth around a wheel, is used to punch holes in kraft paper while tracing an image. A pounce bag, filled with chalk or charcoal, is then used to transfer the design.

Powder brush

This is a full and luxurious brush for adding powder or removing excess powder without disturbing makeup.

Power puff

Usually round, they are always soft, and some are washable. They are great for applying powder very specifically, and for blotting.

Preshow checklist

This is a list of everything that needs to be in place for the show and where, or with whom, it should be. This includes props, costumes, scenery, lighting practicals, effects machines, everything.

Preshrink

Most fabrics should be prewashed before you cut and assemble them into a garment. This allows them to be more their final size before fabrication, so that the sizing of the completed garment will be, and remain, more accurate.

Presentational

This offers a performance where everyone is fully aware that the actors are at work on a stage, speaking and acting out a script, under lights, and in costumes. There is no attempt to disguise the fact that a theatrical performance is taking place to entertain the audience.

Pressure response microphone

This is usually mounted to a flat surface with the attached plate, which increases gain.

Previsualization

Often referred to as *pre-vis*, it means just what you think. It's a way to "see" what the show will look like before you get to the theatre.

Primary

A primary is a color that cannot be created by mixing any other colors together.

Primer

This is a way to make the surface ready to accept your design. Raw wood or fabric soaks in a great deal of the first layer of paint. This is the basis for priming.

Prop breakdown

This contains all information about each prop used in the production. It includes which actor(s) uses it, where they enter from, when they need it, which scene it is in, and where it comes back off stage. Also, and very important, how does the prop get off stage? It should also include descriptions of each prop and anything about the prop that may need to be preset.

Proportion

Proportion is a mathematical thing. It defines the relationship between objects or parts of the same object.

Proscenium

The proscenium arch is what formally separates the audience from the acting area. It creates a frame around the stage just like a picture frame for a painting. It lets you know where to look, and more important, where not to look!

Pry bar

This is made of metal and both ends are designed to be used for different purposes. They are used as leverage for separating objects. Some pry bars are meant to remove nails and do minor lifting. Some are bulky enough to be able to perform demolition.

Q

Quartz envelope
The clear covering over the filament of a lamp is the quartz envelope.

R

Radial arm saw
This works similarly to a circular saw. A crosscut saw blade is usually installed. The blade head is suspended from a long arm, hence the name, in a yoke that allows for selectable degrees of rotation. There is a handle for moving the blade head forward and back while cutting the wood.

Rag rolling
Rag rolling can be done in two ways. You can use a roller and paint a surface, then take a cotton rag that has been bunched into a loose ball and roll the rag ball across the paint to remove paint while also making a texture. You can also do the reverse, by applying paint to the rag and rolling it onto the surface to add paint and texture at the same time.

Rail
This is the horizontal pieces of a frame for a flat.

Rake
An angled stage is called a *raked stage*. The rake also serves as the basis for our modern stage directions. Any part of the stage or house that is on an angle is considered to be on a rake.

Rasp
A rasp is a woodworking tool for shaping the wood. It is made up of a long, narrow steel bar. A handle is on one end while the rest of the rasp has triangular teeth cut into it. When drawn across a piece of wood, it shaves away parts of the wood, very coarsely.

Raster
Raster is a pixel-based technology.

Rayon
Rayon is a very versatile fiber and has many of the same comfort properties as natural fibers.

Realism
This is the representation of nature without idealizing (as in classicism) or inclining to the emotional or extravagant (as in romanticism). The interest in the accurate and graphic may degenerate into excessive detail and preoccupation with the trivial.

Reciprocating saw
This has a straight blade mounted at one end of the body. The blade moves back and forth (that is where it gets its name), much like the action of a jigsaw, but it is much more powerful and versatile than jigsaws. A variety of blade options means it can cut through almost anything.

Reference white
The standard by which you judge all other colors, in actuality, white may not exist in the work. The reference established can be any color that you want the audience to perceive as white.

Reflector
This bounces light from the lamp, gaining brightness until the light comes out the front of the fixture.

Rehearsal schedule
This becomes your master calendar. It should list dates, times, places, and which members of the cast and crew are required.

Removers
These various products are made to dissolve and remove other products.

Rendering
This is a full-color, finished sketch.

Representational
The representational style shows naked truths about ordinary existence within specific situations. This style can be broken into two substyles, realism and naturalism.

Research
Any visual reference that helps inform your choices is considered research.

Respirator
Air-purifying and atmosphere-supplying respirators are used when the face mask is inadequate to protect the worker.

Rip blade
The rip blade is a saw blade for cutting wood. The teeth are designed to cut with, or parallel to, the grain.

Romanticism
Romanticism is the imaginative emphasizing individualism in thought and expression in direct opposition to the restrictive formality of classicism. Other traits of this period are freedom of fancy in conception and treatment, picturesque strangeness, or suggestions of drama and adventure.

Round brush
A round brush is good for lining eyes, etching brows, and applying fine details to special effects makeup.

Router
Routers are motorized tools that typically cut grooves or decorative trims along the edge of a piece of wood.

Rule of thirds
This is the basic rule of composition. An image can be broken into thirds both vertically and horizontally. Each piece of the main image, while having the ability to stand on its own, is an integral part of the whole and directs the viewer's focus.

S

Sandbag
A sandbag is used as a counterweight in a hemp house.

Saturation
Saturation describes the amount of pure color a hue contains.

Scale
Scale is a term that relates to how big or small the object is. This is used in determining relationships and the surrounding proportions of a composition.

Scale rule
A scale rule is normally triangular-shaped with six sides containing 11 scales.

Scar wax
Pliable, yet firm, shaded wax is used to mold simulated injuries and moles.

Scene machine
This is an image projector with a highly efficient light source and lenses that focus the image.

Scenic ground row
Used to ease the stage floor into the backdrop, this is two dimensional and usually has a cutout design on the top to help the transition to the drop.

Scoop
The quality of the light from a scoop is very soft and gentle, creating an even wash covering a large area.

SCR
Introduced in 1958, the silicon-controlled rectifier is still used today. It is controlled electronically.

Scroll saw
A bench-top tool used for freehand cutting of intricate shapes in fairly thin wood, the scroll saw uses thin blades, similar to a jigsaw, to allow for the small radius needed to complete these designs.

Scumble
Putting a small amount of paint on your brush and lightly dragging it across a dry surface is often used as an overlay to a background image, such as creating sunbeams coming out of clouds.

Seam ripper
This is the best tool for opening seams when changes in a constructed garment need to be made, since it is specifically designed for it.

Secondary
Combining any two primary colors creates a secondary color.

Section
This is a visual cut through the middle of important details so that we can see how other parts of the show will relate.

Serger
An overlock sewing machine, or serger, cuts the edges of the cloth as they are fed through, though some are made without cutters.

Shackle
This is a U-shaped device with holes at each end to accommodate a pin or bolt.

Shade
Shade is a hue that has been mixed with black.

Shape
Shape is the definition of any 2D or 3D object.

Sheave
Basically a pulley, it has a groove around its circumference to support and contain a rope and a bearing at its center to permit rotation.

Shield
A kind of insulation that is conductive to protect against electromagnetic and electrostatic fields, this helps keep the buzz and hum away from your audio system.

Show deck
The floor of the theatre is often covered completely with platforms, called a *show deck*.

Shutters
Shutters are shaped pieces of metal inside the leko with a handle on the outside used to shape the beam.

Side view
This is a drawing showing the sides of things.

Sightlines
These are the imaginary lines between the audience's eyes and the stage, also called *lines of sight*.

Sign-in sheet
This chart keeps track of who is at rehearsals and if the person arrived on time or not. It should be posted in the same place at every rehearsal. This is your best and only way to keep track of missing actors and crew.

Signal processor
This can include mixing console, equalizers, reverberation, delay, and amplifiers.

Silk
Silk is a natural protein fiber taken from the cocoon of the silkworm.

Single phase

This line comprises two hot wires (typically one black and one red), a neutral wire (the white one), and a ground wire (the green one).

Single purchase

In a single-purchase setup, the loading floor is on the stage floor. This means a lot of stage space is lost in wings to accommodate the arbors. The advantage of the single-purchase system is that the counterweight required is 1:1; that is, 1 pound of counterweight is added to the arbor for each pound on the pipe.

Sketch

A sketch is the initial drawing of design concepts in black and white or color.

Slip-joint pliers

These are similar to linesman pliers with one major difference, the joint that holds the two sides together is keyed so that the jaws can be opened wider as needed for certain jobs.

Sloper

A basic pattern shape in a variety of sizes. slopers come in different pattern shapes. They help you to get started with a custom pattern by letting you more easily fit the pattern pieces together as you are making adjustments.

Slotted screw

This is a screw with a single straight indent in the top.

Smoke pocket

The guide on either side of the stage that the fire curtain travels within is the smoke pocket.

Snake

Several complete audio cables held together in a common jacket form a snake.

Socket set

A socket set has handle and a series of replaceable heads. Each head has an opening on one side; each opening is a different size to correspond to different sizes of bolt heads and nuts. Sockets work with a ratcheting technology that allows you to loosen or tighten the bolt or nut quickly.

Soft flat

This is the traditional theatre type of flat. It has a soft covering made of muslin.

Soft goods

All fabric items found in the theatre are considered soft goods.

Soldering

Soldering uses molten metal to join two pieces of metal. The metal added during the process has a melting point lower than that of the material, so only the added metal is melted, not the material. Soldering uses metals with a melting point below 800 degrees Fahrenheit. Soldering commonly is used to join electrical, electronic, and other small metal parts.

Spade bit

A drill bit with a straight shaft with a rectangular bottom that comes to a point, it is used for boring holes, typically of a larger size or depth, in wood.

Spanset

Generically known as *roundslings*, this has continuous loops of mono-filament or steel-galvanized aircraft cable in a canvaslike (polyester) sheath.

Spatter

To spatter, you load a brush with a small amount of paint and basically shake the brush at the surface without allowing it to touch, thus creating a loose pattern of dots for texture.

Spatula

A spatula is a tool used for mixing makeup and applying thicker products like nose or scar wax and gel effects.

Speed square

This is a metal triangle containing both 90-degree and 45-degree angles. Measurement markings are along the sides. The important difference between the speed square and other types of squares is that the speed square has a flange on one side that you can use to hold it square against the edge of your material. It is sometimes referred to as a *roofer's square*.

Speed wrench

A speed wrench is similar to a box wrench with one major exception,. it contains a ratchet on both ends.

Spirit level

The spirit level is so named because the little vial containing liquid is actually partially filled with ethanol (alcohol).

Sponging

Sponging is used to create a paint texture by dabbing paint onto, or off of, a surface with a sponge.

Spot block

This is a pulley designed for temporary, and easily movable, connection to a gridiron or other theatre structure.

Spring clamp

Often called a *squeeze clamp* and identified by the size the jaws can open, they are clamps that are strong and lightweight. They differ from other clamps in that they tighten and loosen based on a spring's tension.

Sprinkler system

This is a network of piping and sprinkler heads with water under pressure placed throughout the space.

Square Knot

The basis for so much, it is used for binding together two ropes of the same size. Also known as a *reef knot*, the square knot is secure and easy to untie.

Stage

This is the performance area.

Stage blood

Commercial stage blood has many realistic qualities including color and viscosity. It can come in liquid or powder form for specific effects. It can also come in a peppermint flavor so that, if the blood must be put in the mouth, it is at least palatable. Staining can occur on skin and fabrics, so be careful of this.

Stage left

With an actor standing on the stage facing the audience, to the actor's left is stage left.

Stage right

With an actor standing on the stage facing the audience, to the actor's right is stage right.

Stage manager kit

The kit should include a range of items such as pencils, erasers, highlighters, pads of paper, post-it notes, paper clips, stapler, and so forth—everything you need to do your job, plus spares.

Standby

A standby means the cue is imminent.

Stapler

A stapler binds things together by forcing thin metal staples into the material with pressure.

Stile

The side or vertical pieces of a frame for a flat are stiles.

Stipple sponge

Very coarse, open sponge, it is great for adding texture, such as beards, bruising, and road rash.

String level

A string level is mounted on a string pulled fairly taut between two points in the area you are trying to measure.

Strip lights

Several fixtures built into one, it is used for washing cycs and other large areas, typically made with multiple circuits.

Strobe

A strobe is a machine capable of producing bright flashes of light. Newer models can vary the speed and intensity of the flashes.

Style

Style is the manner of presentation of the production.

Subtractive

In subtractive color system, when all three primary colors are mixed together in equal parts, they "theoretically" make black.

Subwoofer

This is a speaker designed specifically to reproduce very low-frequency sounds.

Symbol

A symbol is a picture, object, or color that stands for something else.

Tab

This is a masking leg turned 90 degrees so that is it oriented upstage and downstage.

Table saw

This works similarly to the circular saw. It is mounted on a table, which gives it more stability and allows for a more powerful engine. A rip saw blade is usually installed. The tabletop gives stability to the material you are cutting, allowing you to cut bigger pieces of wood more easily.

Tack hammer

This is a small hammer usually used for the detail work on finishing projects.

Tailor's chalk

Perfect for marking where you will need to adjust the fit of a garment to an actor, use chalk to make markings before you cut and assemble. The reason tailor's chalk is so good for this purpose is that, when you no longer need the markings, the chalk can be brushed away without leaving any residue. During fittings, it is much faster to mark a garment with chalk than to have an actor stand there while you insert pin after pin.

Tape measure

The tape measure we are most used to seeing these days is the self-retracting pocket tape measure. Its flexibility allows you to measure long lengths while still being easily carried in your pocket. A tape measure blade is usually marked in both inches and feet. Similar in concept to the scenic tape measures yet different in fabrication, it is a soft, flexible tape measure usually about 60 inches long that can conform to the curves of a body well. It is used for taking measurements of people and fabric.

Tertiary

The result of two secondary colors mixed together is a tertiary color..

Texture

Texture represents a 3D. It can be either tactile or nontactile.

Thermal barrier

Some type of item is placed between a heat source and a combustible material to prevent the material from burning.

Thimble

A thimble is a grooved fitting around which a wire rope is bent to form an eye.

Three phase

This has three hot wires (black, red, and blue) along with the neutral and ground.

Thrust

Usually considered to be a hybrid of the proscenium, a thrust stage most often has a proscenium of some kind. The apron becomes much larger and "thrusts" into the auditorium. Many people compare it to a tongue or a fashion runway. There is no rule about its shape or size, just that it extends substantially into the audience area.

TIG

During tungsten inert gas (TIG) welding, the welder holds the welding rod in one hand and an electric torch in the other hand. The torch is used to simultaneously melt the rod and a portion of the project's material.

Tin snips

This scissorlike tool is used to cut thin sheets of metal.

Tint

Tint is a hue that has been mixed with white.

Title block

The title block contains all important information regarding the production and, specifically, the drawing.

TNC

This is a threaded version of the BNC connector. The threads replace the bayonet.

Tone

Tone is a hue mixed with gray.

Top hat

Shaped like a man's top hat, this is used to cut down light spill and help in focusing a light.

Torx

A brand name for a type of screw or wrench with a six-pointed star on the end, it is not the same as Allen.

Trap

This is a hole in the floor with a replaceable plug.

Traveler

Just like a curtain track in your house only bigger and sturdier, the traveler can hold a very heavy curtain and allow it to move.

Triangle

A triangle is a template used to draw vertical and angled lines.

Trunnion

This is mounting hardware for placing a fixture, usually a strip light, on the floor.

Truss

Two or more pieces of pipe fabricated together with cross bracing, this is used in place of standard pipes when you have extremely heavy loads to lift or there are extended distances between lift lines.

T square

Shaped like a T, the short part of the T leans against the side of your table. By sliding it up and down the length of your table, the long part of the T becomes an edge you can use to draw a horizontal line. It is a replacement for the parallel rule.

Tuscan

An order of architecture, the Romans devised Tuscan for use in their temples and other public buildings. Although no Tuscan columns survived, it was thought to originate in Etruscan times.

Tweeter

This is a type of speaker designed specifically to reproduce high frequencies.

Twist bit

A straight drill bit with spiral twists down its length, it is typically used for metal but can also be used on wood, plastics, and many other materials. The front edge of each spiral is a cutting edge. The spiral design helps to remove the debris from the hole as you drill. These bits are usually made from high-speed steel, carbon steel, or tungsten carbide.

Twisted pair

Two center conductors twisted together. Many twisted pairs can share one insulation and jacket. All balanced audio cables are twisted-pair cables with a shield, which further protects the signal being transmitted from introduced noise.

U

Upstage

This is the area of the stage furthest from the audience.

Utility knife

Also known as a mat knife, this type of knife comes in a metal or plastic handle. The blade is retractable, meaning it stores completely in the handle. It uses a two-sided blade. This means when the blade gets dull you can open the handle, pull out the blade, turn it around, and put it back in.

V

Value

Value is the lightness or darkness of a color. This helps describe our perception of a color.

Vanishing point

Vanishing point refers to the point in space where two parallel lines "seem" to converge.

Vector

Vector-based images are created using mathematical formulas to locate each point. Lines are then drawn to connect the dots.

Vise grips

Vice grips are pliers with an adjustable locking mechanism. They come in a variety of sizes and shapes that makes them applicable for many jobs.

Vises

Vises are made from metal and usually attached to a shop bench for stability. Two jaws on the top are usually fairly wide and smooth. and by turning a screw, the jaws are brought together, thereby holding whatever has been caught inside.

Voltage

This is the difference of electrical potential between two points of a circuit.

Vomitorium

This is a hallway where the actors can enter unseen from the middle of the audience. The area usually leads directly underneath the audience risers. The Roman theatre had at least two, one on each side. Not only do actors use these for entrances and exits, but also the audience is often ushered in and out of the theatre using them.

W

Warning

A warning is a verbal signal that a cue is coming up soon.

Wattage

Wattage is the rate at which electrical energy is transferred by an electric circuit.

West Virginia

A mnemonic to remember the mathematical formula to find the watts, volts, or amps if you know two of the three values.

Wet blend

This is done by applying one layer of paint, and while it is still wet, applying a second coat that blends partially or completely with the first.

Wet/dry vacuum

This is a vacuum cleaner with a substantial tank for collecting whatever you're cleaning up. With the flick of a switch, depending on the brand, you can go from vacuuming sawdust to water!

White balance

This phrase often is used when shooting video or film, but it is equally important in the theatre. You "teach" your camera or your eyes what white really looks like, then all other colors are seen in relation, or in perspective, to this newly defined "white."

Winch

Geared mechanisms that can be either hand operated or motorized. They are used to raise, lower, or move heavy equipment. The gearing produces a mechanical advantage in both speed and load capacity.

Wing and drop

This comprises legs and borders often painted to complement the backdrop.

Wings

The areas just off stage, left and right of the acting area are the wings.

Wire rope

This consists of a number of strands of steel wire twisted on the diagonal around a core. Each strand consists of a number of wires also twisted on the diagonal around a core.

Wire rope clip

A U-shaped bolt and a pad with two holes for sliding up the bolt, two small nuts are used for holding the pad in place. It is used for securing wire rope.

Woofer

This is a speaker designed to reproduce low frequencies.

Wool

Wool fiber comes from a variety of different animal coats and not all wools are scratchy. Some are even extremely soft.

X

XLR

With three pins or more, this connector is one of the most commonly used connectors in the sound world. Originally called the *X series* when it first came out, the L represents the added latch, and the R is for the rubber surrounding the internal contacts.

Y

Yankee screwdriver

Also referred to as the *push screwdriver* and is an older style, this screwdriver has a spiral center so that when you press down on the handle the head turns the spiral center so you can drive in or back out a screw by just pushing down on the handle.

Yoke

This is mounting hardware for hanging a fixture that is usually integral to the fixture.

Z

Zetex

This replaced asbestos as a thermal barrier.

OPENING NIGHT AND PAYING CUSTOMERS

There is a superstition in theatre about the opening-night customers. As we all know, some tickets are given away through various connections with the production. These are called *comps*, or complementary tickets. Supposedly, the first customer to be admitted into the auditorium must be a paying customer. This is said to ensure the financial success of the production. House managers have been known to refuse admittance to someone with a comp ticket prior to seating a paying customer.

THE GREEN ROOM

The green room in a theatre is known for being the one room where you can just go and hang out. You can meet with people to talk with before or after a performance. Actors sometimes even meet the fans in the green room. But it is very rare that I've ever seen a green room that is actually green! So how did it get its name?

One story says that the Gaelic word *grian* means sunlit, which is where we get the word *greenhouse*. Since the green room is often one of the few rooms in the theatre with windows, it was labeled the *green room*.

THE SCOTTISH PLAY

Perhaps the most prevalent superstition in all of theatre is about *Macbeth*. We are never supposed to mention the name when we are in a theatre building. It is said that if you say the name, terrible things will happen. Apparently, this is based on the lustful greed for power that takes place in the plot of that play. Everyone calls it the *Scottish play* instead, and we all know what they mean.

Theatre veterans can tell many tales about bad luck happening when the name is said aloud. It is often thought that the supernatural forces of evil are behind this. But you are in luck, because there is a way to break the curse. If you say the name, you must spin around and spit on the floor. They say the spin turns back time and the spit expels the poisonous word from your system.

BREAK A LEG

One possible explanation for this expression is its relation to "taking a knee," which itself has roots in chivalry. Meeting royalty, one would "take a knee"—in other words, bend down on one knee. That breaks the line of the leg, hence "break a leg," a wish that the performer will do so well that he or she will need to take bows.

GREEN IS A BAD COLOR

Don't wear green onstage. Actors used to perform outdoors on the green grass so actors wearing green weren't seen very well. Also, a green light was often used to illuminate characters, and this limelight would make anyone wearing green appear practically invisible.

UMBRELLA PROBLEMS

For over a century, opening umbrellas on stage has been perceived as bad luck. Huggert reports that the belief actually started in 1868, when an orchestra leader named Bob Williams said good-bye to his theatre company before going away for the weekend. He opened his umbrella while standing on the stage, then walked out into a very rainy day. An hour later, he was standing on the stern of a boat, waving good-bye to a group of friends. As it sailed away from the dock, one of the engines exploded and Williams was instantly killed. The publicity seemed to say that the accident and the opening of the umbrella were connected. A theatre superstition was born and lives to this day. As with many of the other superstitions, there is a "counterspell." This was especially needed with this belief, because occasionally an actor must open an umbrella as a stage direction in a play. If an actor opens the umbrella facing the ground, good luck is restored.

"STARS AND STRIPES FOREVER"

In show business, particularly theatre and the circus, this hymn is called the "Disaster March." It is a traditional code signaling a life-threatening emergency. This helps theatre personnel handle things and organize the audience's exit without panic. One example of its use was at the Hartford Circus Fire in July 1944.

MONCKY WRENCH

The Moncky wrench is an adjustable wrench that is rarely used today. Its use has generally been replaced by the adjustable-end wrench, which has a compact head and so is more easily used in confined places. The wrench is named for Charles Moncky, the inventor of it, who sold his patent for $2000.

EVIL CURTAINS

Even the drop curtain contributes its share of stage superstitions, as nearly every actor and manager believes it is bad luck to look out at the audience from the wrong side of it when it is down. Some say it is the prompt side that casts the evil spell, while others contend it is the opposite side. The management, not being sure from which side the bad luck is likely to accrue, places a peephole directly in the center.

BABY DOLL

When baby dolls are off stage during a performance, set them face down on the props table instead of face up. This superstition comes from China. It is believed that if a baby doll is left face up, its spirit (kind of like a poltergeist) will emerge from its eyes and do poltergeistlike things in the theatre.

CHURCH KEY

Church key—the monks made their own ale. To keep the recipes secret, the monasteries were locked. Since the new bottle opener looked a bit like a skeleton key, it was referred to as a *church key*.

CATS

Cats, on the other hand, are thought to be lucky in the theatre, that is, as long as they are content to watch plays from the wings. A black cat is supposed to be an even more infallible source of good luck. It is said that, all around the theatre world, dark felines are treated with the greatest care and consideration. If a cat crosses the stage though, it is thought to be a terrible omen.

WHISTLING

Whistling backstage is a taboo, because it supposedly brings dire results. This superstition quite likely has its roots in the past, when managers hired sailors to run the fly loft, on the premise that the sailors' expertise with knots and raising and lowering sails made them ideal workers. A signal system of whistles cued the sailors. Someone whistling for personal enjoyment could sound like a cue, resulting in a dire event, like a heavy batten falling on actors' heads. Therefore, whistling can be bad luck.

GHOST LIGHT

Many theatres have ghosts, according to resident theatre personnel who will tell you they've seen or heard uncanny visitors, and some insist that to ward off bad-luck spirits there must always be a "ghost light" illuminating the stage when it is not in use. It is turned on as the actors and crews leave and burns all night. If the stage is dark, the superstition has it, ghosties can run free. Or, perhaps, we leave a light on so they can perform.

To me, the reason is less ghostly and more a statement of intense belief: We must be sure that concrete light always is on so that the metaphorical light of the theatre never will disappear. *Dark*, let us recall, refers to a time when there is no show (i.e., "We perform Tuesday through Sunday, but Monday is dark"). We want our art never to become "dark," but instead to remain brightly alive. Or, the stage should never be left dark. A light should always be on to keep the ghost company and happy. The light left on the stage is referred to as the ghost light. Or, a burglar fell off the stage, broke his or her leg, and sued the theatre.

DARK SUCKER

For years it has been believed that electric bulbs emitted light. However, recent information has "proven" otherwise. Electric bulbs don't emit light, they suck dark. Thus, they now call these bulbs "dark suckers." The dark sucker theory proves the existence of dark, that dark has mass heavier than that of light, and that dark is faster than light.

The basis of the dark sucker theory is that electric bulbs suck dark. Take, for example, the dark suckers in the room where you are. There is less dark right next to them than there is elsewhere. The larger the dark sucker, the greater is its capacity to suck dark. Dark suckers in a parking lot have a much greater capacity than the ones in this room. As with all things, dark suckers don't last forever. Once they are full of dark, they can no longer suck. This is proven by the black spot on a full dark sucker.

A candle is a primitive dark sucker. A new candle has a white wick. You will notice that, after the first use, the wick turns black, representing all the dark that has been sucked into it. If you hold a pencil next to the wick of an operating candle, the tip will turn black, because it got in the path of the dark flowing into the candle. Unfortunately, these primitive dark suckers have a very limited range.

There are also portable dark suckers. The bulbs in these can't handle all of the dark by themselves and must be aided by a dark storage unit. When the dark storage unit (or battery) is full, it must be either emptied or replaced before the portable dark sucker can operate again.

Dark has mass. When dark goes into a dark sucker, friction from this mass generates heat. Therefore, it is not wise to touch an operating dark sucker. Candles present a special problem, as the dark must travel in the solid wick instead of through glass. This generates a great amount of heat. Therefore, it can be very dangerous to touch an operating candle.

Dark is also heavier than light. If you swim deeper and deeper, you notice it gets slowly darker and darker. When you reach a depth of approximately 50 feet, you are in total darkness. This is because the heavier dark sinks to the bottom of the lake and the lighter light floats to the top.

The immense power of dark can be utilized to man's advantage. We can collect the dark that has settled to the bottom of lakes and push it through turbines, which generate electricity and help push it to the ocean where it may be safely stored. Prior to turbines, it was much more difficult to get dark from the rivers and lakes to the ocean.

The Indians recognized this problem, and tried to solve it. When on a river in a canoe traveling in the same direction as the flow of the dark, they paddled slowly, so as not to stop the flow of dark, but when they traveled against the flow of dark, they paddled quickly, so as to help push the dark along its way.

Finally, we must prove that dark is faster than light. If you were to stand in an illuminated room in front of a closed, dark closet, then slowly open the closet door, you would see the light slowly enter the closet, but since the dark is so fast, you would not be able to see the dark leave the closet.

In conclusion, dark suckers make all our lives much easier. So the next time you look at an electric bulb, remember that it is indeed a dark sucker.

TRIPPING

If an actress trips on the hem of her dress, she should pick it up and kiss the hem for good luck.

KNITTING

It is unlucky for an actor to knit while on the side of the stage. This is because knitting needles are pointy and can rip expensive costumes, or the needle may fall on the floor and cause someone to fall onstage.

FLOWERS

It is bad luck for an actor to receive flowers before the play begins, though flowers given after the play has ended is considered good luck.

LIPSTICK

When making up, an actress regards it as a sign that she will receive a good contract if she accidentally smears some lipstick onto her teeth.

IN THE LIMELIGHT

This is not a superstition but instead illustrates the way some theatrical terms enter everyday conversation. You've heard of this or that athlete, politician, or rock star having his or her day "in the limelight"? The phrase dates back to 1808, when Sir Humphrey Davy, a British chemist, discovered that a brilliant white light resulted from heating calcium oxide ("lime") to an extreme temperature. This "limelight" became popular to illuminate the important actors on stage. Think *followspot*. It follows, then, *in the limelight* came to mean "in the center of attention," and vice versa.

THE FINAL WORD

Some theatre folks believe it is bad luck to speak the last line of the play before opening night, because the play isn't "finished" until performed. Well, given the number of tech cues associated with that last line—lights, sound, curtain—plus somewhat frenzied blocking to get everyone off stage and in position for the curtain call, isn't it awfully risky not to rehearse it?

Somewhat connected, I've always postponed blocking the curtain call until the very last moment, mostly because doing it says "we're finished," when we aren't. Also, the way a curtain call is blocked necessarily indicates the relative importance of various roles, and I dislike making that statement to the cast, because it violates the idea of an *ensemble*, the creation of which is always one of my directorial goals.

BAD DRESS REHEARSAL—GOOD OPENING

There is a saying that "a bad dress rehearsal will equal a good opening night." It might have started with a producer who had a show underway that had an absolute disastrous dress rehearsal. Not knowing how else to build morale, the producer glibly invented a quick excuse: "Well, you know the old saying that a bad dress rehearsal guarantees a great show!" And that propaganda is hauled out by its hind legs every time a dress rehearsal goes down the tubes. Plah! Most times, a cruddy dress rehearsal means a cruddy opening; a potent dress rehearsal, on the other hand, builds confidence and morale and it is a marvelous high leaping off place for the growth that will follow.

CHAPTER ONE

"Old School/New School" courtesy of Michael A. Fink.

1.1   Image courtesy of Wikipedia as part of Creative Commons License.

1.2   Image courtesy of Wendy Herron.

1.4   Image courtesy of Wikipedia as part of Creative Commons License.

1.5   © 2003 Thomas G. Hines, Whitman College.

1.6   Image courtesy of Wikipedia as part of Creative Commons License.

1.7   Image courtesy of Wikipedia as part of Creative Commons License.

1.8   Image courtesy of Wendy Herron.

1.9   Image courtesy of Wikipedia as part of Creative Commons License.

1.10   Image courtesy of Wikipedia as part of Creative Commons License.

1.11   Image courtesy of Wikipedia as part of Creative Commons License.

1.12   Image courtesy of Wikipedia as part of Creative Commons License.

1.13   © 2005 Michael Brosilow.

1.14   © 2005 Michael Brosilow.

1.15   Image courtesy of Wendy Herron.

1.16   Photo courtesy of Jason Adams, 1869 Bardavon Opera House.

1.17   Image courtesy of Wendy Herron.

1.18   Image courtesy of Katie Kogler.

1.19   Image courtesy of Katie Kogler.

1.20   Image courtesy of Katie Kogler.

CHAPTER TWO

"The Show" courtesy of Michael A. Fink.

2.1   Image courtesy of Katie Kogler.

2.3   Image courtesy of Salvatore Tagliarino.

2.4   "Long Beach" courtesy of Isabella Rupp.

2.5   Image courtesy of Wikipedia as part of Creative Commons License.

2.6   Image courtesy of Wikipedia as part of Creative Commons License.

2.7   Image courtesy of Wikipedia as part of Creative Commons License.

2.9   © Rosaria Sinisi.

2.10   © Rosaria Sinisi.

2.11   © 2005 George Mott.

2.12   Photo courtesy of Carol Rosegg, Shakespeare Theatre Company.

2.13   Photo courtesy of Joan Marcus, Shakespeare Theatre Company.

2.14   Photo courtesy of Carol Rosegg, Shakespeare Theatre Company.

2.15   Photo courtesy of Carol Rosegg, Shakespeare Theatre Company.

CHAPTER THREE

"Urban Panel" courtesy of Michael A. Fink.

3.1   Photo courtesy of Wendy Herron.

3.2   © John Carver.

3.3   "Sunday" courtesy of Isabella Rupp.

3.4   © John Carver.

3.5   © Beth Bergman.

3.6   Image courtesy of Salvatore Tagliarino.

3.7   Image courtesy of Salvatore Tagliarino.

3.8   Image courtesy of Wikipedia as part of Creative Commons License.

3.9   Image courtesy of Salvatore Tagliarino.

3.10   Image courtesy of Salvatore Tagliarino.

3.11   Image courtesy of Wikipedia as part of Creative Commons License.

3.13   Image courtesy of Salvatore Tagliarino.

B

"The Saucerer" courtesy of Michael A. Fink.

4.1   © John Carver.

4.2   © John Carver.

4.3   Image courtesy of Wendy Herron.

4.4   Image courtesy of Wendy Herron.

4.5   Image courtesy of Wendy Herron.

4.6   Image courtesy of Wendy Herron.

4.7   Image courtesy of Wendy Herron.

4.8   Image courtesy of Wendy Herron.

4.9   Image courtesy of Wendy Herron.

4.12   "The Saucerer" courtesy of Michael A. Fink.

4.14   Image courtesy of Wendy Herron.

4.15   Image courtesy of Wendy Herron.

4.16   Image courtesy of Wendy Herron.

4.19   "The Turtle" courtesy of Michael A. Fink.

CHAPTER FIVE

"DDR" courtesy of Michael A. Fink.

5.3   Image courtesy of Wikipedia as part of Creative Commons License.

5.4   © John Carver.

5.5   © John Carver.

5.6   © John Carver.

5.7   © John Carver.

5.8   © John Carver.

5.9   © John Carver.

5.10   © John Carver.

5.11   © John Carver.

5.14   © John Carver.

5.15   © John Carver.

5.16   © John Carver.

5.17   © John Carver.

5.18   © John Carver.

5.121   Courtesy of John Lee Beatty.

5.122   Courtesy of John Lee Beatty.

5.23   Courtesy of George Allison.

5.24   © John Carver.

5.25   © John Carver.

5.26   © John Carver.

5.31   © Rosaria Sinisi.

5.33   Courtesy of John Lee Beatty.

5.34   Image courtesy of Wendy Herron.

5.35   Courtesy of Roger Bardwell, Hudson Scenic Studios.

5.36   Courtesy of John Lee Beatty.

5.37   Courtesy of Scott Pask.

5.38   Courtesy of Roger Bardwell, Hudson Scenic Studios.

5.41   Courtesy of Roger Bardwell, Hudson Scenic Studios.

5.43   Courtesy of John McKernon.

5.45   Courtesy of John Lee Beatty.

5.46   Courtesy of John Lee Beatty.

5.47   Courtesy of John Lee Beatty.

5.48   Image courtesy of Salvatore Tagliarino.

CHAPTER SIX

"Scene Shop" courtesy of Michael A. Fink.

6.1   © John Carver. Model is Chelsea Mason.

6.2   © John Carver. Model is Chelsea Mason.

6.3   © John Carver. Model is Chelsea Mason.

6.4   © John Carver. Model is Chelsea Mason.

8.13 Courtesy of Roger Bardwell, Hudson Scenic Studios.

8.14 Courtesy of Roger Bardwell, Hudson Scenic Studios.

8.15 Courtesy of Phil Grayson, EMU Theatre.

8.16 Image courtesy of William Domack.

8.17 Courtesy of Roger Bardwell, Hudson Scenic Studios.

8.18 Courtesy of Roger Bardwell, Hudson Scenic Studios.

8.19 Courtesy of Roger Bardwell, Hudson Scenic Studios.

8.20 Courtesy of Roger Bardwell, Hudson Scenic Studios.

8.21 Courtesy of John Lee Beatty.

8.22 Courtesy of Roger Bardwell, Hudson Scenic Studios.

CHAPTER NINE

"Red Dawn Mod" courtesy of Michael A. Fink.

9.2 Courtesy of Grace Brandt, Hudson Scenic Studios.

9.4 Courtesy of Scott Pask.

9.5 Courtesy of Scott Pask.

9.6 Courtesy of Grace Brandt, Hudson Scenic Studios.

9.7 Courtesy of Grace Brandt, Hudson Scenic Studios.

9.8 Courtesy of Grace Brandt, Hudson Scenic Studios.

9.9 Image courtesy of William Domack.

9.13 Courtesy of Grace Brandt, Hudson Scenic Studios.

9.14 Courtesy of Grace Brandt, Hudson Scenic Studios.

9.15 Courtesy of Grace Brandt, Hudson Scenic Studios.

9.16 © Beth Bergman.

9.21 © Beth Bergman.

9.24 © Michal Daniel.

9.26 © Rosaria Sinisi.

9.27 © Rosaria Sinisi.

9.28 © Rosco.

9.29 © Rosco.

9.30 © Rosco.

9.31 © Rosco.

9.32 © Rosco.

9.33 © Rosco.

9.34 © Rosco.

9.35 © Rosco

9.36 © Rosco.

9.38 © Rosco.

9.39 Courtesy of Grace Brandt, Hudson Scenic Studios.

CHAPTER TEN

"Mind in Chains" courtesy of Michael A. Fink.

10.1 © John Carver.

10.3 Image courtesy of Wikipedia as part of Creative Commons License.

10.4 Image courtesy of Wikipedia as part of Creative Commons License.

10.5 © John Carver.

10.6 © John Carver.

10.7 © John Carver.

10.8 © John Carver.

10.9 © John Carver.

10.10 © John Carver.

10.11 Photo courtesy of Jason Adams, 1869 Bardavon Opera House.

10.12 Photo courtesy of Jason Adams, 1869 Bardavon Opera House.

10.13 Image courtesy of Wikipedia as part of Creative Commons License.

10.15 Image courtesy of William Domack.

10.16 © John Carver.

10.17 Image courtesy of William Domack.

10.18 Image courtesy of William Domack.

10.20 Photo courtesy of Jason Adams, 1869 Bardavon Opera House.

10.21 Photo courtesy of Jason Adams, 1869 Bardavon Opera House.

10.23 Courtesy of James Thomas Engineering.

10.24 Courtesy of James Thomas Engineering.

10.25 Courtesy of James Thomas Engineering.

10.26 Courtesy of James Thomas Engineering.

10.27 Courtesy of James Thomas Engineering.

10.28 Courtesy of James Thomas Engineering.

10.29 Photo courtesy of Jason Adams, 1869 Bardavon Opera House.

CHAPTER ELEVEN

"House 2 Half" courtesy of Michael A. Fink.

11.1   © John Carver.

11.3   Image courtesy of Wikipedia as part of Creative Commons License.

11.4   Image courtesy of Wikipedia as part of Creative Commons License.

11.5   © Beth Bergman.

11.7   Image courtesy of Wikipedia as part of Creative Commons License.

11.8   Image courtesy of Wikipedia as part of Creative Commons License.

11.9   © Beth Bergman.

11.10 © 2005 George Mott.

11.11 Image courtesy of Wikipedia as part of Creative Commons License.

11.12 Image courtesy of Wikipedia as part of Creative Commons License.

11.13 Image courtesy of Wikipedia as part of Creative Commons License.

11.14 Photo courtesy of Jason Adams, 1869 Bardavon Opera House.

11.17 © Altman Lighting, Inc.

11.18 © Arri Group.

11.20 © Altman Lighting, Inc.

11.21 © Altman Lighting, Inc.

11.22 © Altman Lighting, Inc.

11.23 © Robert Juliat.

11.24 © Altman Lighting, Inc.

11.25 © Robert Juliat.

11.26 © Robert Juliat.

11.27 © Robert Juliat & Altman Lighting, Inc.

11.28 © Selador, Inc.

11.29 Photo courtesy of Matthew Allar.

11.30 © Altman Lighting, Inc.

11.31 © Strong, Inc.

11.32 © Lycian.

11.33 © Lycian.

11.34 © Robert Juliat.

11.35 © Martin Professional.

11.36 © Robe.

11.37 © Martin Professional.

11.38 © City Theatrical, Inc.

11.39 © John Carver.

11.40 © Electronic Theatre Controls.

11.41 © Electronic Theatre Controls.

11.42 © Avolites.

11.43 © Avolites.

11.44 © High End Systems.

11.45 © Sea Changer.

11.46 © City Theatrical, Inc.

11.48 Image courtesy of Ken Billington.

11.49 Image courtesy of Ken Billington.

11.50 Image courtesy of Ken Billington.

11.51 Image courtesy of Ken Billington.

11.52 Image courtesy of D. M. Wood.

CHAPTER TWELVE

"Haiku" courtesy of Michael A. Fink.

12.3   © Carol Rosegg.

12.4   © Carol Rosegg.

12.21 Image courtesy of Wikipedia as part of Creative Commons License.

12.22 Image courtesy of Wikipedia as part of Creative Commons License.

12.23 Image courtesy of Campbell Baird.

12.24 Image courtesy of Campbell Baird.

12.30 © George Mott.

12.45 © Beth Bergman.

12.46 © Beth Bergman.

12.47 © Beth Bergman.

12.48 © Beth Bergman.

12.49 © Patternmaker Software.

12.50 © Patternmaker Software.

CHAPTER THIRTEEN

"Da Gawdaughter" courtesy of Michael A. Fink. Original photo by Lyn Hughes Photography.

13.1 © Ben Nye Company, Inc.

13.2 © Ben Nye Company, Inc.

13.3 © Ben Nye Company, Inc.

13.4 © Ben Nye Company, Inc.

13.5 © Ben Nye Company, Inc.

13.6 © Ben Nye Company, Inc.

13.7 © Ben Nye Company, Inc.

13.8 © Ben Nye Company, Inc.

13.9 © Ben Nye Company, Inc.

13.10 © Ben Nye Company, Inc.

13.11 © Ben Nye Company, Inc.

13.12 © Ben Nye Company, Inc.

13.13 © Ben Nye Company, Inc.

13.14 © Ben Nye Company, Inc.

13.15 © Ben Nye Company, Inc.

13.16 © Ben Nye Company, Inc.

13.17 © Ben Nye Company, Inc.

13.18 © Ben Nye Company, Inc.

13.19 © Ben Nye Company, Inc.

13.20 © Ben Nye Company, Inc.

13.21 © Ben Nye Company, Inc.

13.22 © Ben Nye Company, Inc.

13.23 © Ben Nye Company, Inc.

13.24 © Ben Nye Company, Inc.

13.25 Image courtesy of Linda Mensching.

13.26 © Ben Nye Company, Inc.

13.27 © Ben Nye Company, Inc.

13.28 © Ben Nye Company, Inc.

CHAPTER FOURTEEN

"Speakers" courtesy of Michael A. Fink.

14.2 Image courtesy of Wikipedia as part of Creative Commons License.

14.3 © Sennheiser.

14.4 Image courtesy of Wikipedia as part of Creative Commons License.

14.6 © Yamaha Pro Audio.

14.7 © John Carver.

14.8 Photo courtesy of Jason Adams, 1869 Bardavon Opera House.

14.9 Photo courtesy of Jason Adams, 1869 Bardavon Opera House.

14.13 © Clear-Com Communication Systems.

14.15 Photos courtesy of Sound Associates, Inc.

CHAPTER FIFTEEN

"Studio Star" courtesy of Michael A. Fink.

15.1 © John Carver.

15.2 © Beth Bergman.

15.3 © Beth Bergman.

15.4 Image courtesy of Wikipedia as part of Creative Commons License.

15.8 © Altman Lighting, Inc.

15.9 Photo courtesy of Anne Johnston, Production Resource Group, LLC.

15.10 © Beth Bergman.

15.11 Image courtesy of Geoff Dunbar.

15.13 © Diversitronics, Inc.

15.14 © Diversitronics, Inc.

15.15 © GAM Products, Inc.

15.17 © John Carver.

15.18 © Beth Bergman.

15.19 © Rosco.

15.21 © Rosco.

15.22 Image courtesy of Anne Johnston, Production Resource Group, LLC.

15.23 Image courtesy of Anne Johnston, Production Resource Group, LLC.

15.24 Image courtesy of Anne Johnston, Production Resource Group, LLC.

15.25 Photo courtesy of Anne Johnston, Production Resource Group, LLC.

15.28 Photo courtesy of Jason Adams, 1869 Bardavon Opera House.

15.29 © Rosco.

15.30 © Main Light Industries.

15.31 © Michael Brosilow.

15.32 © Michal Daniel.

15.33 Image courtesy of Tom Cariello.

15.34 Photo courtesy of Curt Ostermann.

CHAPTER SIXTEEN

"A Clipboard Life" courtesy of Michael A. Fink.

16.8 Image courtesy of Andrea Newman-Winston.

16.13 Image courtesy of Andrea Newman-Winston.

16.17 © Great American Market.

16.18 Image courtesy of Andrea Newman-Winston.

16.19 © Global Design Systems.

CHAPTER SEVENTEEN

"Stone Café" courtesy of Michael A. Fink.

Theatre is a big business but really a small one. The industry is far-reaching; in fact, it covers all corners of the world—and everything in-between. It is still small enough, however, that most people know each other or, at the very least, have heard of each other. In researching and writing this book, I was able to call on many companies and individuals for help. All those I contacted offered their assistance in ways I could only dream of. Some went above and beyond my wildest expectations.

I give a special thanks to the following companies; for without them, I would not have been able to add the level of detail to make this book what it is!

CITY THEATRICAL
I N C

GAM PRODUCTS, INC.

HUDSON
Scenic Studio
Christie Lighting
Theatrical Associates

Lighting&Sound
America

matthews
STUDIO EQUIPMENT™

Page numbers with "f" denote figures; "t" tables; "b" boxes.

Complementary colors, 58, 446
Composite, 33, 446
Composition, line
   balance, 50–51
   definition, 41
   line
     direction, 47
     weight, 50–52, 50f
   pattern, 51
   proportion, 50–51
   rule of thirds, 43–46
   scale, 51–52
   shape, 47, 47f
   texture, 47–49, 47f–48f
Compound miter
   153, 155f, 156
Computers
   image types, 70
   Mac *versus* PC, 85
   software, 84–88
Concealer, 446
   makeup, 350–351, 356
Concept, 446
Condenser microphone, 370, 446
Connick, Jr., Harry, 125
Construction drawings, 186–190, 192, 200f, 446
Contact pickup, 371, 446
Contact sheet, 412–415, 414f–415f, 446
Contrast, 446
   in line weight, 50
Controller, lights, 291–292
Conventional lighting, 267, 446
Coping saw, 150–151, 151f, 446
Corinthian, 33, 446
Coriolanus, 36, 37f
Corner blocks, 196–198, 446
Costume breakdown, 423, 423f, 446
Costume designer, 433
Costumes, measurements, tracking forms
   fabrics, 313–316, 316f
   measurements
     men, 325, 326f
     women, 323–324, 324f
   sewing, 325–333
   softwares, 333–334
   tools and. accessories, 316–322
   tracking forms
     men, 328f
     women, 327f
Cotton, 446
Cotton fabric, 313
Counterweight, 249, 446
Coward, Noel, 436
Crayons, 76–77

Crescent wrench, 158–159
Crosscut blade, 150, 446
Crucible, The, 36f
Cue lights, 425–426, 446
Curtain calls, 424, 446
Cutter, 325, 446
Cyc, 446
Cycle play, 10
Cyclorama, 19, 447

D

D-Scriptive, 379–380, 379f
Daily rehearsal report, 417–418, 418f, 447
Dark sucker theory, 299b–300b, 465
Dead lift, 251, 447
Dead-blow hammer, 157, 157f
Deck, 196, 447
Deck plan, 105–108, 114f–115f, 447
Deluge, 447
Deluge system, 137, 138f
Design process, architecture, script, 27–29
   architecture
     styles, 32–33
   design meeting, 33
   director meeting with designer, 29–36
   drawing, rendering, and drafting, 33–36, 185
   kick-off meeting, 190
   research, 30–32
   script
     breakdown, 30
     reading, 27–29, 28f
Designer drawings, 186–190, 447
Designers, 47
Detail brush, 447
   makeup, 349
Detail drawings, 108, 447
Deux ex machina, 184, 447
Digital multiplex (DMX), 291
Dimension line, drafting, 97
Dimensional lumber, 167–169, 168f
Dimensioning, drafting, 100, 101f
Dimmer, 288–291, 447
Dinner theatre, 21
Direct current (DC), 273–275, 447
Direction, 447
   line, 47
Directors, 433
   meeting with designer, 29–36
Distressing, 226, 447
Ditty bag, 325, 329f, 447
DMX, 447
Dome brush, 447
   makeup, 348, 349f

Wood grain, faux painting, 233–235, 234f–235f
Woofer, 374, 375f, 461
Wool, 461
Wool fabric, 313

X
XLR connector, 377, 377f, 461

Y
Yankee screwdriver, 159f, 160, 461
Yoke, 278, 461
Young, Neil, 368b–369b

Z
Zauberflote, 332–333, 340f–341f
Zetex®, 135, 136f, 461